Marcel Moyse: Voice of the Flute

Marcel Moyse (17 May 1889–1 November 1984)

MARCEL MOYSE
Voice of the Flute

by Ann McCutchan

Discography by Susan Nelson and William Shaman

AMADEUS PRESS
Reinhard G. Pauly, General Editor
Portland, Oregon

Endpapers: Moyse's sketch of St. Amour, circa 1943.

ISBN 0-931340-68-3

Printed in Singapore

AMADEUS PRESS
The Haseltine Building
133 S.W. Second Ave., Suite 450
Portland, Oregon 97204-3527, U.S.A.

Library of Congress Cataloging-in-Publication Data

McCutchan, Ann.
   Marcel Moyse : voice of the flute / by Ann McCutchan ; discography
by Susan Nelson and William Shaman.
       p.   cm.
   Includes bibliographical references (p.   ) and index.
   ISBN 0-931340-68-3
   1. Moyse, Marcel, 1889-1984.   2. Flutists—France—Bibliography.
I. Title.
ML419.M69M3   1994
788.3'2'092—dc20   93-33357
[B]   CIP
                                                           MN

788.32092
M938m

Contents

Illustrations follow page 96

Foreword

by Paula Robison

IN the early 1960s a lucky band of American flute players gathered in Brattleboro, Vermont, to study with Marcel Moyse. We were all changed forever. I can only describe the experience as a kind of alchemy: when we walked into Mr. Moyse's studio we were one kind of player, and when we left we were another. We were richer, deeper. We were shaken, exhilarated, and illuminated.

How did he get me to play like that? we asked ourselves. And later, in the waiting stillness of our practice rooms, *How can I ever play that way again?*

In our minds, we tried to recreate his gesturing hands, his sparkling eyes, his voice coaxing and *pulling* the music out of us.

With life! Life! he exclaimed.

But what did that mean? Happy? No . . .

Tender?

Intense?

Vivid?

Strong?

His life was certainly all of those things. Maybe it was all of them together.

His eyes! That's it. Think of his eyes.

As the rest of his body grew frail, Marcel Moyse's eyes burned brighter and brighter. And sometimes he was impatient. Why? He wanted to give us something. He wanted us to understand what he held out to us: the culture of a proud people, a composer named

7

Claude Debussy who could evoke joy and pain in a single note, another named Gabriel Fauré who had the look in his eyes of a lion longing for his far-off home, and whose music was ecstasy contained in a shapely classical form.

But how can I play like that again? How can I find that SOUND again?
Think of his voice now, singing gently.
. . . **Yes** . . .

Sunlight shining through the trees onto the forest floor . . . the brook . . . the line of the mountain range, each curve connected to the next . . . **like the musique de Bach**.

Now, the stamp of a foot, and the strong laugh: **Hah!**

Marcel Moyse's touch turned us into pure gold, sometimes for an instant, for a phrase, sometimes for a whole piece. It then became our task to stretch those moments into a lifetime of artistry. How mysterious the process was! And yet, at the same time, how simple. Marcel Moyse taught us to dream for ourselves. He wanted us, on our own, to become honest interpreters, attentive to both the beauty and the meaning of the music we played, unimpeded by the limits of our instruments.

And above all, Marcel Moyse wished for us to be brave enough to reveal, always, what was in our own hearts.

Paula Robison
July 1993

Preface

by Louis Moyse

IT must be a rather difficult task for any biographer to approach the life of a great artist when his departure from the world is still so close to us. Ann McCutchan had to deal with true and alleged facts, hearsay and accounts more or less accurate (reviews, articles, interviews), international fame, and a legend already well established when my father was living. When he died in 1984, he was almost a century old.

To research his past was not an easy undertaking, especially considering the fact that sixty years of his life were spent on a different continent. In spite of this handicap, Ms. McCutchan faced the challenge with clarity of mind, skill, and devotion, going with strong will and courage to all available sources, close and far away.

She describes my father's life in the context of diverse epochs, skillfully interweaving the musical and artistic world as it was known during those periods. I can only praise Ms. McCutchan for a remarkable achievement. I also thank her for giving me the opportunity to write this Preface.

My father was, at the same time, humble and proud: humble regarding his modest origin and proud to have achieved so much. He was a typical Frenchman, with his roots deeply anchored in his native soil. His short temper was known, as were his other strong character traits (which were not always easy for those around him to accept), but he never really meant to be mean, unless he felt, rightly or wrongly, that someone was questioning his moral or artistic integrity.

During his school years in Besançon, he sometimes astonished his teachers by asking questions (beyond his years) regarding life and the human condition. He was studious, methodical, and disciplined, getting up at four o'clock in the morning, in a heatless room, learning his lessons by the gleam of a candle to be ready for his class. He would not suffer injustice, neither toward himself nor anyone else. He rebelled against any false authority, knowing in advance the price he would have to pay: teachers waiting for him the next morning, at the entrance of the school, with the stick!

When he was a little boy, roaming with other children in the country around St. Amour or Besançon, happy and unconcerned about his future, he certainly didn't have any premonition regarding what fate had in store for him and what he would achieve during a long and successful career.

The "fairies" were generous, providing him with numerous gifts at birth. But these gifts were not given to him on a platter. He had to use them to forge—with courage, patience, intelligence, will, and the love of music—a beautiful instrument, a "speaking" flute. His tone quality was unique, as was the way he expressed feelings through the flute, using the instrument as a painter would his palette.

Life was not easy for him. He had to face great pain (as an orphan, torn between his love for two families), serious sickness (early in his career he became so ill he could hardly blow his flute, and he was refused by the army for health reasons during World War I), other adversities (joblessness and poverty during several periods of his life), and misfortunes (two wars blocked his career). These handicaps might have cut down a man less strong, but not him, with his tenacity to survive and to succeed by overcoming the odds.

Also, in spite of the odds, destiny furnished my father with people who loved and helped him when it was most needed. Among them were "Memée" Perretier, who gave him love and protection when he was born; "Papa" Angelloz, who taught him the flute in Besançon; Joseph Moyse, his uncle, who paved the way to Taffanel, the master of the flute, in Paris; and my dear mother, who married him and was a truly devoted wife, nursing him like a baby when he was sick, his constant companion to her last breath, in

1971. Without these people, his life might have been quite different. Also, his life as a flutist might have been different without the guidance of his teachers: Taffanel, Hennebains, and Gaubert. But I strongly feel that, first and foremost, he was a self-made man. He created his own world and we are grateful for his legacy.

Charles Dorgeuille, the author of *The French Flute School,* dared to question my father's embouchure position. I have no answer to his poor comment but to say that all the flutists I have ever known would have been glad to pay any price to have the glorious sounds of Marcel Moyse! The fact that his embouchure was not perfectly centered didn't bother him, nor anyone else. When the means are adequate and honest, they justify the end. (It reminds me of a nice story about Mozart: Once, he was sitting at the keyboard, playing very low notes with his left hand and top notes with his right hand. He then asked his friends how he could play a middle note at the same time. When no answer came, he played it with his nose! Et voilà!)

I cannot write of my father without thinking of his pipes. They were part of his lifestyle. All were bought in St. Claude, fifty miles east of St. Amour, toward the Swiss border. St. Claude, deeply rooted in the Jura mountains, is well known for two of its best products: wood carving and pipes. I always felt a similarity between the finish of a beautiful pipe and the finest achievement of my father's career—the marvelous smell of the wood and the beautiful sounds of his flute. Years ago I carved a pipe for two from the root of an old wild cherry tree, a big block, raw and shapeless. Flexible tubes were connected to the block (like a narghile, or hookah), and my father and I sat at the two corners of our fireplace in St. Amour, drinking Pernod, talking, thinking, dreaming, looking at the flames.

Another story about pipes. In the '30s, while rehearsing Honegger's *Pacific 231* (the name of a new American locomotive) with the Straram Orchestra, my father once stuck his big curved pipe, lighted, in the left corner of his mouth, and played his flute part at the same time, sending a cloud of smoke all around him! Honegger, standing beside Straram, smoking his own huge pipe, laughed to tears. Those were happy times, when composers, conductors, and players dared to have fun together with a good joke.

Like other well-known artists coming to the U.S. from foreign countries, my father had a problem with the English language. I bring this matter up because I think it explains a great deal regarding the personal "devices" he used for his teaching. He created his own language, with diverse facial expressions, gestures, and attitudes, which could be compared to the mimics of his compatriot Marcel Marceau. If sometimes in his enthusiasm he overacted a little, one easily forgave him, because it was always based on love of music and his eagerness to make his message understood.

I realize that this Preface has to end. Not because I am lacking memories, comments, and stories, but because the reader must be eager to be in direct contact with the life of a great man and outstanding artist.

I loved, admired, and respected my father very much. He was good at heart and a hard worker. He had to fight unfortunate circumstances but his reward was to be able to interpret, with an incomparable mastery, the human emotions contained in a simple melody, like the aria *Fortunio* by Messager. The French text reads: "J'aimais ma vieille maison grise [I loved my old gray house]." It is a heartbreaking song, similar to some of the songs included in *Die Winterreise* by Schubert. My father was able, with just a few notes, to express the meaning and emotions of life, including joy, sadness, hope, suffering, dreams, and realities, the total sum of the human condition. That is the ultimate dream of any artist.

My mother should not be forgotten in this Preface. She was a simple and honest woman, with a golden heart, artistic by instinct. She let her gifts fade away to devote herself to the welfare of the family. I was blessed to be born with such parents and I cherish their memories.

Louis Moyse
January 1993

Introduction

DURING the first months of researching the life of Marcel Moyse, I was tempted to abandon the project several times. Why? Because I quickly discovered that Moyse, then deceased less than five years, wore a robe of mythology thick and purple enough to make even the most fearless fact-checker scream.

Yet myths, stories, and rumors indubitably point to an individual who made a strong impact on others, and in the end it was Moyse's intriguing personality that spurred me on. I set two goals. The first was to describe Moyse's accomplishments in the context of Paris's musical life from the *fin de siècle* through World War II, and that of the United States after the war. The second was to allow a human portrait of Moyse to emerge through the vivid recollections and reactions of people who knew him—family members, friends, colleagues, and students who agreed to be interviewed for this book.

Attempting to meet these aims was often like hunting buried treasure with a faded map. The day I realized that Moyse could not possibly (as he once claimed) have quaffed wine in cafés with the impressionist painter Sisley (who died when Moyse was ten) was a bust. The day I recognized one of *le maître*'s unknown manuscripts in a tattered box at the home of one of his St. Amour relatives was a blast. The search for Moyse was always challenging and never dull. Contact with musicians who had worked with him charged my batteries continuously.

After five years of lively exploration, my task is done. Now I invite readers to discover Marcel Moyse's story for themselves.

ACKNOWLEDGEMENTS

This biography originated in a discussion with my friend Nancy Andrew, one of Marcel Moyse's last students and organizer of his archives, who convinced me to examine Moyse's papers and speak with members of his family. My "study" for the biography was a two-part series published in the summer and fall 1989 issues of *Chamber Music.* Carol Yaple, then the magazine's editor, dubbed the series "The Voice of the Flute: Remembering Marcel Moyse," and from that came the book's title.

In the opening of *Discovering the News: A Social History of American Newspapers,* Michael Schudson writes that "a work of scholarship is a collective enterprise, even if one's style of working is solitary." I cannot agree more; the list of people who helped me weave together Marcel Moyse's story represents not passive interviewees, but active participants in a task that, given the dearth of reliable primary sources on Moyse, was frequently slippery going.

The following colleagues, students, and friends of Marcel Moyse in Europe and the United States offered generous interviews: Robert Aitken, Nancy Andrew, Frances Lapp Averitt, Paul Barrett, Aram Bedrossian, Raymond Benner, Frances Blaisdell, Julia Bogorad, James Brody, Leone Buyse, Paul Carron, Anthony Checchia, Joseph Cobert, Larry Combs, Andrew Crisanti, Charles Dagnino, Michel Debost, Ulysse Delecluse, Elaine Douvas, Alfred Genovese, Bernard Goldberg, Peter-Lukas Graf, Henri Grevot, Raymond Guiot, Jacqueline Hofto, Karl Kraber, David Krakauer, Anton Kuerti, Eleanor Lawrence, Barbara Leibundguth, Elsa Ludewig-Verdehr, Carl Lutes, Richard Mackey, Alain Marion, Judith Mendenall, Raymond Meylan, Philipp Naegele, Aurèle Nicolet, Pat Grignet Nott, Geneviève Noufflard, Alex Ogle, Paul Olsen, René Rateau, Odile Renault, Paula Robison, Sylvia Rosenberg, Susan Rotholz, Robert Routch, Frank Salomon, Peter Serkin, Roland Small, Patricia Spencer, Diana Steiner, Darlene Tillack, Rudolph Vrbsky, Marilyn Martin Wilson, Carol Wincenc, Harold Wright, Ruth Wurster Wright, Trevor Wye, and Richard Wyszynski. Arthur Austin, William Bennett, David Shostac, Steve Dibner, Jorge Mester, Joaquin Valdenpeñas, Donald Wright, and Richard Waller contributed valuable insights, as did countless other musicians, scholars, and friends I spoke with while assembling this book.

Members of the Moyse family in France and the United States who conversed with me at length include Bjørn Andreasson, Christophe Andreasson, Nancy Andreasson, Germaine Chassagnoux (now deceased), Isabelle Moyse Craig, Claude Moyse, Janet Moyse, Michel Moyse, Paulette Routhier, and Dominique Moyse Steinberg. Marguerite Moyse Andreasson was especially helpful. Louis Moyse and Blanche Honegger Moyse offered extensive, painstaking assistance every step of the way; their experiences as members of the family and of the Moyse Trio informed every chapter. I cannot honor them enough.

In the task of research, I have the following individuals and institutions to thank: Joan Bauman, Peter Bay, Shelley Binder, Julia Breen, Virginia Burnham, Doris DeLoach, Paul Douglas, Penny Fischer, Jean Harling, Simon Lippa, Mitch Markowitz, Rolf Meyersohn, William R. Moran, Todd Newmark, Charles Price, Sangjoon "Fritz" Park, Therese Radic, Helen Ann Shanley, Judy Sherman, Rebecca Siegel, Dr. Uri Toeplitz, Nancy Toff, Max Wilcox, Mariedi Anders Artists Management, John Cargher of the Australian Broadcasting Company, the Boston Symphony Archives, Zonn Estes of the Brattleboro Music Center, Clair Van Ausdall of *Chamber Music* magazine, Colbert Artists Management, Jim Pruett and Wynn Matthias of the Library of Congress, Catherine Rochon of the Conservatoire National Supérieur de Musique et de Danse of Paris, Lisa Sullivan of the Curtis Institute of Music, Steve Henner of the Fleisher Collection, Jim Cartwright of Immortal Performances, Dennis Hugh Avey of Robert King Music Sales, Michel Crichton of Alphonse Leduc and Company, the Marcel Moyse Society, Tanya Tabachnikov of Marlboro College, Philip Maneval, Shirley Ann Weekley and Carol Faris of the Marlboro Music School and Festival, Muramatsu, Inc., the New York Public Library, the Paris Opéra-Comique archives, Richard Letts and Holly Brick of Sounds Australian, Chester Lane of *Symphony Magazine,* the music libraries of Boston University, the University of California at Berkeley, the University of Hawaii, and the University of Oregon, Karl Miller of the University of Texas Fine Arts Library, and the staff of the Harry Ransom Humanities Research Center at the University of Texas at Austin.

Special thanks go to my translators, Philip Gottling, Sylvia Bernard, and Kathy Allen-Weber, and to John Ferguson, my dedicated research assistant in Paris. Their services and a research trip to

Europe were funded by a generous grant from the Ludwig Vogelstein Foundation. An artist-fellowship at the Hambidge Center for Creative Arts and Sciences gave me the peace and freedom to organize my materials and draft the opening chapters.

Writers need cheerleaders: fellow wordsmiths who will read a tortured manuscript, furnish reams of constructive criticism, and still tell others how wonderful the book is going to be. Bruce Bruschi, William Burgwinkle, Linda Hartford Huggins, Edd O'Donnell, and Dan Welcher all filled this vital role with seriousness, tact, and good humor. Bruce Kauffman provided additional suggestions and moral support. Discographers Susan Nelson and William Shaman offered helpful comments on the chapters dealing with recordings and delivered a first-rate, scholarly discography for this book, the most thorough available for Moyse. Dr. Reinhard Pauly, Margaret Broucek, and Karen Kirtley of Amadeus Press were my gifted, erudite, patient editors.

Of everyone involved in the birth of *Marcel Moyse: Voice of the Flute,* Nancy Andrew must be identified as the steadfast and priceless midwife. My husband Dan Welcher was the antennaed attending physician; his knowledge, respect for this project, and compatible work habits were everything a partner could ask for.

Finally, I am grateful to my mother, Helen Marden Bond McCutchan, for encouraging me to express myself in both words and music, and to my father, George Morton McCutchan, for expecting me to meet all challenges. This book is dedicated to their memory.

Ann McCutchan
July 1993

Marcel Moyse: Voice of the Flute

Moyse's rendering of the Église St. Amour, circa 1943

France. Église de St Amour. (Jura) m. moyse

St. Amour

St. Amour is the mountain village in the Jura region of France where the flutist Marcel Moyse was born; it is the place he called home, from where he drew inspiration all his life. Even today, St. Amour retains the rustic charm of earlier times. Townspeople in practical garb stroll leisurely through the narrow maze of streets and passageways, stopping at the butcher's and the baker's to fill their string shopping bags. Children's laughter bounces off the high gray walls of houses scored with long, geranium-filled window boxes. And further off, cows and goats browse in the meadows, while young people on bicycles pedal lazily, counting fenceposts for distance, glancing back at the town for a view of the red tiled roofs and Église St. Amour's gleaming, onion-shaped dome.

On the summer day I explored St. Amour, I forgot what century it was.

If the village treasury were overflowing, the citizens would surely erect a statue of Marcel Moyse. He is, after all, their most famous son, the orphan boy who made good. In the 1970s they renamed the town square in his honor. On the north side of the Place Marcel Moyse sits the grand, fadingly functional Hôtel du Commerce where Moyse, as an elderly man, stayed during his annual summer visits. Henri Grevot, the town bandmaster emeritus, lives in a house on the Place opposite the hotel, close to a group of trees where a taxi idles between trips to the railroad station less than a mile away. With little encouragement from this American pilgrim, Grevot pointed to the window of the room where Moyse preferred to be ensconced (second floor, east end, with a flower box), and told proudly how he remembered when the great flutist was a young man. Moyse would have been over one hundred years old on that day; Grevot was in his eighties. It made no difference. Grevot remembered.

Other people in St. Amour were eager to talk, to show the sights. A woman in a grocery performed animated directions to Moyse's birthplace, a dismal four-floor apartment building around the corner, second left, down an alley. The young manager of the copy shop smiled with recognition and understood my embarrassed French perfectly when I asked him to reproduce a newspaper clipping about Moyse. The owner of a hardware store I ducked into during a rainshower turned his business over to an assistant, herded me into his station wagon, and conducted a passionate tour of Moyse landmarks: the wide-windowed house he built for his family, facing the mountains, and the cemetery where he is buried. Expertly navigating the dogleg streets, my impromptu guide described a childhood memory of hearing Moyse play in church, and recommended a visit to the Église St. Amour, where Moyse attended mass as a boy. Inside the dim church, I was startled by the complaints of a sour organ manipulated by an old woman seated high in the loft, hunched over the keyboards like a dried apricot. Along one streaked stone wall, next to a yellow-painted radiator, was a gilt-encrusted reliquary containing the village's very own bone chips of minor saints, the same grim antiques Moyse eyed every Sunday as a boy.

Many people in St. Amour hoard souvenirs of Marcel Moyse's life—a magazine story, a photograph, a recording. But Paul Carron, a large-built man in his late eighties, created his own memento by composing a speech chronicling his idol's career in detail. Carron read it to the populace in the 1970s, during a public ceremony in which Moyse was named honorary Bandmaster of St. Amour. It took thirty minutes to read. Carron has since transformed it into a rhyming epic poem, illustrated it with snapshots, and typed and bound it himself. A publishing house in the region was supposed to print it, he told me, but it went out of business. The project meant a great deal to Carron, who is retired from the defunct marble factory, once St. Amour's biggest employer. All his life he admired Moyse from afar, and during the flutist's last years Carron finally gathered the courage to introduce himself to *le maître*. He was flabbergasted by Moyse's cordiality and his willingness to let an ordinary citizen squire him around on drives through the Jura countryside.

Germaine Chassagnoux, also an octogenarian, was the oldest living member of Moyse's adoptive family. She was surprised to discover that her old box of photographs and newspaper reviews (French, German, Swiss, American) also contained an unfinished manuscript of flute exercises Moyse penned during one of the summers he taught in her home. "My memory is not very good," she apologized. "I don't remember very far back now. But he used to sit in that chair by the kitchen window every day and smoke his pipe." The spot was obviously her own favorite, next to a polished wooden desk glowing with light and color from the backyard garden. But she explained that she always moved her things to another room when Moyse visited. "That was his place," she insisted.[1]

Chassagnoux's daughter, Paulette Routhier, admitted they never fully understood Moyse's career, or classical music, for that matter. He was the patriarch of the family, she said, and everyone in town knew who he was. "When I was little, he invited me along on vacations with his children. He always visited during the holidays, and oh! He played such funny tricks!" With a grin, she added that when Moyse wasn't entertaining his relatives at home with flying spoons and disappearing matchsticks, he loved to stroll around town and greet people, then linger over a restaurant meal of mutton, wine, and local cheeses. He took great pleasure in savoring his pipe for hours after dinner, cooling his throat with the ubiquitous glass of Pernod. Marcel Moyse was never more comfortable than in St. Amour, where he was born in 1889.

CHAPTER ONE

Early Years

FOR most French citizens, 1889 was the year Paris witnessed the hoisting of the Eiffel Tower at the Exposition Univer-
selle. The 984-foot structure had been the object of controversy
since the work's beginning two years before. In a manifesto called
the *Protestation des Artistes,* an impressive list of artists and writers
complained the "ridiculous tower" would obliterate the view of
Notre-Dame and the Louvre. But construction never halted. France
was flushed with exhibition fever—a universal exhibition was held
every eleven years from 1867 to 1900—and the one in 1889 also
happened to commemorate the centenary of the French Revolution. The Eiffel Tower was a monument to French creative
brilliance and an aggressive symbol of the new scientific age in
which the nobility lost clout and the ambitious, self-made man
became king. One typically effusive observer wrote:

> The bounds of space have been destroyed, machines have
> realized what were considered impossibilities, genius has made
> man a Titan, and there is nothing too heavy for him to take on
> his shoulders, no stone that he is obliged to leave unturned.

The Gallery of Machines, an attraction nearly as popular as Eiffel's
folly, was described as

> a palace forty-eight metres high. . . . Through the whole length
> of the room ran four rows of parallel beams to carry the driving
> straps, and two-hundred-fifty horse-power was transmitted

23

through them to an infinity of machines that stood rank and file—the laurel-crowned army of modern civilization ready for new victories.[1]

The thousands of people that jammed the Exposition opening 6 May were so excited they lost all sense of propriety. Normally refined folk rudely jostled one another to gain advantage in the long lines; elegant bowler hats and expensive hair combs flew about like debris in a windstorm. In the early morning of the second day, loiterers discovered a good deal of jewelry left behind in the tracks of the horse-drawn carriages that had swayed dangerously with passengers the day before.

If the technological wonders of the 1889 Exposition announced the future, the unprecedented array of international pavilions celebrated the past. This past, represented by the traditions of alien cultures, was just as mysterious to Parisians as the wondrous telephone. People gawked at the Hindus who served palm wine in the Indian tower just as innocently as they regarded electric generators. The noisy neighborhood of "Cairo" was the most talked-about concoction with its lavish bazaar of jewels, gold-threaded embroideries, and bright carpets. Moorish cafés shuddered with the monotonous rhythms of ancient dances and the bleatings of sand-burnished brass instruments, while one hundred white donkeys driven by barefoot Arabians bore thickly clothed visitors beneath potted palms. France, one of the most centralized nations of the world, was finally embracing the unknown, on home turf.

The hubbub of the Exposition delighted the fourteen-year-old composer Maurice Ravel, who welcomed any distraction from piano practice. The spit and whirl of new gadgets at the fair led to his lifetime fascination with mechanical toys. Elsewhere in the crowd, twenty-six-year-old Claude Debussy gorged himself on exotic music from the Far East. The hollow tones and melancholy scales of the bamboo xylophones, gongs, and tom-toms from Java would soon be absorbed into the musical languages of both composers, transforming French bombast and bravura into delicate ambrosia.

The 1889 Exposition also marked the beginning of the Belle Époque, an era of cliques, clacques, self-indulgence, and pride. Exquisite fads and frivolous feelings bloomed in an economically secure, technologically ambitious time when people beheld themselves as actors in the most dazzling spectacle ever staged. The

Australian coloratura soprano Nellie Melba first trod the boards of the Paris Opéra the third night of the Exposition, and made a magnificent impression with Ophelia's Mad Scene in Ambroise Thomas's version of the revenge tragedy *Hamlet.* A little more than ten years later she and the Italian tenor Enrico Caruso would pair up in *La bohème* and establish the most brilliant operatic partnership of the prewar years. Vincent Van Gogh, whose career as an artist exactly ran the course of the 1880s, rejected such surface triviality. Yet his commitment to the profound expressivity of color and intense belief in a mystic, universal creative force was of the time and could be viewed as the underside of a cultural narcissism that skewed the psyches beneath silk toppers and fancy *chapeaux.* Van Gogh painted his well-known *Self-Portrait* in 1889 during his stay at the Asylum of Saint-Paul in Saint-Rémy, a year before he committed suicide. At the same time, a contingent of French musicians made a pilgrimage to Bayreuth to find out if Wagner had really created a new form of music-drama or was just in love with himself.

Little of this excitement touched the village of St. Amour, where Marcel Moyse was born eleven days after the Paris Exposition opened. Yet, like the impressionable Exposition visitors who wondered where the simple life had flown, Moyse grew to romanticize his origins exquisitely. In some recollections he cast himself as a quiet, pensive shepherd boy who daydreamed for hours on the hillsides; in others, he was a mischievous child who loved rowdy country games and barely managed to do his share of household chores. One fact is certain: Marcel was the son of Christine Josephine Moyse, a young, unmarried woman who was born on 3 April 1867 in the northern Jura town of Besançon.

Christine Josephine was, either by choice or necessity, an independent woman for her time, because when she became pregnant out of wedlock at the age of twenty-one, she bore the social and physical burden with little help or company. Family lore alleges she had a disagreement with her parents and lost any assistance they might have offered; it is not known if the misunderstanding sprang from her predicament as an unwed mother. Christine's lover, a notary student named Bernod, had no intention of marrying her and probably withdrew from the affair because he couldn't afford the cost of this particular family. French notaries in the late nineteenth century were custodians of local morality as well as money. They presided over personal disputes and legal arrangements, collected taxes, served as investment brokers, and often wound up as town mayors, pillars of their communities. The profession was competitive, and required thousands of francs to set up even a modest *étude,* or office. Fathering a child at that time and in those circumstances would have been more than inconvenient to Bernod.

However, the young man took some responsibility and discreetly arranged to send Christine some sixty miles away to St. Amour for the birth and nursing period. The infant would be placed in an orphanage, and Christine could return to Besançon at her leisure. Everything worked according to plan, at first. Sometime before the baby was due, Christine rode the lumbering local train to St. Amour and presented herself at the home of the village midwife, Madame Romand. A few weeks passed quietly, and on the morning of 17 May, Marcel Joseph was born. But just seven days later, on 25 May, Christine died and was buried in the cemetery at St. Amour. The cause of her death is unrecorded, unknown. The baby was given his mother's surname, which means "Moses." He was baptized in the church of Balanod, near St. Amour, on 7 August 1889.

Marcel's father continued to send money to Mme. Romand to care for the boy, but showed no interest in establishing a relationship with his offspring. Within a short time, Christine's parents learned of their daughter's death and, for some reason, were informed that both mother and child had died together. Félicité and Alfred Moyse never fully accepted this story, yet for the first seven years of Marcel's life, no blood relative knew his whereabouts.

Meanwhile, Mme. Romand had her hands full with her own children and the care of other infants and planned to send Marcel to an orphanage run by the Assistance Publique, a government social service agency that offered funds to poor people in exchange for raising abandoned children. At the end of the nursing period, the baby boy was taken by train to a town that supported an orphanage. But on the way he became cranky, then ill, and his guardian turned right around and delivered him back to St. Amour. Wonder of wonders—as soon as the train pulled into the little station at the edge of the Jura, the infant stopped crying, and by the time he was carried into Mme. Romand's he seemed miraculously healed of irritation. Josephine Perretier, a recently widowed neighbor who often attended the midwife, offered to take Marcel into her home with her two daughters. Marcel would remain fatherless, but Mme. Perretier created an exceptionally warm, secure environment on a meager income derived from the family tobacco shop. The affection the boy received from his adopted mother was as honest and simple as their meals of bread and soup and the plain clothing woven by candlelight. "I grew up," said Marcel Moyse, "with a mother and two sisters in a perfect atmosphere of moral and physical health, an ideal that everyone dreams of."[2]

If he was indulged a little as a youngster, Marcel nevertheless had a normal late-nineteenth-century French peasant childhood. He trundled about in wooden shoes typical of the day and announced that when he grew up, he would be the postman for St. Amour—one of the most respected jobs in the village. Indeed, he often said that if he hadn't been a flutist, he would have been a letter carrier. "It would be less trouble and it would be lovely to walk around St. Amour every day," he explained to people. "You stop off at Monsieur X's or Monsieur Y's, and you have a glass of wine and talk, and you deliver his letters. And then you walk along to the next house."[3]

Marcel was raised as a Catholic, said his prayers, and went to mass. He was especially fascinated by the clong of the great church bell that punctuated the country air. Église St. Amour was the center of village life. Wedding feasts, baptisms, communions, and religious holidays were important entertainments for the villagers, as significant as the exuberant festivals that marked the seasons of growth and harvest. Even when he was working in the fields, Marcel was drawn to the sound of the church bell. "It announced mass to me from far away, and evoked in me the feeling of participating in the Sunday celebration of peace. That made me emotional—that's my nature. What is it that gives me this nature? Don't search. My mother, the sky, St. Amour."[4]

One day Moyse trailed the church warden on his way to chime a service, and was invited up to the tower.

> Then I heard the bells up close—boom-boom—and the response— boom-boom—and he said, "You want to try?" Oh, yes! It was a pleasure to ring the bell. I did not understand music

then, but I was impressed by the bell that day. I am told that I failed to let go of the rope because I was afraid of falling, and I found myself on the ceiling of the bell tower with the rope.[5]

After that, Marcel told everyone he wanted to become the town bell-ringer.

In addition to church activities, Moyse participated in the weekday life of the community. The villagers of St. Amour enjoyed socializing in the evenings, meeting in stables and squares to gossip after a long day at the plow or loom. Their rituals were utilitarian and comfortable: men mended tools or whittled hunks of wood while women sorted vegetables or sewed. There might be a version of the ancient game of *boules*—or lawn bowling—set up by the men near the town café. Occasionally there was dancing to a hurdy-gurdy, and Moyse remembered that citizens ate heartily and quaffed bottles of white wine. But talk always took center stage. Everyone told stories—the same ones, over and over. Novelty was not the aim; enjoying the familiar was the point of fun, and innocent dirty jokes and human foibles were the favorite themes. Occasionally, gatherings were enlivened by traveling tradesmen who told silly tales or performed sleight-of-hand tricks in exchange for a meal. Nomadic troupes of actors, mimes, and acrobats commonly seen in the provinces stopped by St. Amour, too. Decked out in mismatched costumes, they amused the villagers with daring stunts and exaggerated sketches of pompous city people, a centuries-old tradition that flowered in Paris as the Opéra-Comique.[6]

Within this milieu, Marcel made friends with neighbors and tradesmen like the baker, the butcher, and the carpenter, in whose shop his aptitude for woodworking might first have emerged. He was small for his age, but outgoing, agile, and feisty. One of his favorite toys was the *bilboquet:* a stick topped with a wire hoop, to which was attached a piece of string with a ball or stone tied at its end. The idea was to thrust the stick so the string would jerk upwards and the ball could be lobbed skillfully into the hoop (this gesture later inspired the jaunty rhythm of the third exercise in his *24 Melodious Studies*). Marcel loved a challenge, and was always ready and willing to stand up for himself when taunted about his diminutive stature. Once, he got even with a foe after observing that on his daily trips to the bakery, the boy always slid his fresh baguette down the handrail of a nearby set of steps. The next day Marcel smeared animal *merde* on the rail and relished a loud hoot over his careless enemy's ruined loaf.

Marcel and his playmates enjoyed a great deal of freedom, spending their time in more instinctive ways than city children. The bright countryside always beckoned, and small boys and girls, whose sensual appreciation of the outdoors was not yet dulled by seasons of labor in the fields, could careen about the meadows with little thought of time or responsibility. All the same, Mme. Perretier did not hide her poverty from the children and occasionally assigned Marcel small tasks in the tobacco shop. She also nursed him through at least one serious bout with bronchial pneumonia, a harbinger of his lifelong struggles with pleurisy and asthma. "My mother—my stepmother—said, 'We are at the bottom. We are to have an awful time—we are to suffer. We are to struggle,' " Moyse recalled. He added that upon meeting the conductor Arturo Toscanini for the first time, he shared this basic, romantic philosophy with the Maestro: "You have to fight life. Life is not funny. You have to fight."[7]

Yet at the time of Moyse's childhood there were many others in St. Amour living off the land, anxious to make ends meet, and it's unlikely he felt more disadvantaged than his neighbors. An early school photograph of him (see Figure 1) shows a bright-eyed toddler staring directly into the camera, offering neither a coached grin nor the grave expression typical of the days when the making of a photograph was a momentous occasion. The little boy's expression is guileless, slightly questioning, with a hint of a smile. A large white collar covers his shoulders, and his arms have been placed across his lap, which is heaped with the plaid fabric of a dress. The leather soles of white shoes poke forth proudly from beneath the skirt, valuable items meant to be seen. But the child's eyes are what capture the viewer's interest. If one gazes very long, his body recedes, like the pre-painted torsos by itinerant artists who put their best efforts into brushing in the heads of their subjects. The face is dominant, honest, and sensitive.

Even at the peak of his career as *premier* flutist in Paris, Moyse spoke of his childhood in St. Amour as the happiest time of his life. "I loved my adopted mother, but the whole town adopted me," he said. His musical teachings were liberally illustrated with memories of the Jura countryside, as detailed as the rural drawings he rendered to illustrate his flute books and the landscapes he painted in his free time. One student fondly remembered Moyse's description of the exposition of the first movement of the Mozart D Major Concerto:

> The opening ascending scale means that you've decided to take a walk—it's a beautiful day! You start from St. Amour, go up the mountain, and through the trees you can see a little stream, bubbling happily. Here the melody turns—you are getting a bit tired, but it's warm, and the sun is shining down! Finally, all the valley is lying in front of you. A cadence, and then . . . you stop and rest, beneath the shade of a beautiful tree.

CHAPTER TWO

First Flute

THERE have been many descriptions of Marcel Moyse's first flute: it was a hollow reed, a piece of pipe, a split blade of grass. He carved it; somebody carved it for him; someone gave it to him as a gift. Moyse himself offered several versions of the story, all featuring his adopted mother, who, he said, showed him how to harvest the branch of a tree that grows near water and whittle it into a primitive instrument. But Moyse probably learned this technique from other children; it was a common pastime.

"You strike the branch with the handle of a knife, and it opens up inside," Moyse explained. " In the hollowing-out process, you make six holes."[1] Marcel was three or four years old when he made his first flute, which was not transverse (side-blown) but played like a recorder. He took to the little instrument immediately, playing by ear the country songs and popular tunes he heard at town gatherings. "I did not let a day pass without trying to perfect it," he boasted. "The biggest trouble was the sharps and flats." (Only a decade earlier, a six-year-old Catalan child named Pablo had become enthralled with his father's *fluviol,* a five-holed pipe similar to a tin whistle, which he taught himself to play. Carlos Casals destroyed the instrument after his son fainted while tootling in a town procession. The family doctor pronounced the cause of the blackout to be the strain of blowing on the *fluviol.* Pablo Casals next took up the cello.)[2]

A child born content in the country could easily pass his life in his home village, and had Marcel Moyse come into the world under

31

normal circumstances in St. Amour, he might never have seen a real silver flute. But when he was seven years old a strange twist of family tragedy occurred that immeasurably changed the child and the adult he would become. Relatives recount this basic story: Charles Moyse, one of Christine Moyse's brothers, died in a military hospital in Perpignan on 11 January 1896, as a result of illness or injury sustained while serving in the French army in Madagascar. News of the loss was delivered to everyone connected to the family, including the midwife who delivered Marcel. As it turned out, Mme. Romand was no longer alive, and the postmaster at St. Amour sent word back to Besançon that the only possible Moyse relative in the village was a small boy in the care of the Perretier family. Felicité and Alfred Moyse suspected he was their grandson.

More than seven years after Christine Moyse traveled the route, her father rode south to St. Amour, excited and determined to embrace a new family member in the wake of yet another loss. But there was no storybook reunion. Marcel was tremendously happy in St. Amour and worshiped Mme. Perretier, whose kindness to him had won the admiration of the whole village. The boy had no reason to doubt that she was his mother, and when a tearful gentleman appeared on a Sunday morning to claim him, he was shocked and dismayed.

Alfred Moyse presented himself as a goodhearted individual with sufficient means to support and educate a bright child, and after a long discussion, Mme. Perretier finally agreed that Marcel should go to live in Besançon. As difficult as the decision must have been for her, it was much more painful for Marcel, and as the child boarded the train bound for Besançon he suddenly tore away from his grandfather, raced across the platform, and plunged into the nearby river. After more protestations and explanations, the situation was smoothed over and Marcel made the journey. Even so, Marcel tried several times to run away, back to St. Amour. Alfred and Felicité understood their grandson's deep connection to the Perretiers and the close-knit village, and wisely invited one of his adopted sisters for a lengthy stay in Besançon to ease the transition. They also arranged for him to spend the summers in St. Amour. As an adult, Moyse would continue to treat the Perretiers as his own people (see Figures 14 and 17), joining them for holidays and including his adopted sisters' grandchildren on family vacations. It made no difference to him that his musical career baffled his adopted mother, who lived to be over ninety years old, never understanding how Marcel Moyse managed to play the flute for a living.

Besançon must have been to Marcel what Baton Rouge is to a youngster from Mamou. In 1896 the northern Jura community supported cultural fixtures such as a civic music school, an art museum (which occasionally doubled as a marketplace), and a literacy rate on a par with that of Paris. Among the artistic people who had lived there was the poet Stéphane Mallarmé, who spent the 1860s in the provinces teaching English and composing some of his finest lyrics, including *L'après-midi d'un faune.* The self-taught eighteenth-century flutist Michel Blavet, often described as the fountainhead of the French flute school, had been a native of Besançon, the son of a wood-turner. The refinements of the town stemmed from the wealth engendered by the local watchmaking industry, a trade introduced by the Swiss in the nineteenth century. Other precision enterprises have flourished in Besançon, as the snowy winters of the heavily forested mountains encourage indoor activities like toy-making, woodworking, and the manufacture of optical goods. The city even tried to cash in on the French tourism boom around 1890 by attempting to establish a resort, but Besançon-les-Bains, a spa said to specialize in a cure for syphilis, failed. It was too far from Paris. New manufacturing industries fared better; Besançon later built the first factory in Europe for making artificial silk from wood pulp.

Like several thousand other men in the Doubs River region, Marcel's grandfather was a watchmaker. Alfred Moyse's ability to dissect and reassemble the fixings of delicate timepieces intrigued the youngster who would someday compose technical exercises for flute with the same thorough craftsmanship. Alfred Moyse was also a passionate, well-read Socialist who conversed with authority and often emerged as the dominant speaker in labor discussions. Union activity was rare in that part of France, and the alliance of watchmakers was an outstanding exception. It has been said that Alfred sacrificed the employee benefits he was helping to secure when he actively supported a factory boss's unsucccessful campaign for political office, becoming, in effect, the man's mouth-piece. Following the election he lost his job and had such a difficult time getting hired elsewhere that he finally set himself up as an independent watchmaker and repairman. One member of the family says Alfred might have enjoyed more business from the wealthy if he hadn't been so open with his Socialist views. Marcel grew to his mid-teens in a home where strong opinion was not only respected but proudly acted upon, even to the detriment of the family's financial well-being.

Although the watchmakers did not continue to benefit from Alfred Moyse's booming voice, the community chorus did. Alfred sang in the bass section of a prominent Besançon choral society that performed in festivals, competitions, and local opera productions. (Standards of provincial performance and presentation varied. Marguerite Japy Steinheil, a member of the Japy family that dominated the Jura watch and machine tools industries, recalled attending a production of Gounod's *Faust* in nearby Belfort, in which a sewing machine had been substituted for Marguerite's spinning wheel.)[3] This group must have been Alfred's main social activity, as it was for the members of the literally thousands of community choral societies throughout France. It meant even more to him after he went into business for himself. And he often took his grandson to rehearsals. Marcel enjoyed them immensely.

Alfred's hobby as an amateur chorister put him right at the center of provincial musical activity, which, for all its energy, lagged far behind Paris. Still, Besançon mirrored the capital in its penchant for opera. Paris was crazy for opera . Music *meant* opera. And in the outlying towns and cities, the huge, aria-borne artform rattled the windows of jewelbox theaters that faithfully mounted the hits touted in popular journals. Even Berlioz had a hard time getting his instrumental works played. Most of the orchestras heard in concert were stage ensembles lifted out of the pit for an evening. The only exclusively instrumental music Marcel regularly heard emanated from Besançon's town band.

Most of the music Marcel enjoyed during his youth was French. After its defeat in the Franco-Prussian War (1870–71), France flew into a frenzy of nationalism, promoting its art and creating various supporting societies and institutions. Notable landmarks in music included the founding of the Société Nationale de Musique by the composer Camille Saint-Saëns and Romain Bussine, a singing teacher at the Paris Conservatoire. The aim of the Société was to support the cause of French music, and it sponsored many premieres of works by César Franck, Emmanuel Chabrier, Édouard Lalo, Ernest Chausson, Paul Dukas, Saint-Saëns,

Debussy, and Ravel. This activity coincided with a blossoming interest in instrumental music and the revival of past French masters like Lully and Rameau.

For a time, the government subsidized orchestras on the condition that they program a certain percentage of French works. Franck, professor of organ at the Paris Conservatoire, exemplified the passionate side of the new French gospel with his views on "the moral obligations of the artist, the need for elevated standards, the consideration of quality over quantity in the students' tasks, emotional sincerity as an absolute prerequisite in all artistic expression, and above all faith as a primary ingredient."[4]

But while Paris was celebrating the first hearing of Debussy's cooly scored *L'après-midi d'un faune,* cities like Besançon were performing sentimental Gounod. Young Moyse heard lavishly melodic operas or excerpts by popular mid-century French composers such as Georges Bizet (*Carmen* was first presented in 1875, at the Opéra-Comique), Jules Massenet, and Ambroise Thomas, whose *Mignon* received more than a thousand performances in France between 1866 and the turn of the century. (Thomas was considered by the French to be the equal of his Italian contemporary Verdi and exerted a great deal of influence on musical life via the Conservatoire, where he began teaching in 1856. Fifteen years later he became director of the school and awarded a teaching position to his former student, the richly mustachioed Massenet, whom Moyse would later pass in the dark halls of the conservatory.) The opulent textures and passionate, language-hewn contours of these operas made a strong impact on Moyse, but it was Louis Ganne's 1899 operetta *Les saltimbanques* that impressed him most. After seeing it three times in a row, he decided he would somehow become involved in music.

Italian works ran second in popularity to French products. By the time Moyse was born, the Théâtre-Italien, established solely for presenting Italian opera to the French, had celebrated a century of existence in Paris. Rossini had made his home there earlier and become the toast of the town, directing the Italian theater and composing new works for that stage as well as for the Opéra. His post as Inspecteur Général du Chant en France, a mostly honorary title, reflected his influence on the French approach to singing, particularly the renaissance of the light, florid *bel canto* style. For a while, the French and Italians seemed to have created a mutual admiration

society. At a typically overwrought gala honoring Rossini, the
French composer François Lesueur raised his glass "To Rossini! His
ardent genius has opened a new road and signalized a new epoch in
the art of music," to which the Italian guest politely responded, "To
the French School and the prosperity of the Conservatoire!"[5]
Although the influence of Rossini, Bellini, and Verdi and other
"southerners" rankled some Parisian critics and musicians, the
lovely, lusty Italian imprint on French music-making remained.

During Moyse's youth, France loosened its attitude toward
German music. Nationalist fervor had earlier stymied the ambi-
tions of Richard Wagner, who desperately wanted acceptance in
Paris, yet didn't seem able to tone down his megalomania when
visiting his sensitive neighbors. In Besançon, Marcel might have
heard some music by the myth-bound composer, whose earlier
operas—*Der fliegende Holländer, Tannhäuser, Tristan und Isolde,* and
Lohengrin—were excerpted in Paris before Moyse was born. In 1869
Jules Pasdeloup dared to present *Rienzi* in its entirety at the Théâtre-
Lyrique, and later the Wagner propagandist Charles Lamoureux
gave *Lohengrin* at the Éden-Théâtre, where the production was
plagued by anti-Wagner demonstrators. But by the 1890s most
traces of anti-German sentiment had evaporated because French
pro-Wagner writers and artists had convinced their colleagues that
the mad builder of Bayreuth was worth listening to. Wagner's work
was finally seen and heard where it counted most in Paris: at the
Opéra.

Alfred Moyse was pleased with his grandson's interest in this
repertoire. Music gave the younger Moyse a means of expression
that was essentially linked to his earlier childhood in St. Amour. By
the time he was ten years old, Marcel had seen perhaps forty operas
in Besançon and knew by heart the arias his grandfather sang at
home. He also became acquainted with two musically talented
uncles who frequently visited, sons of Alfred and Felicité: Eugène,
an amateur oboist, and Joseph, a cellist in the Lamoureux
Orchestra in Paris whose resonant tone moved Marcel so profoundly that the boy hid under the bed in Joseph's room when his
uncle practiced so he could be as near as possible to the sound. At
least once, Alfred and Felicité took Marcel to concerts in Paris. The
three celebrated New Year's Eve there one year and stayed two
weeks, attending the theater nearly every evening. Marcel was especially enchanted by a Mystery play performed in one of the great

cathedrals, by a children's choir. Productions at the Opéra put Besançon's to shame, and he was impressed, he said, in the same way "any kid would be, who passed a heavily rouged woman on the street."[6] But he was hooked, and insisted on attending again and again. Back in Besançon, he begged to see more on the local stage. Once, in the space of a week, he systematically swiped thirty-five bottles of wine from his grandfather's cellar and sold them for ticket money. Finally, Alfred suggested he take lessons on an instrument. The flute, with which the boy continued to dally in amateur fashion, was the obvious choice.

At that time, Marcel played a six-hole metal flute with a little E-flat key, brought to him by a relative from nearby Bourg-en-Bresse. Right away, he was able to close off parts of holes with his fingers to produce more sharps and flats and play in several keys. "I made up variations in G major and went very fast, so that sometimes the F-sharps were F-naturals," he admitted. "I wasn't quite ready."[7] Marcel had already encountered some basic musical training in school. Music was not a regular offering of the French education system (except in Paris), but classrooms in the eastern part of the country, where shifting borders allowed more German influence, were reputed to have pianos and schoolmasters who were musically trained. His grandfather enrolled Marcel at Besançon's municipal music school in the Grandvelle Palace, an imposing structure whose landscaped center courtyard and arched stone breezeways Moyse later sketched for the front cover of his most widely studied book, *Tone Development Through Interpretation* (a drawing of St. Amour is on the back). There, Marcel learned the fundamentals of music from highly educated teachers from Strasbourg, refugees from the Franco-Prussian War. His lessons in solfège were, by his own account, "absolutely extraordinary." The secret, he said, lay in discipline. On Monday, the class learned a new exercise very slowly, singing to the strict slap of a ruler. On Wednesday, the teacher increased the tempo, but only after every child had sung it perfectly at the slower speed. By Friday, the students were expected to execute the material at a quick clip, but not so fast that their articulation blurred or slipped. Every afternoon, Marcel skipped home from school to the tunes of solfège exercises, imprinting the skill exactly, deeply as DNA. He also developed a lifelong abhorrence of speed for speed's sake. "If music goes too fast, one doesn't hear the detail anymore. It has the effect of several concierges chatting among themselves—one doesn't know what the other is saying."[8]

Besançon's handful of semi-professional flutists became Moyse's first role models. The posts these men held were confined mostly to the band, and special performances for wealthy families. Marguerite Japy recounted that her father routinely waved a baton before his own personal band at the family chateau near Besançon:

> Three times a week the band organized by my father came to rehearse at our house. Chamber music did not quite satisfy him, and he founded this band, which numbered forty-five musicians. Ah! Those rehearsals. When the weather was fair they took place under the chestnut trees, but if it rained or snowed the "forty-five" and their conductor would gather in the main drawing-room of the "castle" where two hundred people could have been seated comfortably, or in the dining room, to the despair of my mother, who would ask my father, "Don't you think, Édouard, that your band is just a little too noisy?" My father kissed her laughingly, flourished the baton, and the rehearsal began.[9]

At the civic music school, Marcel began taking flute lessons with an Alsatian musician named Angelloz, whom he described as "a very good teacher—a disciplinarian."[10] His first real metal flute was lent to him by Angelloz, who later made a gift of it to his prized pupil. The instrument presumably featured the Boehm mechanism. The new system—with its large, well-placed tone holes, padded keys, and cylindrical bore—was a great improvement over the traditional transverse wooden flutes whose clumsy key arrangement forced players to invent awkward cross-fingerings or stick to major and minor keys containing few sharps and flats. Boehm perfected his flute in 1847, but it wasn't adopted at the Paris Conservatoire (the arbiter of all pedagogical traditions and developments in France) until the time of Louis Dorus, professor of flute from 1860 to 1868 and teacher of Paul Taffanel, who became one of Moyse's mentors.

Marcel probably worked from the first major tutorial for the Boehm system flute, published by Henri Altès, who succeeded Dorus at the Conservatoire nine years before Marcel was born. Altès was flutist at the Opéra and the Société des Concerts du Conservatoire, the prestigious orchestra comprising conservatory faculty and graduates. Altès also taught Adolphe Hennebains, with whom Moyse eventually studied. Besides providing a well-ordered, encyclopedic text and specific, practical exercises (the current edition runs 372 pages),[11] the Altès method set forth a philosophy of musicianship that reflected the composer-centered concerns of the French nationalist movement. It also liberally quoted the French violinist, composer, and pedagogue Pierre Baillot (1771–1842), the last representative of the classical Paris school of violinists, whose *L'art du violon* (1834) is still considered a standard work.[12] Moyse's teachings a whole century later would echo—strikingly—Altès's point of view. In a section entitled "On Perfection in Execution," Altès wrote:

> The principal quality to acquire in order to play with perfection is neatness. . . . The elements of neatness are: scrupulous observation of the time, exact appreciation of the value of notes, rigid attention so as to prevent confusion in articulation, that is to say, that the tongue and fingers move in irreproachable conformity with each other . . . executing difficult passages with the same ease as simple ones. . . . The result is attained by the assiduous practice of the Daily Exercises. . . .
>
> Beauty of tone consists not merely in that it is emitted pure and limpid with due regard for nuancing and correct intonation, but, if the execution is not to become dry and expressionless, the tone must also be (consistent with the nature of the music interpreted) by turns energetic, pathetic, full, soft, velvety, sweet.

Adding that "music should be punctuated the same as discourse," Altès then offered the words of Baillot:

> "There are two ways of making an accent, one which may be derived from technicality, the other which comes from inspiration. . . . If [the pupil] is born with genius for music, it will be promptly recognized by his manner of interpreting the composer's intentions, but before all things he ought to be accustomed to render with scrupulous accuracy that which the composer has materially indicated.
>
> "When the pupil has become proficient in the technicality of his instrument he is not to fancy that he is at the end of his labors. It is only when every difficulty is overcome that talent can take its upward flight, that it knows no more stumbling

block, and that the artist becomes all that he is fitted to become; expression reveals to his talents new horizons whose limits are the emotions and sentiments of mankind. It is not sufficient to be born emotional, his soul must possess that expansive force, that warmth of feeling that radiates beyond him, which magnetizes, penetrates, burns."[13]

In addition to Altès's weighty tome, Marcel might also have studied with Angelloz books by Louis Drouet (1792–1873), the prolific virtuoso of the old eight-keyed flute whose *Vingt-cinq études célèbres* is still in print. (Drouet reportedly studied composition at the Conservatoire with the flutist-composer Anton Reicha, the son of an Old Town piper who had a predilection for mathematics and the philosophy of Kant. Reicha's legacy includes theoretical treatises and a great stack of woodwind quintets, the best of which Moyse would teach in as much detail as a work by Mozart or Beethoven.)

Although his lungs were permanently weakened by the respiratory ailments he had endured as a small child, Marcel excelled at the flute, and in robust sports like diving and swimming, activities he enjoyed well into his sixties. Physical fitness was a priority of French education in those days; the postwar pride that boosted the arts also turned athletics into a patriotic duty, and by 1880 children in most French schools were required to participate in gymnastics classes four and a half hours a week. The athletic awards Marcel won meant a lot to him and probably elicited wider peer approval than good grades in Latin and reading. With all the world-class honors he eventually accepted as a flutist, he always took pleasure in showing off a particular diving medal he won as a youth.

Besides being physically accomplished, Marcel was good-looking and playful, and he attracted attention with practical gags that preceded the tableware acrobatics and scatological pranks he always delighted in. He was a good student and attended mass (he took his first communion in Besançon) but was not exceptionally goal-driven. Even more than other boys his age, he looked forward to the end of the school year and summertime, when he could return to St. Amour.

Marcel's youth in Besançon was pleasant, but he remained carefree only a few years before he was expected to select and assume his life's work. Like other French middle-class children at the turn of the century, Marcel Moyse did not enjoy the plethora of educational and professional possibilities that exist today. Most young people were counseled to leave school in their early teens to learn standard trades. Although he continued to take lessons on the flute, a musical career did not seem to be an option for Marcel, despite the example of his uncle Joseph. A cello was one thing— there were rows of them in orchestras—but a flute? There were few opportunities: some orchestras, a chamber music milieu that was just beginning to develop in Paris, and circus bands. There was no recording industry nor even a widespread music-education system. At his grandfather's insistence, Marcel attempted successive apprenticeships in law and carpentry, the same trade Pablo Casals's father had planned for him until his mother insisted on sending him to music school in Barcelona. Marcel liked cabinetmaking, also excelled in a course in metallurgy, and began to construct useful objects like chairs and little trunks for his grandparents. Yet these activities were unfulfilling—the restless, energetic young man became quickly bored, and the only desire that arose from these experiments was an impractical one: to become a sculptor. Finally, Joseph Moyse invited him to come to Paris and discover a livelihood. Marcel accepted, and Alfred, greatly relieved, granted his blessing.

Paris Conservatoire

IN 1904 Paris was a gameboard for self-conscious culture and corrupt politics, direct expression and innuendo. For the
fourteen-year-old boy rooted in peasantry, the move to the city was
invigorating and a little frightening. Marcel Moyse was amazed by
what he found.

Marcel moved into his Uncle Joseph's home at 17 Rue Puteaux
near Boulevard de Clichy, on the southern edge of Montmartre, a
tangled district of slanted streets and alleys that had not yet crawled
all the way to the crest of La Butte, the hill recently crowned with the
bright white shell of the church of the Sacré-Coeur. The green
upper slopes were still textured with gardens, vineyards, quarries,
little houses and windmills—a charming area from which to view
the broadening sprawl of Paris. Lower down lay the center of
Parisian nightlife and visionary artistry, France's Greenwich Village.
Montmartre's bohemian culture had already become a cliché by
1900, when the literally starving neighborhood composer Gustave
Charpentier struck it rich with *Louise,* an operatic tribute to life in
the ghetto and hand-to-mouth freedom. Montmartre was a place
where men still dueled and brothels flourished. In cafés decorated
with bold murals and painted statuary, painters, writers, and composers met daily to discuss the latest exhibitions, books, and performances. Montmartre bohemians were interested in fame, not
money, and everyone cultivated at least one idiosyncrasy to advance
his uniqueness. Picasso kept a pet mouse in a table drawer and
carried a pistol. Poet Max Jacob's apartment walls were chalked

with signs of the zodiac; he told fortunes for cash. Playwright Alfred Jarry regularly punctured the apples on his neighbor's tree with a bow and arrow—an innocent gesture compared to the bloody handprints that lined the stairway to his flat, where the windows jingled with crucifixes. Writer Nigel Gosling vividly described the Montmartre artists as "living in the flank of fashionable Paris like a nest of microbes who would soon destroy their host culture."[1]

Joseph Moyse's apartment was located within earshot of the Montmartre cafés, cabarets, and dance halls that shivered with raspy renditions of tart chansons and pounding displays of the cancan. Nearby was the grand and gaudy dance hall the Moulin Rouge, whose neon-complected, overdressed patrons were preserved in gleaming oils by Toulouse-Lautrec. The Moulin Rouge was built the year Moyse was born and was the site where Joseph Pujol, one of the most successful entertainers of the *fin de siècle,* had launched his career. (Pujol earned a dubious honor in Paris's musical history. As the city's most noted fartist, he perfected a novelty act that involved playing the flute via a hose inserted in his anus.) Crouched in the shadows of the infamous palace and its brassy sisters were smaller, less toney establishments that did well enough presenting amateur shows in spare rooms and chairless corners. The iconoclastic composer Erik Satie earned a living for a while playing in some of these cabarets. When Marcel Moyse moved to Paris, the teenaged *chanteur* Maurice Chevalier was warbling in the awninged cafés of the suburbs, hoping for a chance at Montmartre.

A British visitor named Hannah Lynch probably spoke for many ruffled, titillated tourists when, with a sniff of her pen, she referred to the district as "the hill of impropriety." And one Paris author wrote of his neighborhood:

> In Montmartre, there is more intimacy. We commune with the dear dead better. Murger and Offenbach are buried here, Renan and Gauthier, Lannes . . . and Berlioz and Greuze, the exquisite Greuze who had a wretched wife, but how beautiful she was! They represent what is best in France: heroism and wit, subtle art, deep thought and clear language, logic and method, inspiration and recklessness. . . . And that is typically French, Madame, or I am an old fool![2]

The leading composers in Paris could be divided into three camps: the German-inspired romantics such as Vincent D'Indy and other students of César Franck, the classicists represented by Saint-Saëns and Fauré, and the upstart impressionists led by Claude Debussy. Debussy had just been named to the Légion d'honneur (the highest civilian honor in France), and cultivated crowds were still talking about *Pelléas et Mélisande,* a sensation two seasons old, not to mention the composer's desertion of the first Mrs. Debussy for Mme. Sigismond Bardac, née Emma Claude Moyse (a distant relation), a part-time singer and banker's wife. A Polish pianist named Artur Rubinstein was about to offer his Paris debut, and the Spanish cello prodigy Pablo Casals had recently made his first solo appearance there.

In Joseph Moyse, Marcel observed firsthand the life of the average professional musician. Joseph played in the cello section of the Lamoureux Orchestra, or Concerts Lamoureux, a highly respected musical institution founded in 1881 by Charles Lamoureux. The orchestra gave weekly Sunday afternoon concerts that were mainstays of Parisian concert life and often included premieres of new French works such as Debussy's *Nocturnes* (1900). Marcel must have witnessed the 1905 debut of *La mer,* an event that thrilled some critics and bored others. At this time, Concerts Lamoureux was functioning successfully under the direction of the late founder's son-in-law, Camille Chevillard. (According to Louis Moyse, most chairs in orchestras like Lamoureux, Colonne, Pasdeloup, and the Société des Concerts du Conservatoire were, until World War II, unpaid, honorary positions that were nevertheless prestigious and helped players secure jobs that did pay.) Joseph Moyse also performed in chamber or salon concerts and, according to Marcel, may have moonlighted with a gypsy orchestra to supplement his income. Marcel later credited his uncle with introducing him to Hungarian style and said he first played Doppler's *Fantaisie pastorale hongroise* with Joseph.

Most of all, Marcel depended on his uncle to interpret Parisian life and to guide him in determining his place in it. He was sensitive about his rural upbringing and had a great deal of catching up to do, so Joseph Moyse established a plan for his nephew, designed to bring him socially and intellectually up to speed. In the first month, Marcel could do whatever he pleased: attend concerts, visit museums, stroll the streets. Then he would prepare for a career. Because Marcel had announced, tentatively, that he wanted to be a sculptor, Joseph enrolled him in a drawing class at the École Boule.

But Joseph also intended to find a flute teacher for his talented nephew, with the idea that Marcel might be good enough to attend the Paris Conservatoire, the prestigious national music school that offered free tuition to the gifted. Together with Alfred, Joseph Moyse purchased a new flute for Marcel and immediately assigned his nephew several daily practice sessions of forty-five minutes each, interspersed with fifteen minutes of reading from his extensive personal library. Joseph, a strict Catholic, was an austere guardian, well organized and disciplined, and he monitored Marcel's progress closely.

"My uncle would listen to me practicing," Moyse recalled. "Often he would call out, 'Marcel! What are you doing? Where is the beat? I would like an accent. I don't understand!' "

> Sometimes I was afraid. I would ask my aunt if he was home, because I was afraid to practice if he was there. Without being in the room, he would call to me, "Marcel! Your A is too sharp; your C is too sharp; your B, too sharp." Never your A is too flat, your E too flat. In flute we are obsessed with resonance—is the F clear? But my uncle talked about intonation. I found that the way to correct these problems of intonation was in tightening or relaxing the jaws and the lips. My uncle was a good teacher. I was lucky.[3]

Joseph also took Marcel to rehearsals and concerts, and was probably responsible for introducing him to the military élan of John Philip Sousa, who brought his band to Europe five times between 1900 and 1911. Moyse enjoyed the pageantry that accompanied the performances, but it was Sousa's precise, unflagging rhythm that he admired most and praised the rest of his life. *The Stars and Stripes Forever* remained one of his favorite pieces of music.

A week or so before Marcel's fifteenth birthday in May 1904, Joseph presented him to Adolphe Hennebains, solo flutist of the Opéra and a former student of Altès. Hennebains remarked favorably on the boy's abilities and accepted him as a pupil, a decision that brought Marcel one giant step closer to the Conservatoire. It was no secret that young musicians who studied with Conservatoire professors "on the outside" had an advantage at the school's admissions auditions, and Hennebains was assistant to Paul Taffanel, teacher of the Conservatoire flute class (see Figures 3–6).

Hennebains was also a prominent descendant of the so-called

French School of wind playing, which arches back to the founding of the Paris Conservatoire in 1795.[4] At the very least, the "French School" can be described as a continuing tradition in which each flute professor at the Conservatoire is a student of a former professor. However, even the French continue to debate the musical philosophies and technical nuances that constitute this tradition. The chief characteristics of French flute-playing are, like Monet's water lilies, easily recognized but variously perceived. Finesse of tone and dynamics, a clear, singing sound, an infinite color palette, and a spirited yet thoughtful interpretive personality dedicated to the composer's intentions are the qualities most often cited in conversations and dissertations that attempt to define what is French. It has also been suggested that the French style is simply any French flutist's response to the technical possibilities of the Boehm flute. Indeed, many French-trained flutists make a distinction between the pre-Boehm century and the "modern" French flute school, of which Taffanel, the first major virtuoso to wholly embrace the Boehm system (under Dorus at the Conservatoire) and to adapt to the language and style of musical impressionism, is considered the father. Yet others reject the idea of a school or of a well-defined method and philosophy of playing, even for Moyse's time. Artists like Louis Moyse (Marcel's son) and Michel Debost maintain "it just happened" that some very gifted musicians of the late nineteenth and early twentieth centuries chose to play the flute and so blessed the world with superior musicianship via that instrument.

Moyse contributed to the confusion by constantly invoking the great "traditions" handed down to him by his teachers, and downplaying the term "French School." For him, the French flute style was related to French pronunciation. "The French pronounce 'eu' a certain way, and you pronounce it 'oo,' you see," he told an American newspaper reporter. "The position of the mouth and the tongue required to speak French is a natural one to produce the flute tone. In my classes I even notice the difference in sound when a pupil from the south of France plays against one from the north."[5] In a discussion with his grandson Michel, he had more to say:

> One speaks of the French wind school, but it's a vague term which means nothing. . . . From the ethnic point of view, the French have perhaps more facility than certain other groups. It

could have something to do with the fact that France is a temperate country—not too hot, not too cold. There's sweetness, the living is easy.

For the rest, everyone knows that the language plays a great role in execution. One uses the tongue in a certain manner in articulation like the violinists do with their bow. The tongue in Paris is lively, but in the south of France it is accented a little differently than in the north. The north is a little bit heavier, and in the south lighter. . . . The tongue has to become supple according to the demands of the musical phrase; perfect articulation is precise, light, easy, and beautiful. That is really important, because it is the genius of the French School.

In the class of Taffanel, I learned there was a true French School. It's a language. In brief, it's an assimilable language. I know, because the English assimilated it.[6]

Asked about the French School's interpretive approach, Moyse responded simply, "I don't want to be too pedagogical. But when one uses a new language like Debussy, it is necessary to *be* Debussy."

Hennebains was in his early forties when Marcel Moyse came to his studio. By all accounts he was a lighthearted, good-humored gentleman with a weakness for practical jokes, and he once posed for a publicity photograph as Pan, clad only in an animal skin (see Figure 5). He treated his students as if they were his own children, and Marcel often referred to him as "Papa Hennebains." Once, when Hennebains noticed that one of his poorer students did not own an overcoat, he devised a discreet way to buy him one. On the pretext of needing help selecting clothing for his conservatory-age grandson, Hennebains invited Moyse and the coatless student on a shopping trip. The trio browsed in a store, and Hennebains had both young men try on hats and coats to see how they might look on a similar student. When the needy fellow was buttoned into a coat that fit him well, Hennebains declared it perfect for his grandson, and purchased it. Outside the store, Hennebains pressed the package into the boy's arms and without any to-do, insisted he keep it. Moyse, who had been included in Hennebains's plan so his classmate would not suspect anything of the trip, was also entrusted with keeping the matter to himself so his friend could retain his dignity under the circumstances.

Hennebains possessed a free, lively style of playing that, thanks to the recent technological magic worked on 78 r.p.m. recordings, can now be heard on compact disc.[7] If Marcel had developed any unusual technical habits in Besançon, Hennebains probably corrected them, with the exception of his embouchure; he blew more from the left side of his mouth. This did nothing to impede Moyse's artistry and was undoubtedly the most natural embouchure for him, although it may have contributed to some technical weakness toward the end of his playing career. It was Hennebains who prepared Marcel for a successful audition at the Conservatoire just one year later, and it was he whom Moyse first emulated devotedly. Moyse said on occasion that of all his teachers, he had the most in common, stylistically and temperamentally, with Papa Hennebains.

Hennebains had much to offer Marcel through the repertoire of Jean-Louis Tulou (1786–1865), professor of flute at the Conservatoire from 1829 to 1856 and composer of solos that dominated the examination list for the second half of the nineteenth century. The music of Austrian composer Albert Franz Doppler (1821–1883) was also explored, as were pieces by the Danish late classical-early romantic composer Friedrich Kuhlau (1786–1832), whose garden of solos, duos, trios, and quartets for flute is still harvested enthusiastically. (Kuhlau was born sixteen years after Beethoven and outlived him by five years. The composers knew one another.) Kuhlau's works seemed to have left the greatest impression on Moyse during the time he studied with Hennebains.

"I can never forget my first contact with Mr. Hennebains," Moyse said in a conversation with his daughter-in-law, Blanche Honegger Moyse. "I played for him a solo for flute and piano, written by Kuhlau. And he said, 'You don't know this yet, you are too young. But I consider Kuhlau to be the Beethoven of the flute.' "

"If you do not learn Kuhlau deeply," Moyse continued, "you will never be able to play Mozart and Beethoven the right way. If you learn a solo by Kuhlau in a conscientious manner, during two or three months, you will learn almost all of the rules about playing this kind of music. A flutist without knowledge of Kuhlau is not a complete flutist."[8]

To get the most from Beethoven's contemporary, Marcel later made friends with a wealthy amateur flutist named Chabrier (no relation to the composer), who loved to play duets in his free time. Every Monday night for several years, Moyse was a guest in the man's home. From five to seven o'clock in the evening, the pair played billiards in the game room, after which they enjoyed a fine dinner. When the meal was finished they played their flutes together for several hours. Sometimes they were joined by other flutists for larger ensembles. (Moyse later remarked that there was "a great connection" between billiards and the flute. For a long time a large pool table dominated the living room of his last home in West Brattleboro, Vermont, but students report that it was usually piled with flute music and correspondence.) These sessions continued into the early years of World War I and helped Marcel immensely in developing both his ear and the confident, soloistic flair that won recording opportunities and orchestra positions.

He once explained:

> When you are in an orchestra, of course, you play with different instruments. There are the differences between a flute and oboe, or a clarinet, and sometimes you have to fight about dynamics, and many other things. But in Kuhlau, with just two flutes, the challenge is to get a special quality in the tone to highlight [one flute part as distinguished from the other]. This helped me very much to be precise, and to play with good intonation.[9]

He added that because the flute tends to play sharp in the high register and flat in the low register when diminishing from *fortissimo,* the like-instrument duets (one part high, the other low) offered the formidable challenge of adjusting to extreme opposite tendencies.

During the short time he spent under Hennebains's tutelage, Moyse was exposed to the burgeoning new French repertoire for flute, such as the *Suite de trois morceaux* of Benjamin Godard, which he heard Hennebains perform with the composer. (Moyse later played the piece with Hennebains's daughter Madeleine at a soirée given by Moyse's old teacher "Papa Angelloz" in Paris.) He was also aware of Hennebains's close professional relationship with the composer Cécile Chaminade, whose Concertino for flute and orchestra, Opus 107, had been commissioned as an examination piece for the Conservatoire in 1902. Of the competition solos brought to life during Taffanel's fifteen years as flute professor, the Concertino is one of the most charming. Today it is the only regularly performed work of the composer. Chaminade wrote several other pieces for flute (*Serenade to the Stars, Pièce romantique,*

Gavotte), most of which were dedicated to Hennebains.

Cécile Chaminade was the first woman to produce a work for the flute examinations, and one of the first woman composers in France to gain international recognition. She began her career at a huge disadvantage: her father, who felt his daughter's aspirations were unseemly for a woman of the well-to-do class, forbade her enrolling in the Conservatoire even though she was considered talented by one of the professors and invited to study music theory there. Cécile's father did allow her to study theory and counterpoint privately with Conservatoire professors, and for a while she was a pupil of Benjamin Godard, who was known for his salon music.

As Marcia J. Citron suggested in her bio-bibliography of Chaminade, this limited education probably impeded the composer's creative development. Her principal influence was the conservative Saint-Saëns, and she lacked interaction with other students and the opportunity to establish a network of peers. To a large degree, Cécile Chaminade was self-made. An accomplished pianist, she furthered her career by performing her own music, and she toured widely, especially in the two decades straddling 1900. Her early output included large-scale works, but after the death of her father (and the loss of his financial support) in 1887, she turned to portable songs and chamber pieces that were accessible to both amateur and professional performers. Her numerous recitals could be considered promotional tours for the music she published.

Chaminade's early tours were limited to Europe and England. Yet she enjoyed an enthusiastic following in the United States, where her music sold very well. Popular American women's magazines published articles about her, and newspapers occasionally reported her accomplishments. The most striking symbol of her appeal in the U.S. was the proliferation of the Chaminade Clubs, a network of amateur music clubs (mostly female) that developed at the end of the nineteenth century during the rise of women's social organizations. Partly in response to this phenomenon, Chaminade finally made a tour of the U.S. in 1908 (during which she told members of the press that she found Debussy's music "a bit gray" and "wanting in significant ideas").[10] At one point there may have been more than two hundred Chaminade Clubs, and they kept multiplying as late as 1940.

Chaminade married at the shockingly advanced age of forty-four, and held the opinion that conventions of marriage destroyed a

woman's art; the domestic and the artistic could never be recon-
ciled. Her husband, the elderly music publisher Louis-Mathieu
Carbonel, was strictly a platonic companion. Chaminade agreed to
marry him only under the conditions that they continue to live in
their own homes (he in Marseille, she in Paris) and engage in no
sexual relations. Their contact was limited mostly to visits and concert trips.

The Chaminade-Carbonel wedding took place just months
before the completion of the Concertino, and in 1903 Carbonel fell
ill with a lung disease that foreshadowed his death four years later.
In the meantime, the Concertino was taken up by the finest flutists
of the day. Leopold Lafleurance performed it publicly as early as
1904, with the pianist Gabrielle Turpin in the recital hall of *Musica*
magazine. Hennebains performed it several times with Chaminade
at the piano. The reviewer of one of their appearances praised the
interpreter of "this exquisitely original work" and added, "Those
who heard it will never forget it."[11] In 1913, Chaminade became the
first woman composer to be named a Chevalier of the Légion
d'honneur.

The Concertino is really no more than a light nineteenth-
century-style salon piece, equipped with a haunting, noble melody
that poofs out into a fluffy fantasia. The piano accompaniment is
quite simple. Yet Chaminade's salon solo is a good salon solo, one
of the best of the genre. The opening melody especially demonstrates her affinity for songs, of which she composed well over a
hundred.

Hennebains may have been an active booster of new French
styles, but when it came to the latest interpretations of Bach and the
early Viennese repertoire, he was as uninformed as other musicians trained in the days before widespread scholarly knowledge of
baroque style. The landmark figure in the performance practices
movement, Arnold Dolmetsch, first scratched the surface of the
subject the year Moyse was born, and for the next two decades he
worked mainly on the restoration of antique keyboard and stringed
instruments and the building of new ones. It wasn't until 1911 that
he came to Paris to research his book *The Interpretation of the Music of
the 17th and 18th Centuries,* the first comprehensive study of the field.
In the 1920s Dolmetsch turned his attention to reconstructing
recorders, an activity that resulted in specific implications for the
flute and other wind instruments. Wanda Landowska, another vital

figure in the movement, performed on the harpsichord in Paris as early as 1903, but her impact on baroque performance style was not felt until long after Moyse's formal training had ended.

In addition, Bach's compositions for flute had only recently been recognized in Paris concert halls; Taffanel was one of the first to promote them. The nineteenth-century Bach Revival, which yielded the Bachgesellschaft's edition of the composer's complete works, happened mainly in Germany, Austria, and England. Even the 1927 edition of the biblical (and British) *Grove's Dictionary of Music and Musicians* lists only works by Mozart, Spohr, Weber, Beethoven, Haydn, Kuhlau, Reicha, and Schubert as the major literature for flute. Regarding the fecund Dane Kuhlau, the dictionary's "Flute" entry carries this lament: "Indeed, but for a fire which destroyed the composer's manuscripts, their number would be at least threefold. Such as are extant afford inestimable models of construction and originality."

In fact, due to historical ignorance and fallout from the post-war chauvinism of the previous century, only a small number of French wind players before World War II paid much attention to news about the "authentic" delivery of baroque music. The Paris Conservatoire was preoccupied with current works by the country's mainstream composers (Massenet, yes; Satie, no). Alfredo Casella, who studied Bach in Italy before coming to Paris, remarked in his autobiography that none of his Conservatoire classmates knew the great composer's music. It is understandable that Hennebains, like his colleagues, rendered baroque music in rather late romantic, self-disclosing fashion. When asked about his own Leduc edition of the Bach Partita in A minor for solo flute (which Louis Moyse says his father copied from a manuscript—not in Bach's hand—he found at the Geneva Conservatory), Moyse replied, "I did nothing. I just printed everything I learned from Hennebains."[12] His recordings of the Brandenburg Concerto No. 5 and the Second Suite made in 1935 and 1936 with Rudolf Serkin and Adolf Busch support this point of view, yet the Moyse-Serkin-Busch rendition is still beloved because the trio's expressive, symbiotic approach is so satisfying. Perhaps it was through Bach that Hennebains charmed Moyse with the expressive potential in the bittersweet appoggiatura. "Above all, I learned grace and poetry from Hennebains, because he was a poet," Moyse said. "He persuaded me that the appoggiatura says 'I love you.' "[13]

Moyse worked hard under Hennebains but was still not entirely centered on the flute. For a while he pursued his interests in the visual and plastic arts, auditing classes at the École Boule and visiting the ateliers of artists such as Maurice Utrillo, a young painter six years Moyse's senior who worked in the impressionist style. For Moyse, music won over art as a profession because it offered a more secure living (Louis Moyse remembers that when his father's career was expanding in the 1920s, Utrillo was begging for food on the streets of Montmartre).[14] But Moyse's studies at the École Boule resulted in pleasing drawings, colorful, technically proficient paintings, and home woodworking projects that ran all the way from impressive (his summer house in St. Amour) to impractical (an automobile trailer whose walls covered the tires so they could not be changed without sawing into the structure). Moyse's experiments in these areas always exhibited highly personal—some might say quirky—instincts.

Moyse acquired two important tools during his brief venture into the world of visual art: a physical connection to artistic forms, and a language of metaphors. He thoughtfully regarded the construction of human anatomy and the principles of architecture and later applied them to the analysis and performance of music. For example, instead of speaking about melodic and harmonic structure in theoretical terms, he would compare a musical passage or an entire piece to the human skeleton, pointing out the relative importance of shoulder bones, elbows, and fingers. "You see," he'd say, grasping a pupil's shoulder, "Mozart loved this shoulder so much, he put a trill on it." A student might be asked to "make a skeleton" of a melody, a task akin to the linear structural analyses derived from the work of the Austrian theorist Heinrich Schenker. Moyse also used building construction as a metaphor for musical form. The foundation, the frame, the columns—every element was set out in proportion by the architect (or composer). Style emerged from the unique combination of these elements, and was not to be "touched-up" by the performer with a lot of personal gingerbread. This sense of balance and placement encouraged Moyse to develop a penchant for "absolutely indisputable precision."[15]

Moyse's awareness of color also began to mature. He had come to Paris at the end of a time when musicians and artists of the city fraternized daily and even dabbled in each other's fields. Debussy, Saint-Saëns, and Fauré all enjoyed sketching, and Manet and Degas were trained musicians. Painters like Manet, Toulouse-Lautrec, and Pierre Bonnard designed sheet music covers, and fussy Debussy specified hues and typefaces for at least one of his manuscripts. Matisse titled a painting *Harmony in Red,* and Whistler painted *Nocturne in Black and Gold,* while Degas and Toulouse-Lautrec rendered scenes from concerts, operas, or dance. Other artists painted less representational impressions of music they had heard. Composers and artists were often drawn to the same subjects: nature, the countryside, water, children, the Orient and other exotica, birds and animals, the circus, the music hall.[16] Moyse was not actually part of this milieu; his childhood in St. Amour was largely responsible for his imaginative use of rural scenes and situations. But the artistic sympathies of his time encouraged and enhanced such preoccupations. Had this not been the case, it's fair to guess that the explicitly picturesque elements in Moyse's playing and teaching might not have been so pronounced.

At least one more activity attracted Marcel Moyse: cycling. France had been velo-crazy since the 1890s, when two-wheelers with pneumatic tires were standardized and competitive racing became the French national sport. This novel means of mobility helped create the excursion-happy generation that created the demand for the first *Guides Michelin* in 1900. Before the turn of the century, only the well-heeled could afford bicycles. But by the time Marcel got to Paris, bikes were no longer status symbols but mass-produced, affordable vehicles driven by the less exalted. (The rich had turned to automobiles.) At least two Conservatoire students of the late 1890s—Alfredo Casella and Albert Wolff—rode in the Sunday bicycle races at the Parc-des-Princes; Joseph Moyse performed in spring soirées given by the Michelin brothers. Marcel probably obtained a bicycle early on; he enjoyed exercising and watching the races. "If you want to play fast," he once said, "I don't want to hear your flute. [For speed], I prefer to go to the velodrome in Paris, to see the sprinters in the bicycle races. It is exciting, and it is good for the health because you are in fresh air."[17] He also praised the efficient physique of cyclists, and told students that a flutist's fingers should be in fine physical shape, the blood visible and pulsing just beneath the skin, as in the ankles of a velo champion.

Despite the time spent on art and sport, Marcel made such swift progress with Hennebains that after a few months he was invited to audit Paul Taffanel's class at the Paris Conservatoire. If there is a father of the "modern" French School, it is Taffanel (see Figure 3). Born in 1844 in Bordeaux, he went to Paris in 1858 to study privately with Louis Dorus and continued with him after Dorus was appointed professor of flute at the Conservatoire two years later. Since Dorus was responsible for sanctioning the use of the Boehm flute in France, Taffanel became one of the first Conservatoire flutists trained in that system. He gained first prizes in flute (1860), harmony (1862), and fugue (1865), which prepared him for a triple career as flutist, composer, and conductor.

Taffanel had played solo flute at both the Opéra and the Société des Concerts du Conservatoire. He also founded two important ensembles: the Société Classique (a double quintet of strings and winds) and the Société de Musique de Chambre pour Instruments à Vent, which premiered a good deal of new French music. But by the time Marcel Moyse visited Taffanel's class, the venerated musician, then sixty, had been retired from playing for more than ten years. His appointment as chief conductor of the Opéra in 1893 and increased composing activities had forced him to relinquish his Opéra chair to Hennebains, though he continued to teach flute at the Conservatoire. From 1892 to 1901 he also conducted the Société des Concerts, an institution that always attracted a full house. One British tourist complained that foreigners could not hope to get into a concert even "with a golden key."[18] The lady lucked out, though, and wrote of Taffanel in a way that mirrors other contemporary observations:

> M. Taffanel, the able conductor of the Conservatoire Orchestra, cannot compare with the great German conductors, he has not the genius of Mottl, nor the magical temperament of Weingartner, nor the individuality of the French conductor, the late Lamoureux. But in his quiet, measured way, his is an incomparable artistry, to judge him by the results of his lead. M. Taffanel has not a suspicion of affectation or histrionics. He is simplicity itself, the very model of impersonality. He so effaces himself that you are conscious of his presence only by the perfection of his orchestra. He is so easy and subdued that he hardly seems necessary in this admirable triumph of art.[19]

The months Marcel spent observing Taffanel's class were invaluable. He immediately grasped the standard required for admittance, a clear goal to meet. One of his strongest memories from that time was of hearing the older student Georges Laurent play a study by the Danish flutist-composer Joachim Andersen.

> He began with Opus 15 of Andersen, and played in such a beautiful way that I said to myself, "it is possible to learn music with Taffanel only from this book, because it is everything. If I succeed and enter the Conservatoire next year, I will begin with this in November . . . and play it until May, like Laurent." I succeeded [in entering the school]. When Taffanel asked which studies I'd like to take, I said, "The same as Laurent."[20]

Under the guidance of Hennebains and with the approval of Taffanel, Marcel auditioned for and won a place in the flute class at the Paris Conservatoire in the fall of 1905. Moyse left no account of this occasion, but the pianist André Benoist, a student in the 1890s, remembered his initial showing in the impressive, century-old edifice, the former Hôtel des Menus-Plaisirs du Roi on the Rue Bergère, not far from the Opéra.

> I walked down the long, dark corridor that led to the examination hall, escorted by an indifferent usher, and feeling like a lamb being led to his slaughter. The usher opened a door and gently pushed me through. I found myself on a stage, facing a dark, gloomy, rather small concert hall. The stage displayed a concert grand piano, on the music stand of which stood, on opposite sides, a lighted candle. I could think of nothing else but a wake! Through the gloom of the hall, from which the usual "fauteuils" [easy chairs] had been removed, I could discern a long green baize-covered table, at which sat a number of solemn-looking gentlemen, some bearded, some mustachioed, all facing the stage. This, I thought, was the jury. And what a jury![21]

Benoist named Saint-Saëns ("of the sardonic tongue and pronounced soprano lisp"), Thomas, Franck, and Massenet among the officials. "Fortunate for me at that time I had no knowledge of the celebrities who were to pass on my worthiness as a student," he wrote. But his knees persisted in knocking until he spied Émile Decombes, whose piano class he had been allowed to audit.

Suddenly all seemed bright once again, and since my bearded

benevolent professor had confidence in me, I would justify it. . . . I picked my way through several works I had to play and did not do too badly. Then came the sight-reading test, which had to be done from manuscript, to make it more difficult. To make it worse, the manuscript was written for the occasion by Massenet who proverbially wrote fly specks! By that time, instead of being nervous, I was angry! Consequently, I plunged in the best way I could have done under normal conditions (for passing marks, you were allowed three mistakes on a page, but it seems I only made two). When I arose from the piano chair, I thought I could detect some nodding of heads among the critics sitting in judgement.[22]

Three days of "fingernail biting and heart fluttering" dragged by, and at last the official document arrived: "One Benoist (André) is accorded the honor of becoming a student of the Conservatoire National de Musique et de Déclamation at the expense of the République Française (Liberté, Égalité, Fraternité)." The teenager had been admitted to "the shrine of music."

The years 1905–06 happened to be one of the most unstable periods in the history of the Conservatoire, thanks to the fifth annual rejection of Ravel in the prestigious Prix de Rome competition for composers. The First Grand Prize, a four-year residency and stipend at the Villa Medici in Rome, had eluded Ravel four times, on the grounds that his music just didn't follow traditional rules of harmony and counterpoint. The competition jury was notoriously conservative and included Conservatoire faculty who'd never forgiven the composer for his checkered academic record and affinity for mavericks such as Erik Satie, whose bare-bones style and subtle humor floated benignly over the balding heads of the establishment. It wasn't as if Ravel hadn't proven himself beyond the confines of the Conservatoire. By his final attempt at the Prix de Rome in the spring of 1905 he had already written the sonorous, highly virtuosic *Jeux d'eau* for piano, the Quartet for strings, and the orchestral tapestry *Shéhérazade,* which more than established his reputation as a composer equal to Debussy. (*Shéhérazade* had been premiered in 1899 by the very respectable orchestra of the Société Nationale de Musique to a chorus of jeers and whistles from the very respectable audience.) This time, the jury ousted him in the qualifying round and in effect barred him from competing. With the exception of Massenet, the judges' names are now less than footnotes in history. The first *premier grand prix* (first place) winner of the 1905 Prix de Rome contest was one M. Gallois, long forgotten. The first *deuxième grand prix* (technically the third place since there were two first prize winners) went to Taffanel's former student, the flutist-composer-conductor Philippe Gaubert.

Whether or not Ravel baited the judges by refusing to follow "party style" in the preliminary exercises, the jury was obviously so insulated it never suspected a hot reaction to Ravel's disqualification. The public was furious. The press immediately pounced on "L'Affaire Ravel" and revealed that all the candidates who had been accepted in the competition were students of Charles Lenepveu, one of the judges. In a few short weeks, Theodore Dubois, director of the Conservatoire, was forced to resign, and Ravel's teacher Gabriel Fauré—who never attended the Conservatoire and thus also stood outside the establishment—was given the post. Meanwhile, Ravel calmly completed his *Introduction et Allegro* for harp, flute, clarinet, and string quartet, a commission from Maison Érard, the Conservatoire's supplier of harps and pianos. And when the ink was dry, he embarked on an extended cruise aboard the luxurious yacht of Alfred Edwards, owner of *Le Matin,* the newspaper that had spearheaded the furor. It was "all in the family"; Edwards's wife Misia, who presided over one of the last great art salons of Paris, was a former piano student of Fauré.

Fauré's appointment was more than a quick fix for a riot. It marked a deliberate decision by the Ministry of Public Instruction to revise school policy. There were plenty of problems, and few could be solved at once, or with ease. A Commission appointed in 1892 to revise the curriculum had met with such strong opposition from the teachers that it disbanded. Observers complained the Conservatoire was a technical school of craft, not art, which prepared executants to fill spaces, cog-like, on the stage and in the pit. Students were exposed to little repertoire of the past or of contemporary Europe, they said, and the French composers favored were the least distinctive of the lot.

Fauré had barely begun in 1905–06, the only year Marcel attended the Conservatoire. The changes Fauré would make led to a broader, more historically astute study of music and integratation of courses. As a member of the conservatory community, Marcel Moyse would not benefit much from this enlightened philosophy; in effect he was a student of the old regime. The biggest change he witnessed was a revolt among the teaching staff over the formation of admission selection committees. Many of them feared a loss of influence in the selection process, by which—as Joseph Moyse had known—they selected their own private pupils and thus nurtured thriving studios "outside." Old-timers like Saint-Saëns griped about the "mania for reforms" and said the only benefit of the new administration was relief from the sharp nibs of the critics.[23] But when the teachers complained to the Under-Secretary for Fine Arts, he maintained his support of Fauré, a friendly man whose gentle authority hardly matched the overworked decor of the director's office, an imposing den Massenet described in his autobiography:

> The room . . . was reached by a great staircase entered through a vestibule of columns. At the landing one saw two large pictures by some painter or other of the First Empire. The door opposite opened on a room ornamented by a large mantelpiece and lighted by a glass ceiling in the style of ancient temples. The furniture was in the style of Napoleon I.
>
> A door opened into the office of the director of the Conservatoire, a room large enough to hold ten or a dozen people seated about the green cloth table or seated or standing at separate tables. The decoration of the great hall of the Conservatoire was in the Pompeiian style, in harmony with the room I have described.[24]

If the director's office was the throne room, the Conservatoire's great courtyard, onto which classrooms and practice studios opened, was the king's stable. Saint-Saëns, who doted on the Conservatoire's "antiquity—the utter absence of any modern note," nostalgically gushed that he loved "that absurd court with the wailing notes of sopranos and tenors, the rattling of pianos, the blasts of trumpets and trombones, the arpeggios of clarinets, all uniting to form that ultra-polyphone . . . in that ridiculous and venerable palace."[25] Casella, who, as a foreigner, was mocked by his classmates and called nicknames like "Macaroni," was less charitable, calling the Conservatoire a "large, horrible edifice with a courtyard which was murderously drafty." The rooms, he explained, were cramped and inferior "even to those in our most dilapidated music schools. I learned . . . to be punctual with my

[own] conservatory students, remembering those interminable waits in winter in that lugubrious courtyard, where it was impossible to protect my hands from the cold."[26]* (The school was moved to Rue Madrid in 1909, and a few years later, the musty behemoth on Rue Bergère was demolished to make way for a telephone exchange.)

Tradition more than lurked in the corners of the Conservatoire—it engulfed every square foot. Yet as a student of Taffanel, Moyse was part of a fairly progressive class that was already breaking a bit with the past. Before Taffanel's tenure, the flute studio's repertory had calcified. On the whole, the nineteenth century produced little flute music of superior quality, due partly to the primitive mechanics and sonic character of the wooden flute, which had to be blown fiercely to penetrate the thick musical fabrics woven by the romantics. With a few notable exceptions, solo and chamber music for flute was produced by flutists who were not particularly imaginative composers. The list of Conservatoire examination solos for the late nineteenth century reveals Altès's dogged adherence to his own trite showpieces and to those of Tulou and Demersseman; he must never have thought it necessary to invite anyone else to crank something out.

Taffanel shattered that pattern by promoting works of Bach and the Mozart concertos and by commissioning exam pieces by contemporary voices such as Fauré, Enesco, and Gaubert. Besides employing the light, fluid textures of modern French composers such as Debussy, the new solos exploited the greater technical potential of the Boehm flute, unavailable to composers and performers of previous generations. The works of Ravel and Debussy relied on a refined instrument which (as has been noted) offered much more variation and control of tone palette, dynamic range, pitch, and expressive nuance; without Boehm, Debussy's unaccompanied morsel "Syrinx" would never have come about. Paul Taffanel's flute class bridged the gap between the nineteenth and twentieth centuries, and his accomplishments as conductor and composer also made him the most well-rounded musician who had taught flute at the Conservatoire.[27]

While Taffanel's library overflowed with the fruits of new labors,

---

*From *Music in My Time: The Memoirs of Alfredo Casella,* trans. Spencer Norton. Copyright © 1955 by the University of Oklahoma Press.

as well as some chestnuts, his class continued to adhere to a long tradition of group teaching. Students met together three times a week for several hours, taking turns performing prepared materials for critical comment by their master teacher. The accompanist for the class during Moyse's year was Alfred Cortot, who, still in his twenties, was already a prominent figure in French musical life as soloist, chamber musician, and conductor. As a member of the newly formed Cortot-Thibaud-Casals Trio, he occasionally invited his colleagues Jacques Thibaud and Pablo Casals to listen to the flute students or to play for them. Classes were held at the Conservatoire, but Moyse indicated that Taffanel taught privately in his home from time to time.

Like the other professors, Taffanel was accorded great respect by his students. Again, tradition dictated that teachers were not to be questioned. Aspiring performers gladly embraced the roles of apprentices; in a sense, students tried to become their teachers. Many professors held important posts in the city's theater and concert orchestras. Students easily recognized their professional power and submitted themselves to it.

But smart political behavior notwithstanding, Taffanel was genuinely worthy of respect. His distinguished career was widely admired, and his integrity, both as artist and human being, was evidently reflected in his music-making. In his article on the flute in the *Encyclopédie de la Musique,* Louis Fleury described Taffanel's approach as elegant, flexible, and sensitive. Taffanel detested affectation, he wrote, "believing that the text of the music should be respected absolutely. . . . Beneath the supple fluency of his playing there was a rigorous adherence to accuracy of pulse and rhythm. His tone was captivating, and also very full."[28]

Few first-hand impressions of Taffanel's playing have been documented. Moyse said Taffanel had "a really big, beautiful, ample sound—not strong, but generous. And the emotion came out above all. As for comprehension, music didn't dominate him. He was always on top; he saw all the possibilities." Some performers have a tendency to be overwhelmed by the personality of the music they play. Taffanel made music his own. "He always came out of a phrase very big, generous, and deep. He was always at ease," Moyse said.[29]

Information on Taffanel's teaching style is scant. Moyse's former students say their teacher commonly mentioned Taffanel in lessons, but mostly in general expressions of adulation. If a student played well, Moyse might comment, "That is the way Taffanel would have played that phrase." And, in the grand, generous tradition of the self-effacing apprentice, Moyse often remarked (with perhaps some false modesty) that he "learned everything" from his teachers, particularly Taffanel.

"It was Taffanel who took the flute out of the bird range," he said. "Taffanel was the first to make the flute an expressive instrument."[30] "Taffanel was typical of the French School with regard to the flute, and a great man, a kind of God."[31] "Taffanel had a look so direct it was a kind of projector on the music, a musical light."[32]

Georges Barrère, principal flutist of the New York Symphony and a Conservatoire classmate of Philippe Gaubert in 1893–94, left one of the longest descriptions of Taffanel's playing and teaching in three 1921 issues of *The Flutist,* a monthly magazine published in North Carolina during the 1920s to address the concerns of the growing number of American flute players.[33] Barrère wrote:

> Since I have been living in America, the use of superlatives does not mean much to me as we so often hear them abused. But . . . I should like to say with a European's meaning that Taffanel was not only the best flutist in the world, but I doubt if anyone can ever fill his place. Quality as well as quantity of tone and fine technique were only a small part of his splendid characteristics as a flute player.
>
> His musicianship, his style particularly, was highly inspirational. He loathed cheap sentimentality, excessive expression, endless vibrato or shaking of tone, in a word, all the cheap tricks which are as undignified as they are unmusical.
>
> He was very careful to assign his pupils such work as would enable them to progress surely and rapidly. Unlike Altès, he did not pay such strict attention to school routine. Many times we would stay after class to listen to solos which he would play for us in his own inimitable style. While he was teaching one pupil the remainder of the class would listen attentively to every observation or suggestion made to improve our friend's work. Scales and exercises were assigned, but when Taffanel knew the pupil was conscientious, he did not use the recitation period to listen to technical works but would spend the entire time teaching an Andersen study in which he led us to find many beauti-

ful things which would otherwise have passed unnoticed, even though we had thoroughly mastered the technical difficulties of the study. Each pupil was a musical son, and I doubt if there is in the whole world one flute player who has sat at the feet of Taffanel who does not bear in his heart the loveliest memories of that great master, and who does not entertain the greatest veneration and respect for him both as a man and a musician.[34]

Taffanel also shared personal information with his students that others might have kept private. Once, the elderly gentleman even brought a fresh kidney stone to class. "He said, 'I want to show my children what I did last night,' " Moyse remembered. Moyse was impressed that his teacher met with his students even when he felt ill. "I admired the fact that he did his duty. He didn't waste our class time."[35]

Like nearly every other Conservatoire flute professor before him,[36] Taffanel compiled a flute method, but it was not published until fifteen years after his death. With all his teaching and conducting activities, he was simply too busy to assemble his book properly. Gaubert, who was at least as busy, assumed the task when Taffanel died but may have relied on Moyse's assistance to see it through.[37] The Taffanel-Gaubert *Méthode complète de flûte* was finally published in 1923 by Alphonse Leduc and Company. Moyse remembered that Taffanel kept some of his teaching materials in a cabinet at the Conservatoire so students could use them. Some sources believe Gaubert added his own material to the published version, but Moyse maintained that Taffanel was the author, Gaubert the organizer and editor.[38]

At the Conservatoire Marcel also studied chamber music with the celebrated violinist Lucien Capet (1873–1928), whose quartet made a specialty of the Beethoven cycle. Descriptions of Capet's playing usually mention strict adherence to the composer's score. Capet composed and was a highly regarded teacher, particularly of bow technique, which inspired Moyse to seek more variety in flute articulation.

In *The Flute and Its Problems* Moyse recalled that his first few weeks in Capet's class were particularly humbling:

> Never had I felt like such a little boy, so alone, so lacking in ability, as I did among those string players. My doubtful intonation, my feeble articulations and accents, my limited expres-

siveness, my lack of a strong enough tone—there were plenty of reasons to give up hope, especially in front of a Master who was so difficult to satisfy.[39]

But after a short time, he accepted the string players' abilities as a challenge and began to practice pieces from the violin repertoire that lay within the flute's range and contained difficulties that would demand "unusual efforts for a flutist." "I felt that if I practiced in a mood of excitement and enthusiasm, these efforts of imitation would enable me to acquire new qualities in my playing and to perfect those that I already possessed," he wrote. "I was not mistaken."

The year at the Conservatoire must have flown by for Marcel, who had discarded thoughts of an art career and become completely enamored of music. The stinging air of competition at the Conservatoire intimidated him, especially in flute class, where he was afraid to play in front of pupils who remembered him as an auditor from the previous year. "At that time, there was a great difference between us," Moyse said. "But I had it in my heart to show that I had learned, and to play better than they."[40] The chance to excel was perhaps more crucial for him than for young men who came from more privileged homes and enjoyed a wider range of career choices (there were no women in the flute class). Outside of flute and chamber music classes, he played in the student orchestra and attended courses in solfège and music history designed for instrumentalists. The days were not without humor—student memoirs from around that time refer to frequent tension-releasing practical jokes such as the hurling of Chinese stinkballs through a classroom window. Even after he left the Conservatoire, the composer Reynaldo Hahn continued to plague and amuse students and faculty. At a tea-and-cookies party hosted by a professor, Hahn, who loathed tidy soirées, crashed into the room wearing a Spanish toreador outfit and clattered through a fandango, using a tea tray and spoons as a tambourine. Moyse undoubtedly took part in the kinds of witty escapades music students have contrived since the invention of the piano lesson. But he poured his greatest energy into flute practice, anticipating the annual juried examination in July.

It would be hard to overestimate the pressure experienced by students preparing for this event. The exams were not just tests, but public debuts eagerly and noisily attended by the public, and

reviewed and analyzed in the press. The first prize winners represented a Who's Who of the most promising young artists in France,
and anyone vaguely connected to musical life was on hand to form
his or her opinion of the Conservatoire's up-and-coming
virtuosos—singers, violinists, and pianists, in particular. Louis
Laloy, reporting on the 1906 concours for *Le Mercure Musical,* wryly
summed up the passionate audience as

> the same people you run into in the corridors of the Opéra-
> Comique: comrades and laureates from previous years,
> mothers, brothers, fiancés and other relatives of all types.
> Princes of criticism and professional reporters—people of all
> Paris come . . . only because one never refuses a complimen-
> tary ticket.[41]

Candidates with many friends in the gallery received loud bravos
that often had no relationship to the quality of the performances.
Less fortunate students with few fans might evoke "ironic love
murmurings" for a wrong note, a sure challenge to young nerves.
The *concours* audience was a fickle mix of blind devotees and
delighted vultures.

The 1906 *concours* attracted more attention than usual. It was the
first under Fauré's administration, and although critics acknowledged that more time was needed for the new director's reforms to
take hold, they also seized the opportunity to complain about the
Conservatoire's shortcomings. By far the most detailed discussions and criticisms were leveled at the products of the voice
studios—a measure of the great degree to which opera continued to
dominate French musical life. Many observers offered the familiar
lament that beauty and musicality were being sacrificed for the sake
of show-stopping technique and dramatic display. The negative
effects of this approach to singing were being carried over into
instrumental training. Laloy commented:

> If the conservatory wanted to give us good and solid orchestra
> musicians who are not as capable of acrobatics but sure of
> intonation and rhythm, or singers who prefer Schumann and
> Fauré to Meyerbeer and Verdi, there would no longer be a need
> to parade these exercises before a crowd of listeners. Several
> musicians would suffice, in an intimacy fatal to great effects but

marvelously clean and ideal for revealing the qualities of style and feeling.[42]

Using the string bass exam as an example, Laloy censured the judging of young musicians on excerpts and phrases "so gauche" that intonation could only be approximated; feeling and style had no place. "The string bass is made to give the orchestra an unshakable foundation," he continued. "What good is it if it extends itself to climb up into the regions of the violin, with poor, strangled, and out-of-tune notes, or hazardous harmonics?" Moreover, the bass solo and sight-reading pieces were written, respectively, in G major and A minor, easy keys suited to pyrotechnics. Laloy concluded, "One could thus conceive of a prize-winning contrabassist from the Conservatoire who would be unable to negotiate the special difficulties of the keys of F-sharp or D-flat, so frequent in modern music. Our orchestra conductors know very well that this contrabassist is not a myth."

Where did Marcel Moyse and the flute fit into this *mêlée?* In an uncontroversial corner. He couldn't possibly miss the ardent debate over musicality versus virtuosity—the question helped form his musical outlook, one which would always find fault with colleagues and students who possessed superior technical gifts but who couldn't deliver "what the composer wrote." But wind instrument literature and wind instrument players did not interest the public. The flute exams were sparsely attended and barely mentioned in print.

The 1906 exam piece for flute was the *Nocturne et Allegro scherzando* by Philippe Gaubert, who served on the thirteen-man jury. Louis Ganne, whose operetta *Hans, le joueur de flûte* was premiered in Monte Carlo that year, provided the sight-reading piece. As director, Fauré was present. Joseph Moyse undoubtedly sat in the audience. If Marcel was nervous, he did not betray it in his performance of Gaubert's new work. The stretching melody of the nocturne and the skipping, whimsical turns of the scherzo were perfect vehicles for his expressive tone and nimble technique. At the age of seventeen, with only one year of Conservatoire training, Marcel Moyse quietly accepted a first prize and was deemed ready for a professional career.

CHAPTER FOUR

A Career

THIS career is most ungrateful and perfidious, and the facts about musicians who are not destitute of merit but who drag out miserable existences, and literally suffer with hunger, are truly heart-breaking. When one has been for twenty-five years professor in that great artist manufactory which is called the Conservatory of Paris; when one has seen with his own eyes the frightful number of students who have fallen to the level of the *bal public* and the *café concert* from having misunderstood or overestimated their abilities; when one knows how many there are who live by infrequent lessons at twenty sous compared to one who might see his name on a play-bill, it becomes a duty to warn the rash aspirant who seeks to enter this path of danger without the stamp of genius on his brow.

So cautioned the prominent French teacher and music historian Albert Lavignac in an 1895 essay announcing the twentieth-century problem of turning out more trained musicians than the world has time to employ or enjoy.[1] For Professor Lavignac, who labored in the Paris Conservatoire from 1871 to 1915, the mark of "genius," or what enabled one to beat the odds, was rugged, selfless devotion to a personal ideal of "the beautiful." "Such a man as this will turn a deaf ear to all advice that mistaken well-wishers offer to deter him," he preached. "He will go forward against wind and tide; he will suffer, if need be, all privation, indifferent to the comforts of material life." The list of sacrifices goes on.

As melodramatic as this exhortation sounds, it was typical of the period, and Moyse, bolstered by his success at the Conservatoire, boldly faced the dangers Professor Lavignac groused about. He lengthened his practice routine to at least four hours a day and aggressively sought chances to perform. His goal was simple: to make a living playing the flute.

No one remembers Moyse's first professional engagement, but it was probably made possible by a recommendation from Hennebains or Taffanel and might have been a performance in which the student played second or third part to the teacher. Typical first jobs for wind instrumentalists in early twentieth-century Paris included playing a private concert in the home of a wealthy family, sitting fourth part in an orchestra organized for a special event, or substituting for someone in the theater pit. Then as now, young professionals vied for chances to slip into the competitive performance network and prove themselves. Singers, pianists, and composers also hoped to snag private patrons who might be proud to "discover" them and back their careers. But for a flutist, the idea of a private patron was out of the question.

Nevertheless, venues for instrumentalists were increasing, and Moyse's professional life couldn't have begun at a more expansive time. Between the start of his career and the late 1920s, when Moyse was in his prime, the number of concerts in Paris more than doubled to as many as 1880 in one year. Concert activity fell significantly in the 1930s, with economic depression and impending war contributing to the dampening of an artistic scene that never regained the health and vigor of earlier days.[2] But by then, Moyse was so well-ensconced in the most financially resilient ensembles that it would take Hitler's invasion to seriously threaten his position. Moyse's thirty-five-year performing career turned out to be perfectly synchronous with the rise and fall of one of the richest musical bacchanals Paris ever hosted.

Symphony orchestras would eventually become the focus of musical life, but in 1906, opera was still queen of the Paris concert scene, with the Opéra and the Opéra-Comique reigning over smaller theaters that presented comic operas, operettas, and ballets. The flutists who played solo position with the Opéra and

Opéra-Comique were considered to have reached the pinnacle of achievement. In the realm of purely instrumental music, the celebrated Société des Concerts, whose season ran from November to April, was the most prestigious ensemble. But the three popular Sunday afternoon concert series—Concerts Colonne, Concerts Lamoureux, and Concerts Populaires—offered respectable work as well as a connection to the growing middle-class audience for "serious" music. This trio of institutions originated with the enterprising nineteenth-century conductor Jules Pasdeloup, whose Concerts Populaires de Musique Classique of the 1860s played to audiences of nearly five thousand in the Cirque Napoléon. His original idea for bringing music to the masses worked so well that Colonne and Lamoureux followed suit in 1871 after the Franco-Prussian War and put Pasdeloup out of business. (Lamoureux even offered his new middle-class patrons a crash course in highbrow etiquette by insisting they hold their cheers, hisses, and claps until a performance was over.) Colonne and Lamoureux continued to attract new listeners, and eventually Pasdeloup's Concerts Populaires was revived to meet the demand for concerts. In 1920 the venerable series took the name Concerts Pasdeloup in tribute to its founder.

There were many other performance opportunities, indoors and out. The Concerts de la Schola Cantorum (primarily sacred), Concerts Spirituels de la Sorbonne, Concerts Rouge, Concerts Touche, and other associations intoned regularly in baroque salons and chapels, while military bands tooted in the gardens of the Tuileries, the Luxembourg gardens, and the numerous parks and squares bordered by the scalloped awnings of neighborhood cafés. Chamber music wafted through the hushed, posh concert rooms of instrument manufacturers like Érard (maker of harps and pianos; publisher of music), Pleyel (pianos, harpsichords, harps), and Aeolian (keyboard instruments), as well as in elegant private homes thick with upholstery, hors d'oeuvres, and attitudes. The Société des Instruments à Vent, Société Moderne des Instruments à Vent, and Société Diemer–van Waefelghem (dedicated to performing early music on original instruments) were among the most admired chamber music societies. Lucien Capet's string quartet and the Cortot-Thibaud-Casals Trio were bright stars in the constellation of elite ensembles.

Conservatory graduates hoped to be part of these activities but were resigned to accept work, as Moyse did, trilling accompaniments for animals, acrobats, and mimes at the circuses or backing up chase scenes and executions in the growing number of silent-movie houses. If newborn venues weren't visible on the streets, they were known to be hatching elsewhere. The Musée Grévin, a wax museum on the Boulevard Montmartre, contained a theater for operettas, plus a basement that featured representations of the Roman catacombs and a room for "cinematograph exhibitions."

As ubiquitous as they are today, solo wind instrument recitals were uncommon in Paris when Moyse entered the scene. The concept of a debut evening for a flutist or clarinetist had not yet arisen, much less the idea of a solo career. It would take the postwar expansion of virtuoso wind repertoire, the growth of the recording industry, the influence of the booming pianist-violinist-diva-conductor star system, and a surfeit of music degree aspirants to push breath-and-keys specialists onstage with only a pianist for company. Moyse, the "transition" flutist whose nineteenth-century training and early twentieth-century career paved the way for high-profile phenomena like Jean-Pierre Rampal and James Galway, was concerned only with gaining entry to large ensembles, not with engineering a solo concert. No doubt he dreamed of performing a concerto, but the opportunity would come to him within an orchestra to which he already belonged.

Moyse had become one of a handful of flutists in the history of the Conservatoire to qualify for a first prize in one year, but his playing lacked polish, and he knew it. Soon after leaving the school he approached Hennebains for more lessons, but his former teacher turned him down, saying the eighteen-year-old was already an accomplished artist. So Moyse went to Philippe Gaubert, who then played with the Opéra and the Société des Concerts. Gaubert, who had been impressed by Moyse's performance of his concours solo, was pleased to accept him as a private student, every Friday at five o'clock in the evening.

In a sense, Gaubert was part of Taffanel's family. Gaubert's mother had worked as Taffanel's housekeeper when Philippe was a small boy, and the older man had guided the child's musical upbringing. Like Taffanel, Gaubert completed his Conservatoire flute training in just one year and also composed and conducted. In

1906, Gaubert's career was just beginning to fan out; in addition to his success as a flutist, he had recently won the second conductor's post of the Société, trying out on a dare and two conducting lessons from Taffanel.[3] As a composer, Gaubert would turn out a respectable catalogue of chamber, stage, and orchestral works, but his notoriety in Paris came to be based on his conducting. In 1919 he was appointed principal conductor of the Société des Concerts and professor of flute at the Conservatoire, and the following year he became principal conductor at the Opéra. He continued to teach, but eventually retired his flute to a closet and got into the habit of borrowing students' instruments for demonstrations in lessons. Yet he was heard in chamber-music concerts as late as 1930, when he performed Ravel's *Chansons madécasses* at a Ravel festival in Biarritz. Gaubert maintained a strong artistic relationship with Ravel throughout his career. He conducted for recordings of three of his orchestral works and participated in the premiere of the *Introduction et Allegro* in 1907, which Moyse must have attended.

When Moyse studied with him, Gaubert was fairly unformed as a pedagogue; remarks by later students indicate that he usually relied on "show" rather than "tell." The consensus is that Gaubert was so naturally gifted mechanically and musically that he never thought about how he did what he did and thus was unable to put it into words.[4] In any case, Moyse was willing to listen closely for the subtleties in Gaubert's playing and to work to reproduce them. "Gaubert could play everything," he remembered. "He had a fantastic instinct, and was a gifted man in tone, fingering, staccato, everything. It was so beautiful. I tried to imitate it." To catch every detail, Moyse asked Gaubert to play certain passages several times. "M. Gaubert had no time—he was absorbed by many things. I didn't want to ask why do you do this, why do you do that. I didn't want to interfere. So I tried to figure out what was happening, and analyze it."[5]

A Gaubert anecdote Moyse often repeated illustrates how Moyse learned from his last teacher. The story goes that Moyse was waiting for his flute lesson outside Gaubert's studio and overheard him practicing one bar from the Bach B Minor Sonata, over and over. Moyse began to wonder about the reason for this, and when he was admitted to the studio, he asked Gaubert why he repeated the same brief string of notes so many times. Gaubert responded simply, "Because I was trying to get the A-sharp to resolve to the B at the end of the bar." Moyse pondered this and came up with his own personal, picturesque understanding of Gaubert's exercise:

> When I was a shepherd boy in St. Amour, I noticed the mother sheep always knew her baby's cry. No matter how many other lambs were around, the mother knew the sound. So, if you play the A-sharp in a special voice, no matter how many other notes there are, the B will know that he belongs to her.[6]

Moyse remained with Gaubert for about four years. "Gaubert was an instinctive musician," he said. "He played as naturally as someone walks, stepping out with his left foot, then his right, avoiding all obstacles. The musical instinct of Gaubert was like an instinct of the body—music without thinking about it."[7]

Diligent practice, additional study, and a growing number of performing opportunities in the 1906–07 season absorbed Moyse completely. After having studied in Lucien Capet's chamber music class, he continued independently to work through the repertoire for solo violin and eventually added cello literature to his practice sessions, "to try to develop a rich sound, as my uncle had on his cello."[8] He said,

> I don't need to add that I tried to imitate the way Casals and Thibaud performed. But I wasn't copying them; I was attempting to expand my range of expression as far as my instrument would permit. I tried to develop my instrument, not in the way of a cow who wants to become fat by drinking lots of water from the stream, but by looking *into* my sound for a kind of richness.[9]

In 1906 Moyse took part in the premiere of Georges Enesco's *Dixtuor* (or Dixtet) for wind instruments, under the direction of the composer. Like Moyse, Enesco had a peasant upbringing, which was reflected both in his music-making and in his loyalty to his family. His father was a sharecropper. When Georges began earning concert fees, he set aside funds to buy for his father the plot he worked in Romania. Musically, Enesco was a product of the Vienna Conservatory, of Massenet and Fauré at the Paris Conservatoire, and of his native country. His *Poème roumain,* Opus 1, was introduced in Paris in 1898 at the Châtelet when he was still a student, and by the time of the *Dixtuor* he was managing a full schedule as concert violinist, composer, and concert organizer. Enesco was a tall, handsome, and energetic man who spoke five languages fluently. Moyse admired him very much.

As a conductor, Enesco was skilled at imparting fine precision and shapely phrasing, and the premiere of the *Dixtuor* was evidently successful. In an article about Enesco two years later, Jean Huré called him "the most 'modern' " of contemporary composers. "It seems as if the delightful author of *Pelléas* was twenty-five years behind the musician of the Dixtet," he enthused.[10]

Enesco's output during that period also included the 1904 *concours* solo *Cantabile et Presto* for flute and piano. If imitation is the sincerest form of flattery, Gaubert certainly demonstrated his regard for this Enesco work. His *Nocturne et Allegro scherzando* from Moyse's prize-winning year was very much like it, right down to the length: a recording of both pieces by the Swiss flutist and former Moyse pupil Peter-Lukas Graf clocks them at 5' 48" and 5' 58". Both Gaubert and Moyse brought back Enesco's popular piece for the *concours* during their tenures at the Conservatoire.

With important activities like the Enesco premiere beginning to accumulate during his first season out, Moyse was glad to accept a contract with a French resort orchestra for a few weeks. The easy atmosphere there would allow ample time for the personal practice he needed, and the post paid a respectable fee. This type of job was welcomed by good musicians; Casella spent the summer of 1902 playing piano at the Casino in Dieppe, where, in addition to "serious" concerts, Pierre Monteux led a dance orchestra in popular waltzes, polkas, and cakewalks. The exact time of Moyse's engagement and the name of the spa are long forgotten, but it occurred in the summer on the northern coast, not far from Paris, probably in Dieppe. As it turned out, Moyse's time there was cut short by a serious illness, the first of a series that threatened to end his career.

Moyse liked working near the ocean because it gave him a chance to swim, and it was not out of character for him to dive in enthusiastically regardless of the weather. He was probably the only person who braved the waves—with a cold, no less—on the chilly day he became seriously ill with pleurisy and fainted in the middle of a concert. Back in Paris, Moyse's doctor insisted he stop playing for a while, and Moyse failed to argue because he had no choice; he was completely debilitated. Now he realized how vulnerable he really was. It would not be his last physical breakdown.

Moyse was still closely associated with his three teachers, and it must have been difficult for him when Paul Taffanel died in the fall of 1908. Not surprisingly, Hennebains was given the Conservatoire flute class. Moyse always considered Taffanel the center of a professorial triumvirate he likened to three great cathedrals. He said,

> Hennebains, a great artist, I often think of as the Cathedral of Rouen. Gaubert, a great flutist, I compare with the Cathedral of Reims and its flamboyant Gothic details. Gothic art is beautiful and reminds me of the great facility of Gaubert. And in the middle, between these two equally beautiful cathedrals, comes Taffanel, even greater and more encompassing, like the Cathedral of Notre Dame in Paris.[11]

But Moyse also found new heroes among conductors. Ballet and opera concert programs seldom listed the names of the pit orchestra players, and it is difficult to document Moyse's participation in many events, much less name the artists with whom he rubbed shoulders. (A great deal of substituting took place in ensembles as players struggled to juggle work to best advantage, and after he became solidly established, Moyse was a regular sender of subs himself.) But Pierre Monteux, for whom Moyse played as a member of the seasonal orchestra organized for the Ballets Russes, was one man rarely omitted from Moyse's nostalgic recollections of the past. Monteux conducted many important premieres in which Moyse was hired to play, such as Stravinsky's *Petrushka* and *Le sacre du printemps* and Ravel's *Daphnis et Chloé,* danced by the provocative Russian ballet troupe. These startling new works were commissioned by the impresario Serge Diaghilev, who established an annual Paris season for the Russian ballet company in 1909. The Swiss-born Monteux was the Russian's conductor of choice.[12]

Pierre Monteux (1875–1964) was a graduate of the Paris Conservatoire; he entered as a violinist at the age of nine. While still a student, he played viola with the Opéra-Comique and the Concerts Colonne, and he led the viola section at the premiere of *Pelléas et Mélisande* in 1902. At twenty-one he won the post of assistant conductor to Colonne, the first rung on the ladder to an international career that included directorships at the Boston and San Francisco symphonies and the Orchestre Symphonique de Paris.

He was known as a taskmaster in rehearsal, a thorough, disciplined musician with a sharp ear for technical detail and tone color. These qualities impressed Moyse and were not lost on Stravinsky, the recipient of a fairly lengthy letter from Monteux suggesting specific changes in the orchestration of *Le sacre*. On Monteux's list of pre-premiere complaints was a passage in which "it is impossible to hear a single note of the flute accompanied by four horns and four trumpets *FF,* and first and second violins, also *FF.* The first flute plays the theme alone in the middle of all this noise."[13]

When Moyse received his schedule for the Ballet Russes in the spring of 1913, he discovered an unusual number of section rehearsals. In all, seventeen rehearsals were required for *Le sacre:* first, strings alone, followed by separate meetings of the wood-winds and brass. The percussion section was present all along. Monteux reflected,

> The musicians thought it absolutely crazy, but as they were well-paid, their discipline wasn't bad! When at last I put the whole thing together, it seemed chaotic but Stravinsky was behind me pointing out the little phrases he wished heard. We rehearsed over and over the small difficult parts, and at last we were ready for the ballet.[14]

The story of *Le sacre*'s 1913 premiere with the startling chore-ography of Diaghilev's protégé Nijinsky is legendary. Nevertheless, it bears recalling with the thought of what it must have been like to sit in the pit, blaring away on a flute with no hope of being heard through the catcalls. According to Stravinsky, the audience began laughing almost immediately, beginning with a few dumb titters and revving up to an obnoxious din. The composer sought refuge backstage, where he found Nijinsky leaping up and down in the wings like a deranged jack-in-the-box, screeching numbers at the dancers to help them keep time. The dancers couldn't hear the music; the orchestra couldn't hear itself; and at times no one could see what anyone was doing because Diaghilev kept killing the lights to silence the patrons. Moyse's eyes were glued to Monteux, who dared not look up from the score. "I decided to keep the orchestra together at any cost, in case of a lull in the hubbub," Monteux wrote. "I did, and we played it to the end absolutely as we had rehearsed it in the peace of an empty theatre."[15] A year later, Monteux talked Stravinsky into letting him program *Le sacre* on an orchestra concert, minus dancers, because he suspected the uproar was a response to the choreography. Old-timers in the full house, such as Saint-Saëns, were still offended. But the musicians who had played in the Ballet Russes performance found it tamer the second time around.

One of the most common Moyse myths, even among some members of his family, is the "fact" that he played in the premiere of Debussy's *L'après-midi d'un faune.* It wouldn't have been possible—Moyse was five years old at the time. It is likely, though, that he was in the pit in 1912 when Nijinsky performed his openly sexual dance to Debussy's score. Debussy was upset by Nijinsky's undulations, as were most of the critics. (The sculptor Rodin, who commented in *Le Matin* on the dancer's ideal body, was one of the few witnesses who approved.) Though Moyse participated in many of the nouveau chic events of the Ballet Russes, he could never be considered a member of the avant-garde any more than the Juilliard-trained members of the Metropolitan Opera orchestra could be labeled "downtown" musicians when the house mounted Philip Glass's opera *The Voyage.*

Moyse played *L'après-midi d'un faune* under Debussy's baton at least once, probably during or after 1908, when the composer began to conduct his own works. In an interview published in *Musical America,* Moyse said that Debussy, who was not very gifted on the podium, demanded exact, rhythmic playing despite his inability to lead it with the baton. "Four-sixteen is always four-sixteen," the irritated maestro grumbled. "It is never five. Try always to play what I write. If you can't figure out the score, please don't try to collaborate!"[16] "He didn't say much to me," Moyse remembered another time.

> When I played the first phrase in one breath, he didn't even compliment me. He found that natural. Another time, he failed to beat one measure, and I didn't play. He looked at me and yelled, "Stop! What are you waiting for?" I responded, "You!" He thought a moment and then said, "It was I who was waiting for you."[17]

The Russians, the French revolution led by Debussy and Ravel, and the recent housecleaning at the Conservatoire indicated thunderous change in Paris's musical establishment. A daring spirit born of fear, exhibitionism, and real courage led quickly to the careful questioning of tradition, and outright rebellion against what had gone before. The changes weren't limited to the new generation of musicians or audiences inspired by the primordial angularity of Stravinsky and the whoosh and splash of the impressionists. Erik Satie, who had already rebelled once against his stepmother's fawnings over the Opéra and Conservatoire, started his own adult-education movement at age forty by going back to school to study with Albert Roussel at the Schola Cantorum. After accepting a diploma in counterpoint, Satie engineered a second rejection of authority with his series of childlike piano pieces bearing satirical, deadpan quips in the margins. Even grand old Saint-Saëns, at the age of seventy-three, stepped out and became the first prominent composer to write a score for a silent film, *L'assassinat du Duc de Guise,* a landmark of the fertile prewar period in French cinema. Made under the auspices of the innovative Film d'Art company, *L'assassinat* was one of the best early "theatrical" films (as opposed to comedies or crime melodramas) and included actors from the Comédie Française. The story was simple and hardly modern: a duke is warned that a king is after him, ignores the warning, and is murdered by the monarch's henchmen. But the decor and costumes for the film were carefully selected and detailed, and the acting was more refined than the overdone poses seen in earlier, hysterical melodramas. Saint-Saëns's facile, sentimental music was the right match for *L'assassinat.*

The growth of radio broadcasting also had an impact on musicians' careers. The American inventor Lee deForest staged no less a feat than a live telephone broadcast from the Eiffel Tower, in 1908. DeForest's experiment was essentially a publicity stunt for his new deForest Radio Telephone Company, but it made history by planting the first "radio phone" on French soil. With a generator cocooned in its base and antennae draped down its sides, the great contraption of Moyse's birth year began to send signals up to five hundred miles away. What kinds of sounds did deForest transmit? Opera arias, dozens of them, played on a Pathé talking machine. By the following January, deForest, a passionate music-lover, had fine-tuned his system to support a live Metropolitan Opera broadcast from America. It was a double bill—*Cavalleria rusticana,* with Caruso as Turridu, and *Pagliacci.* And although the handful of New York wireless operators and newspapermen who actually heard it complained they caught a lot of ticking sounds and no ecstasy, the occasion begot the inevitable world of broadcast music.

In the midst of this excitement, Moyse met and married a beautiful, almond-eyed dancer named Celine Gautreau (see Figure 8), whom he had noticed at the Gaité-Lyrique Theater in a production of Meyerbeer's *L'africaine*. The morning following the final performance of the Meyerbeer, Marcel showed up for a rehearsal of Massenet's *Don Quichotte* and introduced himself to Mlle. Gautreau.

"We were at the theater together, every night," he recalled fondly. "It was complete communion, from a musical point of view. She sang, she had a certain talent, and loved music very much. At the same time, I was able to teach her what she did not know about it."[18]

Mlle. Gautreau was a serious young woman who had grown up poor in Nantes and come to Paris at the age of sixteen or seventeen to work as a maid for a middle-class family. Louis Moyse said that her first appearance as a member of the regular background troupe of the Gaité-Lyrique was around 1909. She also played small parts in silent films. (For one movie, she was asked to jump through an open window—with people waiting to catch her—but, said Louis, she was horrified by the idea and refused. Cursing furiously, the producer picked her up himself and tossed her through the opening.) When Marcel met Celine, so family legend goes, she was enjoying the attentions of both Massenet and baritone Vanni Marcoux: one brought her flowers; the other gave her chocolates. Celine probably lived in Montmartre. She was undoubtedly ill-paid and may have hoped for a husband to help make up the difference, but her affection for Marcel was hardly conjured for convenience. Celine (born in 1885 on 29 April, which happened to be Josephine Perretier's birthday) was four years older than Moyse and also an orphan. She recognized what the handsome flutist needed. "She knew right away that I was not physically solid," Moyse said, "and she made it possible for me to continue my life as a young flute player without any trouble. She kept all my problems away."[19] Over the objections of Marcel's uncle Joseph, who was a strict Catholic, Marcel and Celine married in a civil ceremony on 12 March 1912, about two years after they had met.[20] In early August of the same year their son Louis Joseph Moyse was born in Scheveningen, Holland, while Moyse was on tour with the Lamoureux orchestra. Marcel was twenty-three.

Celine delighted in Marcel's love and protection and shared her husband's emerging deification of home and family, fed by frequent visits to St. Amour and Besançon. She immediately turned her attention to raising their son (and later a daughter, Marguerite Josephine), whom she taught to read and write before he entered school, and especially devoted herself to Marcel's career, setting an example for the whole family to follow. She insisted on and enjoyed waiting on him at every turn; Marcel rarely stirred the sugar in his own coffee. By all accounts, she became a gracious, supportive wife in the old-fashioned sense. Louis wrote this about his mother:

> At the "Salon de l'auto" of Citroën or Renault, they would show a complete block motor cut in two and functioning at an extremely low speed—carburetor, spark plugs, valves. My mother was an open book like that. She was a wife, a mother, and a grandmother before anything else. She had no other goal. She came from a poor milieu. When she was about ten, she was in charge of caring for her half brothers and sisters. She begged and stole on the piers in Nantes, just to keep from starving. Her mother was drunk most of the time. Celine was not a legitimate child. According to her, her father was an officer in the Japanese navy, and it was a one-night affair with my grandmother.
>
> My mother never went to school. She was pure instinct, intelligent, with a marvelous heart, and completely devoted to the family and intimate friends. She also was stubborn and touchy, and when she argued with my father she was always on the wrong side because he was smarter, using his complicated intelligence to put her down. (Of course, he was never wrong, according to him, and very often transposed facts to be on the right side!) She was defenseless in an argument with him, even when she was right.
>
> She was very gifted artistically. Piano and music were more important than anything when I was young. Before I went to school she taught me reading, writing, and counting. She was also a marvelous inventor of stories. She had a natural way of expressing herself. I remember especially a long story about the life of water. She would start the "long voyage" from a glacier to the sea, with every detail involved during the journey!
>
> She learned how to blow on the flute. She always played the same tune, dear in her heart, but with a terrible sound! It was the Adagio from the Beethoven Violin Concerto. The low C

would never come, but it didn't matter. . . . She stopped the flute after three lessons with my father. He refused to go on because she was beginning to teach him! And of course, arguments would come—battles of words, only, and kissing and peace after.

She was very slim when she was young and her first pregnancy brought her to 170 pounds. She kept it to her death.

She had a common and practical sense of living, which was denied the rest of the family. She was our guardian angel.[21]

By the time of his marriage, Moyse had been out of the Conservatoire six years and established himself as the most talented member of the new crop of flutists, the one to beat in the next major audition. Gaubert offered him regular substitute work at the Opéra, and one year Moyse played solo flute in a summer orchestra at Vichy. The job was a turning point. It paid well and gave Moyse a dose of day-to-day orchestral life. Of this baptism, he said:

I was thrown into pieces of music I'd never seen, and I had to meet the challenge to justify what I'd become! That's the way the profession is. I wouldn't have been able to stand it if I'd made a mistake; then, I wouldn't have dared leave my house, for fear everyone would look at me. Finally, I wanted to justify the confidence others had in me, and the benefits and good deeds done on my behalf, because no one was obligated to do anything. My stepmother certainly didn't have to take me in. My grandparents didn't have much to eat, and my uncle helped me out of love for his sister. I was always careful to show appreciation to my family.[22]

During the 1913–14 season, Moyse spent more than six months away from his family, touring the United States and Canada with the great coloratura soprano Nellie Melba (see Figures 9–10). Although this tour is barely described in the major biographies of Melba, it was an important experience for Moyse, whose sensibilities were increasingly influenced by the singers he admired from the pits of the Paris theaters. The opportunity with Melba came through Gaubert, who had performed and recorded with her the Mad Scene from Donizetti's *Lucia di Lammermoor* and "Sweet Bird," from Handel's *Il pensieroso*. Moyse first accompanied Melba in a concert in London, and his success there led to the tour.

Moyse idolized Melba. Just like any other gifted and vain-glorious diva, the Australian songbird had plenty of detractors within the vocal community. But instrumentalists like Moyse held friendlier opinions of her work. After all, those who performed with her always filled clear-cut supporting roles; none of them experienced, as Mlle. Fritzi Scheff did at Covent Garden, the humiliation of an offstage Melba taking over her high B in Musetta's "Valse" and finishing out the phrase with her. Melba's admirers included the violinist Joachim and the pianists Paderewski and Anton Rubinstein. Taffanel had been associated with her as far back as a soirée in 1887, the first known event at which Mrs. Charles Armstrong billed herself as Mme. Melba. That program showcased the young singer, but Paul Taffanel also played two solos: Mendelssohn's *Chanson du printemps* and a Tarantelle by Rossini.

Melba's 1913–14 traveling company was headed by the violinist Jan Kubelík, followed by baritone Edmund Burke, pianist Gabriel Lapierre, and Moyse. The ambitious junket opened 29 September in Montreal, the same day Moyse was issued an alien certificate by the United States Department of Labor describing him as twenty-four years old, five feet five inches tall, and 145 pounds, with brown hair and brown eyes. The tour ended more than five months later in Hartford, on 3 March (Kubelík stayed on to give a solo recital in London, Ontario). Within that time, Melba and her party delivered sixty-two concerts, from New York (where Moyse was obliged to join Local 310 of the American Federation of Musicians) to Seattle and as far south as Macon, Georgia, enduring such inconveniences as flash floods and a herd of buffalo that dared to stop Melba's private train. At one point in the Rocky Mountains, snow fell so deep that the train was stuck for three days, and some of the men struck out to hunt for food. That evening, Melba's private dining car was filled with the rich aroma of fresh bear steaks, which Moyse found to be excellent.

Melba's programs were selected from her list of greatest hits, such as the Mad Scene from *Lucia,* "Addio" from *La bohème,* and the "Ave Maria" from Verdi's *Otello.* Moyse's most important assignment was to perform the flute obbligato for Lucia's Mad Scene. But he was also featured in the accompaniment to Bishop's "Lo, Hear the Gentle Lark" and to Handel's "Sweet Bird." He occasionally performed solo works, presumably on nights when Melba was especially fatigued. Apparently the diva had a difficult time crossing

the ocean, because the 4 October concert in Montreal began with
Moyse playing the Allegro from the third Flute Sonata of Handel.
Two weeks later in Chicago Moyse provided the same opener,
which irritated *Chicago News* critic Isabel Lowden. "From an artistic
viewpoint the programme was a strange conglomeration and one
wondered why it should open with a flute solo or why there should
be any flute solos at all," she wrote in the next day's paper. "This is
no disparagement of Marcel Moyse, the able flutist, but the
audience came to hear Melba sing."

In freezing Madison, Wisconsin, in the middle of January,
Moyse played three solos—the Handel Allegro, Saint-Saëns's
Romance, and the *Andante et Scherzo* of Louis Ganne—plus the Mad
Scene. Edmund Burke sang five times, and Melba managed three
arias alone. Kubelík was in another city presenting a solo recital,
which was probably why Moyse performed so much that night. He
garnered three sentences in the *State Journal*'s review: "For his
youth, M. Marcel Moyse has gone far in his profession. The sweetness of his work on his beautiful instrument was a revelation. He
was truly artistic in his selection of solo numbers."

Dame Melba was performing well but was past her prime,
having entered that phase of a celebrated singer's life when the fans
flock in appreciation of a career. In his assessment of Melba's 13
October Carnegie Hall concert with the New York Symphony, *New
York Times* critic Richard Aldrich wrote politely that the artist was
"still in the plentitude of her voice," and went on to explain that her
range was not as consistent as it once was. The "flawless perfection" was gone and ornaments were "produced with some effort."
Nevertheless, Melba's technique and phrasing were quite
impressive.

Regardless of Melba's condition, the tour was big news, choice
copy all across the country. One story in the Rochester, New York,
Post-Express bore four headlines, each in a different typeface:

MELBA TALKS TO REPORTER

"GOOD EVENING, GOOD MORNING, GOOD NIGHT," SAYS SHE

PRIMA DONNA SAVES VOICE

**Trail of Great Singer Leads Determined Newswriter Through
Many But Fruitless Events**

It is, of course, an account of how a reporter was repeatedly snubbed by his intended interviewee as she swept in and out of elevators with "the flash of a fur-lined coat."

But the most colorful description of Melba's entourage appeared in the *Minneapolis News* on 14 January 1914. Like the writer in Rochester, the anonymous staffer saw very little of the Aussie star. Still, he managed to find plenty of sustenance for his Underwood.

Madame Melba Yawns in All Keys
Sleepless Night on Train for Diva

All that Nellie Melba could do was yawn when she reached Minneapolis today.

She yawned in G, in B-flat and in F Major, and finally yawned in C. Then, as she stretched, she gave a series of yawns that terminated on the F above high C.

Sleepy-eyed, tired, and travel-worn, the twelve members of the Melba-Kubelík Concert company arrived in Minneapolis at 10 A.M. today, and went directly to the Hotel Radisson. They appear together in concert tonight at the National Guard armory. With them came twenty-eight trunks and thirty-odd pieces of hand baggage.

Wrapped to the eyes in a long, sable coat, Mme. Melba, followed by her maid, was the first of the company to reach the hotel.

When spoken to she yawned politely behind a well-gloved hand and motioned in the direction of Howard E. Potter, the manager. Then she yawned again. Mme. Melba yawned that she was very tired, and would like to be sent to her rooms at once and to bed.

At that juncture Jan Kubelík and Mme. Kubelík arrived, and the virtuoso said something to Mme. Melba in French, but again she yawned and waved him away without speaking and a second later disappeared in the elevator.

Kubelík, like his distinguished concert companion, was tired. He went to his room. So tired was the party that but two breakfasted at the hotel, and thirty minutes later all members of the troupe were reported asleep, tired out from a long concert last night in Omaha, and a tedious all-night trip on a sleeper, where none slept.

The most picturesque member of the company was a gold-and-white turbaned, swarthy Cingalese, who carried under either arm a violin case, containing Kubelík's two instruments. None of the members of the little band knew his name, except to call him "Rajah" and "Dawson." There were so many "C's" and "J's" in it, Manager Potter explained, that he had never been able to either spell or pronounce it.

For twelve years "Rajah Dawson" has accompanied Kubelík over the world. He never leaves the two violins, one, the "Emperor," a Stradivarius, used by the violinist in his concerts, and the other, the "Empress," made by Giuseppe Guarneri, and carried for practise work only. The two are valued at $35,000. With the two instruments the Cingalese carried a third box containing violin strings and fiddlebow hair, brought from Europe, and enough to last the tour out. Rajah Dawson has his meals served in his rooms, sits in the wings of the theaters during the recitals, and day and night guards the two violins money cannot replace.

Besides Mme. Melba, Kubelík and Mme. Kubelík, in the company are Edmund Burke, barytone; Moriel [sic] Moyse, flutist; Gabriel Lapierre, pianist; and Managers Powell and Lowell Powell, the latter of London. Mme. Melba will leave tonight for Madison, Wisconsin, while Kubelík gives a concert the same evening at La Crosse.

As entertaining as this vignette is, the majority of the tour's press coverage focused on the wonders of Melba's singing. In Boston, Toledo, Buffalo, Denver, and all points in between, critics employed ink of purplest hues to describe both her voice and the thousands of ecstatic fans who always seemed on the verge of storming the stage. If Moyse was recognized in a review, it was usually in the final paragraph's list of supporting cast. But there were occasional gems: "facile technique and a mastery of the tonal possibilities of his instrument," "charm of sustained tone, delicacy in bravura and elegance in technique." In Syracuse, Moyse and his flute "ran Melba a close race in the Handel."

With Melba, Moyse was challenged to rise to a musical level he had encountered only as a listener. He also witnessed up close the sort of public glorification of an artist that flutists never received.

Melba was famous; Melba was a living legend; Melba could say and do what she wanted.

The entertainment-hungry American audience amplified Melba's power, too. Serious concert life was evolving in the U.S.; impresarios, music societies, and budding conservatories seemed motivated by a desire for excellence that could be described as wanting to catch up with Europe, ironically, at a time when Europeans were sailing to Ellis Island in record numbers. The cultural inferiority complex which many American presenters and concert goers still cling to (particularly with respect to conductors and composers) is rooted in the late nineteenth- and early twentieth-century births of American orchestras, opera companies, and educational institutions. In his wrap-up of the Chicago Symphony's 1913–14 season, board of trustees president Bryan Lathrop wrote of the orchestra's goal to found "a great Conservatory of Music, equal to any in Europe," which would "greatly strengthen the Orchestra, since the professorships would bring to it the best musicians of Europe."[23]

Moyse already knew that Europeans were valued in America. Georges Barrère had sat as principal flute in the New York Symphony (Melba's Carnegie Hall backup band) since 1905. Moyse used to say that he was offered a position with the Minneapolis Symphony while touring with Melba. The facts lie in unrecorded conversations, but it is interesting to note that in the 1913–14 season, a Danish flutist named Vigo Andersen, said to be a relative of Karl Joachim Andersen, joined the Minneapolis orchestra. The new flutist was probably Vigo, Jr., the son of Karl's brother, Vigo, who was solo flutist of Theodore Thomas's orchestra in Chicago before the turn of the century.

Whatever the situation, Moyse must have found America irresistible, because sometime later—either at the end of the tour or in the following year—Moyse returned to Minneapolis, only to find there was no job after all. With no money for a ticket back to France, he was forced to pawn his flute and earn his passage tending horses on board a cargo ship. As if that weren't enough, Moyse discovered later that while he was raking out stalls, his wife and son were floating comfortably on a passenger liner *en route* to surprise him in the United States; perhaps they wanted to inspect what might become their adopted country. Celine and Louis, a toddler, had no clue they would be turning right around in New York Harbor. The two ships literally passed in the night.

Moyse never performed with Nellie Melba again; her career wound down with the onslaught of World War I. But he always prized his connection with the legendary singer. Most of her twenty-five opera roles were French or Italian, just what a traditional Frenchman would prefer. Moyse paid homage to many of them in his melody book, *Tone Development Through Interpretation*.

CHAPTER FIVE

Opéra-Comique

By the time Moyse returned from the Melba tour and a vacation in St. Amour, a huge percentage of his countrymen were huddling in the muddy trenches of the French frontier. Hostilities marking the beginning of World War I had ignited over the summer of 1914, and by August the German army occupied next-door Belgium. In September the Battle of the Marne brought the fighting just forty miles east of Paris, snuffing the City of Light into blackouts and indefinitely postponing all normal activities, including musical performances. In a short time German airships were buzzing the Eiffel Tower, and Notre Dame Cathedral wore a gaping hole.

Moyse's friend Edmund Burke, the baritone in Nellie Melba's American tour, was in Paris when the war began and managed to dispatch an early report to *Musical America:*

> Paris, the pleasure park of the world, has been transformed. Lightheartedness finds expression only in patriotic exultation. In a sense it is Paris metamorphosed—it is Paris revealing its inner self, its noblest instincts. Never have I seen a Parisian to better advantage. . . . If a Parisian of yesterday was a creature to be loved, the Parisian of today is a creature to be venerated.

French citizens enthusiastically responded to the call for mobilization, then adopted a spirit of grave concern. But, wrote Burke, pent-up feelings were bound to burst out, as in one café on the Boulevard Cravel:

The orchestra began to play the Russian national anthem, and immediately the diners rose *en masse*. Someone called for the "Marseillaise" and the demonstration was continued with renewed vigor. The crowds on the sidewalks surged into the place and waiters and diners were soon jammed together in a solid mass, everyone singing with all possible fervor.

The familiar measures were still in the air when the opening bar of "God Save the King" was played. The Frenchmen knew but a single line, "Dieu Garde le Roi," and they sang the same phrase throughout the hymn. They sang it again and again. Those who were near a table or a chair stood on it and the others measured their height on their toes. I heard the British national hymn in Westminster Abbey at the coronation of King George, and thought I should never again feel the same emotion the majesty of that hymn inspired in me. But in a little French café in Paris I was to feel the full measure of its sublimity.[1]

But the noisy patriotism was short-lived: martial law was declared; military bands were yanked out of the streets; and an eight o'clock curfew was enforced. "We are living in a perpetual Sunday," said one observer. "No commotion, no excitement, and less business." Instead of greeting one another, Parisians kept their heads tilted skyward for signs of destruction.

Only a few months before, the musical in-crowd had blithely participated in an annual musicians' lawn tennis tournament at St. Cloud (William Bastard, the organist, had succeeded Pablo Casals as men's singles champion), while the critics squabbled about debt at the Opéra and an impending strike by underpaid orchestra members, who, it was acknowledged, received about one-third the salary of their colleagues who had emigrated to Boston or New York. Of all the solutions put forth, *Le Monde Musical*'s M. A. Mangéot came up with the most novel one: installing roulette wheels in the foyer of the Palais Garnier. Gambling had the potential to subsidize all the theaters in Paris, he reasoned lightly, and besides, it was less dangerous than alcoholism, "from which the State realizes a huge income."[2]

But in wartime there was no problem because there was no season. Venerable institutions like the Opéra-Comique (whose director was off serving in an artillery corps) bravely reopened to shelter life, not imitate it. Instead of preening divas and racks of petticoats, the Salle Favart's dressing rooms were crowded with entire neighborhoods of homeless women and children who slept in rows, clutching the few possessions they had rescued from the rubble. By the Christmas truce of 1914, nearly every French family had suffered the loss or maiming of a loved one at the front, and Paris had battened down for four years of disarray.

Moyse attempted repeatedly to enlist in the French army, but was turned down every time because of his damaged lungs. The government issued him a certificate of exemption from military service for health reasons in 1911, but his failure to participate in the conflict embarrassed him. Many musicians, including Gaubert, went off to fight, leaving Moyse and others with the precarious and ill-paid work of maintaining what was left of Parisian artistic life. Concerts were canceled or, at best, postponed. Ad hoc performances all but disappeared, and the ranks of the city's orchestras thinned out considerably. Colonne and Lamoureux combined as one ensemble for the duration, and Concerts Pasdeloup suspended its series altogether. Most of the singers who held forth were women; the tenors and baritones were off starring in the pits of no-man's-land.

The war provided a leveling experience for everyone. Jacques Ibert took his *premier prix* in composition at the Conservatoire in 1914 and promptly joined the army. Saint-Saëns toured America in 1915 and donated the proceeds to the war effort; he also demanded the suppression of German music, a sentiment shared by a strong faction of music-lovers on both sides of the ocean. Ravel tried in vain to enlist in the army but was rejected because he was underweight. He finally became a driver in the motor transport corps, but continued to compose, dedicating each movement of his piano suite *Le tombeau de Couperin* (1914–17) to the memory of a war victim. The composer-conductor André Caplet served as a liaison officer near Verdun and wrote music on a collapsible piano he hauled down into the trenches. Harpist Carlos Salzedo wrote optimistically to his manager from the front shortly after the war broke out, "I am still alive! Most likely this war will last till January. For this reason all concert propositions will be impossible for me until that time."[3]

Other musicians left the country. Stravinsky sought safety in Switzerland. Casella returned to Italy to publicize the works of French composers. Darius Milhaud took a job as secretary to his friend, the poet and diplomat to Brazil Paul Claudel, and spent two years in Rio de Janeiro taking in playful Latin American colors and rhythms and tucking them into his musical language. The loner Edgard Varèse moved to the United States in 1915 and stayed. Twenty-one years later he would honor the weighty platinum flute of Georges Barrère with *Density 21.5.*

Moyse's beloved Melba traveled half the world home to Australia: not for yet another farewell recital, but to give concerts to benefit the Red Cross. She also attempted to knit garments for soldiers. "Pathetic memory!" she exclaimed in her autobiography, *Melodies and Memories.* "The wool I wasted, the number of stitches I dropped, the scarves that unravelled themselves at the slightest touch, the socks that would never have fitted any human being!" Challenged by the shrinking pool of traditionally male performing ensembles, the female musicians of Paris—like so many other women in the world wars who proved they could do "men's work" in a time of crisis—boldly took to the stage. One of their best-organized efforts, the Union des Femmes Professeurs et Compositeurs de Musique, lasted six years, presenting concerts by an all-woman orchestra with soloists such as Nadia Boulanger.

In the midst of the shelling, the blackouts, and the growing flood of refugees, French citizens craved a means of escape, and the concert scene was haphazardly revitalized with popular per-formances that benefited war victims and charitable agencies. But the income from these occasions was not enough to live on, and Moyse attempted to keep as many flute students as possible. Teaching, in general, was dismal; schools like the Conservatoire were short on both faculty and students. To Moyse's great grief, Hennebains died in Paris at the start of the war, and Léopold Lafleurance was named his temporary replacement. Like other musicians, Moyse encountered a 50 percent drop in the going rate for music lessons. Food was rationed, with the most generous shares going to citizens in physically demanding jobs. Musicians, a relatively sedentary lot, were accorded small portions. The Moyses, who up to that time had been living in a series of furnished hotels in the 17th *arrondissement,* stayed a year (1915–16) in an apartment on Rue Brochant and in 1917 settled at 49 Rue d'Orsel, in Mont-martre. Even so, the family frequently escaped to St. Amour to avoid the war, and during one country stay, Moyse earned extra money delivering official notices to families whose sons died at the front. Many times, Celine shopped for dinner with a few francs from a flute lesson her husband had taught that afternoon, and occasionally the family went without food for days. Once, Celine took a full week's earnings—one hundred francs from private lessons and odd freelance jobs—and instead of groceries, brought home a big tricycle for Louis, an act that angered Moyse but probably lightened the load of the delighted child.

Marcel managed to improvise a rhythm for his professional and private lives. He socialized little, preferring to bicycle back to the family's Montmartre apartment for lunch after morning rehearsals for the miscellaneous jobs that constituted his wartime career. He practiced at home. Marcel still played flute duets with his old friend Chabrier, and Celine and Louis usually went along for the evening. Louis remembered one night in 1916 when chortlings of Kuhlau were interrupted by the cry "Rush to the cellar—with candles! Lights out!—because 'Grosse Bertha' was bombarding Paris and a huge shell had fallen just two blocks away."[4] Marcel also continued to read for pleasure, thanks to the influence of his uncle Joseph, a frequent visitor. He preferred nineteenth-century French literature, and one of his favorite authors was the prodigious Balzac, whose melodramatic *oeuvre* he savored with pleasure. Though he enjoyed sitting back after dinner to smoke his pipe and reflect on music or current events, he never aspired to intellectualism and in fact hated philosophical jargon and the new rage for psychology so intensely that he abruptly dropped out of the conversation or left the room when talk headed in that direction.

Chamber music limped along, and Moyse was involved. Once again, he was in contact with Debussy, who wrote the Sonata for flute, viola, and harp during the summer and fall of 1915. By that time, Debussy was fifty-three, sick with cancer, and just coming out of a dry spell brought on by the war. In a letter to Stravinsky that October, the composer commented on his creative state:

Music is in a sad condition, one has to admit. It's of no use except for charitable purposes, although we certainly shouldn't complain about that. Personally, I've spent over a year unable to write anything. It's only in the last three months, staying in the house of friends by the sea, that I've been able to think in music again. Unless one's directly involved with the war, it makes thought very difficult. Only that Olympian egoist Goethe could work through one.[5]

Moyse played in one of the earliest performances of the Sonata, possibly at the home of Debussy's publisher, Jacques Durand, with a woman harpist who had just escaped from Munich after spending time in prison. She had been forced to leave Germany without her harp ("worse than losing her leg," Debussy commented to a friend) and played the new piece on a chromatic instrument the ailing composer didn't like.

Moyse and his family managed to survive their precarious situation, but not without considerable stress, and toward the end of the war, the flutist succumbed to a complete physical and psychological breakdown. He was almost thirty, prone to nasty colds of the "walking pneumonia" variety, and pessimistic about his future and the outlook for France. He all but stopped practicing; it seemed to take all his strength just to drag himself to engagements. One day an older colleague, an oboist, took him aside at a rehearsal. "Moyse," he said, "your sound isn't so good anymore—you're vibrating too much. You'd better start practicing or you'll lose everything you have."

Soon after that warning, Moyse awakened one morning to find he could not blow a single note on the flute. His lungs, which still bore the scars of childhood infections and the illness at Dieppe, were so weak that he coughed blood when he tried to play. Celine ran for the doctor, who solemnly predicted the demise of Moyse's career and an early death. For someone else this news would have been reason to quit, but for Moyse it functioned as a good kick in the pants. For several months he abstained from the flute entirely and during this convalescence outlined a strict, progressive exercise regimen for himself. Very gradually, with dogged self-determination, he regained his strength. Early in the process, Moyse's lungs pumped so little air that it took him at least twenty minutes to produce just one low note on his instrument.

"I couldn't do it!" he recalled. "I was so weak. But finally, I decided to fight with life or die."[6] Later he would tell students, "The remedy is within yourself. You have to find it through yourself."[7]

Moyse's *Études et exercices techniques,* sold to Leduc in 1921, came out of this period; it features full-length etudes and numerous tiny technical workouts only a bar or two long, to be repeated over and over. An introductory note states that Moyse intended to assemble a series of studies that would address all sorts of technical issues, particularly tone, precision, legato, and finger technique—most of the basics. The *Exercices journaliers* (Daily Exercises), which Leduc bought the following year, was the flute doctor's prescription for a twenty-six-day cycle of work, a sort of Royal Canadian Air Force fitness program for the flute. Each exercise is lettered, and a calendar-like chart designates the letters to be practiced on each day of the cycle. Some exercises are repeated more than others. By the final day, the flutist will have covered all the material in the order Moyse found most advantageous.

Beginning with these books, Leduc published, over the years, thirty-two volumes of flute exercises by Marcel Moyse (see "Publications of Marcel Moyse" at the close of this book). Some contain strictly original material; others are based on music by different composers for the flute, violin, or keyboard (Chopin and Wieniawski are two examples). Moyse claimed that nearly all the studies were devised for his own use, but he also said that he produced some of them to earn extra cash for a trip or for a new sidecar for his beloved motorcycle. His own flute technique was admittedly hard-won, and he approached each difficulty by inventing studies that contained every possible configuration of a given set of notes; sketches for an unfinished book show his method of setting up a musical scrap with enough bars following to accommodate a complete, predictable round of permutations. The creative work lay in designing the proper fragment and its variations; once they were composed, Moyse had only to fill in the blanks according to the blueprint. "You must include every possibility, every articulation, every interval, every key," he once explained to the British flutist Trevor Wye. "If you don't, someone will always ask, 'Why did you leave *that* out?' That way, there can be no questions."[8] The volumes most used today, such as *De la sonorité: art et technique,* are founded on materials composed by Moyse.

In a small, dark room on the second floor of the Conservatoire, at precisely nine o'clock each Tuesday morning, a bowler-topped cadre of nine assembled around a bronze bust of Beethoven that glared at them from the mantlepiece, the only furnishing present besides a bare table and a piano. These members of the *comité* of the Société des Concerts du Conservatoire administered a musical institution that World War I had wounded as surely as it had the pianists and violinists without fingers, without arms. Yet this governing body continued to serve season ticket holders who so valued their seats that they often willed them to their heirs. Beethoven, the Société's founding inspiration, would have applauded the coexistence of art and battle—wasn't *Wellington's Victory* testament to that? The difference, the *comité* was beginning to admit in its ritual gatherings, was that the hero from Bonn had been a real revolutionary in his day, and the Société had been worshiping at his shrine for nearly a century, carefully ignoring a need for contemporary art music.

The musician-run, Conservatoire-connected orchestra dated back to 1828—the year after Beethoven's death—and adhered to a stack of self-governing rules and statutes weighty as a lead soufflé. From the beginning, when Berlioz's nemesis François Antoine Habeneck led the Société, "active" or voting members of the orchestra were required to be French, over twenty-one, finished with military service (even players born of foreign parents had to have served in the French army), and either a professor or former student of the Conservatoire. There were plenty of rules to cover exceptions. An artist who did not meet the basic criteria could be accepted as an adjunct member, meaning he could play but could not vote on organizational decisions, such as the selection of a new conductor. There were also members-in-training (which might apply to a gifted student invited to play next to his teacher), active aspirants (musicians invited to play but not officially named to membership), casual aspirants (players substituting for sick or vacationing active members), and externals, or temporary "extra" players who played even less frequently than the casual aspirants. The director of the Conservatoire was the ex-officio president of the Société, and the second conductor had to be selected from the ranks of the orchestra, which is how Taffanel and Gaubert both launched their conducting activities. Only the chief conductor could come from outside the Société and the Conservatoire.

The war made all these policies and pigeonholes irrelevant. Somehow, despite the diminishing population, there were still plenty of patrons to be entertained in the Société's acoustically legendary hall, adjacent to the old Conservatoire on a former marsh.

1   Marcel Moyse (front row, left end) with St. Amour classmates, around 1892. Photo courtesy Marcel Moyse Archives.

2   Moyse (second row, fourth from right), a guest at the wedding of Marie Perretier and Alexandre Chassagnoux, circa 1901. Photo courtesy Marcel Moyse Archives.

3   Paul Taffanel. Photo courtesy Marcel Moyse Archives.

4   Taffanel on his three-wheeled cycle. Photo courtesy Marcel Moyse Archives.

5 Adolphe Hennebains as Pan in a publicity photo. Photo courtesy Marcel Moyse Archives.

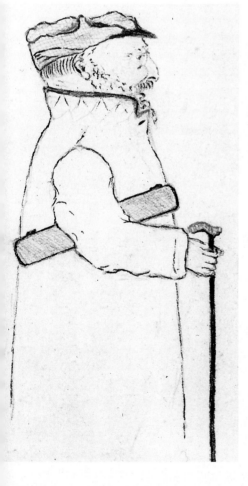

6 Moyse's sketch of Hennebains, circa 1905. Photo courtesy Marcel Moyse Archives.

7   Moyse around the age of twenty. Photo courtesy Marcel Moyse Archives.

8 Celine Gautreau before becoming Moyse's wife, as a player in the Théâtre de la Gaité-Lyrique in 1910 or 1911. Photo courtesy Marcel Moyse Archives.

9 Moyse aboard ship during Nellie Melba's United States tour, 1914. Photo courtesy Marcel Moyse Archives.

10   Dame Melba and Jan Kubelík in the United States, 1913 or 1914. Photo courtesy Marcel Moyse Archives.

11   Moyse in an orchestra conducted by René Baton. Photo courtesy Marcel Moyse Archives.

12　Moyse performing in the De Falla harpsichord concerto, with the composer at the keyboard. Photo courtesy Marcel Moyse Archives.

13　Moyse in a recording session for the Stravinsky Octet, Stravinsky standing, circa 1932. Photo courtesy Marcel Moyse Archives.

14   Moyse's adoptive mother, Josephine Perretier (seated), with Amélie
Perretier, Marie Perretier Chassagnoux, and Surette Chassagnoux in front of the
family tobacco shop around 1925. Photo courtesy Marcel Moyse Archives.

15 Blanche Honegger, Moyse, and his son, Louis, as the Moyse Trio, circa 1936. Photo courtesy Marcel Moyse Archives.

16 Illustration of *le maître*'s flute class at the Conservatoire, 1938. Photo courtesy Marcel Moyse Archives.

17 Marcel Moyse, with his adoptive mother Josephine Perretier and an unidentified family friend, St. Amour, circa 1940. Photo courtesy Marcel Moyse Archives.

18 Moyse in his studio at St. Amour, 1941. Photo courtesy Marcel Moyse Archives.

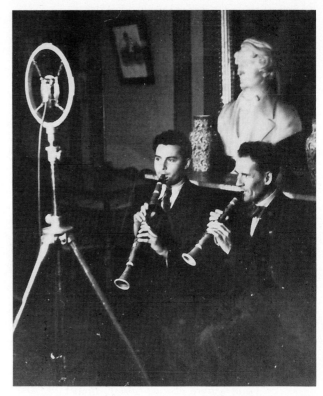

19 Moyse and his son, Louis, at Berlioz's home in La Côte Saint-André, around 1941. After a broadcasting session for French radio in which the Moyses had performed the "Trio of the Young Ishmaelites" from *L'enfance du Christ* with harpist Lily Laskine, a radio official asked them to pose for this publicity picture holding recorders from the Berlioz museum. Photo courtesy Marcel Moyse Archives.

20 & 21   Louis Moyse and daughter Isabelle, leaving St. Amour at the end of World War II. Photo courtesy Marcel Moyse Archives.

22 Moyse and his wife, Celine, in Rio de Janeiro, 1949. Photo courtesy Marcel Moyse Archives.

23 Marlboro's founders in 1951. Left to right, back row: Marcel Moyse, Louis Moyse, Rudolf Serkin, Blanche Moyse, Adolf Busch, and Hermann Busch. Cellist Nathan Chaikin is standing in front. Photo courtesy Marlboro Music, Marlboro, Vermont.

24   Moyse leading a master class of flute enthusiasts, Canterbury, England, 1964. Photo courtesy Marcel Moyse Archives.

25   Paula Robison and Marcel Moyse in a lesson at Marlboro, 1965. Boris Goldenberg photo.

26–28 Moyse conducting a
rehearsal at Marlboro, 1965. Boris
Goldenberg photos.

29   Moyse coaching a woodwind octet at Marlboro, 1974. At left is oboist
Rudy Vrbsky. Woodward Leung photo.

Moyse coaching clarinetist
vid Krakauer at Marlboro, 1978.
orge Dimock photo.

31   Moyse at his home in West Brattleboro, Vermont, 1979. Si Lippa photo.

The hall was tricked out inside like ancient Rome (the gray-green decor seen at its opening in 1811 had been done over in mid-century because of complaints that the drab tints were "damaging to the beauty of the women"). To satisfy its wartime subscribers, the Société had to come up with an orchestra close to its standard ninety-two-man band, and suddenly, nonmembers and ex-members who had retired at the mandatory age of sixty were engaged on a regular basis. Moyse, who qualified as an active aspirant, played with the Société from time to time during the war, probably during the period when Gaubert was on active duty in the French army.

The Société was also obliged to loosen its straitjacketed programming policies symbolized by the deaf genius on the mantlepiece, and it wasn't easy. As early as 1828 Beethoven's ghost clearly hovered when Habeneck turned down a proposal that gave special privileges to soloists. Perhaps the idea would be appropriate, he said, "on the day when the symphonies of Beethoven no longer have the power to excite the public." The day was finally coming, over Habeneck's dead body. After decades of committees whose most consistent program choice was the Beethoven symphony cycle (favored over young composer-virtuosos like Sarasate whose reputations had not been "sanctioned by the public"), the comité had to admit that offspring of the old guard wanted the variety they enjoyed from more forward-looking orchestras like Colonne and Lamoureux. The Société had heard complaints before. Paris critics throughout the nineteenth century griped about its old-fashioned habits, and in its first nineteen seasons, the orchestra never played a multi-movement work in its entirety, for fear of tiring out an audience that seemed to prefer single pearls to necklaces. (Beethoven rated the first full-length performance when, in 1847, the Société delivered his incidental music to August Kotzebue's stage work *Die Ruinen von Athen,* start to finish.) In the Société's first forty seasons, persistent Berlioz was one of a scant handful of living French composers who had a work played by the orchestra.

The music played by the Société during the war years reflected a conscious response to the public's changing tastes and offered Moyse, in his substitute capacity, an opportunity to learn some of the Société's ways with classics as well as the sounds of his own era. The sober guardians of the Société's Tuesday morning club swirled

180 degrees to a propagandist position, and the orchestra began to function as a patriotic state ensemble that performed for charity and civic events such as the Matinées Nationales at the Sorbonne or the decoration of a victorious general. The Société toured various European cities—mostly Swiss—to promote French music, and in the 1918–19 season pulled out the stops with a French propaganda tour of thirty-seven cities in the United States. The Société des Concerts was in Richmond, Virginia, the day the Armistice was signed (11 November 1918) and received a delirious ovation. Later tour highlights included a performance in San Francisco before an audience of eight thousand and an escort of mounted police for a welcoming parade in Indianapolis. From the community stage of Sherman, Texas, to the polished planks of Carnegie Hall, France's musical ambassadors became the focus of American victory jamborees.

Moyse was not part of this tour—he spent a good part of 1918 in Lyon with the Gémier Troupe, a small group of musicians who appeared in a production of Molière's *Le bourgeois gentilhomme,* costumed in the style of Louis XIV. But it was a turning point for him because it resulted in two vacancies in the orchestra's flute section. Gaubert moved out of the solo chair to take André Messager's Société baton at the end of the trip, and Moyse's former rival Georges Laurent, the Société's second flutist, elected to remain in the United States as principal flutist with the Boston Symphony.

Of all the American ensembles that routinely recruited Europeans, Boston had the highest proportion of French players; at one point it was said that a person had to speak French to get along in the orchestra because one-third of the group was Parisian. In the 1913–14 season, the Boston Symphony woodwind section was dominated by Conservatoire-trained Frenchmen, such as flutists André Marquarre, the last *premier prix* student of Altès and a member of the Boston Symphony since 1898, and André Chevrot, who won his top prize in Taffanel's studio the year after Moyse and went to Boston in 1912. Georges Laurent remained with the Boston Symphony for the rest of his career, as content in Massachusetts as Barrère was in New York. Like Barrère, who transplanted the French School to Juilliard, Laurent set down French roots as a teacher at the New England Conservatory.

(Boston's French connection also extended to the podium. In 1918–19, Henri Rabaud left his duties as president of the

Conservatoire and conductor at the Paris Opéra to lead the BSO. For a brief time, Rabaud—a grandson of the flutist Louis Dorus—was the rage on the East Coast; his opera *Marouf* was mounted in New York to great acclaim. It was Rabaud who invited his colleague Laurent to Boston, and although the maestro sailed back to France after one season, Laurent continued to receive cues from familiar faces. Pierre Monteux, hired by the Metropolitan Opera to guide productions of French opera during the war, directed the BSO through 1924 and introduced Boston Brahmins to such new works as *Le sacre du printemps*. The Russian-born Serge Koussevitzky, who earned notches in his baton championing offbeat new music in Paris, followed Monteux with a celebrated reign of twenty-five years.)

With Gaubert at the helm and Laurent in America, the Société's flute section needed a new leader. Gaubert approached his former pupil privately about the possibility, but Moyse was reluctant to consider it, for fear of being accused of profiting from the war situation. But a few months later, the Société voted unanimously to offer him the job, and suddenly Moyse sat in the most coveted flute chair in Paris. According to Louis Moyse, the Société appointment obliged Marcel to quit another new post with the Pasdeloup Orchestra because of schedule conflicts.

When the war ended, the French took to the streets, alternating choruses of the "Marseillaise" with "Dixie." Blazing streetlights replaced shaded lamps, and nighttime Paris once again resembled "Gay Paree." By January the better-heeled citizens had dusted off their tiaras and silk hats and kicked off mid-season concerts with vigor. There was mourning to be done, to be sure, and food was still in short supply, but giddy relief swept thousands of celebrants into the concert halls, and everything sold out days ahead of time, week after week. Moyse was part of the festivities at the Opéra-Comique just before New Year's, when he played in a gala performance of Charles Lecocq's *La fille de Madame Angot,* a production featuring so many brilliant singers that several noted divas accepted minor roles for the first time in years just so they could be seen there. Reynaldo Hahn conducted the affair; the proceeds benefited the children of Alsace-Lorraine. The audience went wild and the curtain had to be hoisted up repeatedly after every act.

During the "spa season" of 1919, Moyse confronted another physical ailment; this time he nearly lost the little finger of his left hand. He was playing at Bagnères-de-Bigorre, near the foot of the Pyrenees, and strained the finger—how, why, no one knows. But he ignored the problem until the digit finally froze. Not one, but three physicians told him the finger was gangrenous and had to be amputated. As Louis Moyse commented, "Those doctors had come from the trenches in the Marne and had seen much worse—for them, it was nothing."[9] Marcel refused to accept their prognosis and began soaking his finger in hot water and herbs several times a day. Little by little, the swelling went down; Moyse measured the progress with Celine's wedding ring; at the start of the treatment, it would not pass the tip of his finger. In the end, it could be slipped all the way down to the base.

Sometime after this, Moyse auditioned for and won the solo flute post in the orchestra of the Opéra-Comique. The exact date has yet to be nailed down; the Opéra-Comique archive at the Paris Opéra has no record of the musicians that played for the company then, and players' names were not listed in the programs. Published biographical sketches identify the year as early as 1913, and Moyse was known to exaggerate that he had had the job as far back as 1909, when he was only nineteen. But Louis Moyse recalls that his father wasn't involved with the Opéra-Comique until after the Armistice, and it makes sense that the seat remained officially vacant through the war years. Moyse could have substituted in the orchestra then, but he probably didn't win the permanent job until he was at least thirty years old—not a boy wonder, but a musician with more than ten years' experience and dues-paying to his credit.

At about the same time, Moyse tried out for the first flute chair at the Opéra, perhaps to prove himself. No one else came close to winning, and the victor was faced with a choice. Considering his allegiance to home and hearth, plus his thirst for the St. Amour countryside, Moyse decided to stick with the less prestigious Opéra-Comique because it offered a more flexible schedule. For years, he shared his duties there with a "second" first flutist named Portré; together, they were responsible for covering all services on a monthly basis. Moyse arranged to take three months off in the summer, with Portré performing all services while he was away. In the fall, the two shared the chair again, but Moyse played more than half the services.

Louis Moyse described his father's treasured summers away from Paris:

The vacations in our little village of Saint-Amour were more than welcome. For one to two weeks he was an exhausted man, sleeping all the time. But after this recovery period, his greatest joy was to drive his sidecar (later an automobile) through the country, living like a gypsy without any schedule, following the Tour de France each year in the Pyrenees or the Alps, going to Italy or to the high passes in Switzerland. He was also very good at repairing his motorcycle right on the road—all kinds of mechanical failures, even major ones. Time was absolutely nonexistent and there was no flute to bother with. Another habit of his was to leave very early in the morning, walking (sometimes alone, sometimes with me) to the little villages surrounding St. Amour, making drawings or watercolors. Coming back home, we would stop at a little café in the village and have a drink of Pernod while playing billiards. During these days time did not exist for him, and very often what was ready for lunch would be served at dinnertime, to the greatest annoyance of my mother. For two months there was no flute, except for lessons given to foreign students who followed him during the summertime. Around the middle of September he would put himself in good shape by practicing five to six hours daily, and going through his repertoire, which was more than one hundred pieces known by heart.[10]

The predominantly nineteenth-century operas Moyse played at the Opéra-Comique have been described as the "repertoire of memory" because the arias were so familiar that everyone knew them by heart. Operas by Rossini, Donizetti, Bellini, Weber, Massenet, Offenbach, Gounod, and Delibes were standard fare, as well as the lighter constructions of Mozart and Verdi, the seductive "verismo" spectacles of Puccini, and of course the Opéra-Comique's crown jewel, *Carmen*. Francis Poulenc, who was a teenager during World War I, called the Opéra-Comique the "true house" of his childhood. From the age of eight he knew "every nook and cranny" of the Salle Favart. "Today I dream in those corridors with no other goal than to pursue lost time," the composer wrote nostalgically.[11]

Moyse came into his own as an artist during the 1920s, one of Parisian culture's brightest decades. The Opéra and Opéra-Comique were settled comfortably as custodians of standard repertory, but the legitimate theater scene sizzled with new productions, and the air hummed daily with radio broadcasts, thanks to the fast development of the medium by the military during the war. Once-banned German music was returned to programs; the Pasdeloup Orchestra resurrected Wagner in 1919 after an audience poll revealed an overwhelming desire for it: 4983 for, 213 against. The popular cinema drew devotees of every class (something the various Sunday concert series had attempted with only limited success), provoking pundits to paint the demise of live, "cultured" entertainment. For many citizens, spectator sports took the place of church-going; technological speed and physical vitality were their obsessions. Concertgoers seeking an aural equivalent followed new music series like Concerts Koussevitzky, which Moyse added to the frantic schedule he managed without a home telephone until 1929.

Moyse admired Serge Koussevitzky, who had immigrated to Paris after the Russian Revolution because he disliked leading his state-assigned orchestra. Koussevitzky was an innovator, not a civil servant; he had conducted the first concert performances in Russia of such works as *Le sacre du printemps.* In Paris he found the freedom and resources to resume his quest for the unusual, and his series ran well from 1921 to 1928, when he had to abandon it for new duties with the Boston Symphony.

Moyse played solo flute for most of the Koussevitzky seasons in Paris (Jean Boulze, solo flutist of the Opéra, is listed in programs for 1928) and was a featured soloist in a new work by Rimsky-Korsakov on the first concert of the 1921 season (see pages 104–105). The repertory Moyse played under Koussevitzky was far more adventurous for its time than the repertory most American orchestras tackle today. Besides one classic, there was almost always a premiere, and an assortment of works from the very recent past. The 12 June 1926 program was typical:

Haydn	"Surprise" Symphony
Hindemith	Concerto for Orchestra (premiere)
Honegger	*Pacific 231*
Bloch	Concerto Grosso No. 1 (for string orchestra with piano obbligato)
Ravel	Suite No. 2 from *Daphnis et Chloé*

Moyse also segued into a closer professional relationship with Gaubert, who, in addition to the chief conductorship of the Société, was named professor of flute at the Conservatoire after the war. Moyse acted as Gaubert's teaching assistant nearly from the start and may have helped him prepare the Taffanel-Gaubert *Méthode complète de flûte* (published in 1923 by Alphonse Leduc and Co.) after Société rehearsals (see note 37, Chapter 3). Working with the flute class sparked Moyse's imagination, and the study table in his flat was always a jumble with scraps and revisions of exercises for himself and the students. In appreciation of Moyse's friendship and artistry, Gaubert dedicated the third movement ("Barcarolle") of his *Suite* for flute and piano (1921) and the *Deuxième sonate* for flute and piano (1925) to his protégé.

The Société des Concerts did not completely abandon its pro-French outlook after the war, but continued to present a respectable amount of new music. This was important to Moyse, whose folder at the Opéra-Comique contained so many beloved chestnuts. A glance at Société programs in the decade following the Armistice reveals titles by dozens of contemporary composers such as Dukas, Roussel, Chausson, Ibert, and (now) lesser-knowns such as Florent Schmitt and Guy Ropartz, whose chamber music for winds has helped carry their reputations to the end of the twentieth century. At the opening of the Société's 100th season in 1926, Henri De Curzon commented in *Le Ménestrel* that an examination of the orchestra's record "would cause more than one surprise, if only to the people who imagine that the Société, which discovered Beethoven, rebelled at each novelty that wasn't consecrated."[12]

The Société played Ravel frequently, and it might have been during one of its rehearsals in 1921 that Moyse approached the composer about an error he had discovered in the score of *Daphnis et Chloé* after playing the premiere nine years before. (As a ballet, the work had not achieved much notoriety, but the two orchestral suites Ravel extracted from it were popular with concert audiences.) The problem centered on a note in the flute solo of the "Pantomime" section of the Second Suite: was it an E-sharp or an E-natural? "Oh, either way," Ravel is said to have responded. "I couldn't care less!"[13]

The Société also continued to tour, not just to French cities such as Bordeaux, Lyon, and Marseille, but to Switzerland and Germany as well. The orchestra was an immense success at international gatherings such as the music expositions in Frankfurt and Geneva. Beethoven was still honored on special occasions. A Beethoven symphony and concerto cycle was presented at the Theater of the

Concert program, Grands Concerts Symphoniques Serge Koussevitzky, 10 November 1921. Harry Ransom Humanities Research Center, the University of Texas at Austin.

GRANDS CONCERTS SYMPHONIQUES

SERGE KOUSSEVITZKY

1er CONCERT : JEUDI 10 NOVEMBRE 1921, à 9 heures précises du soir

AVEC LE CONCOURS DE :

Mme Vera JANACOPULOS

PROGRAMME

1. Ouverture d'**Obéron**. . . . . Ch. M. WEBER
2. **Nocturnes**. . . . . DEBUSSY
   a) *Nuages.* — b) *Fêtes.*
3. Introduction de l'Opéra "**Khovantchina**" MOUSSORGSKY
4. "**La Légende de l'invisible Ville de Kitiej et la Vierge Févronie**". . . RIMSKY-KORSAKOW
   a) *Introduction.* — b) *La Bataille de Kerjenietz*
   (1re Audition) Flûte Solo : M. MOYSE.
5. **Le Vol du Bourdon** . . . . RIMSKY-KORSAKOW
   Sherzo de l'Opéra *"Le Conte du Tzar Sultan"*
   (1re audition).
6. **Shéhérazade** (poème de Klingsor) . . . . M. RAVEL
   a) *Asie.* - b) *La Flûte enchantée.* - c) *L'Indifférent*
   Mme Véra JANACOPULOS.

:: *ENTR'ACTE* ::

7. **Symphonie en ut mineur** (n° 5) . . . . BEETHOVEN
   Allegro - andante con moto - Scherzo et finale.

Orchestre de 100 exécutants sous la Direction de M. SERGE KOUSSEVITZKY

LE 2e CONCERT aura lieu le JEUDI 17 NOVEMBRE 1921
avec le concours de M. EDOUARD RISLER
Au Programme : Œuvres de Rimsky-Korsakow (suite du " Conte le Tzar Saltan ",
1re audition). Francesco Malipiero, Florent Schmitt, Beethoven, Wagner.

Champs-Élysées under Walter Damrosch after the war to benefit former pupils of the Conservatoire, and the Société gave a Beethoven centenary concert at the Sorbonne in 1927, with Rabaud in charge of the Fifth Symphony and D'Indy leading the Ninth. (Louis Moyse, then fifteen, remembered being "squeezed" into the Beethoven orchestra by his father and the trombonist Raphael Delbos so he could sit in the midst of the music. He wore concert attire, but did not play. Louis said that on that occasion, Gaubert also led the "Emperor" Concerto with pianist Édouard Riesler, and "Adieu à la bien-aimée" with Marthe Chenal. No one questioned Louis's mute presence on stage.)[14] The Société also welcomed guest conductors such as the up-and-coming Bruno Walter.

Critics of the Société's concerts in the 1920s frequently praised Moyse in lavish, poetic terms. Pierre de Lapommeraye, who covered the Société series for *Le Ménestrel,* reported in 1926 that Moyse played so irresistibly in the B Minor Suite of Bach that the audience demanded an encore of the Minuet, "which he played alternating with the cello in exquisite manner. A full sound, warm, never strident, poetic, playful, elegant, and spiritual, makes of the flute, under the breath of M. Moyse, an instrument of dreams and enchantment."[15] The success of that particular evening could not have been better timed, because, according to his son, Moyse had been undergoing another breakdown in morale, which he attributed to overwork and psychological stress.

> Nothing was interesting him anymore, not even his flute. But after that performance, on the way home, he said to my mother and me, "Something has been happening in my brain—now I realize I've been driving myself for nothing. But I think I have the courage to come back."[16]

The following year, M. Lapommeraye singled out Moyse for his work in *L'après-midi d'un faune:* "The flute of M. Moyse, light, enveloping, wrapped us up in mythological and sunny landscapes. What poetry, what warmth, what fullness there was in the notes of M. Moyse. The listener forgets the instrument, and succumbs to the performer, the evocator."[17] If Moyse had experienced a rough year, his audiences did not seem to notice.

At the Opéra-Comique, Moyse began to listen more admiringly and intently to the singers, with the idea of adapting the vocalist's vast range of expression to the flute. Although he later took pride in calling up memories of Melba and of Caruso, whom he knew best from recordings, the singers he heard regularly—such as Sybil Sanderson, Mary Garden (creator of the role of Mélisande), and the bass-baritone Vanni Marcoux—were the ones who consistently impelled him to expand his trademark belief: that the flute could be as evocative as the human voice. Marcoux's strengths were similar to Moyse's: he had a weakness for sentimental songs and was gifted at "making magic out of unlikely material." The emotional content of his art was so technically controlled that he could suggest tears in his voice without disturbing the musical line. And because Marcoux's voice was so bright in character, it sounded high and light even at the bottom of the staff and enabled the words to project clearly.

"What is the flute? Nothing but a poor piece of pipe," Moyse used to say, with a shrug. But by emulating the range of emotions singers achieved through the subtle use of tone color, dynamics, diction (especially French), and the rest of the vocal palette, Moyse came to believe that a flutist could rise above his fate as an unseen key-pusher and sing out splendidly within—or over—the orchestra. His method of accomplishing the singer's dramatic potential did not depend on imitation, but on informed awareness that worked from the inside out and fed on personal emotions. If flutists could learn the articulated text of a song or aria as well as its psychological meaning, and strive to deliver the sorts of inflections, tone colors, and phrase shapes they would use if they were singing, they could render any melody intimately and profoundly. Moyse knew more than one hundred opera arias by heart, and he practiced them on his flute. In the 1920s, he became a real child of the Golden Age of opera.

Moyse's famous melody book, *Tone Development Through Interpretation* (published in 1962), is a mother lode of tunes from the operas he played night after night and inadvertently describes the quirky differences between the repertoire of the Opéra and that of the Opéra-Comique during his career. For example, three minor works by Gounod are represented in Moyse's book, but not *Faust,* because even though it originally contained spoken dialogue—one of the earliest defining features of the genre of *opéra-comique*—it "belonged" to the more prestigious theater. Gounod added recitatives ten years after its premiere so it would qualify as "grand opera." The first version of *Faust,* with spoken dialogue, was revived in 1932, but, strangely, at the Opéra, not the Opéra-Comique. Yet even though *Carmen* was commonly heard outside Paris with added recitatives instead of the original dialogue, the Opéra wouldn't touch it, ostensibly because the recitatives were added after Bizet's death. More than one aficionado complained that the arbitrary line of demarcation between house repertories did more than confuse the public: it prevented healthy competition that might have motivated both theaters to improve their products.

In a practical sense, it is much easier to understand why Moyse knew Offenbach's *Les contes d'Hoffmann* and missed out on the Ring Cycle. Compared to the Palais Garnier, the Salle Favart, inaugurated in 1898 (fire destroyed the original building eleven years before), was a modest theater with a relatively shallow stage, mediocre acoustics, and a tiny orchestra pit. The facade and entryway of the Salle Favart's "railway-station-baroque" exterior turned away from the boulevard, as if embarrassed to show itself. The arrangement stemmed from the odd requirements of an eighteenth-century bill of sale for the land.

Albert Carré, director of the Opéra-Comique in Moyse's early years with the company, was dedicated to mainstream works during his long and influential tenure (1898–1925, with a break during the war), but nonetheless gambled on Charpentier's controversial *Louise* and Debussy's *Pelléas et Mélisande* around the turn of the century. After the war Carré was less adventurous—a growing middle-class clientele and mounting costs forced him to be—and one of the few chances he took was the 1923 premiere of Milhaud's *La brebis égarée,* the story of a biblical "lost sheep" with a libretto by the poet Francis Jammes. The performance was very important to the outlaw Milhaud, who hoped it would propel him into the mainstream musical establishment. But the composer's hopes were crushed on opening night, when reactionaries in the audience protested indelicately during the first act. Louis Moyse was there, courtesy of his father, and recalled part of the event:

> In one aria, the heroine sings, "Oh, where would I go, where would I go?" And a guy in the top of the hall, sick and tired of hearing the same words, yelled at the top of his lungs, "Well, go to the movies!" Unanimous laughs from everyone, including the audience, the orchestra, and people onstage, except for Carré and Milhaud, who sat in the first loge.[18]

The police were brought in to quell the disturbances, but the damage was done. *La brebis égarée* closed after a handful of performances, and Carré backpedaled to Massenet and company.

During the 1920s the Opéra-Comique began a chaotic series of management changes that frustrated everyone, public and employees alike. In 1925, the elderly Carré stepped down and Louis Masson took over with a plan to update the house repertory and pull the Opéra-Comique kicking and screaming into the twentieth century. Among his projects was the first Paris production of Ravel's *L'enfant et les sortilèges* (February 1926), which, in his review for *Le Figaro,* André Messager begrudgingly praised as a progressive step for the new management, even though he didn't like the piece very much. The following year, Milhaud got a second chance with his forty-five-minute chamber opera, *Le pauvre matelot,* a "mistaken identity" tragedy on a libretto by Jean Cocteau. Paris received it coolly, but Milhaud fared well anyway. Attracted by the modest forces *Le pauvre matelot* required, small opera houses all over Europe, particularly in Germany, adopted it and turned it into one of the composer's most-performed works.

Masson's efforts were admirable, but not sufficient to balance the Opéra-Comique's books, which ran up a hefty deficit by the end of the 1931–32 season. All Paris's show houses were having problems during this time and blamed the French government for unjust taxation; on 29 March 1932, all theaters, cinemas, and entertainment halls protested by bolting their doors for a day. Although the Municipal Council of Paris had recently increased its subsidies to the four national theaters, including the Opéra-Comique, Masson was forced to give up his post to M. Gheusi, wartime director of the company and a seasoned impresario known to be contributing a personal investment of several million francs. Artistically, Gheusi had a reputation as a commercial crowd-pleaser, but critics also hoped he would reform lax personnel policies that undermined the quality of productions. In an article titled "The Crisis at the Opéra-Comique," Henri Prunières commented,

> It is important to recognize that a theater like the Opéra-Comique has nothing to do with an avant-garde scene. The presentation of repertoire is its principal object. Let it be sung in tune by melodious voices, and may the orchestra rehearse sufficiently so that we don't have to sit through any more massacres,

as were committed in these last years—when, by the third performance a third of the orchestra was composed of substitutes,
painfully sight-reading the parts. That is what the public has a
right to demand, and what we are waiting for with confidence
with M. Gheusi.[19]

In addition to renovating the Salle Favart's interior, lowering
ticket prices, and opening the 1932 season with *Carmen,* one of
Gheusi's first acts was to take away the orchestra players' right of
hiring their own substitutes, a privilege Moyse frequently took
advantage of, given his multitude of outside engagements. The
French musicians' union was willing to comply with the stricter
rules because Gheusi paid well. Moyse, who had trod closely
enough in his grandfather's footsteps to become an outspoken
member of the union, must have found himself in a catch-22.
Gheusi's administration increased the earning potential of the
orchestra members, but it probably forced Moyse to limit his
freelance work for a while.

Moyse's name appeared regularly in published listings of
chamber-music performances both before and after that particular "crisis." On 18 October 1923 at the Opéra he played in the
premiere of Stravinsky's Octet, and he probably participated in a
limited-edition pressing recorded the following month. (Stravinsky
probably passed the record out to a few friends and colleagues; the
Finale is incomplete because the wax ran out. Moyse played on the
commercial recording for Columbia nine years later with
Stravinsky—see Figure 13 and Discography nos. 64–65.) In June
1926 Moyse took part in a highly publicized all-Ravel concert sponsored by *La Revue Musicale* at the Salle Gaveau, joining the young
harpist Lily Laskine (who had earned her *premier prix* at the
Conservatoire the year before Moyse), clarinetist M. Hamelin, and
the Pro Arte Quartet in the *Introduction et Allegro,* with Ravel
conducting. The Pro Arte also played the Quartet, and pianist
Robert Casadesus performed *Miroirs.* Moyse collaborated with
Ravel again the following year (September 1927), this time in
Amsterdam, in a recital of chamber music sponsored by the American patroness Elizabeth Sprague Coolidge, who had commissioned all the works on the program. Ravel's *Chansons madécasses* was
the "keeper" on the concert that included music by Francesco
Malipiero, Gabriel Pierné, and N. T. Berezowski. Madeleine Grey

sang the *Chansons,* with Moyse on flute, Hans Kindler on cello, and Ravel at the piano.[20]

Moyse was also a fixture at special events, such as a 1926 festival of French music sponsored by the Confédération des Travailleurs Intellectuels in the Salle Gaveau. One hundred and twenty artists participated, and Moyse was one of a handful singled out for mention in the press.

By 1926 Moyse had become solo flutist with Concerts Straram, an important addition to the postwar music scene. Walther Straram, who enjoyed the financial sponsorship of the wealthy widow Ganna Walska, was not an outstanding conductor, but he respected his musicians and was committed to presenting new music as well as the neglected eighteenth- and nineteenth-century chamber orchestra repertoire. With Straram, previously ignored

---

MAISON GAVEAU (SALLE DES CONCERTS)
45-47, Rue La Boétie, 45-47

CONCERTS
WALTHER
STRARAM

SAISON 1927

PROGRAMME
du
ONZIÈME CONCERT
JEUDI 7 AVRIL
à 9 heures du soir

ONZIÈME CONCERT

Jeudi 7 Avril 1927

PROGRAMME

BACH . . . .   Concerto Brandebourgeois n° 1
                         Allegro non troppo - Adagio - Allegro -
                         Menuetto - Polacca

MOZART . . . . . .   Concerto pour Flûte et Harpe
                     Allegro - Andantino - Rondo, allegro
                     Mlle Lily LASKINE
                     et M. Marcel MOYSE

LARMANJAT   Divertissement (1re audition)
                         Allegro - Tempo di minuetto - Alle-
                         gretto - Andante - Finale, allegro
                         giocoso
                         Piano : M. Maurice FAURE

HONEGGER . . . .   Pastorale d'Été

POULENC . . . . . .   Mouvements perpétuels
                      (1re audition)

RAVEL . . . .   Le Tombeau de Couperin
                        Suite d'Orchestre
                        Prélude - Forlane - Menuet - Rigaudon

Prix de Vente : **2** Francs

Concert program, Concerts Walther Straram, 7 April 1927. Harry Ransom Humanities Research Center, the University of Texas at Austin.

music by Monteverdi, Purcell, Bach, Vivaldi, Handel, Rameau, and others surfaced in Paris, as well as seldom-heard symphonies by Haydn, Mozart, and Stamitz. Straram also welcomed important guests. In 1931 Richard Strauss led the orchestra in a program of his music; it was his first visit to Paris since the beginning of World War I.

Moyse continued to reserve summertime for the annual family pilgrimage to St. Amour. A few years after the birth of his daughter, Marguerite, in 1923, he designed and built, with his trombonist friend Raphael Delbos, a large home there, on a wide corner lot at a crossroads on the edge of town. The quantity of long, vertical windows gives the house a modern appearance, and the yellow-on-blue sunburst design of the wide front gable further declares Moyse's individuality. Marguerite recalled that "as a small girl, we would visit people in the village, and my father would say to them, 'Remember when I used to sit in this spot as a boy and eat my lunch . . . ?' He knew everybody, and everybody knew him." The house was owned jointly by the Moyse and Delbos families and shared until Moyse could afford to take full possession in 1939.

Moyse also found a way to combine his love of travel with his penchant for tinkering and nailed together what might have been the first RV, according to Marguerite.

> We called it a chicken coop. It had the chassis of a car, and on the back he built a little house with a pointed roof. It had sleeping quarters, and the back panel opened and unfolded to make a little table inside, so if it was raining we could still stop and have a picnic.
>
> Once we went to a bicycle race, and it was raining, so we opened the back, and suddenly a man on a bicycle and one on a motorcycle stopped because they thought it was a refreshment stand! My mother was deeply offended.[21]

Everything worked beautifully until the contraption suffered a flat tire on a junket to Italy. That was when Moyse noticed that the low edges of the jerry-built cottage obstructed the rear wheels, and he was obliged to borrow a saw from a roadside restaurant and cut a slab out of one side so he could change the tire.

The Moyse family's Paris headquarters was a flat on Rue d'Orsel in Montmartre. After the war the eccentric neighborhood grew less artsy and more touristy to satisfy visitors from abroad who lusted after a taste of naughty Parisian nightlife. Cabaret proprietors went to greater extremes than the prewar gang of intellectuals and creative sad sacks had ever witnessed. A cabaret called Le Ciel became a medieval dining hall, complete with waiters in Wagnerian costumes who addressed customers as "My Brother" and delivered blasphemous sermons and benedictions to amused foreigners. Le Florida's colorfully lit, glass dance floor predated the American disco environment by decades when it was installed around 1925, the same year one of Berlioz's former Montmartre residences was demolished. Cynical journalists filled space with sidewise warnings: "Two shiploads of savages just arrived at Cherbourg—watch out, Montmartre." To old-timers, the district had become Las Vegas. Even the poor stopped sleeping in the grass on the hill below Sacré Coeur on hot nights. But Montmartre mustered its original spirit on occasion, such as the September 1926 auto race up the slopes of La Butte, in which the top prize went to the car that took the longest time to ascend.

Toward the end of his life, Ravel wrote an essay for *Excelsior,* addressing "musical youth" with a little less hand-wringing than Albert Lavignac had expressed a generation earlier. In it he pointed to the diminishing feasibility of staging large-scale works and predicted a time—soon to come—when other musical venues would take over:

> What will these young people do? Their situation is particularly distressing. The lyric theater, in its traditional form, is moribund. Throughout the world, people are turning away from this type of spectacle, which must be revived at all cost. Present economic conditions no longer warrant the composing of large symphonic works, and even less those which require the addition of large choral groups. All that is too expensive today.
>
> Only the phonograph recording, the soundtrack film, and the radio can save music, which is now in jeopardy. Unfortunately, producers of recorded music have other preoccupations. They have earmarked the phonograph recording exclusively for commercial success, instead of commissioning new works especially for it. The soundtrack film, which could be the most important form of lyric expression in today's art, spurns the collaboration of genuine musicians, and permits very little

access to its studios. There remains the radio, which has also been indifferent to this problem until now.[22]

If, as Albert Lavignac had suggested, there were too many trained, unemployed musicians drifting about Paris in 1895, the situation, according to Ravel, was about to become intolerable in the 1930s. Ravel's concerns centered on composers, but the growing difficulty of performing giant works and the rising strength of the broadcast and recording industries were to modify the public's perception of musical art and artists, and affect the artists themselves. Whatever the consequences for the future, Moyse was in the right place at the right time when opera-driven record companies began to take a greater interest in purely instrumental music.

Instrumental soloists had been preserving everything from potboilers to sonatas since the early days of acoustical recording. But it was a new technological advance that turned Moyse and his fellow wind players into home entertainment. In 1925 a breakthrough in the electrical recording process improved the quality of platter production: performers could finally play into a portable microphone instead of screeching down a horn or tube that erupted out of a box or wall like a practical joke. The flute had always been relatively easy to record; its basic sound is acoustically the purest of all the wind instruments, and its full practical range (with the exception of the extreme high register) could be picked up by antique systems that failed to register extreme highs and lows. (In early orchestral recordings, tubas and bassoons often played the bass lines because the double bass could not be imprinted. Piccolos recorded surprisingly well—better than the flute—but the high harmonics of the violin tended to vaporize. Even high-pitched percussion fared poorly. Early record-buyers had to take virtuosity on faith when an ascending xylophone run thinned out into a patter of wooden clicks.) New recording and reproduction technology made flutes sound even better, but Moyse made at least one major adjustment to the medium. It was at that point, he said, that he began consciously to employ vibrato as a means of enriching his sound on records. But he cautioned students who would imitate him to listen to singers, not string players, for proper examples. "We cannot imitate the violin's vibrato because it has one source for tone (the bow) and another (the fingers of the left hand) for vibrato," he maintained. The flute tone colored by vibrato should imitate the motion of a piece of wood floating on water, he said. The waves undulate, but the piece of wood does not. On numerous occasions Moyse called jazz vibrato "the chewing gum of the ear." On record, his tone comes across remarkably alive, full and supple; his propensity for playing sharp—a species-wide tendency many flutists faithfully continue to uphold—also contributes to the brilliant effect.

Of all the French flutists whose sounds are embedded in the thick 78s of the 20s, 30s, and 40s, Moyse chalked up by far the largest catalogue. Gaubert and Hennebains were caught on disc toward the ends of their performing careers, most often in short ditties that would fit easily on a four-minute side; Hennebains was also featured on some multi-disc sets. Barrère recorded extensively in the United States, and there were others, such as Laurent, who turned out a handful of recordings each. Moyse's only competitor in Paris was René Le Roy, a popular chamber-music performer who attended the Conservatoire ten years after Moyse. Le Roy cut more than two dozen records. Moyse surpassed him, partly because of his close ties to orchestras.

Moyse's first outing as a soloist in a recording studio is believed to have been 21–26 March 1927, when he cut four solo selections for flute and piano for the Compagnie Française du Gramophone (Discography nos. 1–4; also see no. 164 and notes concerning the "Étoile" label). One of these, Genin's "Carnaval de Venise," was immediately popular and sold thousands of copies in the major Paris department stores such as Galeries Lafayette. Moyse signed on with the Columbia Graphophone Company, Ltd. ("French Columbia"), soon after and recorded several works, including Debussy's unaccompanied work "Syrinx," on 16–18 January 1928 (Discography nos. 14–17). That year, the July issue of *La Revue Musicale* offered a one-line review: "For Columbia, Moyse plays Debussy's piece "Syrinx," and the "Andante pastorale" of Taffanel. The sound is utterly beautiful."[23] Moyse also began working for Odéon in late 1927 or early 1928; his Odéon recording of Debussy's Sonata for flute, viola, and harp (Discography nos. 8–13) dates from that time. His first known orchestral recording is with L'Orchestre Symphonique de Paris in the "Aquarium" and "Volière" movements from Saint-Saëns's *Le carnaval des animaux* (Discography nos. 169–170), produced in 1927.

The recording and reproduction processes of the 20s and 30s were to current standards and practices as frying a hamburger is to preparing a gourmet meal. The methods, although sophisticated for their time, were simpler, and the results bore far less subtlety. In general, the French used "dead" studios with lots of drapery, while the English preferred more reverberant concert halls (which, to the French, cluttered the sound). The 1932 recording of Stravinsky's Octet, with Moyse on flute and the composer conducting (Discography nos. 64–65), sounds less sonorous than it would up close in a padded room. The performance is also not up to today's technical standards; not all individual parts are note-perfect, and the ensemble is occasionally ragged, illustrating the standard limit of two or three "takes." Even divas who might have demanded excessive time marched into the studio, delivered the goods in short order, and left, satisfied that the wax master was up to snuff.

Balance, that subjective factor that continues to bedevil performers and recording engineers, was basically achieved by varying the placement of a single microphone or the position of the musicians in relation to it and to each other. Two or three microphones might be used for an orchestra; the performance would be picked up by all three, and the best of the lot would be used (occasionally more than one recorded version of the same "take" was released). Of course there was the problem of fitting pieces or sections of larger works on one side of a 78 r.p.m. record. All one has to do is imagine playing to a stopwatch to understand why tempos were frequently erratic. Soloists known for dizzying finales were motivated by more than the need to impress: they were trying to get the whole piece in before the wax ran out.

Although Moyse recorded most for the Gramophone Company and Columbia Graphophone, he was associated with a variety of companies throughout his career in France. Some of the recordings listed in his extensive Discography are orchestral performances in which he was known to have supplied a prominent flute part, and there are numerous orchestral recordings that feature his sound but are insufficiently documented for attribution, the most notable being the 1930 Straram Orchestra rendering of Debussy's *Prélude à "L'après-midi d'un faune,"* which won a Grand Prix du Disque (Discography nos. 180–181). Most of Moyse's known records are of solo and chamber music. In late March 1930, he made the first French recording of Mozart's Concerto No. 2 in D major (Discography nos. 40–43), supported by an orchestra conducted by Piero Coppola. It won a Grand Prix du Disque in

1932 (see Notes to the Discography, items nos. 40–43) and became, for many European and American flutists of the next two generations, "the first flute record I ever heard."

Le Maître

IN the middle of the 1931–32 season, Philippe Gaubert was promoted to music director of the Opéra and gave up his flute class. In February, Marcel Moyse succeeded him as professor of flute at the Conservatoire. Moyse's link to the French School's chain of artist-pedagogues was officially forged. The prestige and responsibility he accepted that year didn't garner the popular coverage that the Italian maestro Toscanini was receiving, but in the professional musical community, it was big news.

Moyse's appointment was not unexpected. He had assisted Gaubert at the Conservatoire for about ten years, and observers predicted the student might someday take the teacher's place. René Rateau, who won his *premier prix* in 1928, said that although he was registered as a member of Gaubert's class in the mid-1920s, he always considered himself a student equally of Gaubert and of Moyse. Reminiscing in his memorabilia-filled Montmartre apartment in 1991, Rateau, whose career included chairs in the Boston and Chicago symphonies and the French Orchestre National, said that Moyse taught Gaubert's flute class at least half the time and gave some Conservatoire students weekly private lessons in his home. "Gaubert was extremely gifted—he could play anything," Rateau recalled. "But he was not good at explaining things. Moyse made up many exercises to solve problems."

Louis Moyse, who studied piano from an early age but didn't take up the flute until his late teens, attended the Conservatoire for two years—Gaubert's last and Marcel's first. "Look at the list of first prize winners in Gaubert's class, even in 1921. They all studied with my father! He worked with them in class, and after they won their first prizes, most of them went back to him to have lessons." He added that during his year with Gaubert, he heard his teacher play only once:

> It was at the end of the class. He stood up, opened his flute box, and played the "Minuet" and "Dance of the Blessed Spirits" by Gluck. It took a few seconds for his embouchure to adjust under his mustache. It was incredibly easy flute playing, a beautiful sound, like pure water coming from an invisible source. At the same time, to be honest, I judged that the interpretation could have gone deeper—at home, I was used to a different approach; Orpheus was literally crying his sufferings through a marvelous palette. But what a master! He probably hadn't opened his flute case in weeks, and his mind was full of big scores for concerts and opera. This little piece w ͻ for him just an aperitif before a huge meal.[1]

Moyse's arrangement with Gaubert was casual but predictable. "The Société des Concerts rehearsed on Friday mornings," said Louis, "and almost every week, Gaubert would look down from his stand and say, 'Moyse—you'll replace me today?' "[2] Louis was one of three in his father's first official class who gained top honors in July 1932 performing Gaubert's *Fantaisie,* the same work Gaubert had assigned his first class a dozen years before.

Besides his strong ties to Gaubert, Moyse was known for his growing catalogue of exercise books. By the time Leduc bought *Le débutant flûtiste* in 1933, the publisher had already issued more than a dozen other volumes by Moyse. (*Le débutant flûtiste* is a beginning tutor that systematically presents all the notes of the flute, beginning with those that are easiest to produce. The emphasis is on quality of tone and interval placement, the equivalent in ballet of learning the five positions in slow, exact motion before a mirror.) Moyse's many recordings also assured him an advantage over other well-placed flutists who might have been considered for the Conservatoire job. His virtuosity was recognized throughout Europe and across the Atlantic; the year before the Conservatoire appointment, the American record journal *Disques* had called Moyse "one of the foremost flutists of the day" in a review of his Debussy recording with Lily Laskine and the violist Ginot.[3] His accomplishments as solo flute with the Société des Concerts, Opéra-Comique, and Straram orchestras, as well as his appearances with nearly every other professional ensemble in Paris, constituted the ideal master's pedigree.

Moyse locked into the school's traditions with ease and pleasure, continuing to accept about twelve students (the official limit) for the flute classes, which still met three times a week. He taught from many of the same materials that Taffanel, Hennebains, and Gaubert had used and increasingly insisted on a singing style as his symbiotic feeling for the operatic voice intensified. In reference to Moyse's coaching of the G major etude from Andersen's *24 Grosse Studien,* Rateau said, "He told us that every *note* is a song—chante, chante!" Rateau also remembered that students were expected to perform exactly as Moyse did: "He didn't like it if you didn't play his interpretation."

The Swiss flutist and scholar Raymond Meylan studied with Moyse for seven years, beginning in 1936 at age twelve, after having become enthralled with his parents' recordings of Moyse performing the Mozart D Major Concerto, the Stravinsky Octet, and Gluck's "Dance of the Blessed Spirits." In the first few months of study, he worked from Moyse's simpler books, beginning with *Le débutant flûtiste,* and thereafter followed a diet of Tulou, Demersseman, Kuhlau, Doppler, Boehm, Andersen, Berbiguier, and other exercises and etudes Moyse had mastered under his teachers. The main difference was that Moyse added his own concoctions to the smorgasbord. Meylan also encountered solos by Bach, Handel, Chaminade, Taffanel, Gaubert, Fauré, and others. The few contemporary works he studied were among those Moyse had performed, such as Jacques Ibert's Concerto, Arthur Honegger's *Danse de la chèvre,* and Frank Martin's *Ballade.* Although Moyse's choices could never be described as stylistically groundbreaking, they reflected his commitments to teaching the repertoire he knew best and to extending the pedagogical tradition with his own flute studies.[4]

Moyse's influence as a teacher in Paris was widespread but difficult to track. The Paris Conservatoire maintains a list of forty-five Moyse students who received prizes or certificates between 1929 and the early years of World War II, and eighteen recipients from 1946 to 1949, but it doesn't count important flutists from the Gaubert years such as René Rateau, or Moyse's close friend André

Jaunet, who took his *premier prix* in Gaubert's final year of teaching and won first prize in the 1939 Geneva International Competition (two other Moyse students placed second and third that year). Jaunet taught at the conservatory in Zurich and sent his best students to Paris to study, as he had, with Moyse. This "Swiss connection" brought now-prominent Swiss flutists such as Aurèle Nicolet and Peter-Lukas Graf to Moyse's studio after the war.

Moyse used to say that, in all, he had taught seventy-seven *premier prix* pupils. Sometime in the early 1950s he jotted down a list of several dozen prominent students who dated all the way back to Gaston Crunelle, a 1920 *premier prix* winner in Gaubert's first class who succeeded Moyse as professor of flute during World War II. How long or to what extent Gaubert's students worked with Moyse before, during, or after their time at the Conservatoire can only be speculated, but it is fair to guess that Gaubert's students considered Moyse to be at least as important in relationship to Gaubert as Hennebains had been to Taffanel when Moyse was a student. In the postwar period when Moyse assembled his list of successful former pupils, the flute sections of the Paris orchestras were populated with Moyse products; in the Opéra-Comique, for instance, there were Crunelle and Caratgé (another Gaubert class graduate), and in the Orchestre(s) de la Radiodiffusion Française, nine protégés were listed. Beyond Paris, Moyse had representatives in dozens of orchestras and conservatory teaching positions worldwide, from Tokyo to Tel Aviv, Copenhagen to Chicago. The branches of the Moyse tree around 1950 extended across France and out to Switzerland, Germany, Hungary, Czechoslovakia, Austria, Spain, Italy, Sweden, and Norway, down to Chile, and over to the United States, Australia, and Japan. Some of these flutists, such as the players in the Swiss and Scandinavian orchestras, had been sent by their governments to study at the Conservatoire. Others worked with Moyse in the summer at his St. Amour house, which the locals—whose hotel and cafés enjoyed brisk, seasonal business from flutists—nicknamed "Le Petit Conservatoire International."

Several Americans made their way to St. Amour in the late 1920s and throughout the 1930s. Among these flutists were Arthur Kitty, Robert Cavally, and James Pappoutsakis, who went on to play with the Chicago, Cincinnati, and Boston symphonies, respectively. Another student was the late American flutist Harry

Moskovitz, who studied with Laurent in Boston and Barrère in New York then won a scholarship to work with Moyse in Paris about 1931. Moscovitz later helped pave *le mâitre*'s way in the U.S. via magazine articles on flute recordings and flute playing. Frances Blaisdell, another student of Barrère, studied with Moyse in Paris and St. Amour in 1932. Blaisdell encountered disapproval in Moyse's home village because, as she put it, "No nice French girl would travel three thousand miles to study the flute."[5]

René Rateau remembered Moyse as a rather authoritarian teacher, and indeed, by the time he took over the Conservatoire flute class, Moyse was fully convinced of his sovereignty as a musician. If originally (as people said) he would have been content to play second flute in an orchestra, a transformation had taken place by virtue of the unusually focused, self-absorbed drive to achievement that in some people kicks in hard after the initial surprise of success.

Moyse belonged to an autocratic, "I Am Right" generation of cultural leaders that included podium dictators like George Szell and Toscanini, whom Moyse idolized. Orchestra players accepted the manipulations of these maestros as quietly as some acceded to Hitler or to Mussolini; ticket-buyers and the new media publicity machines were also enamored of powerful baton wielders. In this context, Moyse never shook the notion that he was a peasant. In the act of teaching, he played it to advantage, drawing disarmingly on events and emotions from a less sophisticated life. But among professional colleagues, he often felt compelled to puff himself up, to insist upon recognition where a man more confident of his position might calmly expect and receive it.

Yet as he grasped greater authority, Moyse also developed a capacity for almost excruciating patience with young, inexperienced students—often females—who were open and willing to submit themselves to his rigorous demands. One example is Geneviève Noufflard, who came to Moyse in 1939 and was one of the few women ever admitted to his class.[6] Noufflard was nineteen and had studied the flute for only two years, with René Le Roy, the highly regarded chamber-music and recording artist.

(Moyse considered Le Roy *mondain* because he was adored by the private society concert set that Moyse loathed and ridiculed. Louis Moyse described his father as "a typical Frenchman, with the need to *épater le bourgeois*—startle the old fogeys." Once, at a concert reception in Switzerland, a bejeweled matron bustled up to gush, "Maître! What were you thinking of as you played this marvelous *Danse de la chèvre?*" Whereupon Moyse lifted his chin and replied sarcastically, "Chewing grass, Madame!")

Geneviève Noufflard knew that the age limit for admittance to the Conservatoire was twenty but auditioned for a place in the flute class anyway, aware that she did not meet advanced standards. It was, she said, mostly an experiment in coping with pressure.

There were two parts to her entrance exam: first, the performance of a work she chose, and on another day, a work selected by the Conservatoire committee. Noufflard was not technically equipped to handle the committee's selection. "But the piece I had studied, I played very well," she related. "It was the *Fantaisie* of Fauré. I was musical, but I had no technique whatsoever." As it happened, war broke out after the first round, and the flute class shrank overnight. More students were needed to fill the vacancies, and the standards were suddenly relaxed. Noufflard wasn't required to play the second test; Moyse accepted her on the basis of her sensitive rendering of the Fauré.

"Not only was I the only girl in the class, but the others were not terribly nice people on the whole, and it was not fun to be with them," she recounted. "They made fun of me because I was not technically advanced. But I had a nice tone, something musical, and Moyse liked me very much right away because of that. It was a difficult period for me, but he was very nice." Slowly and carefully, Moyse put Noufflard through the simplest paces, such as fifteen minutes of the same handful of tones, repeated laboriously, one after the other, until they all matched in timbre and intensity, with a B-flat dropping seamlessly out of a C that melted down from a D. Moyse's great patience with Noufflard probably exacerbated the taunts of other students, but it earned him a devoted follower. When the war finally forced Moyse to hide in St. Amour, Noufflard risked crossing enemy lines to continue her studies with him in the country.[7]

One day in the spring of 1932, Moyse got a message from Ernest Ansermet, conductor of the Orchestre de la Suisse Romande, that his services were wanted, last-minute, for a performance of the fifth Brandenburg Concerto. There had been a tragedy; the Suisse

Romande's first flutist, a former student of Moyse named Welsch, had committed suicide. Would Moyse come play the part?

Of course he would. And in his typical way of cramming unplanned or out-of-town appearances into his schedule, he drove all night from Paris to Geneva and arrived just in time for the morning dress rehearsal. Onstage he was greeted by Ansermet and the principal cellist Henri Honegger, who in turn introduced Moyse to the solo violinist for the Brandenburg, Honegger's twenty-two-year-old sister, Blanche. Their mother had volunteered Blanche's fee to help pay for Moyse's appearance so, for the sake of her daughter's budding career, the show could go on.

Blanche Honegger's memory of the rehearsal is vivid.

> Ansermet had told me, "Oh, Moyse has such a unique *sonorité*!" and I was nervous and very eager to hear him. I remember very well when I heard him start to play. I wondered, "Oh, my God, is that the flute *sonorité* they were talking about?" Because all I heard was breath. I thought, "This is not a flute tone—this is full of impurities."[8]

She had no idea Moyse had not slept in more than twenty-four hours and was struggling to remain alert.

To spare the orchestra the cost of a hotel room, Mme. Honegger invited Moyse to be a guest of the family during his brief stay. He rested in the Honegger home on the afternoon of the concert, and following a good meal and a glass of wine—a pre-concert ritual that he said promoted circulation in his lips—he was ready to perform. Moyse rarely warmed up extensively; a few minutes of tone exercises sufficed. With the first entrance of the flute in the Bach, Blanche Honegger's impression of Moyse changed. "It was very beautiful. I had always thought a flute should sound like a bird—that was my training! But immediately I appreciated that incredible, rich tone. It was very easy to play with him." The concert was a big success, and Moyse complimented Mlle. Honegger on her performance. She was too shy to reciprocate: "Of course, I did not say a word to him." Moyse barely grunted to the harpsichordist, whom he had not liked.

The concert in Geneva proved to be more than a quick job for Moyse and a rescued opportunity for Blanche; it was a catalytic event that would lead to important personal and professional gains for both. Moyse enjoyed his visit with the cultured Honeggers and was particularly delighted to learn that M. Honegger shared his love of the night sky; the pair spent hours peering through Honegger's telescope. When the conversation turned to Blanche's plans to follow her mother's and grandmother's interests in homeopathy and study medicine in France, Moyse offered to help. That fall, Blanche moved to Paris, into a rented room the Moyse family had found for her near their flat in Montmartre. Within a few months she was eating dinner regularly with the Moyses, and in the following year, 1933, she came to live with them.

The moods of the household shocked Blanche at first. Marcel and Celine were stubborn individuals who argued so frequently that the quiet Swiss woman wondered if they might divorce soon. Yet as partners, the Moyses were so loyal to their family that an outsider might come to one of two conclusions: either the quarreling was just a style of communication, or the integrity of their union rested on a deep understanding that superseded domestic strife. "My father always said that our parents were the highest people in our lives," Marguerite Moyse Andreasson remarked at age sixty-four. "The family had to be perfect—you could not express a bad feeling toward a parent. It was sometimes constricting, this feeling. I had to come to middle age, with children of my own, to realize that family is a lot, but it is not always everything." As Blanche wavered between the possible explanations for the decibel level of the household, she also found the whole family to be "generous beyond reason" and supportive of her activities.

Blanche Honegger spent just one year studying medicine before she realized that music was her truest calling. Despite the amount of time she spent in the company of test tubes and animal parts, she continued to practice several hours a day and took lessons with Enesco, who told her he would not teach the violin, but he would, if she wanted, teach her music. Blanche was the youngest child of a musical family. She began violin lessons with an uncle at the age of five, studied piano, and went on to earn a diploma at the Geneva Conservatory. For several years she worked intermittently with Adolf Busch of the renowned Busch Quartet, who, like Moyse, first visited the Honegger home in conjunction with a concert. Busch was impressed by the diminutive twelve-year-old girl who played Bach cantatas at the keyboard from memory, and he talked her parents into jettisoning her academic education so she could spend her days practicing. He became a good friend of the family, and by the time Blanche was in her late teens, Busch and his young colleague and future son-in-law, the Austrian pianist Rudolf Serkin, stopped by the Honeggers' regularly.

During her student days in Geneva, Blanche played in a string quartet she founded with her brother Henri, and the group won first prize at the Geneva competition in the first year quartets were invited to compete. Their quartet was the only one that entered. ("I suppose they could have not given us a prize," Blanche reflected. "I don't know that we were that good.") The group disbanded when Henri went to Paris to study with Casals; his subsequent career with the Suisse Romande lasted thirty-five years. Blanche traveled in the summers and twice attended Wanda Landowska's chamber music classes in Paris, recalling most fondly the times Landowska gathered her students together in her private concert hall and played Chopin for them. Blanche was also an early private student of the young guitar virtuoso Andrés Segovia. One summer she stayed with his family as a sort of apprentice and sat with his wife for hours, listening to Segovia practice. But after three years of study, the guitar—like the piano—had to be abandoned in favor of the violin. At nineteen, Blanche Honegger made her solo debut in Geneva with Ansermet and the Suisse Romande in the Beethoven Violin Concerto.

After his emergency Brandenburg appearance and Blanche's move to Paris, Moyse was invited to take Welsch's place as professor of flute at the Geneva Conservatory. Every other week for several years, he burned up the roads between Paris and Geneva, often with his family in tow, leaving Paris at midnight, arriving in Geneva at noon, teaching all afternoon, and returning to Paris in time for a rehearsal at nine o'clock the next morning. Friends marveled at Moyse's stamina and waited for a physical or psychological breakdown, which never occurred. For a time, Blanche taught at the conservatory in Neuchâtel and was a regular passenger on the trip. If anything went wrong in transit, Celine took over. Moyse never monitored the gauges, and the car regularly ran out of gas in the country. Always, Celine trudged several miles for help while Marcel waited by the road, smoking his pipe. When his schedule permitted it, Moyse stopped in St. Amour *en route* and visited Josephine Perretier (his adoptive mother) and other family members (see Figure 14). In Geneva, he sometimes played with the Société de Musique de Chambre, organized by the composer/pianist Frank Martin; Henri Honegger played on the series, too.

It was at the Honeggers' watering hole that Moyse met Adolf Busch. (Busch moved from Germany to Switzerland in 1933, when Hitler came to power.) The men liked each other immediately, "which was very strange," according to Blanche, "because one was as French as the other was German. Yet right away, Adolf wanted to perform with him. That's when it all started."

So began an artistic alliance between three musical families— Busch, Honegger, Moyse—that would grow, transform itself, and survive for decades, well past the point of their public musical collaborations. From the beginning, Moyse, Busch, and Serkin toured successfully with works like the Bach Concerto in A minor for flute, violin, keyboard (Serkin played piano), strings, and bass (BWV 1044). Louis Moyse and Blanche joined them in outings with the Busch Chamber Players, which included the Busch Quartet (Busch, Gösta Andreasson, Karl Doktor, and Hermann Busch) and Henri Honegger. The relationship between Busch and Moyse required compromise; Moyse did not always agree with Busch's way with Bach, but he usually deferred to him because he respected and liked him so much. Moyse also admired Serkin, and once commented, "I never played the Brandenburgs with him without him thanking me. Me? I was bowled over. It was *I* who should have thanked *him* for playing the piano part."[9]

Everyone in the Busch Players had to contend with Moyse's motoring habits, which held up more than one concert. Once, Marcel, Louis, and Blanche were speeding through the mountains from Pisa to Florence to meet the Busch party for a performance, and their car, wheezing and spluttering, plowed into a ditch. (Blanche: "Naturally we got stuck—we always got stuck.") A wheel was lost; the threesome were inexorably detained, and they finally puttered into Florence three hours late. The only person not distraught was Moyse. Busch graciously held his tongue. The music-making was worth it.

Perhaps the most lasting product of that period was the October 1935 recording of the Brandenburg Concertos in London for Columbia Records, the culmination of the Busch Chamber Players' European Bach cantata and concerto tours that included members of the Busch Quartet, Marcel and Louis Moyse, Blanche and Henri Honegger, and Serkin, who took to the London sessions his new bride, Adolf Busch's eighteen-year-old daughter, Irene. (The group stayed at the Grosvenor Hotel, whose restaurant rated poorly with Marcel because Brussels sprouts appeared on the menu every day.) Moyse played solo flute in the second, fourth, and fifth concertos, and Louis played second flute to his father in the fourth. Adolf was the solo violinist, and Blanche participated in the tutti strings; Serkin, of course, was the pianist (see Discography nos. 88–93). In 1936, Moyse and the Busch Chamber Players returned to London to record J. S. Bach's Suite No. 2 in B minor (BWV 1067) for the Gramophone Company (Discography nos. 114–119).

While Moyse helped build a multi-family musical relationship with Adolf Busch, he simultaneously headed an alliance at home. The Moyse Trio came into existence the moment Blanche stopped auditing physiology classes at the Sorbonne. With Marcel on flute, Blanche played violin or viola, and Louis provided piano or harpsichord accompaniment (see Figure 15). Louis also joined his father in flute duets, sometimes with Blanche at the keyboard. Marcel explained:

> Because we took pleasure in making music together, and since I already had a certain influence, I had the idea to explore the beauty of certain pieces—little pieces, but good ones—written by our musical ancestors, like Bach's sons and Telemann. I said, why make a repertoire of things that are destined to disappear? There are treasures in the attic.[10]

The Moyse Trio was founded at a time when public interest in chamber music was rising. The celebrated achievements of a few seasoned ensembles such as the Cortot-Thibaud-Casals Trio (which celebrated its thirty-fifth anniversary in 1931) as well as the rediscovery of baroque music inspired the formation of intimate groups that sometimes served as showcases for string players and pianists who had—or wanted—solo dates. Moyse's career was at a brilliant peak; his eminence would have been secure had the Trio never played a note. But for the other two members, the Trio offered an opportunity to establish themselves. Louis had recently graduated from the Conservatoire, having studied flute with Gaubert and his father, piano with Isidor Philipp and Joseph Benvenuti, and harmony and composition with Eugène Bigot. As a flutist he was, like it or not, overshadowed by his father, and his versatile position in the group showed him to be cut smartly from the same cloth, but in a unique pattern. Blanche was new to Paris; her name was not as familiar as those of prodigies in short pants such as Yehudi Menuhin and Ruggiero Ricci, and the Trio was an excellent means of introduction.

The way Louis and Blanche tell it, the three just decided one day to "make a trio" and began rehearsing. Moyse took the lead; there was little talk of style or detail. His primary concern was sparking a rhythmic vitality that would brighten and sustain the character of everything they played. For Blanche, playing in the Trio was like going to musical finishing school: she tried her best to imitate Moyse and rarely questioned him. In 1933, the year the group started out, she spent the summer with the Moyse family in St. Amour and studied Kuhlau flute duets with Marcel, which they played together. "He was always pushing me to be more of a prima donna, which was good for me—I needed it," she admitted.

Louis recalled that there was something very special about the Moyse Trio.

> We never had to discuss anything, musically. The "magic" was that the three of us had the same deep feeling for music, based on traditional interpretations by great masters. We knew in advance where one would take a little ritard, or make a crescendo, and we had exactly the same feeling—absolutely the same feeling! It was as simple as sitting at a table for a meal. No problem.
>
> Of course I had played so many times with my father. Blanche was very good by herself, but her contact with my father and Adolf Busch gave us so much in common. We hardly rehearsed as the Trio Moyse! We would read through a new piece once or twice, and O.K., it was fine. When the works were settled for good in our minds and fingers, we did not take the trouble to rehearse before a concert. It was a job, and that job became routine, part of our living system.[11]

Though Marcel was the star attraction, the Trio presented a limited number of solo flute pieces and focused instead on a range of literature that allowed as much mixing and matching as possible. A repertoire list from the height of the Trio's career gives names of composers, not titles of works, and it may be assumed that the group performed more than one trio sonata by, say, Bach, or Telemann. There are seventeen "classical" composers (Bach to

Kuhlau) listed under flute, violin, and piano trios, and sixteen living ones. For other combinations of instruments (including flute and piano pieces and violin sonatas), there are 103 listings, plus eight concertos for two or three instruments and orchestra, twelve flute concertos, and eight violin concertos. At the very least, the Moyse Trio's repertoire numbered 164 compositions.

A typical program featured Marcel and Blanche each in a solo sonata accompanied by Louis, a piece for two flutes and piano, and a group of flute, violin (or viola), and piano works. Interpretations were fresh but controlled, especially when the Trio began to make recordings. Their most successful project on record was the Bach Trio Sonata in G (BWV 1038), which won a Grand Prix du Disque (Discography nos. 132–133). To prepare for the limitations of the 78 r.p.m. platters, the threesome rehearsed the Bach in strict tempo until they could play each movement in the same number of minutes and seconds, every time. When the recording date arrived, the Moyse Trio could play perfectly with their backs to one another, eyes shut: one, two, ready, go. This rhythmic discipline helped out even in freak circumstances. In a concert in Angoulême, Marcel and Blanche were performing a three-movement duet, and discovered at the end of the slow (second) movement that the music for the third movement was missing. After a split-second exchange, the two launched into the second movement again, this time at double speed. "No one noticed," said Louis. "It was a big success—lots of applause!"

The Trio toured regularly in Europe, starting in the mid-1930s. By this time, the Moyses had moved from the flat on Rue d'Orsel to a larger, four-level home at 52 Rue Durantin in Montmartre, which had an immense living room, dining space, and kitchen on the first floor, a studio for Marcel on the second, and bedrooms on the third and fourth floors. Blanche continued to live with the family because, in a sense, she had been adopted.

During the Trio's first year, Blanche's father had suffered severe financial setbacks in his real-estate business and was forced—as were other Europeans struggling with the widespread economic depression that contributed to the tensions that produced World War II—to give up major assets. To reduce living expenses and improve his failing health, he moved with his wife to a smaller home in the mountains. Blanche's mother begged her to come back to Switzerland; Ansermet had assured Madame Honegger that her daughter could have a position with the Suisse Romande, and the Honeggers needed the income.

The Moyse family enjoyed a comfortable living and proposed a magnanimous alternative. If Blanche were allowed to remain in Paris, they would send the Honeggers an amount every month equal to what she could earn playing in Geneva. As Blanche acquired more engagements, she would contribute to that sum. The Honeggers accepted, and Blanche stayed.

As the career of the Moyse Trio grew, so did the separate professional lives of its members. Louis frequently accompanied Marcel or played second flute to him in duo engagements; one typical father-son appearance took place in December 1936 at an all-Reicha concert sponsored by l'Association des Amis de Tchéchoslovaquie (Friends of Czechoslovakia) to celebrate the centenary of the composer's death. Their performance of Reicha's Variations for two flutes (along with a string quartet played by the Calvet Quartet, trios for horn and cello, and the inevitable wind quintet, with members of the Orchestre National) helped promote a reevaluation of Reicha, whose reputation had supposedly suffered because he had been a sworn enemy of Cherubini. Marcel and Louis received flowery letters from conductor Maurice Emmanuel and M. Onufsky, an official of the Czech ministry who praised their "masterful execution" of the music of his "illustrious compatriot." Another example of Marcel and Louis's work together was a 1938 performance of Enesco's *Dixtuor,* led by the composer and rehearsed in the Moyse home.

The father and son recorded most frequently as soloist and accompanist, but their 1948 recording of Domenico Cimarosa's Concerto in D for two flutes with the Lamoureux Orchestra under Marcel's old Conservatoire classmate Eugène Bigot (Discography nos. 160–163) was a delightful exception. This time, Louis, who played in the Lamoureux flute section, was showcased equally with his father to beautiful effect. Louis performed often as a soloist and chamber music artist apart from his father. In 1937, *La Revue Musicale* described his rendition of a new work by Italian composer Cesare Brero as a perfect opportunity "to show off his pure sound and the supple agility of his instrument."[12] A few months later, the same publication reported on a performance of Bach's triple Concerto in A minor (BWV 1044) featuring Louis, Blanche, and the pianist Heinz Jolles:

The concert was performed with love. Nothing has a more direct effect on the audience than a passionate faith which perceives music intuitively and thus owns it. Heinz Jolles and his collaborators, the violinist Blanche Honegger and the flutist Louis Moyse, with a chamber orchestra led by P. Duvauchelle, carried off a success of which they have a right to be proud."[13]

Blanche performed extensively on her own as well. Her arrival in Paris was marked by a highly praised concert of baroque music at the church of Montmorency with Wanda Landowska, Henri Honegger, Louis Bas (oboe d'amour of the Opéra and one of a handful of woodwind players Moyse revered) and mezzo-soprano Mlle. Tatianoff. Soon after, Blanche performed a Mozart concerto with the Lamoureux Orchestra under Bigot. When Blanche abandoned her medical studies, Busch assisted her more aggressively in building her career. A week before her 1936 Lausanne radio broadcast of the Beethoven concerto, Adolf wrote the following to his brother Fritz (who had been based in Copenhagen since 1933, when the Nazis forced him from his directorship of the Dresden Staatsoper): "I am telling you once more, she plays the Beethoven, especially, more beautifully than I ever heard it—some things, even a lot of things differently than I do them, but I could *not* say less well." Fritz Busch accepted his brother's recommendation of "Blanchette," and after she performed under his baton in Copenhagen, Fritz communicated to Adolf, "Blanche Honegger was an absolute joy, and she had an almost sensational success. I already wrote her today with various possibilities, and hope to be able to to help her further in launching her solo career. She deserves it in every way."[14]

Blanche's growing reputation as a soloist inspired two well-known composers to write flute, violin, and orchestra works for Marcel and Blanche to play. Jean Françaix was one; in 1937 he completed *Musique de cour,* which Marcel and Blanche introduced with the Orchestre Philharmonique under Charles Munch the same year. The other composer was Martinů (whose birth story is nearly as romantic as Moyse's: his mother gave birth to him in the belfry of a church in Policka, Czechoslovakia, where his father, a shoemaker, moonlighted as the tower watchman). Martinů lived in Paris in the 1930s with his wife Charlotte Quennehen, a French dressmaker who stitched full-time so her husband could compose. His music was well received, but by the end of the decade the couple were still subsisting in a pair of rented garrets. The Martinůs became good friends of the Moyses and spent a summer with them in St. Amour. Blanche remembered Martinů as "a very understated man, very subdued, very soft-spoken, gentle, very shy. His wife talked all the time, but he said very little." But, she said, "Inside, musically, he was very strong. He was not shy at all as a musician. He was very forceful. He knew exactly what he wanted, every detail." In her lively memoir, *My Life with Bohuslav Martinů*, Charlotte Martinů wrote of the visit:

> I remember our stay in the summer of 1936 in the Jura, at Saint Amour, in the villa of Marcel Moyse, the famous flutist and professor at the conservatory. Thanks to Mrs. Marcelle de Lacour, a harpsichordist, we travelled through the entire Jura range. Bohus felt at ease with Marcel Moyse because they understood each other perfectly.[15]

For the Moyse Trio, Martinů completed both the Concerto for flute, violin, and orchestra and the Sonata for flute, violin, and piano (dedicated to Celine in honor of her fine cooking) in 1936. Blanche remembered that in Martinů's first draft of the Concerto, the flute part was much more virtuosic than the violin part, and she asked for more impressive material to play. Martinů obliged. Marcel and Blanche premiered the Concerto at the Société des Concerts under Gaubert and later performed it with the Orchestre National Radiodiffusion in Czechoslovakia and on tour, but the work fell into obscurity when their European careers ended after World War II. Henri Honegger, however, continued the family connection to Martinů when in 1945 he premiered the Sonata da camera for cello and orchestra, a work written for and dedicated to him. The work helped propel Henri to a solo career.

Of all the conductors who visited Paris during the 1930s, Arturo Toscanini made by far the biggest impression on Moyse. The domineering Italian's appearances in France were infrequent; at that point in his career he had relinquished his post at La Scala and was spending the bulk of his time with the New York Philharmonic. But for most of the decade he managed to lead concerts in Paris about once a year, always to packed houses that sold out the day tickets went on sale.

Toscanini had a strong affinity for French music—even the Paris critics raved about his revelatory interpretations—and his Paris programs and the character of events themselves marked this in a manner one might describe as "typically French." Twice when Toscanini visited, statuary was involved. On 17 June 1932, he was one of four conductors (along with Gaubert, Pierné, and D. E. Inghelbrecht) to preside at a program in the Théâtre des Champs-Élysées for the unveiling and dedication of the Debussy monument designed by Jean and Joël Martel. The grand rock bears a bas-relief on either side; the face wears a stone tapestry suggesting the principal works of Debussy, and the simple inscription, "Claude Debussy, *musicien français.*" On the back, "Le Concert Symbolique" represents the composer at the piano and an orchestra populated by his closest friends and interpreters, many of whom (Mary Garden, for one) performed at the dedication. At the base of the monument is a motto taken from Debussy's writings: *"Il faut chercher la discipline dans la liberté, n'écouter les conseils de personne, sinon du vent qui passe et nous raconte l'histoire du monde* [Discipline must be sought in liberty; heed the counsels of no one, unless it be of the wind that passes and recounts to us the history of the world]." Toscanini conducted *La mer* for the sanctification of the majestic boulder. Moyse proudly played solo flute for him in the Orchestre du Festival Claude Debussy; the program for that day was one of a scant batch of playbills he saved from his entire Paris career.

Four years later, Toscanini was brought in for another weighty occasion, donating his services to headline a festival concert of French music at the Salle Pleyel. The proceeds of the evening went to build a monument to Saint-Saëns, who took his place in the heavenly orchestra three years after Debussy. Toscanini liked to impress the French with his knowledge of their musical culture and often served his Paris audience forgotten or neglected works by their countrymen. This time, he chose the honoree's fourth Piano Concerto (with Robert Casadesus), the Love Scene from Berlioz's *Roméo et Juliette,* one of Ravel's *Daphnis et Chloé* suites, and then, to everyone's surprise, Bizet's "Patrie" overture and *Les Éolides* by Franck.

Between these galas, Toscanini returned to his annual conducting of the Straram Orchestra, which retained its name after the founder's death in 1933 and functioned as an ad hoc ensemble. These programs were given in the Théâtre des Champs-Élysées in a series of two or three per visit. French works, Wagner, and an occasional Italian piece were the usual fare; an all-Wagner evening in 1933 was so well received that it enjoyed an unplanned repeat the following night.

Moyse cultivated a friendly relationship with Toscanini and served as a mediator whenever a dispute erupted between the conductor and a musician or theater manager. A classic situation arose at the second performance of the 1933 Wagner concert, when Toscanini arrived to discover that two violinists were missing, hardly surprising given the last-minute scheduling. Mad as a bear, Toscanini snapped his baton in two and stalked back to his hotel. The house manager panicked, collared Moyse, who was backstage warming up, and pleaded with him to go after the maestro. Moyse insisted that the manager, his secretary, and the concertmaster join him at Toscanini's hotel room, but when the conductor opened the door of the deluxe suite, Moyse's accomplices pushed the flutist inside and scurried down the hall. "They were afraid!" Moyse exclaimed at the memory. "And Toscanini was so surprised! I mentioned how beautiful the concert was yesterday, and he asked if I had been there. He was nearly blind—he did not know I was playing! Then he said, 'You were very nice!' and he kissed me, and five minutes later he came back with us to the concert."[16]

Like many others in the orchestra, Moyse admired Toscanini for his interpretations of Ravel and Debussy and for his allegiance to musical text. Under Toscanini, "liberties" were eliminated from standard repertoire and commonly edited works regained their original mileage. On one occasion, however, the maestro added notes to a score. After an oboist in rehearsal failed to understand the phrasing Toscanini wanted in a solo passage, the conductor took Moyse aside and asked him to double the line in the concert. Moyse played along. The shape of the melody improved, but the oboist never noticed Moyse. The incident obviously meant little to Toscanini because when Moyse asked him the following season if he wanted the same oboe player, the perfectionist mused, "Oh, him. He's married, with two children, isn't he? Yes, go ahead and hire him."

Toscanini's image as a vigorous, temperamental "legend" was far advanced in the 1930s; Moyse's lifelong adulation of the conductor and investment in his own legendary status suggests he might have drawn inspiration, consciously or not, from Toscanini's behavior. In 1929, David Ewen sneaked into a rehearsal of the New York Philharmonic under Toscanini and published a description that offers striking parallels to what Americans would later experience in sessions with Moyse, whose English, like Toscanini's, was never very good.

> He stands quietly in front of his orchestra, a handkerchief twisted around his neck, and with almost superhuman patience and understanding, he guides his men. I have seen him explain minutely and carefully to one of the performers how to attain a certain effect and then, when the performer had failed a second time to get it right, begin his explanation all over again. . . .
>
> But once in a while his Italian temperament manifests itself. Because of his meager knowledge of English, he could not convey his meaning clearly. The violinists played the theme stiffly; he wanted it to sound limply, liquidly. In desperation, Toscanini took out his handkerchief and dropped it slowly to the floor. "You see—like this play it—the music should float—like these here handkerchief—" he said. But the violinists could not attain the effect and after many minutes of trial, Toscanini threw down his baton and shrieked out a volley of Italian curses and imprecations that re-echoed in all the corners of the hall.

Ewen reported that Toscanini had other methods for surmounting the language barrier. When words failed, he indulged in highly physical demonstrations: acting, singing, mimicking. In a rehearsal of Respighi's *Feste Romane,* Ewen continued,

> he wanted to show the clarinetist how to play a certain trill flippantly, so he hunched his back, raised his two hands and shook his fingers rapidly. In indicating to the trombonist how to perform a certain vulgar sound, he kicked his leg out, clenched his fist and emitted a deep, resonant groan. He dances, rants and postures in front of his men in attempts to convey the mood of his music. In a high-pitched voice he imitates the sound he wants. He has an almost unbelievable understanding of sound. What to another would be merely an interval of a fifth is to him a long-drawn sigh, and he insists the player thereof obtain that effect. When, in the *fortissimo* climax towards the end of the work he did not hear a sigh from the cornet, he stopped the whole orchestra.

Ewen watched Toscanini go over the Respighi minutely from beginning to end,

> working slavishly at every little phrase, at every nuance, at every effect. Once he reached the end, he began to go backwards to the beginning, repeating his former instruction, showing how one part blends into another, explaining how to build up a climax with fastidious delicacy. Every effect of his is merely for the glorification of a monumental whole.

Toscanini worked straight through every two-hour rehearsal, with no breaks. At the end Ewen noticed that "every player is thoroughly fatigued, and so is Toscanini."[17]

Toscanini's effect on Moyse would become apparent later when his teaching style became more animated in response to both his English-speaking students and his declining ability to demonstrate on the flute exactly what he wanted. It would be wrong to say that Moyse imitated Toscanini's personality. Moyse was a self-made man with a strong sense of who he was; he hardly needed to clothe himself in someone else's persona. What Moyse got from Toscanini was an exaggerated method of communicating musical ideas and emotions, which he tailored to fit his own opinionated, imaginative, and playful self.

Throughout the 1930s, Moyse recorded extensively, taught exhaustively, and maintained his posts with the Opéra-Comique and Société des Concerts (see pages 140–142). He relished and jealously guarded his supremacy as Paris's top flutist, telling admirers that his accomplishments came from hard work, not extraordinary gifts, then taking deep offense if anyone else offered the same analysis of his talent. But Moyse also worked tirelessly because he wanted the income. The year before he took Gaubert's place at the Conservatoire, the French government increased the average annual salary for professors from about 10,000 francs to 15,000, to account for inflation. But the improved pay was still less than what a second flutist could earn in one month's work in an American sound studio.

"My father's career was not what people think—that he was touring all the time all over the world," Louis explained.

Flutists didn't have careers like that, then. My father was a hard worker, with rehearsal from nine o'clock to twelve or twelve-thirty; then he had just one hour for lunch at home before starting another rehearsal, a recording session, or the flute class at the Conservatoire. That would last until four-thirty or five, then he would rush home in a taxi, and teach one or two private lessons from five-thirty to seven-thirty. At seven-twenty he would ask my mother to serve him dinner on the corner of the table while he was finishing the last lesson. At twenty, twenty-five of eight, he'd be rushing out, jogging, to be at the theater at eight o'clock. And at midnight, he'd come home, absolutely tired, you know? There were many days like that!

The more special engagments Moyse took on, the more he found himself hiring substitutes at the Opéra-Comique. The year 1934 marked his fifteenth season there as solo flute, and though the management still frowned on excessive nights off, Moyse seemed to get away with it. He was, after all, a sought-after performer and a strong presence in musical circles. But he rarely missed premieres or appearances by singers he admired.

Moyse was much less inclined to bow out of a concert by the Société des Concerts, where he shone, in clear view and earshot of everyone. Geneviève Noufflard insisted that some people came just to hear Moyse in the orchestra, even when he didn't have a special solo. Moyse's daughter Marguerite said the whole family attended Société concerts as faithfully as the devout go to church; she was taken to concerts and opera productions from an early age.

Other children were kept at home, but I was lucky! There were a lot of well-known artists, actors, and writers at the concerts, and my mother would tell me their names. My godmother was a seamstress, and she made me a black velvet dress with a white lace collar to wear. When it got too short, she made me a red velvet dress with the same lace collar. I still have that collar.

Marguerite remembered most clearly her introduction to a children's author because she had just been given his book on the life of ants. But the most glorious images for her float in a wondrous, whirling fog of well-dressed men and women on the steps of the great halls: the Salle Favart, the Champs-Élysées, and the two huge opera houses that, to the little girl, loomed like

Concert program, Société des Concerts, 12 October 1930. Harry Ransom
Humanities Research Center, the University of Texas at Austin.

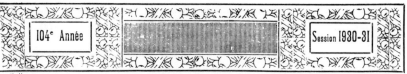

 104ᵉ Année

 Session 1930-31

SALLE DES CONCERTS
2bis, RUE DU CONSERVATOIRE

CONSERVATOIRE NATIONAL DE MUSIQUE

SOCIÉTÉ DES CONCERTS

DIMANCHE 12 OCTOBRE 1930
à 15 heures précises

Iʳᵉ Série **PREMIER CONCERT** Iʳᵉ Série

avec le concours de

M. Maurice RAVEL = Mˡˡᵉ Madeleine GREY

MM. M. MOYSE et A. CRUQUE

PROGRAMME

1. **La Flûte enchantée,** Ouverture. .. .. Mozart.

2. **Symphonie en sol mineur** .. .. Mozart.

3. **Trois chants hébraïques** . .. . Maurice Ravel.
   Mˡˡᵉ Madeleine GREY

4. { **Pavane pour une infante défunte**
   { **Menuet antique** (1ʳᵉ audition au Conservatoire) Maurice Ravel.

5. **Chansons Madécasses** (1ʳᵉ aud. au Conservatoire) Maurice Ravel.
   Mˡˡᵉ Madeleine GREY, M. Maurice RAVEL.
   MM. MOYSE et CRUQUE.

6. **Boléro** (1ʳᵉ audition au Conservatoire) .. .. .. Maurice Ravel.
   sous la direction de l'auteur

7. **Daphnis et Chloë** (2ᵉ suite) .. .. Maurice Ravel.

Piano GAVEAU

Le Concert sera dirigé par **M. Philippe GAUBERT**

LOCATION. - S'adresser : 2 bis, rue du Conservatoire, tous les jours, sauf le lundi, de
10 h. 30 à 12 heures, et de 14 h. 30 à 17 h. 30; le dimanche, de 10 h. 30 à 11 h. 30.
Téléphone : PROVENCE 57-94. Chez MM. DURAND et Fils, 4, Place de la Madeleine et
à la Boîte à Musique, 133 et 135, Boulevard Raspail (VIᵉ).

SOCIÉTÉ DES CONCERTS DU CONSERVATOIRE

Chef d'Orchestre : M. Philippe GAUBERT

ARTISTES DE L'ORCHESTRE

Iers Violons	P. Gaillard.	Violoncelles	Flûtes	Bassons	Tuba
	Séru.				
Merckel.	Savoye.	Cruque.	Moyse.	Fr. Oubradous	Appaire.
Luquin.	Fourment.	J. Dumont.	Manouvrier.	Ferd. Oubradous	
Besnier.	Eiselé.	Gurt.	Lavaillotte.	Basson et	
Candéla.	Lovisolo.	Deblauwe.		Contrebasson	Harpes
Debruille.	Lepetit.	Gaudichon.	Hautbois et	Guilloteau.	
Lestringant.	Benedetti.	Hérouard.	Cor anglais		Cœur.
H. Dumont.	Maché	Frécheville.		Cors	Mlle Lautemann
A. Le Métayer	Chédécal.	Ladoux.	Bleuzet.	Vuillermoz.	
Pascal.	Huot.	Delacourcelle	Gobert.	Delgrange.	
Poirrier.			Boudard.	Morin.	Timbales
Guérin.				Epinoux.	
Hardy.					Perret.
Lespine.	Altos		Clarinettes	Trompettes	
Carembat.	Villain.	Contrebasses		Vignal.	Batterie.
	Drouet.		Costes.	Carrière.	
	Seitz.	Gasparini.	Guyot.	Harscoat.	Laval.
2mes Violons	Ch. Le Métayer	Pickett.		Lamouret	Clayette.
	Michaux.	A. Charon.	Clarinette-	Trombones	
Tracol.	Elissalde.	H. Boucher.	basse	Couillaud.	Orgue
Serret.	Lagardère.	Brousse.		Delbos.	
Dony.	Seigneur.	Larmée.	J. Loterie.	Tudesq.	G. Jacob.
	Desestre.	Alb. Charon.			

PRIX : 2 FRANCS

glittering castles. In the lobbies, the bright pops of flashbulbs revealed where celebrities posed, peeling off their gloves, before the whole sauntering parade pressed its way through the inner doors to private boxes and plush seats. To Marguerite, everything in that period seemed to thrive endlessly in "a big, beautiful basket."[18]

Moyse also played with Triton Concerts, a series dedicated to twentieth-century music. Triton's performers were among the top soloists of Paris, and the series presented important new works. For example, a 1933 program in which Moyse contributed to a now-forgotten Concertino for flute, viola, and bass by Schulhoff also featured an exciting hearing of Béla Bartók's Second Rhapsody for violin and piano, played by its dedicatee, Zoltán Székely. Another Triton concert in February 1937 showcased music by Alexandre Tansman, Milhaud, Stravinsky (the *Three Pieces* for clarinet, played by Louis Cahuzac), and Pierné, whose 1927 Sonata da camera, Opus 48, Moyse offered with cellist Pierre Fournier and pianist Lucette Descaves. Moyse was involved with other chamber groups as well, and in the early 30s he participated in Déjeuners Concerts, a live lunchtime radio series broadcast twice weekly. Moyse was the lone flutist in the show's chamber orchestra, which never rehearsed.

On 25 February 1934, Moyse premiered Jacques Ibert's Concerto for flute and orchestra, with Gaubert and the Société des Concerts. For flutists everywhere, the work, written for Moyse, signified the re-birth of the flute as a solo instrument after a century of neglect and inspired observers like *La Revue Musicale*'s Suzanne Demarquez to encourage composers to look beyond the piano for a solo concerto instrument. "Musicians should, with flute players, rejoice, for one of their own has finally dedicated a concerto to an instrument within the orchestra," she wrote. After a full discussion of the work's merits, she complimented the performers: "Philippe Gaubert conducted as an artist in love with the rare lines of the Concerto, of which Marcel Moyse is the ideal interpreter: delicious sound, lushness, virtuosity—he unifies all of that in the most supple understanding the composer could hope for."[19] Moyse recorded the concerto the following year (see Discography nos. 102–105).

In the summer of 1934, Moyse performed the G Major Concerto of Mozart in Salzburg at the invitation of Bruno Walter, who had recently led the Straram Orchestra in a series of Mozart concerts. The prestigious offer helped motivate the French government to name Moyse a Chevalier de la Légion d'honneur, even though the Salzburg concert was not well attended.[20] Moyse's membership in the Légion was quite appropriate; he enjoyed international recognition as an artist and had evolved as a powerful member of several French artistic institutions. Moyse served on policy-making bodies such as the Comité National de Propagande pour la Musique, the Conseil Supérieur de la Radiodiffusion Française, and the Paris musicians' union and could be counted on to deliver strong opinions on everything from government politics to the going rate for a rehearsal. His correspondence from the 1930s and 40s demonstrates his aggressive networking among conductors, administrators, critics, and former students, with the goals of influencing decisions that had broad impact on musical life and securing jobs for his students and dates for himself and the Trio. Flutists wrote to him in supplicating language of their undying devotion, at the same time requesting Moyse's recommendation for, say, a second flute post in Zurich. Musicians in general liked or at least respected Moyse, but also criticized him for his bluntness and refusal to change his mind or compromise, even when it might be to his benefit to do so. Occasionally Moyse exercised a propensity to coldly sever a friendly relationship over a disagreement or criticism, real or perceived. It was—to put it mildly—an advantage to be on his good side.

For a time, Moyse was chairman of the Société des Concerts *comité,* in which capacity he occasionally went head-to-head with Gaubert. Prior to the opening of the 1936–37 season, the Académie Française proposed an extra performance to honor a recently deceased Conservatoire faculty composer named Albert Doyen. Doyen's catalogue was negligible. He had written no music for orchestra alone, so the *comité* decided it would perform a piece of his for chorus and orchestra, using an amateur choir. Since this was Doyen's only suitable work, the balance of the evening would be filled with Beethoven's Ninth Symphony, with the same raw voices.

Gaubert had originally agreed to put one orchestral work by Doyen on a regular subscription concert, not to organize a special event. In a long letter addressed to Moyse (as chairman of the *comité,* not as a friend), he expressed his displeasure in a fashion that revealed his own strong personality as well as the typical concerns and machinations in the life of a union member.

> Who will pay for this concert? It would astonish me if the *comité,* which is so demanding of fees when it concerns a gala of Fauré or Debussy at the Champs-Élysées, would happily accept no payment for a Doyen concert that no one obligates us to put on. And if twenty Société members aren't free that evening, who will pay for the replacements? What concerns me is that you are demanding two or three rehearsals and a concert plus my personal worth for a very long piece which I will probably conduct only once. It also comes at a bad time, because on the 24th I revive *Alceste* at the Opéra, a work I've never conducted before and which I want to work on a lot, given the small amount of time that remains. . . . Why should I kill myself at an age when one should be doing less?
>
> I don't know this choir—they're only amateurs and I understand they want the satisfaction of making music with a great orchestra. We would not get the same satisfaction. . . . From a union standpoint, we don't have the right to play with amateurs, and there are enough cynical union members on the *comité* who

will not like it. . . . I don't understand, coming from union members as ardent as you are, your enthusiasm in glorifying a musician who always did wrong to the organization by giving concerts with amateur choristers and musicians. This is not a comment against Doyen, who was a comrade at the Conservatoire, but a disagreement with these principles. You're a Socialist, they say. I knew Doyen very little, but all his life he did wrong to the organizations of professionals in conducting underpaid concerts. . . . The most striking thing is that all of you, Socialists and non-Socialists, are discontent because I, your conductor, your leader, do not have the same opinion you do.

Thus, do not count on me for the Ninth or whatever in this concert in memory of Albert Doyen. I prefer to make a gift to the *comité* for his monument, because there is one (although Fauré and Saint-Saëns haven't gotten theirs yet). At least I won't do anything wrong, either to the chorus or the professional musicians. There you have it, dear Moyse. You see that I am also a Socialist and a union man as you are—even more so![21]

Although there is no record of Moyse's reaction to this letter, no hard feelings were maintained, and Moyse probably respected Gaubert all the more for his position. Two years later, when tension in the orchestra between older traditionalists and younger players motivated Gaubert to resign from the Société, Moyse begged him to reverse his decision. Gaubert explained to him in a letter why he wanted to leave after nearly twenty years at the head of Paris's oldest orchestra, and what he thought of the state of the Société.

I am very touched by what you want to do. I have read your letter to the members of the Société. I'm leaving because . . . I want the time to practice, to fly with my own wings outside of France, where I will do what needs to be done for French art. Believe me, the Société can no longer live in this hall. It is crushed by the competition, and it is not the Société's fault. It is dying and I'm leaving before the agony begins. If the spirit of the young people were different, the patient could be healed. But the young people only come there to do business, not art. . . . if it weren't for the subsidy from the state and radio, we would have closed the house a long time ago.

As for the expression, "M. Gaubert is very clever"—that's

worthy of the Apaches' vocabulary! Twenty years of conducting, of devotion, and artistic contributions, to arrive at that—that's unspeakable! After that you can understand why it's impossible for me; it would be odious to withdraw my resignation. The respect due to those who have responsibility no longer exists, and one speaks to a conductor as one would speak to a boy in the orchestra. It will all end up with fighting at the Société, and so as not to be present at this fight, I am leaving. Just in time.

Fifty-nine-year-old Gaubert closed with this advice for his best-known student, who was now close to fifty himself: "You have talent, a personality. Don't sacrifice it to those who are justly jealous. . . . That's the way it is these days, more than it ever has been. . . . I thank you. Come to see me. Affectionately yours, Gaubert."[22]

Charles Munch was named the Société's conductor effective in 1938–39, only six years after his professional conducting debut with the Straram Orchestra. Moyse, upset by Gaubert's exit, sent Munch a letter at the end of Gaubert's final season saying he might leave the orchestra. Munch tried to telephone Moyse, but in vain— the flutist had posted his ambiguous note as he was departing on the *Normandie* for an appearance in the United States. So the maestro, who had recently conducted Moyse and Blanche in Françaix's *Musique de cour,* responded in writing:

> You say you regret that circumstances might prevent you from working with me, but I assure you I would regret it even more if I should be deprived of collaborating with your immense talent. An artist like you is irreplaceable, and I hope we can keep you among us. Believe in my most cordial sentiments.[23]

Nevertheless, Moyse resigned.

Moyse made another major change in his life around that time: he retired from the Opéra-Comique. Put simply, he was too busy teaching, recording, and playing with the Trio to continue his commitment to the orchestra he had served for twenty years. He was also producing several original manuscripts or new editions per year—his contracts with Leduc between 1927 and 1940 covered almost thirty different projects—and in the late 1930s he signed an agreement to endorse a special Moyse model flute for the instrument manufacturer Couesnon. His solo dates outside Paris continued to accumulate; one of the most memorable was a 1937 performance of Ibert's Concerto in Prague, with the composer conducting. At a post-concert reception hosted by the French Embassy, the ambassador's wife asked Moyse if he would "play something" for the guests. Sensing the flutist's discomfort, Ibert announced he would compose something new for the occasion and set to work at the parlor table. In less than an hour, Moyse premiered Ibert's *Pièce pour flûte seule.*

The Danish flutist Poul Birkelund studied with Moyse during that period and told the British flutist Trevor Wye about an incident that illustrated—to Birkelund's amazement—how Moyse handled his packed schedule. Birkelund was walking around Paris one day when he ran into his teacher, carrying a flute case as naturally as one wears his own arm. Moyse invited Birkelund to stroll with him, and after a time Moyse slowed down in front of a large building. "I have to go in here," he told his student. "Do you want to come in with me?" To Birkelund's surprise, an entire orchestra was assembled inside around sprays of microphones. Moyse twisted his flute together, sampled an A, and launched into an electrifying performance of a flute concerto. When it was all over, Moyse packed up quietly and motioned Birkelund to follow him out for more exercise. It was a beautiful day for a radio broadcast, an even better day for a walk.

Moyse made several recordings in 1938, among them Ravel's *Introduction et Allegro* with his old friends Lily Laskine (harp), Ulysse Delecluse (clarinet), and the Calvet Quartet (Discography nos. 128–131). At the Société Nationale, the Moyse Trio premiered Martinů's Sonata for flute, violin, and piano, which led immediately to a recording (Discography nos. 124–127). ("We worked very hard on the Martinů," Blanche said. "Very hard. I remember some mistakes we had in concerts—none that anyone else noticed, but we knew, . . . so when we made the recording we really had it perfect. The scherzo was very difficult.") In March, the Trio went to Czechoslovakia to play in Prague, Brno, and Bratislava and happened to be traveling back home through Austria on 18 March, the day Hitler invaded the country. The Moyses spent the night in a little inn and moved on to Switzerland the next day with no delays. But the landscape frightened them. "There were swastikas all over the country," said Louis, "on people, animals, farms, buildings, trees, cars, churches, chairs, hotels, windows, rooms, beds, clothes, on everything. . . . Swastikas as small as a postage stamp, glued to a fence, or as huge as a flag, covering a monument."

In the summer of 1938 Moyse and the Trio were invited to perform in the United States, a welcome break from the frantic activity in Paris and the political tumult in Europe. As usual, the whole family went first to St. Amour, and, as usual, Moyse was greeted there by a handful of foreign flutists who had come to study with him. One of these was Uri (Erich) Toeplitz, now retired from the Israel Philharmonic. Toeplitz was upset by Moyse's plans to go to America, but resolved to get as much instruction as possible in a short time. Moyse told him that the number of lessons he could have was only dependent upon money (50 francs a session), so Toeplitz appeared at the Moyse home as frequently as possible. One Sunday morning Moyse taught still clad in his pajamas and a jacket; afterward, with Louis accompanying, he played the first movement of the Mozart D Major Concerto. "I had the honor of a private concert," Toeplitz wrote in a 1992 memoir.

> This was so impressive that I cannot forget it. Moyse, then at the height of his career, had a very clear tone when playing *piano,* but some air was heard in the *forte.* This did not disturb me at all, as it added to the enormous intensity of his playing. He did put his flute a little off to the side of the middle of his lips, but when I tried the same, he said, "Me, not you!"[24]

Sometime before Moyse's departure for America, Gaubert sent this last, treasured note (undated), written in reply to an obviously praising letter from Moyse:

My Dear Moyse,

> Your letter touches me infinitely. I never doubted your affection and your attachment. You were my pupil, and my friend, moreover, when you were already an artist. Since then you have become a great artist. I'm proud of this, as our master Taffanel would have been. Why do you speak to me of my modesty? Is it so great? An artist is never too modest when he wants to improve himself. To improve, he looks above himself; one can *always* look above oneself. Beethoven found himself a small boy next to Bach. And God knows what a man he was!
>
> You probably want to speak about "publicity." People have

written a lot of good things about me, but I've never made anything of it. Others do it, as you say—are they more appreciated? It's the artist in a true sense who makes a reputation as
an artist, and not photos and press releases. An audience made
enthusiastic by an artist or a work does more for the name of a
man than all the clichés. I don't have to tell people who I am.
People judge me, and that's all. Photographs poison me for a
couple of months after they appear, and I believe that my head
has been published in all the newspapers of the world since I
was director of the Opéra!

Have a great success there. Play Bach for them, and don't
forget, if you have the chance, to play my second Sonata, which
is dedicated to you, and which is known there. Or the Sonatine,
dedicated to Barrère. Bon voyage, from the bottom of my heart.
I embrace you affectionately.

Gaubert[25]

Three summers later, Philippe Gaubert died.

Moyse's invitation to America in 1938 came from two
conductors: Koussevitzky in Boston and Toscanini in New York.
Toscanini arranged Moyse's American radio debut in a Mozart con-
certo with the NBC Symphony under William Steinberg (15
August) and also helped the Trio set up a broadcast concert.[26] At
Tanglewood, Koussevitzky welcomed Marcel to the Boston
Symphony for the Berkshire Music Festival's fifth season. Georges
Laurent had taken the summer off to go to France, and Moyse was
to be his illustrious replacement. The "Berkshire Symphonic
Festival" spanned two long weekends then, and six concerts were
given in 1938 between 4 and 14 August. The repertoire was familiar
to Moyse: Beethoven's Sixth and Ninth symphonies, Respighi's
Pines of Rome, Ravel's Mother Goose Suite, Debussy's La mer, a Bach cantata, an all-Wagner program, and so forth.

In the words of a clarinetist in the orchestra who was present
that summer, Moyse's time at Tanglewood was "not successful."
Part of the problem was pitch. In those days the Boston Symphony's
A was set around 442. René Rateau, who had recently joined the
orchestra as second flute, found it necessary to give up his French
instrument (A = 435) for a higher-pitched American one, a Powell.
Moyse preferred his Couesnon, the mid-quality instrument he had

played since the late 1920s and had endorsed in advertisements for the company.[27] He was undoubtedly out of tune with the Boston musicians.

Others have remarked that Moyse's playing in the late 1930s exhibited some signs of decline. It is true that Moyse's later recordings reveal occasional unclear passagework or inadequate breath support; these slipups resulted from Moyse's tenuous physical condition rather than lack of practice and took little away from his breadth of expression. His publicity flyer from this period pictures a grinning, robust man who seems ready to leap to the stage at the slightest nod and launch into a concerto. But the spirit was always hardier than the body. In 1938, Moyse's resources were not quite as dependable as they had been ten years earlier.

At the end of the summer of 1938, the Moyse Trio sailed back to France, first class on the *Normandie*. Louis was in particularly good spirits. On the way out of Lenox, Koussevitzky had offered him a contract to play second flute in the Boston Symphony for the 1939–40 season. The maestro also joined the Trio on their voyage; he was headed for a vacation in Savoy. The four disembarked in France just before Germany bit into Czechoslovakia. War was inevitable, and the guests at Paris's big music party continued to dance, with one eye on the ballroom door.

CHAPTER SEVEN

War

W E decided we would leave Paris when the front got within a day of the city. So as soon as we heard the Germans had attacked behind the Maginot line, that they were only seventy kilometers away, my parents got up and put everything in the car. I remember my father telling us later that the Germans arrived by the evening of the day we left for St. Amour.[1]

In May 1940, Marguerite Moyse peered out the back window of her father's Rolls-Royce, wondering if the snail-like procession of automobiles, motorcycles, bicycles, and pedestrians that crept out of Paris could possibly squeeze past the city limits by nightfall. The sky was cloudy; rumor had it that the French government had ordered an artificial fog to hide the exodus. And as the highway stretched into the countryside, Marguerite, her parents, and Blanche, who was two months pregnant with twins, eyed the fuel gauge as if it were about to register disaster. More and more cars were abandoned at the side of the route for lack of gasoline. Soon the Rolls had to be left behind, and the Moyse family anticipated joining the silent lines of beleaguered humans and farm animals disappearing into the hills on foot. They were fortunate; at a train station they secured seats in a railroad car bound for the Jura.

151

The Moyses had been preparing for this trip since the first day of September 1939, when the Nazis invaded Poland, and France and Great Britain declared war on Germany. These developments had their greatest impact first on Louis, who held a reservation on a ship bound the very next day for Boston. Louis planned to join the Boston Symphony that season, putting an end to the Moyse Trio and marking the beginning of an orchestral career an ocean away from the gathering war. Marcel supported his son's decision to leave, and expected to join him on the voyage to help establish himself in the United States.

All of that changed dramatically. Within hours of his scheduled departure, Louis was drafted into the French army; and, moved by the wartime passion that inspires people to make such decisions, he asked Blanche to marry him. He was already serving with his regiment on the Rhine when he returned to St. Amour for the wedding on 7 November 1939. Louis served in the Maginot line for eight months before being transferred to Meaux (about sixty kilometers east of Paris), where he was in charge of a unit of army postal workers. Danger was imminent, but not yet overt, and he was able to visit his family for a week in March. When the Germans invaded Paris in May, Louis and his compatriots fled with the rest of the French army to the south of France and stayed in Montauban, north of Toulouse. France formally submitted to Germany on 22 June 1940; Louis's unit moved to Vichy and demobilized in July, and he joined the rest of the family "secured in their insecurity" at St. Amour, which lay in the unoccupied region of France.

Nonetheless St. Amour was not entirely safe. Soon after the Moyses settled into their summer home, word came that a German outfit had bombed a train three kilometers north of the St. Amour railroad station, at a point where the railroad lines to Paris and Strasbourg intersected. The residents of the village scrambled to prepare for their assailants, and when bombs could be heard pummeling ground a few kilometers away, the Moyse clan—ten, including relatives—jammed themselves into and onto a little automobile and puttered away from the noise. They spent one night at the house of a friend, Marcel Gaillard, in Chamirey-Mercurey (near Chalon-sur-Saône) and planned to push on the next day. But a few kilometers out, the Moyses were met by a band of German troops who threatened them with guns. Everyone in the car began praying to heaven. Blanche's ability to speak German subdued the soldiers, who desperately needed an interpreter to obtain provisions from their French hostages. "Don't go any further—we're everywhere," an officer told them. "Go back to the home of your friend." Moyse wheeled the auto around, and Blanche spent the next day going house to house with the Nazis, requesting food for their troops and engaging in increasingly heated conversations along the way.

> They talked to me about Hitler and said French girls were all whores, and Jews were lice, and I said, "I have friends who are Jews, and I like them very much! And French girls are not whores just because they wear lipstick." And the soldiers said, "We know they are, for a fact," and I said, "You were told lies." They got mad, and I got angrier and angrier—I wouldn't agree to anything they said. And their captain told them, "Leave her alone. She has the right to her own opinion." That was because they still had orders at that time to be perfect gentlemen. They were very correct—the boys were handsome, blonde Siegfrieds. They told me, "Soon we will go to England, and it will all be finished." So I asked, "What will your wives say if you're all dead, instead?" And they answered, "Our wives will be proud and happy to have given us to our Motherland." And I said, "You're all brainwashed!" And they were.[2]

St. Amour was spared for the moment, but the summer was difficult for everyone. Moyse retreated behind his pipe. Doubtful of the future and lacking access to his funds in Paris, he arranged to perform every few weeks on the radio from Lyon, about seventy-five kilometers south of St. Amour, and when Louis arrived, the Trio took to the airwaves in half-hour broadcasts, twice a month.

Regardless of the situation, there was to be a Paris season, and Henri Rabaud, who was still director of the Conservatoire, wrote to Moyse in St. Amour, asking him to return to teach in November. Rabaud hoped for his cooperation, but Moyse replied that he could not fulfill his teaching duties while Paris was full of Germans. Rabaud named Gaston Crunelle to replace Moyse.

"We are not going back," Moyse told his family. "We are going to buy a cow, we are going to transform our garden into a farm, and we are going to live here and wait, and see what happens." Aside from his memories of World War I, he abhorred the possibility of performing under German or collaborationist command and was afraid that he might be mistaken for a Jew, although the spelling of

his surname (which means "Moses") in that case would have been
Moïse, not Moyse. Most of all, he was concerned for the safety of his
family. "The real and simple truth," Louis explained, "is that we
were all scared, not knowing what the future would bring. We were
waiting, like most French people." By this time, hundreds of musicians had fled Europe; the Serkins moved to New York in the last
weeks of 1938, and Adolf Busch and his wife joined them in the
spring of 1939. By 1940 the whole Busch Quartet had arrived in the
United States and begun concertizing.

The Moyses adapted to country life in a region whose ability to
support them was severely diminished by wartime rationing, the
depletion of the work force, and the confiscation or destruction of
resources by the enemy. The family brightened considerably
during the winter of 1940, when Blanche was able to cross the
border to her parents' home in Geneva for the 16 December births
of Claude and Michel. The babies inspired optimism in everyone,
with a deeper sense of devotion to family than before.

The Moyse Trio continued the Lyon broadcasts, which offered a
new set of risks. According to Louis, these broadcasts took place at
night, sometimes as late as eleven o'clock. With the city under
curfew, and no available transportation back to the home of Jean
Augier (Marcel's former pupil, flutist in the Lyon orchestra), where
they stayed, the Moyse Trio often found themselves leaving the
radio station on foot at a time when anyone seen on the streets
might be arrested, or shot. Louis recalled,

> We were careful to walk in the middle of the street, because if
> you tried to hide in a doorway, the Germans would fire first and
> ask for papers afterward. One musician we knew was killed that
> way, coming home from the radio. There is now a plaque at the
> Lyon radio station that commemorates the event.

Marcel and Blanche retained their teaching posts in Geneva and
Neuchâtel as long as they were permitted to cross the Swiss border
(which officially closed in October 1941). Blanche's friendship with
a Swiss foreign policy official afforded them the privilege when
others were turned away. "At customs I asked them to call his office
for permission and they were mad about it, but they took us each
time," she said. All these trips were made in trains so cold in winter
that there was ice on the seats. Once, in the fall of 1940 or 1941,

Marcel and Louis went to Berlioz's native village, La Côte Saint-André, to play the "Trio of the Young Ishmaelites" (from *L'enfance du Christ*) with Lily Laskine on a radio broadcast honoring the composer. The broadcast took place in Berlioz's home, and afterwards, father and son posed for a publicity photograph holding a pair of recorders from the Berlioz museum (see Figure 19).

For the most part, though, the Moyses remained at home in St. Amour. Food was scarce, and the family photo album from the war proves that everyone slimmed down on their diet of parsnips, turnips, and salt pork, except for Celine, who over the years had grown stout, but strong. "She walked miles to get food—perhaps just a little rancid butter!—from the black market," Blanche remembered. One of Madame Moyse's ploys was to wheel an empty baby carriage through back roads to a food source, load the illegal goods, cover them carefully with a blanket, and return to St. Amour, humming a lullaby. More than one policeman nodded approvingly as she strolled by innocently, clucking maternally at a sack of flour, singing her eggs to sleep.

Lack of sustenance deepened everyone's true colors, especially when treats were involved. For two years, each member of the family hoarded a small allotment of sugar. Louis and Blanche saved their few ounces for the children, who numbered three when Isabelle was born in 1943. Celine's foremost aim was to comfort her husband, and she often tried to please him by baking a favorite dessert, having asked Louis and Blanche to contribute their portion of sugar. Most of the time, however, the young couple refused; they knew well that the lion's share of the cake or pudding would go to Pépé.

The preoccupation with food was shared by everyone, including Moyse's friend, the critic Émile Vuillermoz, who with his wife fled Paris for Marseille. In June 1941, the Moyse family managed to send a box of food to Vuillermoz, a gourmand who found available provisions intolerable. Vuillermoz replied:

> After six months we no longer know what butter is. The contents of your box have renewed our contact with civilization in a place where foodstores shamelessly post notices of cheese guaranteed without fat, mayonnaise guaranteed without oil or eggs, and sausage guaranteed without pork. The sight of your magnificent buttery breads, pure, frank, and honest, loyally

accomplishing their secular mission, which consists in operating the most subtle and savory synthesis between the alchemies of the animal and vegetable kingdoms, fills us with a sort of religious aspect. These are the great symbols and the great ancestral forces which take on at this time a profound and touching meaning.[3]

To this, Vuillermoz added news of heads rolling at the national radio in Paris, and a pledge to work with Moyse on a plan for reconstructing it after the war. A few months later, he wrote again to acknowledge receipt of a package of potatoes and beans that, due to humidity, "arrived in flower," and mentioned his plans to turn down the Vichy government's request that he become music director of the radio. After the war, Vuillermoz discovered that his journalist license had been suspended, and he was forced to wage a legal battle to resume his profession.

The Moyses eventually developed a ready-to-eat menagerie of several dozen chickens and rabbits and a dairy cow. With a lot of time on his hands, Marcel observed the caged rabbits closely and derived a lesson from them. "Among the rabbits were some who jumped, some who threw themselves around, and some who twisted up in the air and then started up again," he told his grandson Michel.

> That surprised me. Then one day I was in the country, sitting on a rock, and I heard a dog bark. A hare passed in front of me. He was running across an intersection there. I looked—and he jumped up, just like that! Others told me he jumped so the dog would not be able to follow the track—that was his defense. That is how I learned that the rabbit's movements in the hutch were exercises to keep himself in shape.[4]

Moyse continued to practice, but the isolation wore him down. His playing declined, and he grew desperate for news, gossip, anything that would help him divine the future. "My father-in-law always dreamed, projected, planned," Blanche explained. "He spoke about how the war was going, why we could hope that this or that would happen—always comforting himself with talk of how things would be." Moyse was, above all, determined that his colleagues in Paris accept and respect his decision to remain in unoccupied France. A letter to his student Geneviève Noufflard contained an anxious list of questions: "What did Girod tell you; what are the students doing; what is musical life doing? What is Crunelle doing? What do you know of the Conservatoire? What is your situation with respect to this *grande maison?* What has become of music? What has become of my good friends?" He complained that he grew tired from practicing long hours—his main activity, besides writing more flute exercises—then launched into pedagogical advice: "Always work on the exercises for tone. You can stop for two or three days between the four series. *But don't ever leave the studies!*" After recommending more Kuhlau and solfège, Moyse concluded, "I will never give courses by correspondence. Not even through radio—it's too difficult. I need to read in the eyes of the student whether he has understood. But don't be afraid of bothering me—ask me as many precise questions as you wish. I will be happy to answer."[5]

Noufflard had left the Conservatoire when Moyse did and spent one year, 1940–41, at her parents' country house. She traveled to St. Amour several times for visits of three or four weeks and lived with the family of a baker who permitted her to practice in the oven room. "It was terribly hot, after the baking of the bread," she remembered. "But I went every other day to have a long lesson with M. Moyse. It was wonderful." She also tutored Marguerite in English, a skill Moyse's daughter would find useful later. Geneviève Noufflard returned to the Conservatoire in the fall of 1941, armed with miles of new exercises copied from Moyse or written down by him. She studied with Crunelle, but quit school in 1942 to join the Resistance movement.

Moyse taught a handful of other determined students, including Aurèle Nicolet, a young pupil of André Jaunet in Zurich, who took a few lessons from Moyse in a Geneva café then worked with him at the nearby La Chaux de Fonds Conservatoire, a music school where Moyse taught. (Nicolet's family came from a town in the Jura about a hundred kilometers from St. Amour.)

Despite undependable means of communication, Moyse maintained connections with sympathetic friends who might help him professionally. Jaunet attempted to line up some concerts for Moyse and the Trio in Switzerland, but, as he explained to Moyse in a letter of 13 March 1942, he met with resistance from administrators who thought an "essentially French" event would compromise Swiss neutrality. Most concerts were run under the auspices of the International Red Cross anyway, he wrote. After Moyse could no longer teach in Geneva, Raymond Meylan kept him apprised of the political situation and of the devotion of the flute class there. Moyse and Frank Martin exchanged letters on the topic of a new work for the Trio, but Martin had to bow out because his schedule of commissioned works was full. D. E. Inghelbrecht, who had conducted for the Opéra-Comique and Pasdeloup and had founded the Orchestre National de la Radiodiffusion in 1934, wrote Moyse to express distress over the deplorable musical conditions in Paris and to offer warm wishes. Moyse also corresponded with Straram's son Enrich regarding the creation of the Fondation Walther Straram, an organization dedicated to training young conductors. The Fondation was officially established in March 1945, with Moyse as the salaried director of the artistic committee (or faculty), which included Roger Désormières (director of the Opéra-Comique), André Cluytens (soon to take Désormières's position at the Opéra-Comique and later to direct the Société des Concerts, after Munch), Olivier Messiaen (who taught at the Conservatoire), and Marcel Darrieux, former concertmaster of the Opéra-Comique and the Straram Orchestra.

At some point during their exile, the Moyses were tracked down by journalist Jean-Roger Rebierre, who published a "puff piece" painting Marcel and the Trio as a band of happy campers, communing contentedly with nature for the sake of France. The Moyse house, wrote Rebierre, was like "the dream come true of a couple of retirees." But within lived the great Marcel Moyse, "an artist of simple tastes."

> I find myself on the gravel drive which leads to the house. All is clear, agreeable, and breathes the joy of life. A good-looking athlete with an open smile comes to meet me, his hand extended. It is Louis Moyse, son of the master, and his designated successor. "Come this way—my father is waiting for you," he says.
>
> We go into the welcoming house. Marcel Moyse is resting there, smoking his pipe, seated in an armchair. "I've just come back from Geneva, where I gave a series of master classes. Ah—I assure you that traveling is no longer a pleasure. Before the war, I went here and there by car. Now I'm reduced to taking the train like everyone else."

The interviewer then invites Moyse to describe his childhood as an orphan: "I made flutes from willow branches while guarding the cows in the field—that field over there, which belongs to me, now," Moyse responds, gesturing toward a window. The histories of Moyse's career and the Moyse Trio are recounted in the article, and finally the reporter tears himself away, letting the reader know that

> the conversation of Marcel and Louis Moyse is so charming I find it difficult to leave. I finally get up. Marcel Moyse accompanies me to the gate. In passing through, I salute Madame Honegger-Moyse, who distributes snacks to Michel and Claude. I return to the road, enchanted by the two hours spent in the company of great artists—very French—who have carried to the outside world the renown of French music and are excellent ambassadors of our country. I turn around once more to see the "Little Conservatory." In his native village, Marcel Moyse leads a peaceful life which indisputedly proves his wisdom.[6]

Sometime late in 1943 or in the early spring of 1944, Marcel and Louis made a short trip to Paris and confirmed their suspicion that someone had reported Marcel to be a Jew. He was arrested, brought before the Gestapo, and forced to show that he was circumcised. Moyse demanded to know who had named him, to no avail. But he was released when a French musician, a collaborator, defended him, saying Moyse had been wrongly denounced. The flutist was stunned—his defender was an orchestra player he barely knew. When Moyse asked why he went out of his way to save him, the man replied, "Because I have known you for more than twenty-five years. I know what kind of person you are. I wanted to help." Moyse obtained official records of his lineage, and the authorities issued him a *Certificat de non-appartenance à la race juive*—a "Certificate of Non-Belonging to the Jewish Race"—protecting him from further inquiry. Celine had no records, but her maiden name, Gautreau, was obviously not of Jewish origin. After the war, Moyse tried to locate his protector (whose name has disappeared from the memories of those who know the story) in order to return the great favor, but never found him.

Moyse also questioned every possible source to learn who had given his name to the Gestapo and finally learned that his betrayer was a flutist and former student with whom he had performed often, a man who had been a friend of the family: Louis Moyse had served as "garçon d'honneur" at the man's wedding. Marcel and his son returned to St. Amour, more discouraged than ever.[7]

"He was absolutely crushed by what was happening—he was in tears, completely broken," Blanche reflected. Louis described his father as "furious! ready to assault anyone." Yet Moyse never seemed despondent in the presence of his three grandchildren. He entertained them, played games with them, taught them tricks. Once he walked the twins by a great walnut tree that stood on a neighbor's property and showed them how to strike the trunk hard with a heavy stick so the walnuts would tumble down. Satisfied with their harvest, Moyse and his grandsons quickly crammed the nuts into their pockets before anyone observed them. Claude Moyse remembered his grandfather "picking up his flute and leading the three of us in a parade, playing *Carmen*—things like that."

The Moyses led a fairly pastoral life, albeit one without adequate food, communication, or meaningful work. As the months ticked by, the threat of ruin increased, and Marcel and Louis were obliged to take part in "community" activities, such as this one, recounted by Louis:

> Starting with the fall of 1942, the Germans decided, through the Vichy government, to have the railroad in the territory guarded at night, two Frenchmen per kilometer. Once a week, my father and I (together or with another man) were assigned to watch the kilometer around the station, connecting with other men in the next valley. The idea was to prevent the Resistance from blowing up trains, but of course it never worked for the good reason that in each village, people like us, who knew the train schedules, had connections with members of the Resistance hidden around in the hills and informed them. Like all systems, this one was not guaranteed 100 percent! But most of the time, the Resistance managed to blow a few meters of railroad that could not possibly be guarded.[8]

Usually, the French mechanics on the locomotives were warned in advance of the Resistance traps and prepared for derailment by clinging to the tops of the cabins to avoid having their legs cut off, a common injury in that situation. If a citizen in charge of a destroyed length of railroad was caught by the Germans, he was either killed on the spot or sent to a concentration camp. But if he was lucky enough to reach the local gendarme before the Germans did, he fell under the protection of the Vichy regime. Most of the time, the gendarmes themselves were anti-German, but anyone connected with missing track was never really safe, and most in that predicament found a way to disappear—usually into the hills to join the Resistance. "We had many friends who were not that fortunate," Louis said. "But we were lucky. The railroad never 'blew up' in our section, but two or three kilometers farther, yes."

By 1944 the Red Army was battering the German front, and Allied forces were planning an invasion; Nazi soldiers, sensing the possibility of defeat, began to run amok in the villages. When a group of them walked into St. Amour one day and shot three picnickers, Marcel and his family escaped into the hills for a night. Everyone, including the little boys, was on foot, except for baby Isabelle, who rode on her father's shoulders. The Moyse family lost a beloved member during that period of time; on 9 May Marcel's adoptive mother Josephine Perretier died at the age of ninety-two.

On 6 June 1944, British and American troops landed in Normandy and began to push the Germans in the northeastern section of France back over the border. Reporting in *The New Yorker*, A. J. Liebling wrote that peasants living in the battle zones refused to leave for the sake of their cows.

> The Germans have been trying to evacuate people and their livestock before them as they retreat, but the peasants hide themselves and their beasts. When American troops start fighting around their farmhouses, our Civil Affairs officers attempt to get the peasants to move back of our lines, for their own protection, but they usually say they won't go unless they can take their cattle with them, and since they can't take their pasture along with the cattle this is not practical.[9]

Down in St. Amour, the Moyses fretted over their one cow, who had given her best for the war effort and was quite unfit for a quick escape. The Allies were surging forward on French soil, but no one knew how close they were. In mid-August, truckloads of Nazis clad in leafy camouflage rumbled into town and warned citizens they would burn St. Amour the next day if the Resistance launched one more ambush; they had been attacked twenty-two times on the way from nearby Bourg-en-Bresse. Soldiers prepared stacks of wood and hay for inflammation. The Moyse adults put the children to bed but remained awake all night, dressed for flight. Marcel wanted to run to the hills and hide in the forest, but Blanche put in that her ability to speak German might save them one more time. The family stayed indoors, lights out. By the early morning of 16 August, American troops had debarked in the Mediterranean and advanced to an area a few kilometers away, and the Nazis had fled without lighting so much as a match. Within hours, Moyse's grand-children were among the youngsters of St. Amour who raced to the square to greet the Americans and clamber aboard the victorious tanks.

Paris was liberated on 25 August 1944. In November, the Moyses paid their last respects to the cow, who would serve them a few months more in the form of the freshly canned meat the women packed for the trip back to Paris.

Moyse may have been at the center of things before the war, but exile had made him a permanent outsider. As his former Conservatoire student Raymond Guiot put it, Moyse had been sur-rounded for four years by cattle and sheep instead of students and concert halls; music had, quite plainly, gone on without him. He had failed to make formal arrangements to leave his posts temporarily, leaving plenty of opportunities for younger rivals (many of them former students), who quickly claimed Moyse's chairs in chamber groups and orchestras. Moyse, whose own career had developed under similar circumstances thirty years before, well understood what had happened, although he was quick to point out that during the first war, fill-ins such as himself con-sidered their positions temporary and were more than willing to return their chairs to the flutists who had served France honorably.

But in 1944, everything was different. People were already talking about a talented young flutist named Jean-Pierre Rampal, who had served in the French army under the Occupation and went AWOL when he heard his outfit was going to be sent to Germany for forced labor. After dodging the police for a while, Rampal entered the Conservatoire and, with just five months' study under Gaston Crunelle, received his *premier prix* shortly before Moyse came back to town. After Paris was liberated, Rampal was invited to perform the Ibert Concerto, Moyse's vehicle, on the radio. The specter of a new generation crowned by an artist Moyse had not taught added to his depression over the loss of his positions and the state of concert life in general. When he returned to Paris, Moyse was fifty-five years old, still an intense, vital man with a long, brilliant performing career, but one that he was physically and politically incapable of prolonging at fevered pitch.

What mattered most now to Moyse was his throne at the Conservatoire, and he seethed when he learned that Gaston Crunelle had been awarded the permanent flute professorship by the new director, Claude Delvincourt. If Moyse had established any understanding with Rabaud about returning to the Conservatoire after his self-imposed exile, it wasn't strong or specific enough to transcend the extremes and confusion of war. As the fighting ground on and Moyse remained practically incommunicado in the Jura, the Conservatoire proceeded to change. Claude Delvincourt was popular with musicians; he won the Prix de Rome in 1913 (sharing it with Lili Boulanger) and suffered a crippling wound fighting in World War I. During the Occupation, he organized an orchestra that sheltered French musicians who might have been forced to join the German army. When the war was over, the French government ruled that all collaborators be suspended from their posts. Delvincourt was placed in that category, but he was so well liked that the Conservatoire administration suspended him for a grand total of one minute. When Moyse emerged from hiding after four years to take back the flute class, Delvincourt was surprised by his expectations.

What followed was a struggle between Moyse, the Conservatoire, and the Ministry of Arts. Stuck in the middle of the fracas was Gaston Crunelle, a good man, fine flutist, able teacher, and former student of Gaubert and Moyse. The Conservatoire liked him; there was no reason for him to step down at that point. On the other hand, many observers agreed that Moyse deserved to return to the faculty. After two years of lengthy meetings and unpleasant tiffs, Moyse grudgingly accepted the Conservatoire's proposal for compromise: Crunelle would stay, but a second flute class would be created for Moyse.

Le maître was hardly idle during his fourteen-month wait for a flute class. Like the prisoner who scratches a chalk mark on his cell wall every day he is incarcerated, Moyse composed a variation for an original melody every day he remained outside the Conservatoire. There were 440 variations, all written in a minor key, except for the last. Yet Moyse did not hide away from the world. He accepted invitations outside France to teach or perform, building on his international reputation and his network of former students. In the late summer of 1945, he gave a series of master classes at the Internationale Musikalische Festwochen in Lucerne, attended by André Jaunet's Zurich students such as Aurèle Nicolet, Raymond Meylan, and Peter-Lukas Graf, a teenager who had tried and failed to obtain a copy of *De la sonorité* during the war and wound up laboriously copying Jaunet's copy by hand. The following July, Moyse performed the Ibert Concerto with the Concertgebouw Orchestra under Clarence Raybould, in Interlaken. In the fall of 1945, at the behest of Blanche, he moved the family from Rue Durantin to a rented home in Rueil-Malmaison, in the suburbs. It was safer than the center of town and offered Moyse's grand-children fresh air and room to play.

In 1946, Moyse's engagements included a Scandinavian tour with the Moyse Trio, packed with chamber-music recitals and per-formances of concerto repertoire, such as the fourth Brandenburg Concerto, Martinů's Concerto for flute and violin (with the Danish State Radio Orchestra in Copenhagen), and the Ibert and Mozart D major flute concertos (with the Selskap Philharmonic in Norway). That fall, he finally met his new class at the Conservatoire. Geneviève Noufflard was back, and several of Crunelle's students, such as Nicolet (who had entered the Conservatoire when the war ended), Raymond Guiot, and Jean Doussard, switched from Crunelle to Moyse. There were other pupils, too, notably nineteen-year-old Charles Dagnino, from Nice. Graf came the following year. According to Conservatoire records, Moyse began with thirteen students. In 1947 he taught fifteen, and in 1948, sixteen.

The class schedule was the same—three afternoons a week. More and more, Moyse insisted on teaching in his home instead of in the drafty, inhospitable Conservatoire. Presiding in his personal studio, Moyse could comfortably describe to his pupils the various qualities of *joli son*—beautiful sound—the basis, he said, for all musical expression.

Nicolet, Graf, Guiot, and Dagnino unanimously recall Moyse's intense intuitive and physical energy. He had been a good educator before the war, but upon his return he seemed absolutely driven to teach, to hammer home the importance of expression so deeply that each student would somehow be changed forever. The images he used from physical surroundings or emotional landscapes could be summed up, according to Nicolet, as "eye-ear-heart." "Moyse is

like a computer chip—the seat of memory for certain musical principles," he said.[10]

Graf, who occasionally attracted Moyse's wrath by, as he puts it,
"chattering too much during class," still vividly remembers one
lesson on melody.

> It was a very simple melody by Reicha, one I would not accept in
> my eighteen-year-old state. It wasn't great music, but by singing
> it, and pointing out subtleties that could be added to individual
> notes, Moyse showed that playing this melody on the flute
> could be very difficult! A bad flutist can play a melody by Bach
> or Mozart, and there is still Bach and Mozart, but to play some-
> thing less in a way that brings it to life, you must be in control of
> the sound, and of expression.[11]

Nicolet, too, remembers three lessons "imprinted in my head
and on my heart," all relating to the ideals of sound, to the relationship of singing to flute-playing, and to the art of declamation on the
flute. Moyse "was like an actor in the French theater," he said. "His
magic was in his power of suggestion, through physical gestures,
descriptions of pictures, and, of course, singing."

But as animated as Moyse could be during flute class, he was
still unhappy. One student from the postwar years described him as
"an angry old man, a dictator." Moyse resented the presence of
another flute professor at the Conservatoire and often criticized
Crunelle during lessons. He also seemed bent on proclaiming his
Catholic origins, afraid (as other French people were) that war
might break out again. "Always, he had to repeat that even though
his name was Moyse, he was not Israeli," Graf remarked. These
behaviors bothered Moyse's pupils, but most of them learned to
separate the disgruntled man from the brilliant musician.

Moyse made a handful of recordings after the war. In July 1947
the Moyse Trio went to London to record the J. S. Bach Trio Sonata
in G (Discography nos. 152–153); in the same sessions Marcel performed some solos that were never released (Discography nos. 154–
157). In 1948 Moyse recorded the Gennaro "Aubade printanière"
for two flutes and violin and the Scherzo from Louis's Suite in C for
two flutes and viola, with Blanche and Louis (Discography nos.
158–159) and also the previously mentioned Cimarosa Concerto
for two flutes and orchestra, with Louis playing second flute and
Moyse's old friend Eugène Bigot conducting (Discography nos.

160–163). There were solo dates, too, such as a Mozart concerto appearance in Koblenz with the Südwestfunk Orchestra, for the inauguration of a new radio station (25 January 1947), and a Christmas recital with organist Marie Dufour on 5 December 1948.

The Trio, which Moyse still managed on his own, continued to perform in Paris and on tour. The threesome gave concerts in England during 1947; among them was a recital of French music at Wigmore Hall with baritone Camille Maurane. February 1948 brought a concert with the Société des Concerts under the baton of composer-conductor Henri Busser. The Trio turned in its well-honed fifth Brandenburg, and Marcel and Blanche performed Françaix's *Musique de cour,* not in the orchestral version, but with Louis on piano. Moyse must have been gratified to see the press notices that praised his virtuosity and acknowledged the predominance of his students in orchestras all over the city.

The Trio also played again with the Busch Ensemble and made a last record for HMV that was never released. In the summer of 1948, with the assistance of Andrés Segovia, the Moyse Trio toured South America. They were appreciated there and could not help comparing the milieu to the social and professional climate of postwar Paris. In cosmopolitan Buenos Aires, they became acquainted with an established community of cultured French expatriates who listened sympathetically to Moyse's account of his experiences at the Conservatoire. They, too, refused to believe the war was over. No one had confidence in the government, they declared; France was changed for the worse. They urged the Moyse family to emigrate before Louis could be drafted again. Plans were being drawn up for a new conservatory in Mendoza—wouldn't the Trio like to serve on the faculty? There was no firm proposal, but—just as in Minneapolis thirty-four years before—Moyse was intrigued by the possibility of a good position in a new place. This time, he felt he had nothing to lose and much to gain: safety and opportunities for his family and the chance to turn his back on the people and institutions he felt had undermined his status and career.

After giving more than forty concerts all over the continent, Marcel, Louis, and Blanche departed Buenos Aires on 2 September and arrived in Cherbourg on 17 September. Two weeks at sea failed to dampen Marcel's enthusiasm for South America, but other family members were not as excited about his dream of moving thousands of miles away. "I remember my mother sitting in the kitchen and crying," recalled Marguerite, "and I said, 'Well, Maman, should we tell him we don't want to go?' And she said, 'No! Because I know what he would do—we would stay, and he would go!' " Blanche was not happy about Moyse's plan, either, but Louis was seriously worried about staying in France, for fear of being drafted for another war, and Blanche's parents promised the clan financial assistance for travel. The grandchildren, who had spent the summer at the Honegger home in Geneva, were the last to hear the news. "We didn't really know what it meant," said Claude, who was not quite seven at the time, "except that my mother was crying on the train when we were on the way back to Paris, to pack."[12]

In the fall of 1948 Moyse requested a leave of absence from the Conservatoire for the winter, but did not mention to anyone that he was thinking of leaving. In November the Moyse family auctioned off their furniture, including Louis's piano, and left their rented home in Rueil-Malmaison for good. They spent most of December and January in Switzerland.

Roger Cortet, a former student of Gaubert and Moyse, was quickly hired to take over Moyse's flute class, and on the evening of 13 January, a disappointed throng of current and former students gathered at the Restaurant Jean down the street from Moyse's former home on Rue Durantin to bid farewell to *le maître*. The souvenir menu from that evening reads, "The undersigned flutists extend to M. Moyse, the artist, professor, and man, the homage of their profound gratitude and the assurance of their enduring devotion." There are thirty-one signatures, including that of an American student, Joseph Cohen, who had arrived the year before to study with Moyse on the G.I. Bill. The laudatory inscription appears to be in the hand of Gaston Crunelle.

Moyse, who presided over this "Last Supper" from a dais, was flattered by the group's tribute. But his good humor was short-lived, and a thick streak of righteous indignation took charge as the evening wore on. Soft asides about the shabby treatment he had received from colleagues and from the Conservatoire grew into quite audible, angry statements, and he finally delivered what some witnesses describe as a prepared speech that contained bitter darts for officials, rival flutists, and musical Paris. The members of the assemblage, who had heard these complaints before, were ill at ease and saddened by the outpouring. They departed quietly, bidding their *maître* and friend farewell.

Joseph Cohen, who became a Francophile under Moyse's tutelage and later changed his name to Cobert, explained Moyse's behavior this way: "You know how people get to a point in life where they can no longer tolerate being kind and they're going to tell the truth? That's what that cruelty was. It means, 'I can't be bothered. I'm sick and tired of telling you the same things. I don't want any more—this is it.' " Moyse would employ this surgical method of severing close relationships again. Alongside that, Moyse's narrative definitions of "sincere emotion," as remembered by Cobert, illustrated a deep vein of sentimentality:

> A man goes off to war. Sitting in the train, he looks out the window and sees his wife, pregnant, with a baby in her arms and a small child holding onto her dress. He knows he's going to the front. He looks again at his wife and children, and he holds back his tears so they won't be upset, even though he is sure he will never see them again.
>
> Then there is the baker. His son is a baker, too. The army is stationed in their village. The moment comes when the baker must bid farewell to his son, and he grabs him, and hugs him, and cries so hard he can barely speak, and he knows damn well his son is only walking around the corner to deliver bread to the army.[13]

On 29 January, the Moyse family and thirty-nine pieces of luggage boarded a steamship in Antwerp bound for Morocco with a haul of dynamite. They were the only passengers. Every day, the children watched as the crew watered down the explosives. At Casablanca, the dynamite was unloaded, and the boat proceeded to Buenos Aires, Argentina. The Moyse twins recall a stop in Cape Verde, where a man tried to trade a small boy for Blanche's cache of Swiss chocolates. There was a storm off the coast of Africa that frightened everybody. When the craft crossed the equator, the ship captain upheld maritime tradition and baptized the eight travelers.

In Buenos Aires, the Moyses were met by a French violin dealer named Viret, whom they had met during the 1948 tour, and by a reporter and photographer from *Le Quotidien,* the newspaper for French-speaking citizens of Latin America. *Le Quotidien* published a glowing portrait of Marcel, and the family was ready to believe in a secure artistic future there. Concert life in Argentina's metropolitan communities was impressive. Symphony orchestras and concert societies were sprouting in the provinces, and the 1949 season saw a third professional orchestra added to Buenos Aires. That year, the three orchestras programmed mostly Beethoven, Wagner, Mozart, and Mendelssohn. Schubert and Richard Strauss tied for fifth place. As usual, a plethora of European and American soloists and ensembles visited that season: violinists Isaac Stern and Szymon Goldberg; pianists Walter Gieseking, Arturo Benedetti Michelangeli, and Witold Malcuzynski; the Vienna Boys Choir; the Hungarian String Quartet; and the Moyse Trio drew the most attention. Opera had been a mainstay since the nineteenth century, and Buenos Aires's crown jewel, the 3500-seat Teatro Colón (where the Moyse Trio performed during its 1948 tour), featured more than a dozen productions in 1949, including Bellini's *Norma* with twenty-five-year-old Maria Callas in the title role and the first Argentine production of Roussel's *Padmavâti* (whose Paris premiere Gaubert had conducted in 1923), with the French mezzo Hélène Bouvier.

The Moyses stayed with the Virets about two months, while other contacts found them a house to rent in Arguello, a village near Córdoba. There was only one problem: there were no teaching jobs there, or in Mendoza, the city they had originally planned to make their home. In the short time between the summer tour of 1948 and March 1949, someone connected to the Perón government had quashed the idea of the Mendoza school, and Moyse's French friends were in no position to question a ruling party that was both pro-German and contemptuous of upper-class ideals. Juan Perón had been president of the Republic since 1946, and his reforms included taking over the universities (and firing 70 percent of the faculty) and nationalizing foreign-owned enterprises such as the British gas companies and French railroads. Moyse was unaware of the situation and had never requested written confirmation for any of the opportunities that had tempted him. The month the Moyses docked in Buenos Aires, the Perón government promulgated a new constitution that allowed a president to be reelected indefinitely. There was no choice but to scrape around for an alternative. The Moyse Trio was unemployed.

Córdoba remained the Trio's base for practicing and presenting the few concerts they were able to schedule. Meanwhile, the children were bereft of friendly playmates, and one of the twins became ill with mononucleosis. It became increasingly clear that South America had turned out to be a wrong turn, a bad dream.

CHAPTER EIGHT

A New Life

By the summer of 1949, Moyse and his family were not merely disenchanted with Argentina, but frightened. The adults encountered pro-German sentiments in the cities, the children experienced racial and cultural prejudice on the playground, and no one knew how to make a living. The women in the family were more than willing to return to France and admit South America was a mistake, but Marcel refused to consider it.

At the lowest point, Blanche wrote to her parents in Switzerland, hoping to make contact with Adolf Busch and Rudolf Serkin in the United States. The Serkin and Busch families had been in New York since the beginning of the war and had established country homes in Guilford and Brattleboro, Vermont. Serkin, who was then head of the piano department at the Curtis Institute of Music, had connections with a new college in nearby Marlboro that wanted to create a music department. If the Moyse Trio were to relocate in the area, the Honeggers suggested in their reply to Blanche, they might be hired to teach. For once, Moyse was ready to listen to outside advice, and he responded positively. In a short time a letter arrived from Serkin himself. "Please come to Vermont," he said. "There are positions for you at Marlboro College, and you will be among friends."

In September 1949, the Moyses once more observed the transfer of their worldly belongings to the hold of a ship. The original itinerary included at least one Moyse Trio concert *en route,* but when they stopped at Montevideo, Uruguay, the three canceled the event and hid in their cabins. Moyse still harbored postwar paranoia, and the family had only tourist visas to show for so much luggage. What if someone tried to stop them from leaving? The safest course was to burrow deep into the lower quarters of the boat and wait for someone above to announce the appearance of the Statue of Liberty.

When their ship docked in New York Harbor, the Moyse family were greeted by a man sent by Serkin who lunched with them at Grand Central Station and saw them off on a train to Massachusetts. Irene Serkin met them in Greenfield and drove them to a white frame house she had rented for them in "Harrisville," a community of three homes clustered on a little hill near Marlboro. The area reminded the Moyses of the French countryside. "Snow, ice, and cold welcomed us," Louis remembered. "The table in the house was ready, with a huge cooked ham. This was the first contact we had with marvelous American hospitality."

Soon after the Moyses arrived in Vermont, Joe Cohen came up from Philadelphia to help them settle in and wound up staying several years. He was fully adopted by the family and placed himself at Moyse's disposal as interpreter, manager, and all-round "gofer" in exchange for room, board, and flute lessons. Family members acknowledge his inestimable help to Marcel, whose English was "atrocious." Without Joe Cohen, Marcel could not have begun teaching right away.

Woodwind Magazine, a publication for American wind players, had predicted Moyse's arrival as early as February 1949, before the flutist even landed in Argentina.[1] So when *le maître* actually set foot in the U.S., the magazine wasted no time announcing his presence to the instrumentalists participating in the postwar explosion of school bands and orchestras. "The woodwind world has been waiting expectantly for some word as to his plans," an unsigned reporter noted in the December 1949 issue. "Idle rumors have been floating about for months, but the final word was forthcoming only two weeks before *W. M.* went to press." The article informed readers that Moyse would head a new Marlboro College music school in Brattleboro, Vermont, and give courses in flute, chamber music, conducting, harmony, and solfège. Louis would teach piano and flute; Blanche would teach violin and viola. The faculty also included Adolf Busch and his brother Hermann, the cellist; vocalists Maxine Stellman and Joseph Caruso; and music theorist Chaloner Spencer. (Spencer, not Moyse, actually taught the harmony courses.) Serkin, a member of the music school's advisory board, would join these faculty artists in a campus concert series.

The following month, *Woodwind Magazine* published an ebullient profile of Moyse, with the following disclaimer by the editor:

> *Woodwind Magazine* has scrupulously followed a policy of impartiality in its columns. To be of greatest service to our readership, we have refrained from editorializing, subtly or obviously; whenever publishing an opinion representing one side of any issue, we have attempted to counter with the opposing position as well as a mediation between the two. The following interview with Marcel Moyse, the French flutist, is a glowing tribute by one of our editors. We consider it an impartial estimate of the greatness of a man which can be objectively substantiated. It is the opinion of the writer of the column that Moyse is one of the world's great living musicians. The staff of *Woodwind Magazine* feels that it is not going out on a limb in concurring.[2]

The profiler wrote that Moyse's face reminded him of French "energy, eagerness, alertness, and agility." "Moyse treats music as a young man treats his first love," the writer enthused. He went on to sketch an inspiring lesson—heavy on singing, light on English— and described Moyse's plans to establish an American school of woodwind playing that would "challenge the best anywhere in the world."

The way for Moyse's entrance to the United States had been partly paved for some time. *The Flutist,* a publication that spanned the 1920s and encouraged the founding of dozens of flute clubs across the country, had printed plenty of articles about the French flute school and Moyse's countrymen Barrère and Laurent, who headed the New York and Boston flute societies. Despite *The Flutist's* quirky tone—characterized by editorials on subjects such as prohibition, law enforcement, and the importance of attending church (not to mention a regular sprinkling of racist jokes, written in dialect)—the North Carolina–based magazine helped foster an interest in the flute that no other wind instrument could then claim. The demise of *The Flutist* came with the Depression, just as Moyse began his international recording career. But despite the lack of a major flute publication in 1950, there were more organized bodies of flutists than ever, eager for contact with the French School. *Wood-wind Magazine*'s article represented Moyse's first chance to impress Americans in print. (Another piece, "Marcel Moyse on Flute Playing," appeared in the June/July 1949 issue of *Symphony*, which, like *Woodwind Magazine*, was edited by James Collis.) Between 1949 and 1952, Moyse was featured eight times in *Woodwind Magazine*, whose publications included a two-part discography by his former student Harry Moskovitz. The cover of the October 1950 issue displayed Moyse with pipe in hand and wearing a casual, open-collared shirt, an image that contrasted sharply with American flutists' stilted, formal portraits. In 1952, *le maître* published his own article, headlined "The Battle Page," in which he took an unsuspecting Murray State College student to task for a series of articles on flute teaching, and challenged him to a public debate under the auspices of *Woodwind Magazine* and the New York Flute Club. Not surprisingly, the student, who had graduated and moved to Arizona to teach Navajo children, wrote in to "bow humbly, as a student to a great master, and withdraw from the battle."[3]

Moyse's persona may have dazzled readers of the sincere little journal, but at Marlboro, a remote school whose New England–style, white clapboard buildings then housed about two hundred students, the man was working in relative obscurity, teaching a few raw beginners elementary skills such as scale playing and sight-singing. After all the Moyses had endured since the beginning of the war, they were grateful for modest positions and a home on the edge of the Green Mountains, where, Blanche said, "seasons happened at the times we expected them, and there were grass and trees, and nature that's friendly." In 1951, the Moyses bought a rambling, two-story house on Western Avenue in West Brattleboro, in which Marcel created a unique inner sanctum, a second-floor room transformed by paint and plywood into a rough-hewn Gothic chapel that today might be considered folk art. Moyse lined the walls with plyboard into which he sawed or carved Gothic arches, tracery, and other ornamentation; to the ceiling he nailed slabs of wood painted ultramarine blue and studded with signs of the zodiac. Every window, shelf, and cranny was crammed with memorabilia ranging from a picture of Taffanel to a reproduction of a bust of Nefertiti that Moyse painted bright canary yellow to match its shelf. (There was a yellow Venus de Milo, too.) In this space oddly reminiscent of both Église St. Amour and the bizarre studios of

Belle Époque artists, Moyse practiced and listened to opera records for hours, every day. The acoustics in the room were terrible. Students who took lessons there said the atmosphere was more important to him than resonance.

With Marlboro as a base, the Moyse Trio attempted to establish itself in the new country. Assisted by Serkin and Bernard R. LaBerge Management, a well-known agency that represented European artists in America, the group gave several tour concerts right away. In 1950 the Trio was hosted by such institutions as the New York Flute Club (29 January), the Boston Conservatory (8 February), the Library of Congress (10 March), and La Société Pro Musica Montréal (12 March). This itinerary, together with announcements of the Trio's work at Marlboro College, attracted the attention of immigration officials, and in their first American summer the Moyses were informed that their tourist visas had run out and everyone would be deported. The whole clan fled one more time— to Canada—while friends arranged to have them admitted legitimately at St. Albans, Vermont, as a family of educators. The following year the Trio appeared at such wide-flung events as the annual Bach Festival at Kalamazoo (2 March) and Tanglewood (25 July). In 1952 the Isabella Stewart Gardner Museum in Boston presented them (19 October), as did Cabell Hall Concerts in Charlottesville, Virginia (25 November). (The Moyses became U.S. citizens on 4 November 1959.)

Bernard LaBerge died soon after these tours began, and the fledgling firm of Colbert Artists immediately arranged with the manager's widow to take over LaBerge clients who needed representation. The Moyse Trio moved to Colbert's roster sometime in the 1951–52 season. Henry and Ann Colbert were new to the business and added the LaBerge name to theirs for prestige and to identify the members of LaBerge's stable. The Moyse Trio stuck with Colbert-LaBerge for a short time—a program from a 12 April 1953 concert at the Arts Club of Chicago indicates they were still receiving bookings—but they weren't entirely happy and talked of engaging new management. Yet when Moyse heard that Columbia Artists would require him to audition, he put an end to the idea. Naturally, Louis and Blanche would be asked to display their talents, he said, but Marcel Moyse was internationally recognized; to ask him to play under those circumstances was insulting.

At the same time, there were strong signs that the Trio might not be able to function much longer. Moyse suffered from frequent asthma attacks, and Blanche was frustrated by a persistent pain in her bowing arm that she later attributed to wrongful habits in posture and position formed when she was young. Perhaps in response to the possibility of permanent impairments, Moyse privately issued two original LPs, mastered in his own kitchen around 1954. The first, *The French School at Home,* featured excerpts of studies by Soussman, Fürstenau, Andersen, and Moyse. The second, *Tone Development Through Interpretation,* was a collection of opera melodies and movements from chamber works that he recorded with Louis or the Trio. Louis engineered the recordings (Discography nos. 199–221). Moyse later issued several albums of previously recorded music, transferred from 78s (see Discography, "Marcel Moyse Records, U.S.A.," under "X: Long-Playing Reissues").

By the mid-50s, the Moyse Trio concertized infrequently, mostly in Vermont at Marlboro or in association with the Brattleboro Music Center (BMC), a highly successful community music center Louis and Blanche had founded. The nucleus of the Center was a chorus, which Blanche directed. Louis accompanied and occasionally played flute under the BMC's auspices.[4] Marcel considered himself semi-retired as a performer ("I began to be the third member of the Trio," he said), and, disappointed with the lack of advanced students at Marlboro College, he resigned early, passing his handful of duties to his son and daughter-in-law. The Moyse Trio's last official public appearance was a Sunday afternoon recital at Marlboro on 30 June 1957.[5]

The question remains why no major conservatory grabbed Moyse after he arrived. The East Coast schools and orchestras had been raiding France's wind sections for decades; Laurent and Barrère had cinched an American tie to the French School long before, and had sent their students back to Paris to study. Yet Moyse was courted by no major institution, at least not in a manner he would have accepted. There were rumors that influential flutists felt he was a threat to their own studios. Some observers opined that Moyse lost potential support when the sixty-year-old *maître* failed to perform his best in the Moyse Trio's recital for the New York Flute Club, only three months after they had arrived in the United States (and some witnesses said he played very well). Others offered that a few key musicians sneered at the old-fashioned exercises and repertoire Moyse would undoubtedly insist on teaching, thus poisoning the idea for their impressionable students. Whatever the reason, Moyse did not take on a major-league professorship but encouraged his family's nesting instincts in Marlboro, and because he needed the income and wanted to establish himself, he created independent private studios in several cities, to which he commuted. His Manhattan studio developed a rather "underground" character because some of its regulars were also students of leading New York flutists who might have objected to an outside influence.

"It was pretty obvious there was a clamp on anyone there who recognized Moyse," said Marilyn Martin Wilson, who had come to work in Manhattan after studying with Moyse's former pupil Robert Cavally at the Cincinnati Conservatory. Wilson had sought Moyse on the recommendation of Cavally, and along with a few other devotees, spent an entire day each week in a Conservatoire-style class with the French master. Beginning in the spring of 1951, Moyse taught in a ground-floor studio apartment he had rented for the purpose on West Fifty-sixth Street, in the neighborhood where his daughter Marguerite had moved with her new husband, Bjorn Andreasson (violinist with the New York Philharmonic and son of Gösta Andreasson, second violinist of the Busch Quartet). Since Moyse was in town only on Fridays, he invited three flutists to live there practically rent-free, thus giving them an opportunity to live and study in a city they could not otherwise afford. The only hitch was that they had to clear the space for him on class day. The arrangement worked well for several years, although Marilyn Wilson remembers that some found it hard to remain free of educational and professional obligations during the entire class period, which ran six to eight hours. Moyse reprimanded those who ducked in and out too often. The Conservatoire system works, he said, because everyone listens to everyone's lessons. You learn from the examples of others—it is not enough to take your turn to play, then leave. Moyse might have added that the generous stretch of time gave him a chance to unravel and develop his ideas, nonstop, in front of an audience, without having to switch gears every hour. Occasionally he threw barbs at his students' teachers, who he felt could learn from him, too. "If Mr. Taffanel were alive today, I would go on my knees all the way to Philadelphia to take lessons from him again," he proclaimed.

Moyse also commuted to Boston and Montreal. In Boston he taught at the School for Contemporary Music; in Montreal he gave lessons at the Conservatoire de Musique. For a time he also taught at the Haynes Studio on West Fifty-first Street in New York and at the Hartt School of Music in Hartford, Connecticut. His former student Arthur Kitti, assistant principal flutist of the Chicago Symphony, brought him to Chicago in 1951 for three weeks of master classes.

Moyse was bitter over what he perceived as a unified snub by the major conservatories. But he was also energized by the idea that a few flutists were willing to discover him for themselves. He was sought out in three cities and—perhaps best of all—beholden to no institution. After many years of to-and-fro between Paris and Geneva, he still loved driving, and he usually hit New York and Boston in one outing.

Joe Cohen accompanied Moyse on many of the Boston–New York trips, rising with him at four or five o'clock in the morning on a Friday in time to make New York by midday. Moyse taught until eight o'clock in the evening without stopping for lunch. Cohen supplied him with sandwiches during the session and then took the wheel of his teacher's green Chevrolet for the mad dash to Boston, where Moyse worked the following morning. In the first hour northbound, Moyse would sit silently, thinking of the students he had just taught, recalling what he had assigned each one. Cohen knew to remain quiet until the process was completed. In the second hour, Moyse indicated when he was ready to converse. He spoke of music and flute playing, reminisced, complained about the past, and harped on the present. Cohen mostly listened. After Cohen left Vermont in 1954, Moyse brought Celine on the trips, and later his youngest granddaughter, Dominique (born to Louis and Blanche in October 1950), who was allowed to skip school a few times to go to New York with Pépé. Dominique still remembers the postwar highway landscape she and her grandparents regularly traversed:

> On the way, between Brattleboro and Wethersfield [Connecticut], there was a giant banana on the side of the road, and then there was a giant milk bottle! We always stopped for breakfast at the same Howard Johnson's in Wethersfield. All the waitresses knew my grandparents, and my grandfather always had an English muffin with marmalade. Then there was a Kinney's shoes, where my grandparents bought me my first pair of shiny

black shoes. And then we would count the bridges. My grandfather said there were eighty-two overhead bridges between
there and New York. So after eighty-two, we'd be in New York
and we'd stay with my aunt and her family. My grandfather gave
his music lessons, and my aunt and my grandmother yelled at
each other, and everyone had a wonderful time. Traveling
fifteen hours a weekend didn't bother my grandfather one iota.
He was just so self-sufficient. He didn't need the invasion of
other people's ideas, voices, opinions. He could sit behind the
wheel and drive, and all he asked was that my grandmother not
talk to him.[6]

By the late 1950s Moyse switched his New York base to an apartment with several rooms. And when Björn and Marguerite
Andreasson had a son and moved to a larger home in 1962, Marcel
relinquished his rented studio and, with little warning to his
daughter's family, commandeered his grandson Christophe's bed-
room for teaching. The New York lessons ended soon after. According to Marguerite, who dared not refuse her father the room (and
undoubtedly resented the imposition), there was a problem with
thin walls. "I got all kinds of little hints from my neighbors, and
finally complaints that it was not possible to have four hours of the
flute on Saturday mornings," she said. "We had to tell him to stop.
My mother took it very badly."

A few times during the 1950s, the Moyse family halfheartedly
entertained the idea of leaving Vermont. Once, Blanche and Louis
were invited to consider teaching at a girls' school in Connecticut.
The salaries were extravagant compared to those at Marlboro
College, but the couple turned down the offers. There were too
many rules and regulations for students and faculty. "When we
visited that school it was like being in a cage," Blanche recalled. "We
looked at each other, and knew we would never be able to stand that
atmosphere, never. We preferred being poor in a free place."
Indeed, Blanche and Louis seemed happily incapable of con-
forming to strict academic policies and valued the flexibility
Marlboro provided. Soon after settling in the U.S., they (and the rest
of the family) instituted annual August pilgrimages to St. Amour
(never Paris) that did not conclude until after Marlboro's fall term
had begun. At first no one said anything, but after a few students
and faculty complained, Blanche and Louis were informed they

would forfeit pay if they continued to miss the beginning of school. They weighed this information. After that, the Moyses sometimes returned on time and sometimes did not. Isabelle Moyse Craig remembers growing up with a sense that "we were all special; we should have special privileges."[7]

Moyse worked hard to develop his grass-roots, city studios during the winters, but his most important activities in terms of establishing his reputation in America lay with the fledgling summer Marlboro Music School and Festival, an enterprise separate from the music courses offered by the college during the academic year. When the Moyses first arrived, Adolf Busch spoke with them about the possibility of starting a summer chamber music retreat, an artistic oasis in which Adolf and Hermann Busch, "Rudi" Serkin, and the Moyses could make music together with a small, invited community of advanced students and professional players of like mind. The aim would be to exchange ideas and explore repertoire in a friendly setting, free of normal per-formance pressures. No one would be paid to play, and public per-formances would be the byproduct, not the goal, of rehearsals. As Louis Moyse put it, "There was a need for all of us to make music, at any cost."

Around March 1950, Marlboro College agreed to sponsor a summer music session based on Busch's ideas. There was no time to adequately publicize or organize the project, however, and when the student violist Philipp Naegele saw a tiny mimeographed notice about it on the bulletin board at the Yale School of Music, he was puzzled. "There were the names: Moyse, Busch, Serkin," he recalled, sitting under a tree at Marlboro in 1991. "And I said to myself, 'Wait a minute—what's going on here?' "

Naegele wrote to Marlboro College for information but received no reply, so he asked his parents, who knew Hermann Busch indirectly, to inquire for him. The message came back, "Tell him to come."

"I was picked up at the train station in Brattleboro and brought to the college," he remembered.

> And in the dining hall sat the family Moyse, with Marcel and Louis drinking Pernod, Blanche pregnant [with Dominique] and Hermann well into several beers. They were having a plan-ning session as to what they could possibly do, because almost

no one had been recruited. A few people drove up, looked around, figured this was not for real, and left. And the Moyses told me, "Just be patient. Adolf will come tomorrow and we'll arrange something." And the something was that Hermann Busch borrowed a car and his daughter Trudy drove me and her father to Adolf's twice a week to play chamber music. That was my chamber music course for the summer.[8]

Philipp Naegele was the lone string student at Marlboro in 1950, a summer so hastily organized that the Marlboro Music School and Festival does not count it as year one, even though a catalog exists for it. A few pianists and flutists wandered in to study with Serkin and Moyse (including Arthur Kitti's student Darlene Rhodus Tillack, who went to New York to work with Moyse and then became the first of a long line of flutists who moved to Brattleboro for year-round study). But there were not enough players to form good ensembles. A handful of public concerts were presented under the banner of the Marlboro Music Festival, including one by the Moyse Trio on Sunday, 2 July, that featured *MOYSIANA,* a duet for two flutes on the names Marcel, Louis, and Moyse, by André Thiriet. The musical name themes are printed in the program, notated on tiny staves. The following year (1951 — considered the official beginning of the summer school and festival) more players showed up. Counting the resident artists, there were fifty-four participants. Eight were flutists who had come to study with Moyse. Nine more played oboe, clarinet, bassoon, or horn. Voilà! *Le maître* could coach woodwind quintets.

Marlboro's concerts that summer included student wind players in works like the Mozart Quintet (K. 452), the Schubert Octet, and the Haydn Concerto for flute in D major (Hob. VIIf:1) with Joe Cohen as soloist. Marcel and Louis Moyse also played the Cimarosa Concerto with a small orchestra conducted by Adolf Busch. Some of the most memorable music-making of the early years never reached the ears of the public. After supper in the dining hall of Marlboro College, the Busch-Serkin Trio frequently indulged in Strauss waltzes. Everyone danced, all were exuberant, especially Busch, whom Louis described as a perfectionist in his own playing, a deep musician, yet "the kind of man who'd invite anybody—an amateur—to play duets. It didn't matter if someone played a wrong note or played a little out of pitch; he didn't care.

What was important was to be expressive through music, and enjoy it." Once in 1951, Serkin engaged some local folk fiddlers for polkas and square dancing; the same summer the festival staged an informal fest affectionately dubbed "Circus Busch" (also the name of a famous circus in Germany). Everyone converged on the dining hall in costume, and Serkin played marches on the piano.

The summer of 1952 marked an early turning point in the festival. Adolf Busch died on 9 June. On Sunday, 13 July, Rudolf Serkin delivered the first concert of the season, opening with Busch's Piano Sonata in C minor, Opus 25. Serkin was joined by Hermann Busch in the Beethoven D Major Cello Sonata; the program closed with Beethoven's Piano Sonata in E major, Opus 109. It was a fitting tribute.

The loss saddened everyone. Without Adolf Busch's guiding spirit, how would the festival proceed? Serkin and Moyse had always deferred to Busch. Now there was a vacuum, a need for someone to take charge. For about two years, Blanche took responsibility for running Marlboro, until "Rudi," who was closest to Busch and in the prime of his career, emerged, perhaps reluctantly, as artistic director. The move was not without tension; the Moyses understandably preferred to see Blanche in charge. Marcel had no designs on the post himself; at that point he had no desire to exercise the diplomatic skills necessary to lead a growing institution, and by the family lawyer's account, the flutist had no patience for business details, which may explain why he seldom balanced his checkbook and often suspected and accused people of owing him money. Moyse was not interested in managing anything. Instead, he walled himself off from the rest of the campus by building (with his own hands) at the edge of the grounds a stocky practice and teaching cabin of four-by-fours, bolted together and reinforced so well that, in the words of his grandson Michel, "if you drove fifteen tanks into it, it would remain standing."

What Moyse did want from the Marlboro community was recognition of his stature and respect for his ideas, and the degree to which he was acknowledged by Serkin and others came to directly affect his contentment there. That contentment came and went in cycles, in response to both musical and philosophical differences he experienced with his colleagues and to minor incidents and encounters around campus that he perceived, correctly or incorrectly, as personal slights. What seemed to bother him most at

Marlboro was what he called the "second-rate" treatment of wind music and wind players. The strings and piano have the richest literature, he acknowledged. But the winds can be just as expressive in their own repertoire, and transform it, make it much more exciting than some tired rendition of Brahms. Why, he asked more and more, was this not acknowledged in the programming, and in the way in which he was regarded as an artist?

Marlboro retained the light and color of Busch's original vision throughout the 1950s. News of the little utopia spread, and enrollment swelled to eighty or more musicians in the second part of the decade. Some of the first young players to take a chance on the secluded Vermont workshop became prominent artists. Pianist Anton Kuerti and violinist Sylvia Rosenberg were both fifteen years old when they came to Marlboro in 1951. Bernard Garfield, who became principal bassoonist of the Philadelphia Orchestra, was there at the start, as was Harold Wright, the future principal clarinetist in Boston. Concert pianists such as Gary Graffman, Claude Frank, Lee Luvisi, Van Cliburn, Malcolm Frager, Richard Goode, Eugene Istomin, Gilbert Kalish, and Leon Fleisher spent summers there. The strings included such world-class chamber musicians as violinists Felix Galimir (Galimir Quartet) and Arnold Steinhardt (Guarneri Quartet); violists Walter Trampler (New Music Quartet, Yale Quartet, Chamber Music Society of Lincoln Center) and Michael Tree (Guarneri Quartet); and cellist Leslie Parnas (founder, Chamber Music Society of Lincoln Center). Leading wind players such as hornists Myron Bloom (Cleveland Orchestra) and Richard Mackey (Boston); oboist Alfred Genovese (Metropolitan Opera, Boston Symphony); clarinetists Richard Waller (Cincinnati Symphony) and Andrew Crisanti (Fort Worth Symphony); and bassoonists Jane Taylor (Dorian Quintet) and Arthur Weisberg (New York Woodwind Quintet, Contemporary Chamber Ensemble) were part of this extraordinary mix.

In 1955, the French baritone Martial Singher, a veteran of the Opéra, was invited to establish a vocal program at Marlboro. The following year, violinist Alexander Schneider, who had just begun his second tenure with the Budapest Quartet, was asked to participate. With Felix Galimir already in residence, Schneider's presence might have been discomforting to Blanche, who continued to deal with her arm ailment. Marcel grew jealous of the attention Serkin and the students paid Schneider, who had collaborated with Pablo

Casals at Prades and was very influential on the New York string scene. Moyse wanted notoriety for himself and tried to distance himself from Schneider, to show that he was different.

Moyse was not doing badly; he drew so many flutists to Marlboro that the festival admitted many more than were necessary to populate ensembles. In the early years there were at least twice as many flutists as any other species of wind instrumentalist. Every week, each one attended a flute class, a woodwind class, and a private flute lesson. The most advanced players were assigned to mixed chamber ensembles that met two or three times a week and were coached by an older professional, usually Moyse. In the beginning, Moyse's standards for acceptance to Marlboro were not very selective. The higher the numbers, he felt, the faster his reputation would spread, and Louis was on hand to teach the less gifted players. The patience he had begun to develop in Paris with novices like Geneviève Noufflard was tested frequently, but he was more than content to work from the ground up if the student submitted completely to his instruction; he was even happier if the student was pretty. Most of his American flute classes were female, as opposed to the overwhelmingly male enrollment at the Conservatoire. Yet some of the early notables in the Marlboro flute classes were men such as Karl Kraber (Dorian Quintet), Bernard Goldberg (principal, Pittsburgh Symphony), and the Canadian concert artist Robert Aitken. *Maître*—as everyone called Moyse—managed a summer load of twenty to twenty-two hours a week.

As word of Moyse's woodwind coaching got around, more and more oboists, clarinetists, bassoonists, and hornists applied to Marlboro. In 1959, for example, there were twenty-nine wind players on campus, more than enough for a Mahler symphony. Some, like Harold Wright and Alfred Genovese, were Philadelphia friends of Joe Cohen, former members of the Symphony Club, the free music school for gifted students founded by the yarn manufacturer and music patron Edwin A. Fleisher.[9] Moyse was particularly fond of them, partly because they seemed predisposed to Moyse's approach from their work with the oboist Marcel Tabuteau at the Curtis Institute of Music.[10] Tabuteau was as vociferous a coach as Moyse; he often taught private students in his apartment at the Drake Hotel, close to Curtis, and it is said that the master's exhortations could be heard down the hall and in the street. Tabuteau also took over the string ensemble classes at Curtis during the war, and many string players who were coached successfully by Moyse at Marlboro had worked with the oboist. Violinist Diana Steiner, a Curtis graduate who first went to Marlboro in 1951, said, "They were both 'madmen' in the French style."

In contrast, Roland Small, who at this writing plays second bassoon with the Boston Symphony, was one of many Moyse disciples who came from less sophisticated backgrounds. Small had grown up in Dayton and read about Moyse in *Woodwind Magazine*. To the teenager trained within the roar of a school band, Moyse's breadth of musical expression was a revelation, while *le maître*'s pipe, Pernod, and throaty accent demonstrated the cultural possibilities beyond Ohio. Darlene Rhodus Tillack, a Marlboro participant in 1950, 1952, 1954, and 1955, said Moyse's flute sound so overwhelmed her on first hearing that she unconsciously tore all the corners from the music she held in her lap.

The poetic, spontaneous musical thought Moyse had dispersed at the Paris Conservatoire underwent a second flowering at Marlboro in direct relation to the waning of his performance career. In Paris, a certain efficiency had characterized his studio, and though he was well known for his ideas, particularly his devotion to operatic style, Moyse was so busy playing that his gifts as a teacher were only partly revealed. However, with the loss of his ability to play in public, Moyse, the quintessential autodidact, had the time and freedom to turn every musical question over and over, like colored rocks in a stream.

Musicians who studied with Moyse in the 1950s describe a man who was bent on a mission of cracking dull heads and bogus traditions in order to release the instinctual, sensuous beauty of music. One of his favorite mottos was "There is no bad music, only bad musicians." Moyse accomplished his goals in several ways, according to his analysis of the student in question and the presence or absence of a class audience ("It is all *psychologie,*" he said). First, he continued to play for students. "His playing had an enormous octane level," Philipp Naegele recalled. "That was inspiring. He never made a sound that was routine. He never let anything happen that wasn't experienced." Moyse also used metaphors, stories, singing, physical gestures, praise, and humiliation to stimulate his pupils. Many examples of these devices became stock-in-trade Moyseisms, repeated for new listeners (and imitated affectionately behind his back) over the next thirty years, but no less animated or effective than the thousandth rendition of a classic fairy tale or ghost story that continues to move each new generation of youngsters. Few students fail to recall his description of the low register of the flute. "It is like a mayonnaise," he insisted—the best, homemade kind in which the richest farm-grown ingredients separate from the rest and ease to the bottom of the jar. Lush low notes, Moyse said, like thick ingredients, must be spooned up deliciously from the bottom.

In a spiritual sense, Moyse returned to a youthful, self-centered state of wonder. The innocence of the simplest folk melody visibly delighted him more than ever, a chugging little accompaniment made him laugh. He expressed his emotional reactions to music verbally and physically, as delicately or flamboyantly as he would on the flute. Of Moyse's relationship to other human beings, including his family, his daughter-in-law said, "He did not communicate *with* people—he communicated *himself* to people." This need to express, to constantly pour forth with little concern for the reactions of those on the receiving end, was undeniably selfish. It was also at the heart of his charisma. "When Moyse held on to you, it was like being grabbed by a baby," explained Alex Ogle, a long-time student. "You know how babies are—they grasp you completely." Surrounded by a devoted family for which he no longer had to provide, Moyse gained a kind of authority and magnetism that would be impossible to sustain in any other environment. For those who were caught up with building careers, he became a touchstone, a point of reference for the feelings that had drawn them to music in the first place.

So out flowed the images of St. Amour. A Mozart tune and its echo were two birds calling to one another across a meadow. The high point of a melody was bright and lofty as a red-tiled village roof or a shining star. A perky allegro evoked a country festival ablaze with color. Students as far back as 1950 still recall their favorites, which they often recorded in diaries and notebooks. In an ornamented line of Bach, Moyse said, the melodic notes should gleam through the ornaments, "like the sunlight shining through the trees." The individual notes of a buoyant accompaniment in a Reicha wind quintet had to bounce along "like rubber balls," whereas the soft underpinnings of the Mozart E-flat Wind Serenade's Adagio were to be played "like a rumor" whispered around town. The flute's cloudy middle E, Moyse lamented, is "like a fish—it slips!"

There were strong emotional images, archaic and naive. Appoggiaturas were meant to evoke the weeping of Greek women. A minor-key adagio was the voice of a young farmer who missed his wife. To demonstrate the strength of emotion he sought, Moyse might sing an entire etude with the words "je t'aime—oui—je t'aime." To a young female who played woodenly, he would sidle up and whisper, "Do you have a boyfriend?" A nod, a pause. "Do you like to kiss him?" A nod, perhaps a shiver, and another, more successful attempt at expressivity. If a player grew frustrated trying to achieve a beautiful sound on a particular note, Moyse might cajole her into affection and patience for the troublesome tone. "You *love* your B! You *love* your B!" he would repeat encouragingly. The breath taken before a final phrase was to be executed as "a souvenir," a memory. There were gestural metaphors. Rough playing reminded him of a child pulling the limbs off a doll. A performer was supposed to phrase "like a fencer, not a boxer."

In addition to these brief images, Moyse used lengthy stories to communicate musical concepts. Some of these were extended, nature metaphors; others were human sagas. The entire exposition of a concerto might be described, phrase by phrase, as a walk in the woods, complete with changes in weather and terrain and encounters with animals. A happy event or a tragedy (birth, death) could be woven deftly within the melody, harmony, and rhythm of a sonata movement as if the music had been created to accompany a film Moyse watched in his head. *Le maître* also drew on two kinds of memories from his life in Paris. If the students at hand were flutists, he was most inclined to worshipfully recall the attributes of his teachers—Hennebains, Taffanel, and Gaubert—and to scatter quotes from his lessons with them, especially Taffanel. He recited anecdotes from experiences with great musicians such as Stravinsky, Ravel, Debussy, and Toscanini, not just to offer musical insight, but to establish his own authority as an important member of that generation. Moyse also reminisced about life in Paris: late-night discussions of art in Montmartre cafés, glamorous concert-goers at the Salle Favart, the holy mission of the Conservatoire.

Moyse loved to joke in class, to make a point for a favored student or just savor the limelight. Once, after Karl Kraber completed a quick, nervous rendition of a particularly lengthy work, Moyse looked at him matter-of-factly and asked, "Kraber, aren't you driving to New York this afternoon?" "Yes, *Maître,*" came the answer. "If you drive like you play," said Moyse, "you'll be dead before you get to Massachusetts. Go back to the beginning again." Everyone laughed, and the second performance was far more relaxed. Another time, a young woman who was painfully con- scious of historical performance practices questioned Moyse's use of vibrato in Bach. "This man had twenty-two children—and you think he wouldn't want vibrato?" Moyse shot back with a wink. Moyse couldn't help being entertaining. Everyone who studied the Dvořák Serenade with him one particular year remembers the time he pulled off his beret in the middle of a run-through to reveal a large, stinky wedge of cheese perched on his scalp. Moyse con- tinued waving his arms in time to the music until the entire group dissolved in laughter.

Not every moment was magic or fun. Moyse's temper erupted frequently when he wanted to shake or shock a student or when he was genuinely angry or disgusted with something. The trick was to figure out how one really stood during a typical Moyse barrage. Nearly every former student recalls his telling someone that he or she "played like shit." A student who did not catch on to him should "go tend cows." An insensitive musician was told, "You play like a Nazi!" Other exclamations such as "You know nothing! Nothing about music!" or (with a great shrug and a shake of the head) "Nothing to do! Nothing to do!" provoked and perplexed the victims, who doubled their efforts or failed to show up the following summer. Some disciples backed up everything he said. Eleanor Lawrence, who worked with Moyse in the 1960s, said, "Many of my own students who worked with him were enraged over what they considered cruelties, but I never heard him say anything that I didn't feel was justified. Going to a Moyse seminar was like submit- ting to a litmus test—you could almost see his nose turn blue!"

Moyse always communicated with his body, in action and at rest. Often, he listened to pupils while seated, silent and expres- sionless, with his eyes closed. Those who did not know better were certain he was asleep. Raymond Benner, a Marlboro regular throughout the 50s and former associate principal bass of the Detroit Symphony, declared Moyse's presence had a "mysterious quality—even when he said nothing, he made you play better. He let the silence work." A pupil might have completed a movement of a piece or an entire concerto before Moyse registered any response; by then, the room would be so tense with anticipation that anything he said had enormous impact. Moyse might utter flatly, "You play well," and—after sensing everyone's relief—launch into a rigorous coaching of the work, phrase by phrase. But he was just as apt to deliver a withering assessment. More than once, his first remark after a new student's performance was a question: "Who is your teacher?" When the student gave the name, Moyse pronounced simply, "He is robber."

Some class meetings never had a moment of silence. Moyse could be totally animated from the start, interrupting a student's attempts over and over again with advice or exhortations, singing along in a gravelly baritone that wavered with emotion. If the repertoire was operatic, Moyse was more likely to treat his classroom as a stage. When he conducted a chamber group, his arms slashed downward, as if he were flagging race cars. He loved props and used anything at hand: a hat, a scarf, his pipe. Once he even employed his own flute by flinging it across the room at a student who had the impudence (or naïveté) to inquire whether he should perform his assigned piece in the style of William Kincaid, Julius Baker, or Laurent.[11] "Of course," added Albert Genovese, who witnessed the incident, "Moyse was careful to throw the flute so it landed in a chair, unharmed."

Most students clearly remember Moyse's face, the eyes in particular. "There were three things that you could read in them," said one: "Moyse's perception of you as a person, his reaction to your music-making, and his absolute will to change you." It isn't surprising that the American students who performed best under his supervision submitted themselves entirely to his judgment. Some became devoted acolytes who carried Moyse's music or ran errands for him. Many of his favorites happened to speak French; Moyse took a long time to learn English and always slipped back into his native language when he could not find the right words to convey his meaning. Talented students who could understand him in either language had an advantage.

If Moyse was hell-bent on communicating his musical ideals, he had no desire to explain, technically, how music should be played on the flute or any other instrument. His approach was entirely through the eyes, ears, and heart, which is why some pupils, especially those still grappling with the physical challenges of keys, mouthpieces, and their own breathing apparatus did not feel comfortable with him and, in some cases, developed bad habits in their efforts to produce the effects he wanted. When Moyse had exhausted his possibilities for improving these players, he gave up, usually in a blunt fashion that still contained a sliver of his message: "There is nothing I can teach you," he would say. "Go out and watch the sunset." Or he might, without comment, play an opera record, as if that were all that was left to demonstrate what he meant. Those who were successful under Moyse sent their own protégés to him only when they had become technically proficient. Moyse, as the embodiment of a heightened, natural musical spirit, was ideal as a finishing school, not as a tutor of instrumental skills. "He was always trying to get us off the earth, to shoot for something unreachable—and trying for that was the great adventure," said Raymond Benner. "He was a teacher for everybody. The instrument didn't matter. He was a teacher of music."

CHAPTER NINE

Expanding the Legend

IN 1959, Marcel Moyse became an American citizen. He could look back on a performing career of more than thirty years and a lifetime of teaching: four decades in France and one in the United States. His contact with France consisted of summer visits to St. Amour, correspondence with a few former students, and pension payments from the government.[1] The last time he saw any French flutists was in 1953, when the band of the Garde Républicaine de Paris, led by Moyse's student François-Julien Brun, toured the U.S. (One of the band's soloists was another former pupil, Henri Lebon, featured in an arrangement of the Fauré *Fantaisie.*) Moyse's Paris colleagues were long retired or deceased, and most young French flutists were not even aware he was alive. Some of Moyse's exercise books continued to sell in his home country, but *le maître* was mostly a historical figure to the students of Jean-Pierre Rampal, who took over the Paris Conservatoire flute class when Crunelle retired. For a long time, no one from France came to Vermont in search of Moyse, and he delighted in his American pupils, whom he began to praise as superior to the French.

Nevertheless, except for the musicians who had stumbled across the Marlboro experience, the American musical community of the 1950s, which revolved around a handful of conservatories and orchestras, barely knew Moyse was available. Some artists of his vintage might have accepted complete retirement, but because Moyse was far from his original milieu and endowed with a stubborn will to make an impact, he maintained a messianic urge to teach—to anyone who would listen—what music in the pre-electronic age had been about, before everyone on earth was seduced by cold speed and clutter.

By the late 50s Marlboro had stabilized and begun to flourish under Serkin's guidance. A recording program with Columbia Records inaugurated in 1957 helped publicize the fine work being done in idyllic seclusion, and Moyse conducted one of the earliest productions, the Beethoven Octet, Opus 103 (Discography no. 223), which helped promote his reputation as a chamber-music coach. Moyse did not conduct so much as drive and cajole his players with hand gestures, eye contact, and the intensity of his presence. The energy is palpable on disk; it is as if in putting down the flute, Moyse simply picked up another instrument, one with multiple mouthpieces and a hundred keys.

As a leader of mixed instrumental ensembles in Marlboro concerts, Moyse was most visible in 1959, when he directed eight works: the Mozart Sinfonia Concertante in E-flat major, K. 297b; the Beethoven Octet in B-flat, Opus 103; the Cimarosa Concerto in G for two flutes (with Louis Moyse and Ornulf Gulbransen); Richard Strauss's Sonatine No. 1 for sixteen winds; Mozart's Serenade No. 10 in B-flat, K. 361, and Concerto No. 4 in E-flat for horn, K. 495 (with Myron Bloom); Ravel's *Introduction et Allegro* for flute, clarinet, harp, and strings; and the Stravinsky Octet.

Even so, Moyse grumbled increasingly about his situation at Marlboro. His complaints usually had to do with administrative foibles and the feeling that he, as a wind player, was not given as much respect and attention as the senior string participants. A rehearsal schedule posted without his input could throw him into a rage, and he was unhappy when Serkin deferred to Alexander Schneider on artistic matters. Moyse did not fume silently, but indulged in bitter asides to students and friends. He also expressed himself in letters, such as a lengthy one he wrote to Serkin in September 1958. The epistle, drafted in Moyse's birdlike script on lined paper, includes all sorts of grievances, from unpleasant comments about Schneider's influence to a balanced, well-thought-out list of suggestions for improving the festival's administration, including establishing rehearsal schedules further in advance and mailing the summer catalogue earlier than Tanglewood and Aspen.

"Each year the quantity of stupid incidents, bruised egos, failures of tact, etc. make the atmosphere of the school more and more heavy," Moyse concluded unhappily in the letter. "Work becomes more and more painful. The wind instrument department is more difficult to direct." Still, the remarks contained in the letter were, he insisted, "inspired by love of music, love of the school, the affection I have for you, and by the desire to pursue in America my musical ideal, in a school which I would still like to consider as mine."[2]

Raymond Meylan, a Moyse student who warmly accepted his teacher's greatness as an artist and his shortcomings as a human being, received a lamentation from Moyse in 1959 and offered this advice in return:

> I have heard you complain several times about the decline of the musical world, speaking of the masters that you have known, and despairing whether any new ones will rise up. It's a very natural sentiment, but as has been proven in all periods, [greatness] must result from the evolution of style in general. We can't judge future tastes (imagine Beethoven judged by the aesthetic of Bach). It's necessary then to content yourself with excellence within, and to offer the most brilliant message possible.
>
> I truly believe that you have realized a career of the first order. Therefore, why don't you drop these bitter judgements. . . . Keep a tranquil heart. Little by little the diffusion of your school is on one hand a sign of your excellence, and on the other, the sign of an expanding musical world.[3]

In another letter, Raymond Meylan added to previous message:

> You shouldn't wait for your disciples to be identical to you. Something of your work can be found everywhere, like an element of civilization. You can be happy that your school has overflown the borders of France and is now in Germany; even the Italians follow it. The records, the rapidity of exchange, the radio—all contribute to create a musical Europe with less dif—ferentiated regions. And in this new world, it is really your school which is on top.[4]

Around that time Moyse issued privately on LP a group of his best recorded performances from the 1920s and 1930s. Perhaps hoping to revive his name in France, he sent one of his self-produced records to Jean-Pierre Rampal; and in July 1959, Rampal replied, thanking him for the gift and praising his work: "Even though I have never worked under the direction of Moyse, I have always had the deepest admiration for his inspired talent. You can be sure that his distance does not prevent him from being present in the hearts of flutists."[5]

Moyse also continued to foster ties with his Swiss students such as Aurèle Nicolet, who had left the Berlin Philharmonic to pursue a career as soloist, recording artist, and teacher. Recuperating from an operation one year, Nicolet posted a long letter that Moyse must have appreciated. In it he wrote:

> I know several French players of the "new school" of Rampal, etc., whose technique and facility I admire, but I always have the impression I am searching for something other than what they look for. I feel myself nourished from another tradition, coming from another school. Once I was a member of a jury with Crunelle. He told me how much he admired you, and we agreed that although the technical level of the current candidates is extremely high, it is rare to hear a flutist who is sensitive to color and beauty of sound, and who uses his means toward the service of expression.
>
> The things you made me work on are always at the base of my teaching, and I love this work, which is perpetual creation and the best personal discipline. I'm lucky to have lots of pupils, and many talented ones. One of those who gives me the most satisfaction is a young Frenchman, from Besancon. . . .
>
> I would also like to say, that even after fourteen years I am still so full of your remarks, perceptions, images, expressions that all of them spring involuntarily in each lesson that I give, in each musical phrase that I play. . . . Thanks to you, the expression of the flute has gone beyond the pretty and the gracious, it has become frank. I am trying to disseminate this heritage well, and to make it known.[6]

As gratifying as these communiqués from Europe must have been, Moyse remained sour on Marlboro and threatened to quit several times. What pushed him to the edge was the entrance of the great cellist-turned-conductor Pablo Casals, whom Serkin invited to Marlboro in 1960.

Casals was eighty-four that year, Moyse seventy-one. Of the two, Casals had the more visible musical reputation as an artist, plus a general image as a humanitarian and political activist that sprang from his public stands. During World War II he had made headlines by refusing to perform in Nazi-dominated countries. He also played concerts in France to benefit the Red Cross and his fellow Catalan exiles, and in 1946, refused to play in any country that recognized the Franco regime. After the war Casals created his important music festival at Prades to commemorate the Bach bicentenary, the forerunner of the annual festivals in Puerto Rico. Unlike Moyse, who preferred seclusion in St. Amour and Vermont, Pablo Casals was comfortable with a sort of international citizenship that gilded his activism and attracted top musicians and patrons of the arts. He also enjoyed close professional ties with Serkin and Schneider. Marlboro's administration undoubtedly hoped Casals's participation would create more interest and financial support for the festival.

The *Brattleboro Reformer*'s 6 July account of the 1960 season's first concert reflected the changed, more celebrity-conscious atmosphere brought about by Casals's presence. The review opened with notes on the virtuoso's appearance in the audience and his upcoming activities at Marlboro as cello teacher and chamber-music coach.

"It is not certain that the world-celebrated cellist will make any professional appearances before the public," the reporter wrote. "When he entered the concert hall just before the opening number on Sunday's program, the audience gave Casals a spontaneous and thunderous ovation."

And following laudatory comments on the reading of a Mozart string quartet and a group of Fauré songs (rendered by the baritone Martial Singher, a young quartet, and the seventeen-year-old pianist Richard Goode), the reviewer praised the efforts of another senior musician:

> Perhaps the most popular and most fascinating item on the program was the concluding number, the rarely-heard Octet for Winds in E-flat, Opus 103, by Beethoven. This was performed under the baton of Marcel Moyse, the uniquely gifted director,

one of the original founders of the Marlboro Festival. The work
was played with dash, brilliance, nuance, and a keen perception verging on delicate humor which brought down the house
and won such thunderous and insistent applause that the final
movement had to be repeated.[7]

Marlboro regulars from that time recall that Casals was treated
with a deference they had never witnessed there before; a few feel he
was exploited. Pablo Casals became the first musician to receive
generous pay at Marlboro, a situation that a former board member
admits generated bad feelings. Someone was always pulling out his
chair, parking his car, waiting with an umbrella when the maestro
needed to walk from the studio to the dining hall in the rain. The
Marlboro audience, which was increasingly made up of vacationing devotees from New York, Connecticut, and Massachusetts,
was enamored of him, and concerts began selling out well in
advance. The press was frequently on hand, and the Marlboro story
began to receive the depth of coverage reserved for institutions,
not experiments. After ten years with no superstars, Marlboro
suddenly had one. But for all the advantages Casals brought, a
number of participants and observers felt his celebrity marked a
shift in the utopian atmosphere originally sought by Adolf Busch.

Moyse had worked assiduously to preserve his niche as self-
styled patriarch of Marlboro. Being eclipsed by Casals was hard to
take, and although Moyse respected the cellist as a musician, he did
not hide his irritation with the publicity machine. Serkin, whose
temperament was nearly the inverse of Moyse's, quietly sought a
way to demonstrate that *le maître* was important to Marlboro
without sacrificing his own goals for the festival. He was aware that
the more selective enrollment policy recently instituted would rule
out the overflow of flutists who had flocked to Marlboro in the 50s,
and he knew that Moyse could no longer manage his outpost
studios in New York and Boston. Serkin felt it was necessary to fill
the gap for his friend; he cared about Moyse and wanted to maintain harmony in the Marlboro community. Frank Salomon, who
joined the administration in 1960, recalled that "Serkin felt that
Moyse, Casals, and Schneider all had something special to offer
Marlboro, and Moyse was in a category of his own." So in 1961,
when a group of five woodwind players who had been turned down
by Marlboro convened in Brattleboro anyway and asked Moyse to

coach them independently, the festival administration offered to help organize the situation.

Tony Checchia, a Curtis graduate and former Marlboro bassoonist who had been taught by Moyse and worked in the Marlboro office, took on the project. Checchia understood Moyse as well as anyone. His own father was an immigrant, the same age as the flutist. "One had to take into consideration the cultural background, the expectations of a European," he explained. Checchia was also a warm, thoughtful diplomat, someone the entire Moyse family trusted. His offer to run the new woodwind "seminars" was a master stroke that helped ease the tension between Moyse and Serkin and gave the flutist room to expand his reach.

The 1961 coachings of the upstart wind quintet were held in the kitchen of a garage apartment rented by bassoonist Roland Small, two houses up Western Avenue from the Moyse manse. The atmosphere was casual, and hours were long. Refreshments, including Pernod, were served, and after an exhausting session Moyse would unwind in a monologue of memories. The following year, with Checchia's assistance, Moyse offered two seminars, one for woodwinds and one for flutes. Each ran for about a week, separately, and took place before Marlboro's season opened. The format roughly followed that of Moyse's Paris Conservatoire classes. Players attended one three-hour session a day and frequently convened around Moyse in the evenings as he held forth on Paris, opera, his teachers, and musical ideals. During the 1960s, most of the seminars took place in a music studio at Marlboro College. Later they were held in St. Michael's Episcopal Church (1970–71); Moyse's boxy living room with its monstrous billiard table (1972); Michel Moyse's painting shed (1977–81 and 1984); Dalem's Chalet, a motel (1982); and the West Village Meeting House (1983).

During the years in Michel's unheated studio, a scholarship was awarded to a flutist willing to arrive early and fire up the wood stove, and someone was usually assigned to drive Moyse to and from the sessions because *le maître*'s driver's license was usually in a state of animated suspension from a speeding ticket or fender bender. (At one point the state tried to revoke Moyse's license for good, but his lawyer proved successfully that the elderly flutist couldn't earn a living without it.) The students stayed in rooming houses, motel rooms, apartments—whatever accommodations could be rounded up each year—and lived nearly like monks, attending class and practicing constantly, staging a few late-night poker games for sanity. Moyse's seminars were intense retreats, where players willingly blocked out all other concerns and lived only for music and *le maître*. Looking back later, Moyse explained his goals: "I knew there were many people of technical talent in America who lived very far from musical centers, and I made a course that would give them the principles of music, or of the flute, as I was trained in the school of Taffanel, Hennebains, and Gaubert. Voilà!"[8]

The first year a flute seminar was offered, a twenty-one-year-old Juilliard student named Paula Robison mailed in her registration, packed her bags, and headed for Brattleboro like a pilgrim racing toward the Promised Land. She had discovered Moyse in the typical way: a friend who had gone to Marlboro told her he was really and truly "alive and well and living in Vermont."

"I play the flute because of him," she says now.

> It was his recording of the Mozart D Major Concerto that my father used to listen to; he was always haunted by the sound. Then when I was ten or eleven, I started to play. I always heard Moyse's name, but I didn't know he was alive any more. My teacher gave me his books to work with. Still, Moyse was just a legend, a magical name to me.[9]

At Juilliard, Robison studied happily with Julius Baker, but, she said, "There was something poetic I was searching for—something spiritual." When she learned Moyse occasionally taught in New York, she joined his outpost class, but, like others who studied with Moyse on the side, did not inform her "official" teacher. "Some teachers feel very strongly that their students shouldn't take lessons with anyone else," she reflected. "But if someone who is studying with me wants to go work with someone else, I think that's great. Any way a student can achieve enlightenment is fine."

In her first New York flute lesson with Moyse, Robison was spellbound by his musicianship and personality. "Even though he was no longer playing publicly, there was so much energy in his sound that your whole being was drawn to it," she said, echoing the impressions of others who had come before her. "Someone said he could get music out of a stone. It was really true."

In 1961, Robison made a highly successful New York debut under the auspices of Young Concert Artists, and the following summer she was in Moyse's first flute seminar. The next season she took part in the Marlboro Festival, where she was a regular for eight years (see Figure 24). In 1966 Robison became the first American flutist to win the Geneva International Competition, which brought her a solo performance with the Orchestre de la Suisse Romande and other opportunities that ensured a fine, visible career. Her acknowledgement of Moyse in the midst of her success played no small part in advertising *le maître*'s existence in America.

Word of the flute and woodwind seminars spread quickly through other channels, too. Prominent orchestral musicians and college and university teachers began to take part, then send their students. Another link to Moyse's growing popularity was the 1962 publication of what became Moyse's most widely used, signature exercise book, *Tone Development Through Interpretation,* a compendium of opera arias and instrumental melodies, all lifelong favorites that Moyse used for "the study of expression, vibrato, color, suppleness, and their application to different styles."[10] Also, the press continued to play a role. Of a Marlboro concert on 4 August 1962, *New York Times* critic Alan Rich wrote:

> Something of a miracle took place at the beginning of last night's chamber concert at the Marlboro Music Festival. An octet of wind players at the center here was conducted by Marcel Moyse in Mozart's Wind Serenade in E-flat, and the result was the kind of playing this listener never expected to hear this side of heaven.

Rich then described the sense of style the seventy-three-year-old musician achieved with players of divergent backgrounds, "a kind of sonority from the group that was astonishing in its mellow smoothness." Moyse "imparted to the players an elegance of phrasing that made Mozart's slight entertainment sound like a masterpiece."[11]

By the mid-60s, two woodwind quintets and fifteen flutists were on the seminar books. (Afternoon classes began on the late side, at three o'clock instead of two to accommodate Moyse's addiction to the TV soap opera "As the World Turns.") Admission was granted on a first-come, first-served basis, and there was always a long waiting list. Those who inquired too late were invited to audit the classes for a lower fee, but, said oboist Pat Grignet Nott, who took over the administration of the woodwind seminars from Tony Checchia in 1970, "If someone wasn't willing to audit, he didn't want to hear about them when a participant spot opened up. He said if you're not willing to listen, then you don't understand what this is all about." Indeed, the auditors usually outnumbered the participants, and in the busiest years, the seminar site required a rented portable toilet. Flutists were expected to bring etudes by Boehm, Fürstenau, Soussman, Berbiguer, Andersen, and Moyse, plus solo works like the Bach sonatas, a Quantz concerto, the Mozart concertos, Doppler's *Fantaisie pastorale hongroise,* and Moyse's *The Golden Age of the Flutists,* a book of solos. Woodwind ensembles studied quintets by Rossini, Cambini, and Reicha, plus the contents of the Andraud book of quintets (Beethoven to Taffanel), and octets or other large pieces by Beethoven, Bernard, D'Indy, Dvořák, Enesco, Gounod, Haydn, Mozart, and Strauss. Seminar participants attended concerts at Marlboro; some of them worked as ushers there. Likewise, Marlboro musicians were welcome to drop in on Moyse's classes. Pianist Peter Serkin, who counts Moyse as one of his greatest influences, came to the seminars consistently for years and taped over one hundred hours of them.

As his seminars developed, Moyse received offers to teach master classes elsewhere. One of the most significant opportunities came about in 1964, when he was invited to give two weeks of flute master classes at the Artist's Home in Boswil, Switzerland, near Zurich. It was the first time since coming to America that Moyse had been asked to return to Europe to teach, and the event, which came just a few months after his seventy-fifth birthday, was a huge success.

The sessions were held in the quaint little church in Boswil, which had generous acoustics and a handsome altar. Every day, flutists from all over Europe, America, and Japan waited their turns in a semicircle around Moyse, who presided from a large upholstered chair. There was a piano in the sanctuary, but Moyse wanted no accompaniment; he said it might obscure the details of the flute-playing.[12] *Le maître* stayed in the renovated vicarage, which was the center of a quiet artists' colony. In conjunction with the classes, a festival was held in Zurich to mark the master's seventy-fifth year. It was headlined by three prominent Swiss flutists whom Moyse had taught in Paris: Peter-Lukas Graf, Aurèle Nicolet, and Raymond Meylan.

Boswil was designated an annual happening, and word of it spread. The next year, 1965, the village was jammed with more of Europe's top young flutists, an International Who's Who of artists such as James Galway, William Bennett, and Trevor Wye. Two years later, Wye founded the Flute Summer School in England for the purpose of bringing Moyse to the British. Many of these flutists were gaining exposure to Moyse for the first time. Aurèle Nicolet described it as "a big flute meeting." "If a bomb had fallen on that church," he said, "there would suddenly have been a lot of major flute jobs available." As a result, Boswil became the place for flutists to be, a European annex to the Vermont seminars. Moyse returned every year until 1976.

In 1966, Moyse resigned from Marlboro. He had been ill that spring and had undergone a gall bladder operation. On the surface, he was moved to quit because Serkin, who had a known aversion to hospitals and was in and out of town, had not visited him. But beneath that complaint lay Moyse's frustration with a musical retreat that welcomed press coverage of Queen Elisabeth of Belgium driving to a backwoods concert in a limousine. Tony Checchia says Moyse's resignation was due to "a personal misunderstanding not resolved." The door was left open for Moyse to return, and Marlboro continued to loan music for Moyse's woodwind seminars. Louis left Marlboro in 1966 too, citing his reasons more directly in a letter bearing the same date as his father's (11 April 1966). Louis wanted time to compose and to do more editing work for the G. Schirmer Company. In addition, he wrote, he was being given fewer assignments at Marlboro and felt more like a substitute player than a primary member of the community. Frank Salomon acknowledged that the 60s transition from open-enrollment summer school to select festival was more difficult for Louis since he, as the Moyse who still performed, was simply absorbed into the group of professional participants while the administration helped set up a special venue for his father.

(Marlboro did not lack fine flutists after Moyse left. Paula Robison was there nearly every year from 1963 through 1971. Ornulf Gulbransen, who had first come in 1959, was a regular during that time. Gulbransen was one of a succession of Danish flutists trained in the French School, beginning with Andersen, connecting on through artists such as Poul Birkelund and the Kuhlau Quartet, four Danish flutists who worked with Moyse at

Boswil. And there were other stars, such as Bernard Goldberg of the Pittsburgh Symphony and the Canadian flutist Robert Aitken, to name just two who also happened to be devoted and influential students of Moyse.)

Moyse's resignation from Marlboro may have had as much to do with his health as his mood, but he did go on to Boswil in 1966. In 1967, he underwent surgery twice more. Still, the seminars thrived, as did Moyse's winter studio in Brattleboro. Alex Ogle was one of several East Coast flutists who organized carloads of friends for group lessons in the Moyse family's new home, a chalet built in the soft hills above West Brattleboro. "We'd go up from New York about once a month—we'd have kind of a party in the car going up, and a party going back, and these wonderful four-hour lessons with Moyse in the afternoon. It was our own little seminar."[13] Ogle later worked with Moyse at Boswil and at St. Amour as one of a succession of prize students invited to join *le maître* on vacation in his home village. New Yorker Eleanor Lawrence was part of the stream of flutists who pitched camp temporarily in Brattleboro to take lessons. One summer, she rented an apartment there for three weeks and had a private lesson with Moyse every day, an unusual situation, since most lesson experiences with Moyse were master classes. Lawrence's isolation and the intensity of Moyse's input were so great that, as she put it, "I was going a bit around the bend. One day, Moyse asked me, 'Is there anywhere you can go? Is there any place here you can make friends?' I'd never said a word, but he realized the solitary business was getting to me. He told me to go away for the weekend and not practice too much."[14]

Moyse, who seemed to come dangerously close to death nearly every year, turned eighty in 1969. In New York, a large group of current and former students gave him a birthday party, complete with a flute choir rendition of "Happy Birthday" (gifts included a new television set for *le maître*'s soap-opera viewing pleasure and a necklace for Madame Moyse). After that he led a month of seminars in Vermont; flew to England to teach two weeks at the International Summer School at Canterbury, Kent; gave master classes in Copenhagen; spent time at St. Amour; and taught at Boswil in late August.

Karl Kraber went to Boswil that year and took notes on Moyse's classes. The first day went like this:

August 20, 1969

First class, 2–6 P.M. About 35 of us. Who'll begin?

1. A Canadian girl volunteers. Moyse gives long talk (all in English). Object: to talk with the flute, to be expressive, to be interesting.

No formal organization to the course—to leave things to chance is to be fresh and not stale.

The girl played Tulou's *13th Solo in A,* and quite well. Very expressive, lovely sound, took time for nuances, had mastered the hard "licks."

A bit slow, I thought, and not very dramatic. Moyse went through it with her, note by note, phrase by phrase.

The elegance of Tulou is something to be brought out, made much of, he says. Demersseman is boxing, Tulou is fencing. Opening two notes: *en garde!*

2. A Swedish girl was next, with the first four of M's *24 petites études.* Big sound, swooping. He remained interested, worked with her a half hour. Then a break.

3. A Norwegian girl was next, very nervous, started with No. 13 in *Tone Development (Fortunio* of Messager), stopped several times.

Then went to *L'Arlésienne* violin solo, No. 49. M told the story of two old people, a shepherd and a grandmother, who talk about love and their pasts, only to realize that they were in love with each other when they were young, but because the shepherd felt the woman was above his station, he never proposed to her, and there she is, old, and still thinking of him. They pray and cry together while the violin plays.

4. Then there was a pause and K. K. volunteered to put himself on the chopping block with Bach Sonata No. 7 in G minor [now known to be by C. P. E. Bach]. Smashed through it, more nervous than for any audience. After making a wreck of the entire first movement, I did a little better as he took me through it, bit by bit. How much I hadn't thought about—how I rush, am tempted to play everything fast like jazz, with quick rhythm but no shape or long line. *Thoughtless!* (I would do well to learn

his articulations from his edition before bringing him the sonata and spending class time trying to learn them).

Then, home for dinner of cheese and fruit, go over the music with a pencil only, and back to the Alte Kirche for an 8–10 P.M. lesson.

Kraber's notes from classes at Boswil and Brattleboro in the late 60s and early 70s contain plenty of Moyse's trademark utterances and observations. Here are some examples:

Why is everything loud like an elephant, or always soft, like a giraffe?

Did some musicologist say you have to start every trill on the upper note? This reminds me of the Duke who went to the bathroom and forgot to fasten the bottom button on his vest. From that moment on it became the rule to leave that one undone.

Seventy-five years ago there was a French School. It's disappeared now. . . . If you want to play Berio, that's your business. If you want to play with the flute backwards, you can do that, too.

Story: A king asks his cook for his best dish. That evening, seven tongues, exquisitely cooked, are served. The next day, the king says, "That was delicious. Now make me something awful." That evening the cook again presents seven tongues. "Why tongue again?" asks the king. "Because," answers the cook, "with the tongue we make the best things and also the worst."

If the music is not like you want it to be, don't play it. I don't like your nose. Can you change your nose?

Nothing troubles me more than when someone plays "Syrinx." Even good players think they can do what they want. Debussy wrote what he wanted. Think: who wrote the fantasy? Play the composer's fantasy, not your own.

My personality? I tried to be like Taffanel, like Gaubert, like Hennebains, and finally I became Marcel Moyse. Also [I am who I am] because of my mother, God, my village, and being an orphan.

Moyse: I had three great teachers: Hennebains, Taffanel, and
Gaubert.
Student: Do you play like Taffanel?
Moyse: No.
Student: Why not?
Moyse: Because I can't.

In 1970, the Marlboro School and Festival invited Moyse to
return for its twentieth anniversary, but he turned down the offer
and went on with his seminars. The passing of two decades did not
seem to impress him. The next year, however, time staked a claim
when Celine died at the age of eighty-six. Celine's health had been
unstable for a while. She had become depressed, suffered from loss
of hearing and high blood pressure, and was prone to falls that have
been interpreted as brief heart failures. Toward the end of her life
she became quite childlike, and the habitual arguments between
husband and wife ceased; the pair watched TV together, holding
hands.

Moyse was heartbroken by the loss of his partner. There was a
memorial service in Brattleboro; Moyse deposited some of his
wife's ashes in a little jar, which he carried about with him for
months. Some students recall a few instances in restaurants when
he drew out the jar, placed it on the table, and spoke to it. From that
time on, Moyse frequently expressed his desire to join Celine in
heaven. Sometimes he referred to himself as "Marcelily," a combination of "Marcel" and "Celine." Regardless of the friction in
their relationship, Moyse began to look back on his fifty-nine-year
marriage as a lasting, idyllic tryst.

Celine's death foreshadowed another profound change in
Moyse's personal life because around that time, Louis and
Blanche's marriage began to unravel. This turn of events surprised
people partly because the couple had achieved so much together.
In 1972, the Brattleboro Music Center, their foundling, celebrated
its twentieth anniversary with the premiere of Louis's musical epic
The Ballad of Vermont ("dedicated to the State of Vermont: its natural
beauty, its independent people, its untamed spirit"). The Center
and the lifetime accomplishments of Louis and Blanche were featured generously in *High Fidelity/Musical America*.[15]

If Moyse had no control over the loss of his wife, he must have
felt he could influence the fate of the rest of the clan, and in his own

indomitable way, he did. As the patriarch of a close, long-lived musical family and a "traditional Frenchman" who turned a blind eye to love affairs and abhorred divorce under any circumstances, he disagreed with his son's decision to leave Blanche for a woman who worked at the Brattleboro Music Center. But Louis stuck to his plan, and after he remarried at age sixty-two in the summer of 1974, his eighty-five-year-old father, whose household then consisted only of himself and Blanche (then sixty-five), refused to acknowledge his new daughter-in-law. This behavior understandably alienated Louis, but Marcel remained rigidly set on the issue for the rest of his life. Friends and acquaintances dreamed of reconciliation scenes, but no one really expected one to materialize. Louis's departure from the home, where three generations had coexisted under the same roof, spelled the end of his professional connections with the Brattleboro Music Center. The father-son relationship was never restored.[16]

CHAPTER TEN

Grand Old Man of the Flute

TOWARD the end of the 1960s Moyse began to strengthen his connections with Japan. As the sort of elderly master traditionally revered in the Orient, he attracted to the Boswil master classes an increasing number of Japanese flutists, who latched onto his books and records. In 1970 the Japanese flute-manufacturer Muramatsu struck a deal with Moyse to reissue his Vermont-produced LPs and remastered 78 recordings as a set; the move seemed wise at the time, but the contract was written so that distribution did not extend to the United States—at this writing, Americans can obtain the set only if they purchase it abroad (see Discography, "Muramatsu," under "X: Long-Playing Reissues"). In 1972, forty Japanese flute students came to Boswil, and in 1973, Toshio Takahashi and the Suzuki Talent Institute invited Moyse to Japan for a month, where he coached flutists in Tokyo, Matsumoto, and Kobe, before assemblages that swelled to a thousand. It was the first time Moyse had held seminars before such large audiences; he returned in 1977 for a similar round of appearances.

In October of 1973, Pablo Casals died. The following summer, on 2 June, the Brattleboro Music Center sponsored a gala concert at Marlboro to celebrate Moyse's eighty-fifth birthday. Seminar students performed the Mozart Serenade in E-flat and the Beethoven Octet with Moyse and joined Blanche, the Brattleboro Music

Center Chorus, and the Marlboro College Chorus in the Bruckner Mass in E minor. Rudolf Serkin appeared backstage in the green-room to congratulate his colleague, and by Sunday, 28 July 1974, *le maître* had publicly returned to Marlboro, directing (from an over-stuffed chair) his seventh Marlboro performance of the Mozart Serenade in B-flat, K. 361.

Summer 1974 also marked the first time a French flutist came to Marlboro, and it was none other than Michel Debost, principal flute of the Orchestre de Paris and former first flutist in the Société des Concerts du Conservatoire. Debost, forty, had completed his Conservatoire training in 1944, just as Moyse was returning to Paris after the war to reclaim his position. Debost had worked with Moyse at Boswil, an experience that, he said, "transformed me," and his presence brightened Moyse's restoration to the Marlboro fold. At last, a leader of the modern French School had crossed the ocean in search of the old traditions. Somewhere beneath French soil, Taffanel, Hennebains, and Gaubert were trilling with delight.

During the 1974–75 academic year, Moyse traveled monthly to the Curtis Institute of Music in Philadelphia to coach the Aulos woodwind quintet in a pilot program for advanced chamber-music study. Rudolf Serkin was director of the conservatory at that time (he held the post from 1968 to 1976; the Aulos quintet also studied with bassoonist Sol Schoenbach). Three of the Aulos members (which included Judith Mendenhall, flute; Rudy Vrbsky, oboe; David Singer, clarinet; Alex Heller, bassoon; and Bob Routch, horn) had worked with Moyse at Marlboro. Once, in a spirit of adventure, the group tried to persuade Moyse to listen to their con-temporary repertoire. The idea fizzled when he claimed he could not decipher the Villa-Lobos score they pressed on him. But instead of rejecting the piece outright, he insisted first on being driven to Woolworth's for reading glasses more powerful than the thick lenses he already wore. The new spectacles, he concluded, were of no use, and at the next coaching he made a show of tossing the Villa-Lobos score in a wastebasket. Nevertheless Moyse fostered a warm relationship with the Aulos players, and several of them usually joined him for dinner at the Barclay Hotel after rehearsals. The hotel dining room posted a dress code the young men were rarely prepared to meet, and more than once they convened in Moyse's room first to don his spare coats and ties. Moyse always ordered frogs' legs, followed by a generous pipeful of Bugler tobacco.

Also in 1974, Moyse published one more exercise book: *Comment j'ai pu maintenir ma forme,* with an English translation of the text (by Marcel and Louis Moyse's Canadian student Paul M. Douglas) titled *How I Stayed in Shape.* This was written during an extended visit in Metz with his former Conservatoire pupil Charles Dagnino (to whom the book is dedicated). Teaching and writing continued to satisfy Moyse while his household was undergoing the transformation from an old-fashioned patriarchy to a situation in which an aging man depended completely on his daughter-in-law. Blanche Honegger Moyse took on the main responsibility of caring for Marcel after Celine's death and her own divorce, as much out of love and duty as the practical realization that, because she was part of his household, she could accomplish it best. She admits she was often frustrated by her father-in-law's behavior, but at the same time she was quite able and determined to continue her busy professional life with the Brattleboro Music Center, Marlboro, the New England Bach Festival (which she founded in 1969), and many other pursuits.[1] When Marcel was invited to teach out of town, Blanche accompanied him; her willingness to be his constant companion made these activities possible. At home, there was usually a live-in flute student/helper who attended to Moyse's meals and local travel. Blanche had guided many of the family's business dealings and continued to act as Marcel's agent. Occasionally he expressed gratitude, but most of the time he took his daughter-in-law's role for granted. Observers say that without Blanche's intellectual energy and strong will as daily stimuli, Moyse might have declined quickly. As long as he had someone close by whom he respected and who was willing to butt heads with him, Moyse could remain relatively lively and positively ornery.

In 1975, Moyse expanded his seminars and named them the Marcel Moyse School of Wind Playing. Enrollment peaked between 1975 and 1982, a period which spanned, incredibly, Moyse's eighty-sixth and ninety-third birthdays! In the heaviest years, Moyse presided over seven sessions: four for woodwinds, three for flutes. Flute and woodwind seminars ran concurrently; from mid-May to the end of June, he taught two three-hour sessions a day, with one or two days off per week. It was a nightmare to organize, but thanks to Pat Grignet Nott's devoted (and unpaid) administrative skills, it ran splendidly. The 1976 seminars had to be canceled entirely after Moyse underwent a cataract operation in the spring.

But in 1977, the school was up and running again.

Moyse was also sought by professional ensembles. One of the first was Tashi, formed in 1973 by the Marlboro foursome pianist Peter Serkin, clarinetist Richard Stoltzman, violinist Ida Kavafian, and cellist Fred Sherry. Tashi expanded its instrumentation to accommodate more diverse repertoire, and when it was preparing to record the Mozart Clarinet Quintet and the Quintet for piano and winds, Peter Serkin invited Moyse to coach them in his New York apartment.

Bob Routch, hornist of the Lincoln Center Chamber Players and a former member of both Tashi and the Aulos quintet, recalled that he and his colleagues played much better under Moyse, "getting the wave, somehow, just being around him," becoming "deconservatoried." Moyse was noticeably frail by then. Routch said, "His eyes were the most powerful tool of expression that I remember. But sometimes I saw him looking quite inward, when he was alone and no one was talking to him. There was a dark side of the moon."[2]

Outwardly, Moyse always rallied for admiring students and the promise of good music-making. His wardrobe grew more flamboyant as he aged: striped pants, plaid jackets, and an odd-color shirt topped with an ascot were typical, accessorized by a beret or cap and the pipe of the moment (his favorites were briar pipes made in the Jura town of St. Claude). Entering a classroom on the arm of a favorite student, he would shuffle slowly through the crowd, giving one pupil a gleeful pinch, another a good-natured pat on the head. Occasionally, he would pick up his old, corroded flute, bring it slowly to his lips, and carefully produce one pure note to show what he wanted. As lessons progressed, he nursed his pipe and a tall tumbler of watered Scotch or Pernod that would have rendered anyone else useless. ("How does one execute a clear, resonant note?" he asked. "Listen to the tap of the pipe against the glass.") He ate little of the food he ordered in restaurants and seemed to exist solely on pipe tobacco and spirits.

Sometime in the mid-70s Moyse visited Charles Dagnino in Metz and was introduced to Alain Marion, the new professor of flute at the Conservatoire. Marion, a protégé of Rampal, was bowled over.

"I spent two days and two nights with Moyse," Marion reminisced. "We didn't sleep. At four o'clock in the morning, he

was drinking coffee—with eight or nine sugars in a small cup!—
white wine, and the whiskey, and the cognac—Moyse was
unbelievable!"

What did the pair talk about during those forty-eight hours?

"All about music, the flute, composers like Chaminade, stories
about the orchestras he played in, musical philosophy, the relationship between pupil and teacher." Moyse also spoke tartly of his
problems at the Conservatoire after the war and his refusal to visit
Paris ever again. And he insisted on playing for Marion, alone. "He
brought out his flute, and he played, just three or four notes: A, C,
B, A. . . . I started to cry, of course. It was such a clear sound, completely different than on his records. Completely different. On
records it is very strong. Live, it was like Gaubert: very free, very
simple."[3]

Marion left Metz determined to bring Moyse back to Paris and
secured funding for le maître's return in January 1977 for a week of
public master classes at the Conservatoire. Between two and three
hundred people attended, and French Radio taped nearly every
minute and edited it down to five programs that were broadcast that
April (see Discography nos. 194–198). Moyse's final class appearance culminated in an ovation that lasted close to half an hour, with
luminaries of the contemporary flute crop offering golden tributes
to the Grand Old Man. Nevertheless, Moyse was still impelled to
retaliate for past grievances and indulged in nasty asides to acquaintances, the essence of which was that the French School had slid
downhill into a pile of mud. Recipients of these comments were
offended, perplexed, or embarrassed.

If the opposite side of Moyse's habitual animosity was pure,
unbridled sentimentality, the Paris trip was a constant flip-flop.
Every reunion with a cherished place and person reminded Moyse
that the past was long gone. When Marion first brought Moyse from
the train station to the entrance of the old Conservatoire, the elderly
flutist wept unabashedly. Later, Marion accompanied his guest to a
gathering and witnessed the reunion of Moyse and his old friend
and favorite second flutist, Albert Manouvrier, who had sat next to
Moyse in several orchestras and recorded Berlioz's "Trio of the
Young Ishmaelites" with Moyse for Decca.

"I had Moyse on my arm, walking very slowly, you know?" said
Marion.

And there was Manouvrier standing there, eighty years old. And I said, "Mr. Moyse, try to see—just in front of you is your friend." And Moyse stopped, and Manouvrier came up to him, and Moyse said softly, "You are Manouvrier." And he started to cry again. Thirty years—thirty years since he'd seen him.

As he approached his ninetieth birthday, Moyse slowed down considerably. "My body is like my flute: full of holes," he told people. His tempos in chamber music were much more leisurely and sometimes uncomfortably sleepy, like a music box winding down. Those who performed under his guidance were not always sure whether to follow Moyse or look to the flutist or first oboist for leadership. Some players felt they should follow Moyse no matter what; others thought it would be more respectful to carry on in the style and spirit he would have created twenty years before. When thirteen early Marlboro alumni gathered at Boston's Symphony Hall in 1980 to record the Mozart B-flat Serenade under Moyse's direction, they found that some of his tempos had relaxed significantly. And yet, said Richard Mackey, the Boston Symphony hornist who had organized the recording session, Moyse's legendary energy still drove the ensemble. The result was a warm, shapely interpretation that was released nearly ten years later, on the short-lived Nautilus label (Discography no. 225).

Moyse also became even less tolerant of others. If it is true that personality traits become exaggerated in old age, Moyse was a textbook case. His granddaughter Dominique, who is a sociologist, said, "I think my grandfather always wanted immediate gratification, and when he was old and sick, he became very demanding, childlike in some ways. Also a little paranoid, which is another Moyse tendency—it's why they compensate with criticism, you know."[4]

Besides Blanche, the only people who experienced this up close and on a daily basis were the student flutists who came to live in the Moyse household and helped to care for le maître in exchange for lessons. The prospect of constant access to the great artist was exciting, but the reality of day-to-day life wore most of the young women thin. Moyse was jealous of their time, their outside interests, and their social lives. Every one remembers getting the silent treatment for days because she took a weekend off with a boyfriend or excused herself from another evening of listening to opera records to do her laundry.

And yet, those who encountered this behavior remained devoted students. At this point one has to ask (emphatically) why? A good number of musicians who had had contact with Moyse in his later years were not enamored of him. They came to a seminar or Marlboro coaching, experienced the elderly master's abuse, and left, understandably unwilling to submit to insults or bitter rips about circumstances that had nothing to do with them. A few highly respected artists, Marlboro alumni interviewed for this book, feel that Moyse was "a phony." But for those willing to sacrifice emotional energy for a musical god, Moyse was still worth the effort. Flutist Susan Rotholtz kept a thick notebook from her lessons, full of quotes she reads aloud reverently: "The silence must be so soft it becomes music." "When you leave an expressive note, leave it with regret." The French flutist Odile Renault, a student of Moyse's Conservatoire pupil M. Gillet, came to live with Marcel and Blanche in 1980 and likened her experience to psychoanalysis. She went back into her past to understand the present, she said, and returned to Caen with a rich knowledge of late-nineteenth-century musical style (plus the wisdom that the "personal lives of famous people aren't always interesting"). The distinguished soloist Carol Wincenc sought out Moyse at that time and underwent a musical/spiritual transformation not unlike what Paula Robison had encountered nearly twenty years before. Yes, Moyse said mean things. But, if one was patient and thoughtful, they did not take away from the musical messages, which remained whole, and vibrantly imparted.

Marcel Moyse turned ninety in 1979. The year began with a trip to Hawaii in January, arranged by seminar alumnus Paul Barrett, principal bassoonist of the Honolulu Symphony. Moyse conducted members of the symphony in a concert of chamber music at the University of Hawaii then flew back to Brattleboro to prepare for his seminars and another round of honors, including an honorary doctorate from Marlboro College. On 20 May, two hundred students, colleagues, and friends from all over the country gathered at Brattleboro's West Village Meeting House to surprise the Grand Old Man with a boisterous reunion and birthday bash. There was a slide show about Moyse's life, a performance of the Mozart K. 361

Serenade with Moyse conducting, a rendition of "Happy Birthday" for twenty-two flutes and piano (Peter Serkin did the honors), and speeches from every generation of musicians who had worked with Moyse at Marlboro and in the seminars. *Le maître* was also presented with a facsimile copy of the K. 361 Serenade, published by the Library of Congress.

The weekend of 7 and 8 July, Moyse conducted on two concerts (the Dvořák Serenade and Strauss Serenade in E-flat major, Opus 7, respectively), which were advanced by a major profile of Moyse in *The New York Times*.[5] Later in the summer, he led the Marlboro Festival Orchestra and soloists (Neil Black, oboe; John Bruce Yeh, clarinet; Kenneth Munday, bassoon; David Jolley, horn) in the Mozart Sinfonia Concertante in E-flat major, K. 297b, on 29 July, and on 3 August a fresh group of initiates in the Mozart B-flat Serenade, K. 361. After Marlboro, he took his usual trip to St. Amour, where the whole village threw its most distinguished son a birthday party.

In 1979 Moyse gave a few master classes in Texas. He was quite difficult to understand then; even the pupils who had studied French had a hard time. At the University of North Texas in Denton, Judith Mendenhall stood between her students and Moyse's overstuffed throne to help translate. At Baylor University in Waco, the faculty wind quintet bravely asked Moyse to coach them in front of their pupils. Despite the barrier of spoken language, his message inspired everyone; the Baylor Quintet traveled to Brattleboro in the summers of 1980, 1981, and 1983 for additional work.

The seminars were still popular, and Moyse continued to coach and conduct at Marlboro, but his delicate health required a lighter schedule. He tired easily and complained that his life was too long. When he was ninety-two, Moyse made his debut in Avery Fisher Hall, conducting a chamber group from Marlboro in the Dvořák Serenade and the beloved Mozart B-flat "Grand Partita." Naturally, he led the players from an overstuffed chair that dwarfed him. Elaine Douvas, now principal oboe at the Metropolitan Opera, remembered vividly what happened in rehearsal when the players complained they could not see him well. "In Fisher Hall, the podium comes up out of the floor, so they put his chair in the middle of it and raised it up," she recalled. "But Moyse thought he was too close to the group, and he started scooting his chair back."

Before anyone could stop him, Moyse had tipped backward off the podium. Douvas jumped up and grabbed the arm of Moyse's chair but wound up falling too, and suffering a bent oboe. "He was just lying there on his back, in the armchair," she said. "He looked kind of stunned. That was the moment of fear for me—we had no idea if he was hurt."[6]

The whole ensemble was upset about the incident, except Moyse, who allowed himself to be helped up and within an hour was entertaining everyone in his dressing room. Later, when Douvas escorted him onstage for the performance, he chided her gleefully, "This time, don't fall down!"

The 1983 seminars drew a devoted batch of players, including the Oregon Symphony Woodwind Quintet, which had given its debut concert the previous season and applied the proceeds toward the trip to Vermont. This would be Moyse's last year at Marlboro. In 1984 he carried on with the seminars and celebrated his ninety-fifth birthday, his last. Congratulations poured in from all over the world, former pupils everywhere played concerts in his honor, and somewhat belatedly, the state of Vermont bestowed on Moyse the Governor's Award for Excellence in the Arts. On 9 June, in Brattleboro's Latchis Theater, filmmakers Claude and Michel Moyse premiered a documentary about their grandfather, "Marcel Moyse, Grand Old Man of the Flute." Narrated by James Galway and featuring interviews with artists such as Jean-Pierre Rampal, Rudolf and Peter Serkin, Paula Robison, Claude Frank, and Blanche Honegger Moyse, the film is a beautiful tribute to the complex life of a man who was blessed with the ability to see it in elemental terms. "Our instrument is limited in many ways," reads one Moyse quote in the film. "For example, it lacks amplitude. When the sound is forced, it doesn't become ample; it becomes hard. But this stays within material dimensions. What augments the sound of the flute is the spirit which spreads, and I observed long ago that sound derives from generosity of the heart."

Later that month, Moyse contracted pneumonia and was hospitalized. He improved a little in the summer and rested at home, but canceled his annual trip to France. His diminished form required constant care, and at the beginning of the fall musical season, Blanche transferred him to a nursing home. He seemed comfortable there and occasionally managed to torment the nurses with pranks and demands. But by that time, students had begun traveling up to visit, aware that this time, the end really was in sight. All that seemed to be left of *le maître* was a huge forehead, nose, and jaw. There was a record player in his room. All Moyse would listen to were his own recordings, over and over. When someone tried to play a record of Hennebains, he found fault with it and complained, "That's not me; it's not me." Occasionally, a flute duo or wind quintet came to play for him in his room, and he even taught a few short lessons there, under the careful gaze of a nurse.

On the last day of October, Moyse came home. On 1 November (All Saints' Day) 1984, he died while sleeping. Blanche discovered him. His face glowed with peace and happiness; a very long, full life had floated away like a grace note.

Yet as frail as he was in his last years, Marcel Moyse never stopped practicing and searching for new ways to sing on the flute. After one of his last illnesses, Pat Grignet Nott went to visit him in Vermont and found him sitting alone in his kitchen, playing short, high peeps.

"I'm learning again to play the high register," he told her, "and this time, without effort."[7]

Postlude

IN the year following Marcel Moyse's death, musicians throughout the world offered concerts in his memory. Among these events were a New York concert featuring Peter Serkin and the Y Chamber Symphony in Mozart's Piano Concerto No. 13, K. 415 (17 and 18 November 1984) and a Grand Memorial Concert in London featuring Edward Beckett, William Bennett, Poul Birkulund, Charles Dagnino, Michel Debost, Peter-Lukas Graf, Susan Milan, Aurèle Nicolet, Trevor Wye, and other noted flutists (6 January 1985).

On the afternoon of 10 August 1985, Blanche Moyse and other family members watched as Marcel and Celine Moyse's ashes were interred in a ceremony at the cemetery of St. Amour. The town band played for the occasion, dressed in black uniforms. The entire citizenry was present. Among the graveside floral tributes was a huge spray with a red sign embossed in gold: "Au Grand Maître Flûtiste Marcel Moyse—Souvenir Muramatsu."

News of Moyse's death was reported worldwide by United Press International and the Associated Press. Burt A. Folkart's obituary for Moyse in the *Los Angeles Times* (2 November 1984) recalled a 1979 interview with Jean-Pierre Rampal, in which Rampal described Moyse as "the first to imagine that a flute player can be a great soloist. For my generation, he was king." The *London Times* called Moyse the "doyen of flute players." Similar acclamations were published in other major newspapers in the United States and Europe.

In 1988 a group of musicians founded the Marcel Moyse

217

Society to sponsor the preservation of Moyse's library and recordings and to promote educational and scholarly projects related to Moyse. This active, international organization, which is hundreds of members strong, also publishes a newsletter of interest to all musicians and music-lovers. The mailing address of the Marcel Moyse Society is P.O. Box 5602, Baltimore, MD 21210, U.S.A.

Moyse's memory was celebrated *en masse,* throughout 1989, *le maître's* one hundredth birth year. During the week of 17 May, about two hundred Moyse alumni met at Marlboro and Brattleboro for celebratory exhibits, dinners, and two concerts that featured many of Moyse's top American pupils in the repertoire he loved best: French flute solos, Kuhlau flute quartets, Beethoven and Taffanel wind quintets, Bach trio sonatas and chorales (conducted by Blanche Moyse), and the Mozart Serenade in E-flat, K. 375, a work Moyse often said he wanted to have played at his grave. Commemorative events in Europe on 17 May included a rousing, narrated retrospective concert in London with flutists William Bennett, Trevor Wye, and Edward Blakeman of England plus Charles Dagnino and Raymond Guiot of France. In August of that year, the National Flute Association honored Moyse's legacy in New Orleans at its annual convention with the Moyse Society's exhibit of memorabilia and a gala Centennial Celebration concert. The roster of participants was again distinguished and international. Perhaps the most moving portion of the concert belonged to Louis Moyse, who conducted Émile Bernard's *Divertissement,* Opus 36, and his own Marlborian Concerto No. 3 for four flutes (William Bennett, Charles Dagnino, Bernard Goldberg, and John Barcellona) and orchestra.

In the years since, Moyse's influence has been evident in the growing use of Conservatoire-style master classes, the continued sales of his exercise books, and the reissue of many of his recordings. His students populate music school faculties and professional ensembles throughout the world, all employing their own methods of sharing Moyse's passions and ideas with new generations of musicians.

Notes

PROLOGUE
1. Germaine Chassagnoux died in 1992, a year after my visit.

CHAPTER ONE
1. Kaufmann 1891, 239–242.
2. Moyse, Claude and Michel, 1980.
3. Author's interview with Trevor Wye, 1991.
4. Moyse, Claude and Michel, 1980.
5. Moyse, Claude and Michel, 1980.
6. Zeldin 1977, Vol. II, Chapter 6, "Happiness and Humour."
7. Estevan 1976, 83.

CHAPTER TWO
1. Moyse, Claude and Michel, 1980.
2. Kirk 1974, 37.
3. Steinheil 1912, 12. Marguerite Japy Steinheil grew up in the Jura, married the painter Frederick Steinheil in 1890, and moved to Paris, where she presided over an elegant salon that was frequented by the composer Massenet. She was later accused of murdering her mother and husband, and spent two years in prison before she was finally exonerated.
4. Hill 1924, 45.
5. Quoted in Weinstock 1968, 132. The gala took place in 1823.
6. Moyse, Claude and Michel, 1980.
7. Ibid.
8. Ibid.
9. Steinheil 1912, 12.
10. Estevan 1976, 81. Louis Moyse adds that Angelloz operated a shoe store in Besançon called "The Golden Mule." Angelloz later sold his

shoe business and moved to an apartment in Paris near the Place Clichy. During the 1920s, the Angelloz family and the Moyses socialized occasionally.

11. The current French-English-German-Italian edition of the venerable *Méthode pour flûte système Boehm* omits translation of Altès's general music theory text so that, in the words of one longtime American flute teacher, "English-speaking students just go at it blind." This edition, revised by Philippe Gaubert's student Fernand Caratgé and published by Leduc in 1956, contains a publisher's note to the effect that all flute teachers have their own ways of teaching theory, so translating that portion is unnecessary.

12. Altès' invocation of Baillot is not surprising. Standard orchestral stringed instruments and their methodologies developed well before the Boehm flute was accepted. Most woodwind tutorials and etude books of Altès's vintage mirror nineteenth-century violin studies, right down to the omission of breath marks. In addition, Altès and his younger brother Ernest Eugène (1830–1899) were taught the violin and fife by their father when they were very young. Ernest entered the Conservatoire violin class in 1843 and undoubtedly studied from Baillot's books. He enjoyed a long career as a violinist, composer, and conductor in various posts at the Opéra and the Société des Concerts du Conservatoire.

13. Altès 1880; 1906 ed., 286. The unattributed translation is cleaned up in later editions; for example, "pathetic" (from "*pathétique*") becomes "moving." Baillot's elevated perfectionism, which so strongly informed Altès, included an abhorrence for pyrotechnics. He was willing to hear Paganini perform, but supposedly hid his face when the Italian virtuoso indulged in harmonics, long staccato passages, and left-hand pizzicati.

CHAPTER THREE

1. Gosling 1978, 74. Also see Roger Shattuck, *The Banquet Years: The Origins of the Avant Garde in France, 1885 to World War I* (New York: Random House, 1968).

2. Quoted in Steinheil 1912, 39. Jean Greuze (1725–1805) was a portraitist and painter of moralistic, yet sensuously rendered genre paintings.

3. Lawrence 1979, 9.

4. Some historians trace the French School to the pre-Conservatoire days of Michel Blavet (1700–1768), a contemporary of the German flutist Johann Joachim Quantz.

5. Lippa, 1979. Reprinted with permission from *WWD*, 8/17–24/79. Copyright 1993 Fairchild Publications. A Capital Cities/ABC Inc., company. All rights reserved.

6. Moyse, Claude and Michel, 1980. In a letter to the author (24 November 1992), Louis Moyse pointed out that English speakers, who tend to "shrink" or swallow vowels, are perfectly capable of developing

outstanding lip and tongue techniques. "The fact is," he wrote, "music is a language by itself and you can learn it, on any instrument, whether you are white, black, yellow, or red."

7. In 1990 Pavilion Records released "The Great Flautists," a two-disc set (GEMM CD nos. 9284 and 9302) of remastered recordings by Moyse, Hennebains, Gaubert, Barrère, and Le Roy (see Discography, "X: Long-Playing Reissues," nos. 10 and 11). After he immigrated to the United States, Moyse produced an LP titled "The French School of Flute Playing," which contains performances by Hennebains, Gaubert, and him (see Discography, "Marcel Moyse Records, U.S.A.," under "X: Long-Playing Reissues").

8. Moyse, Blanche Honegger, 1975. Hennebains was one of many who called Kuhlau the "Beethoven of the Flute." The flute method of the Italian-American flutist Leonardo De Lorenzo included an etching of Kuhlau, with the inscription, "Il Beethoven del Flauto."

9. Ibid.

10. Citron 1988, 22–23.

11. Quoted in Citron 1988, 184.

12. Author's interview with Alain Marion, professor of flute, Paris Conservatoire, May 1991. Moyse introduced his version of the Bach Partita on tour with the Busch Ensemble in Florence, Italy, sometime in the mid-1930s. He said the Partita frustrated him. In the Allemande, for example, he occasionally remarked that in attempting to enrich or lengthen the melodic pitches in this quick-paced, sixteenth-note movement, the flutist is forced to produce a harsh sound. On a violin, he explained, one can make a chord or a special bow stroke to highlight certain notes without distorting rhythm. But on the flute, the choices seem to be to exaggerate the length and alter the rhythm or to change the color and accept punchy articulation.

13. Moyse, Claude and Michel, 1980.

14. Louis recalled that Utrillo often passed by the family home on Rue d'Orsel,

> imitating a bugler with his hand (sucking his thumb), and yelling *fortissimo* the children's call from *Carmen:* "La garde montante!" Three doors away from our building was a small café-restaurant. Some musicians, colleagues of my father, had lunch there. Often Utrillo would come begging for a Pernod or a glass of wine or a meal. He would say, "I will pay you with a drawing or a painting." He would take any material available as a canvas—napkin, paper, cardboard, even a calendar—anything! and start work while talking, drinking, eating. Three or four francs was the price of a masterpiece! Some musicians (not my father) were smart enough to keep them and made good money later on. (Letter to the author, 24 November 1992)

15. Moyse, Claude and Michel, 1980.

16. For a detailed discussion of the relationships between visual artists and musicians, see Brody 1987, Chapter 6, "Music and Art."

17. Moyse, Blanche Honegger, 1975.
18. In his memoirs, Saint-Saëns described the Société des Concerts in the 1850s as "a paradise, guarded by an angel with a flaming sword, in the form of a porter named Lescot. It was his duty to prevent the profane defiling of the sanctuary." According to the composer, the marvelous sound of the Société orchestra was for a long time attributed to the hall. But after the Russian pianist Anton Rubinstein caused a ruckus by wrangling permission to play there with the Colonne orchestra, opinion changed. The Colonne orchestra sounded nothing like the Société. The credit finally had to go to the musicians, not the environment.
19. Lynch 1906, 62.
20. Lawrence 1979, 8.
21. Benoist 1978, 19. Reprinted by permission of T. F. H. Publications, Inc.
22. Ibid., 20–21.
23. Saint-Saëns 1919, 23–24.
24. Massenet 1919, 97. The description applies to the room during the tenure of Ambroise Thomas, but most of the same furnishings probably remained during Moyse's time.
25. Saint-Saëns 1919, 14.
26. Casella 1955, 39–40. Casella also mentioned that his piano teacher, M. Diemer, "took pleasure in telling me before the class that I was lazy, like all Italians." Casella's nationality didn't seem to bother Phillipe Gaubert, who chose him to be his accompanist in the first public performance of Fauré's *Fantaisie,* Opus 79, in 1901.
27. Taffanel was better known as a conductor than a composer. His output for flute included the "Andante pastorale and Scherzettino" for flute and piano and several fantasies and variations on popular themes.
28. Quoted in Dorgeuille 1983, 16.
29. Moyse, Claude and Michel, 1980.
30. Author's interview with Josef Cobert, 1989.
31. Moyse, Blanche Honegger, 1975.
32. Moyse, Claude and Michel, 1980.
33. In 1920 *The Flutist* reported the first instance of an American university's allowing flute as a major subject. The University of Oregon had this distinction, and Miss Beulah Clark of Portland was the beneficiary.
34. Barrère 1921. Text edited by the author.
35. Moyse, Claude and Michel, 1980.
36. With François Devienne in 1794, there began a nearly unbroken chain of flute methods published by successive Conservatoire flute professors. Gaubert updated Devienne's method for the Boehm flute; all other tutorials devised before Altès's have long been out of print.
37. In a 28 March 1982 interview with Penelope Fischer, Moyse mentioned that he assisted Gaubert in editing the Taffanel method. Louis

Moyse contends that his father's statement was incorrect. In a 24 November 1992 letter to the author, Louis writes, "My father was never involved with that method. It was directly published by Leduc from Taffanel, via Gaubert."
38. Fischer 1982, 146.
39. Moyse, Marcel, 1973, 3.
40. Moyse, Claude and Michel, 1980.
41. Laloy 1906, 154–157.
42. Ibid.

CHAPTER FOUR
 1. Lavignac 1895, 488. Addressing this issue half a century later in his 1951 Charles Eliot Norton lecture on music education, Paul Hindemith predicted that if a (hypothetical) country (such as America) had five thousand music teachers, all of whom in their lifetimes produced two more music teachers each, then in the fifteenth year, "every man, woman and child in the United States will be a music teacher, and after about twenty years the entire population of our planet will consist of nothing but music teachers."
 2. Zeldin, Vol. 2, 140.
 3. Described in an account by Gaubert in the 31 December 1938 issue of *Le Monde Musical,* quoted in Fischer 1982, 19.
 4. Fischer 1982, 33–34.
 5. Moyse, Blanche Honegger, 1975.
 6. Author's interview with Judith Mendenhall, February 1989.
 7. Moyse, Claude and Michel, 1980.
 8. Ibid.
 9. Ibid.
10. Pincherle 1961, 112.
11. Lawrence 1979, 3.
12. The Russians' presence in Paris was not new; that nation's music and musicians showcased at the 1889 Exposition had broken ground for cultural exchange with the French, who were weary of German influence, particularly the hoopla over Wagner. Gounod responded quickly with pilgrimages to St. Petersburg and Moscow, and from that point on, the number of performances of Russian works in Paris steadily increased.

   Diaghilev cannily rode the crest of the wave supporting an impressive roster of protégés. He was a savvy politician who mingled with creators and connoisseurs in all the arts, including painting, France's great pride. When the Salon d'Automne in 1906 mounted retrospectives of Gauguin, Courbet, Carrière, and the architect Dobert, it also unveiled a twelve-room section of Russian art. The theatrical presentation on gold-brocade walls was executed by none other than Léon Bakst, Diaghilev's stage designer. The exhibit committee included a wealthy countess who ran the Société Musicale, and the head of the committee was the great Russian organizer himself. Three years later the Ballets Russes came to town.

Diaghilev's cultivation of gifted young artists is well known; it was he who introduced Stravinsky to Paris. The composer made his first visit to supervise the premiere of *Firebird* in 1910, given on 25 June at the Opéra with Gabriel Pierné on the podium. The following June, *Petrushka* was given its first performance at the Théâtre du Châtelet, and this time the up-and-coming Monteux conducted.

13. Craft 1984, 53.
14. Monteux 1965, 89. Excerpt from *It's All in the Music* by Doris Monteux. Copyright © 1965 by Doris Monteux. Reprinted by permission of Farrar, Straus & Giroux, Inc.
15. Ibid.
16. Hiemenz 1975, 15.
17. Moyse, Claude and Michel, 1980. Louis Moyse says his father embellished this story over the years, and that it probably involved the conductor Walther Straram, not Debussy.
18. Ibid.
19. Ibid.
20. According to Louis Moyse, his father's rift with Joseph Moyse lasted only a few months. Louis also recalls being told that his parents had a private religious marriage ceremony near St. Amour when he was about ten years old. The witnesses were the trombonist Raphael Delbos and his wife, who became godparents to Marguerite Moyse and with whom the Moyses shared their St. Amour home.
21. Letter from Louis Moyse to the author, 24 November 1992.
22. Moyse, Claude and Michel, 1980.
23. Otis 1924, 256.

CHAPTER FIVE
1. *Musical America,* 29 August 1914, 22.
2. Quoted in *Musical America,* 15 August 1914, 21.
3. Quoted in *Musical America,* 19 September 1914, 5.
4. Moyse, Louis. Letter to the author, 24 November 1992.
5. Lesure and Nichols 1987, 280.
6. Estevan 1976, 84.
7. From a group of quotes mounted in a "Souvenir from Seminar, June 1969" photo album assembled by Janet Parry-Hill Wyatt.
8. Wye 1985a, 36.
9. Moyse, Louis. Note to the author, November 1992.
10. Moyse, Louis, 1985, 36.
11. Perrin 1960.
12. *Le Ménestrel,* 5 November 1926, 466.
13. Hiemenz 1975, 15.
14. Moyse, Louis. Note to the author, November 1992.
15. *Le Ménestrel,* 5 March 1926, 107. Louis Moyse remembers that his father's encore was not the Minuet (in which the flute doubles the

strings and is hardly heard), but the entire finale: *Polonaise—Double et Badinerie.*

16. Moyse, Louis. Note to the author, November 1992.
17. *Le Ménestrel,* 16 December 1927, 522.
18. Moyse, Louis. Note to the author, November 1992.
19. *La Revue Musicale,* September–October 1932, 305.
20. Kindler played the premiere of the work the year before, along with Jane Bathori, Alfredo Casella (piano), and Louis Fleury (flute).
21. Author's interviews with Marguerite Moyse Andreasson, August 1988.
22. *Excelsior,* 28 November 1933. Quoted in Orenstein 1990, 402. *A Ravel Reader* by Arbie Orenstein, 1990, © Columbia University Press, New York. Reprinted with the permission of the publisher.
23. *La Revue Musicale,* July 1928, 317.

CHAPTER SIX

1. Moyse, Louis. Note to the author, November 1992.
2. Author's interview with Louis Moyse, August 1990. The Conservatoire attributes students to Moyse as early as 1929, when two pupils were granted *accessits* (certificates of merit) under him.

    Of his son's desire to be a musician, Marcel Moyse once said, "It wasn't I who put the career of a flutist in his hands. It was his decision, not mine. I wanted to make him a doctor, nothing else" (Moyse, Claude and Michel, 1980). To this, Louis responded, "My father's comment is true, but he was referring to me as a seven- or eight-year-old. Later, he rather encouraged me, which was not too difficult! It was just like being born in a circus and watching the parents perform a show thirty feet up on a wire—I could not dream of anything else!" (Note to the author, November 1992)
3. *Disques,* January 1931, 464.
4. "Mein Studienplan bei Marcel Moyse," *Tibia,* January 1985. Another comprehensive list of repertory prescribed by Moyse is contained in a letter Moyse wrote to Charles Delaney in 1950, in response to an inquiry about private lessons. The letter was published in the Marcel Moyse Society newsletter, Vol. 3, No. 1, April 1992. The list is similar to Meylan's, although an order of study is not given.
5. Author's interview with Frances Blaisdell, March 1992.
6. Mlle. Marguerite Artis had gained a *premier prix* in Moyse's class the year before. She is the first female prize-winner recorded under Moyse, but there may have been a few other women in his Conservatoire classes who did not reach that level.
7. Author's interview with Geneviève Noufflard, June 1991.
8. All quotes of Blanche Moyse are from interviews with the author.
9. Moyse, Claude and Michel, 1980.
10. Moyse, Claude and Michel, 1980. Outside the Busch-Serkin-Moyse alliance, the Moyse Trio frequently performed the Bach A Minor

Concerto and the D Major Brandenburg Concerto (Blanche, violin; Louis, piano).

11. Author's interview with Louis Moyse, July 1990; personal notes to the author, November 1992. To his description of the Moyse Trio's work schedule, Louis Moyse added:

> I personally feel that is the only real way to make music in a group. If one has to spend so much time rehearsing, he or she has the wrong partners or is in the wrong business. With adequate technique and knowledge, it should be as easy to make music as it is for a baker to bake bread.

12. "Quelques concerts dans les salons de la Revue Musicale," *La Revue Musicale,* August–September 1937, 198–199.

13. "La sonate—M. Heinz Jolles," *La Revue Musicale,* June 1938, 388.

14. Serkin 1991, 349, 356.

15. Martinů 1978, 43.

16. Hiemenz 1975, 15.

17. "Rehearsing with Toscanini," *Musical America,* 25 March 1929, 19 ff.

18. Author's interview with Marguerite Moyse Andreasson, June 1992.

19. "Jacques Ibert: Concerto pour Flûte et Orchestre," *La Revue Musicale,* March 1934, 224–225.

20. Moyse's name does not appear in the Salzburg Festival program book, but Louis Moyse recalls that the performance took place at four o'clock in the afternoon and drew no more than seventy-five people. Marcel was disappointed and expressed this in a letter to Bruno Walter, who did not conduct the concert. Walter's apologetic reply, dated 31 August 1934, is in the Moyse Archives.

21. All Gaubert correspondence quoted is from the Marcel Moyse Archives.

22. Marcel Moyse Archives.

23. Marcel Moyse Archives.

24. Toeplitz, Uri. "Studying with Marcel Moyse in 1938," unpublished memoir, 1992.

25. Marcel Moyse Archives.

26. There is no record of the broadcast in the NBC Radio archives, but Blanche and Louis agree that the session took place close to the time of Marcel's concerto performance.

27. Moyse admitted that the Couesnon was not the most sophisticated instrument available, but he appreciated it as a well-built tool or container, "into which he could pour any beverage he desired." Louis Moyse said his father was opposed to instruments made with a "built-in quality of tone," that is, flutes with so fine a basic, characteristic sound that a young player is fooled into thinking he or she is responsible for producing it and goes no further to develop personality and variety. Over the years, Moyse was responsible for some changes in the Couesnon flute, such as the spacing between tone holes, which slightly improved the scale. His disk-like appendages to the left-hand A and G keys and a longer appendage for the left-hand G-sharp key contributed to a more natural hand position.

CHAPTER SEVEN
1. Author's interviews with Marguerite Moyse Andreasson.
2. Author's interviews with Blanche Moyse. All following quotes come from the same interviews.
3. Letter from Vuillermoz to Moyse, dated 22 June 1941 (Marcel Moyse Archives).
4. Moyse, Claude and Michel, 1980.
5. Contents of an undated letter translated orally by Geneviève Noufflard during an interview with the author, 1991.
6. The article, titled "Une famille de musiciens—le Trio Moyse," has not been attributed to a publication; it was probably printed in Lyon. A copy is in the Marcel Moyse Archives.
7. Moyse's betrayer had remained in Paris to play in Nazi-run ensembles. According to Louis Moyse, the man's son became disgusted with his father's opportunism and betrayal of friends and joined the Resistance movement.
8. Moyse, Louis. Note to the author, December 1992.
9. Liebling 1964, 158.
10. Author's interview with Aurèle Nicolet, June 1991.
11. Author's interview with Peter-Lukas Graf, June 1991.
12. Author's interview with Claude Moyse, July 1991.
13. Author's interview with Joseph Cobert, February 1989.

CHAPTER EIGHT
1. *Woodwind Magazine,* February 1949, 1. The premature news might possibly be attributed to the magazine's contacts in Paris, who may have misinterpreted Moyse's plans. It is also not unlikely that Moyse, in his passion for clearing out of France, told some people that he was going to America, instead of South America.
2. *Woodwind Magazine,* January 1950, 1.
3. *Woodwind Magazine,* February 1952, 6.
4. Under Blanche Honegger Moyse's direction, the Brattleboro Music Center (founded in 1952) grew into a nationally recognized community music school.
5. That program, which opened the 1957 Marlboro season, included the Trio Sonata in C minor from "The Musical Offering," S. 1079, of Bach; a Handel Sonata in E minor for two flutes; Haydn's Trio No. 1 in C major, Hob. IV:1, for two flutes and viola; "Aubade printanière" for two flutes and violin by Marcel Gennaro; Louis Moyse's Suite in C minor for two flutes and viola; and the "Syrinx" of Debussy, played by Marcel Moyse.

In the 1950s and early 60s, Louis and Blanche Moyse revived the idea of a Moyse ensemble several times. One year, the pair toured Switzerland, Denmark, Norway, and Sweden as the Moyse Duo. Around 1960, Blanche, Louis, and their friends cellist Nathan Chaikin and pianist Denise Bidal began rehearsing as the Moyse Ensemble and played a few concerts in Switzerland. That effort was short-lived, but the Moyses and Bidal (who lived in Lausanne) continued for a while as a new Trio Moyse, which Marcel approved of wholeheartedly. The group performed publicly several times, including a trip to Argentina, but soon folded when Blanche's bowing arm ceased functioning. Her last appearance at Marlboro as a violinist was in 1966. At that point, Blanche dedicated herself to the study and performance of the choral works of J. S. Bach.

6. Author's interview with Dominique Moyse Steinberg, 10 February 1989.
7. Author's interview with Isabelle Moyse Craig, July 1990.
8. Author's interview with Philipp Naegele, July 1990.
9. The Symphony Club was founded in 1909; students attended music-theory classes and were trained in orchestras led by professional conductors. Half the rehearsals were spent on sight-reading new or unfamiliar pieces, most of which Fleisher collected himself. In 1929 Fleisher donated his collection to the Free Library of Philadelphia, and it continued to grow. With over fifteen thousand compositions, the Fleisher Collection is now the largest body of orchestral performance material in the world. Scores and parts are loaned to organizations for a nominal handling charge. Fleisher disliked vocal music and never purchased works that included a chorus. Today, however, the Fleisher Collection includes orchestral parts for major compositions for chorus and orchestra.
10. Tabuteau emigrated from France to play with the New York Symphony Orchestra in 1905, the same year as Barrère. He was first oboe at the Metropolitan Opera under Toscanini and later played with the Philadelphia Orchestra until he retired in 1954. Tabuteau was two years Moyse's senior and also won his *premier prix* from the Conservatoire at age seventeen.
11. In another account of the event, the offending student asked Moyse about fingerings to use in the piece. To Moyse, fingering choices were trivial compared to the musical ideas he was teaching, and he would have perceived such a question as evidence of a limited imagination.

CHAPTER NINE
1. Moyse received no royalties from sales of his exercise books published by Leduc; the contracts provided only for a flat, one-time fee upon receipt of each manuscript. Moyse's last volumes for Leduc were *Exercices Fürstenau* and *6 grandes études Fürstenau,* both published in April 1940. Louis Moyse recalled that around that time, his father signed a letter from Leduc which carefully proposed that he stop producing exercise books. In all, Leduc had published twenty-eight books by Moyse (see "Publications of Marcel Moyse" near the close of this volume).
2. Moyse Archives.
3. Letter dated 10 May 1959. Moyse Archives.
4. Letter dated 9 January 1961. Moyse Archives.
5. Letter dated 7 July 1959. Moyse Archives.

6. Letter dated 15 December 1961. Moyse Archives.
7. *Brattleboro Reformer,* 6 July 1960.
8. Moyse, Claude and Michel, 1980.
9. Author's interview with Paula Robison, February 1989.
10. Description from the title page of the book, published by McGinnis and Marx. *Tone Development Through Interpretation* is dedicated to Louis Moyse.
11. *The New York Times,* 6 August 1962. Reprinted by permission. Copyright © 1962 by *The New York Times.*
12. According to Louis, one of the organizers had written to Moyse, suggesting that Louis take part as class accompanist. Moyse declined without sharing this idea with his son. Louis interprets the decision as evidence of Moyse's ever-increasing need to be "the only one." Around the same time, Blanche asked her father-in-law to direct Boswil's overflow applicants to a summer school she and Louis were trying to establish in St. Prex. Marcel did not oblige.
13. Author's interview with Alex Ogle, February 1989.
14. Author's interview with Eleanor Lawrence, February 1989.
15. *High Fidelity/Musical America,* September 1972, MA 22–23 ff.
16. Louis and his wife Janet eventually moved to Westport, New York. The breakaway, he said in 1992, was the starting point of his freedom to be his own man, an individual artist. Throughout the 1970s and 80s he enjoyed engagements as a performer and teacher: two years each as a guest professor at the University of Toronto and Boston University and master classes and concerts in Europe, Canada, and the United States. Louis Moyse appeared regularly at the National Flute Association's annual conventions, the last being the 1989 gathering in New Orleans, where he conducted an ensemble of his father's former pupils in one of the convention's several Marcel Moyse Centennial events. Louis still runs his own summer flute seminars in Westport.

   In an article published in *The Flutist Quarterly* ("My Father, Marcel Moyse: The Man, the Artist," Vol. 10, No. 4, Summer 1985, 35–38) after his father's death, Louis wrote:

   > Although circumstances in my life brought about an impasse in the relationship between my father and myself for the last twelve years of his life, I know that his love for me remained as strong as ever. . . . By blood, spirit, and our common heritage I feel fully qualified to evoke a past in which we were close together for nearly half a century as flutists, musicians, and partners.

   And in a note to the author in 1992, he recalled two instances when he attempted to reconcile with his father but was rebuffed. He wrote,

   > Well, I have done what I could. He kept a friendly relationship with many other people who have done worse than I. He always had a paternal smile for them. I didn't have that luck. To finish the story, he was on the losing side, because for myself, I keep in my heart my love, admiration and respect due to an outstanding man and artist. Even the terrestrial Gods have their shortcomings.

CHAPTER TEN

1. In 1978 Blanche Moyse founded the Blanche Moyse Chorale, part of the Brattleboro Music Center, an institution which currently supports a faculty of thirty, plus three hundred students, a chamber series, and a chorus and orchestra for the area's amateur musicians. Six years later she took the Chorale to New York for a performance of the *St. Matthew Passion,* an event cited by *The New York Times* as the "Best Bach of the Tercentenary Year." In 1987 Blanche debuted in Carnegie Hall, conducting the Orchestra of St. Luke's and the Blanche Moyse Chorale in the Bach *Christmas Oratorio,* and in 1990 she returned to Carnegie Hall to conduct the same ensembles in the *St. Matthew Passion.* In October 1993, Blanche Moyse marked the twenty-fifth anniversary of the New England Bach Festival with another performance of that work. She continues to conduct Bach cantatas every year at Marlboro.

   Blanche Moyse is a Fellow of the Vermont Academy of Arts and Sciences, and received the Vermont Governor's Award for Excellence in 1977, six years before her father-in-law. She has honorary degrees from Marlboro College, Southern Vermont College, the University of Vermont, and the New England Conservatory of Music. In 1990 she was named one of thirty-five outstanding Vermont citizens by Governor Madeline Kunin, and was cited by the Vermont Council on the Arts as one of twenty-five residents who had made major contributions to the arts. She has been featured on national radio and television, and has been guest conductor for a number of choruses and orchestras. At this writing, Blanche Moyse is eighty-three.

2. Author's interview with Bob Routch, February 1989.
3. Author's interview with Alain Marion, May 1991.
4. Author's interview with Dominique Moyse Steinberg, February 1989.
5. Hinton-Braaten, Kathleen, "The Grand Old Man of the Flute," *The New York Times,* 1 July 1979, 19, 24.
6. Author's interview with Elaine Douvas, February 1989.
7. Author's interview with Pat Grignet Nott, May 1989.

Selected Bibliography

Ahmad, Patricia J. 1980. *The Flute Professors of the Paris Conservatoire from Devienne to Taffanel.* M.A. Thesis, University of North Texas.

Aitken, Robert. 1979. "Marcel Moyse: A Long and Productive Life." *National Flute Association Newsletter* (February): 1 ff.

Altès, Henri. 1880. *Célèbre méthode complète de flûte.* New ed. Paris: Alphonse Leduc, 1906. Rev. and exp. ed. F. Caratgé. Paris: Alphonse Leduc, 1956.

Andrew, Nancy. 1989. "Marcel Moyse Centennial." *The Flutist Quarterly* (Spring): 25–26.

Andrew, Nancy, and Blanche Moyse. 1987. Letter to the Editor. *The Flutist Quarterly* (Fall): 6.

Andrews, C. E. 1928. *The Innocents of Paris.* New York and London: D. Appleton & Co.

Armes, Roy. 1985. *French Cinema.* London: Secker and Warburg, Ltd.

Arrigo, Ellen, and Darlene Rhodus Tillack. 1961. "Marcel Moyse." *Flute Forum* (Spring): 8–9.

Baker-Carr, Janet. 1977. *Evening at Symphony.* Boston: Houghton-Mifflin Co.

Barrère, Georges. 1921. "The Flutist Biographical." Trans. Lola M. Allison. *The Flutist,* Vol. 2. Nos. 2–4 (February, March, April): 316, 319 ff.; 340–342 ff.; 364–366.

Barrilet, Sophie. 1989. Written interview with Louis Moyse. Trans. William Cloonan. Unpublished.

Bauman, Joan Marie. 1989. "The Living Heritage of Marcel Moyse." *Flute Talk* (May/June): 17–20.

———. 1990. "Peter Lloyd Remembers Moyse." *Flute Talk* (March): 12–13.

Benoist, André. 1978. *The Accompanist: An Autobiography of André Benoist.* Ed. John Anthony Maltese. Neptune, N.J.: Paganiniana Publications, Inc.

233

Bertrand, Laurence. 1985. "Marcel Moyse." Trans. Rachel Wood. *Pan* (June): 43–50. First published in *L'Âme et la Corde,* 121 Blvd. de Magenta, 75010 Paris.

Blaché, Alice Guy. 1986. *The Memoirs of Alice Guy Blaché.* Trans. Roberta and Simone Blaché, ed. Anthony Slide. Metuchen, N.J.: The Scarecrow Press, Inc.

Blakeman, Edward. 1983. "Paul Taffanel—The Father of Modern Flute Playing." *Pan* (April): 7.

————. 1984. "Philippe Gaubert—A Born Flutist." *Pan* (March): 10.

————. 1985. "The Sound Which Sings." *The Listener* (23 May): 36.

Braun, Gerhard. 1979. "Glückwunsch für Marcel Moyse." *Tibia* (2): 325.

Brett, Adrian. 1982. "300 Years of the French School." *The Flute Worker* (November): 1 ff.

————. 1983. "The French Style in America." *The Flute Worker* (December): 1 ff.

————. 1985. "The Other French Players." *The Flute Worker* (Winter): 1 ff.

Brody, Elaine. 1987. *Paris: The Musical Kaleidoscope 1870–1925.* New York: George Braziller, Inc.

Casella, Alberto. 1955. *Music in My Time.* Trans. and ed. Spencer Norton. Norman: Oklahoma University Press.

Citron, Marcia. 1988. *Cécile Chaminade—A Biobibliography.* Westport, Conn.: Greenwood Press.

Cobert, Josef Nathan. 1972. *A Thematic Index with Pedagogical Commentary to the Flute Works of Marcel Moyse.* D.M.A. Dissertation, Florida State University.

Craft, Robert, ed. 1984. *Stravinsky: Selected Correspondence,* Vol. II. New York: Knopf.

Damrosch, Walter. 1930. *My Musical Life.* New York: Charles Scribner's Sons.

De Curzon, H. 1917. "History and Glory of the Concert-Hall of the Paris Conservatory." *Musical Quarterly* iii: 304.

De Lorenzo, Leonardo. 1951. *My Complete Story of the Flute.* New York: Citadel Press.

Dorgeuille, Claude. 1983. *The French Flute School, 1860–1950.* Trans. and ed. Edward Blakeman. London: Tony Bingham, 1986.

Eksteins, Modris. 1989. *Rites of Spring: The Great War and the Birth of the Modern Age.* Rpt. New York: Anchor Books.

Estevan, Pilar. 1976. *Talking with Flutists.* New York: Edutainment Publishing Company.

Étienne, David Eugene. 1988. *A Comparison and Application of Select Teaching Methods for Flute by Henri Altès, Paul Taffanel–Philippe Gaubert, Marcel Moyse, and Trevor Wye.* D.M.A. Dissertation, Louisiana State University.

Fenelon, Fania. 1977. *Playing for Time.* Trans. Judith Landry. New York: Atheneum.

Fischer, Penelope. 1982. *Philippe Gaubert (1879–1941): His Life and Contributions as Flutist, Editor, Teacher, Conductor, and Composer.* D.M.A. Dissertation, University of Michigan.

Flanner, Janet. 1972. *Paris Was Yesterday: 1925–1939.* Ed. Irving Drutman. Rpt. Orlando, Fla.: Harcourt Brace Jovanovich, 1988.

Fletcher, Kristine Klopfenstein. 1988. *The Paris Conservatoire and the Contest Solos for Bassoon.* Bloomington: Indiana University Press.

Galway, James. 1979. *An Autobiography.* New York: St. Martin's Press.

Gold, Arthur, and Robert Fizdale. 1980. *Misia: The Life of Misia Sert.* New York: Knopf.

Goldberg, Bernard. 1979. "Tone Development Through Interpretation: A Tribute to Maître Marcel Moyse for His 80th Birthday." Pamphlet, *W. T. Armstrong Co.*

Gosling, Nigel. 1978. *Paris 1900–1914: The Miraculous Years.* London: Butler and Tanner.

Gundry, Alfred. 1985. "The Marcel Moyse Grand Memorial Concert." *Pan* (March): 30–31.

Hammond, Paul. 1975. *Marvellous Méliès.* New York: St. Martin's Press.

Hansen, Polly. 1984. "Marcel Moyse: Joyful Music." *Flute Talk* (May): 1–4.

Harding, James. 1970. *Massenet.* London: J. M. Dent and Sons.

———. 1972. *The Ox on the Roof: Scenes from Musical Life in Paris in the Twenties.* Rpt. New York: Da Capo Press, 1986.

Hiemenz, Jack. 1975. "Marcel Moyse, Master Flutist: 'I Imitate Caruso.' " *High Fidelity/Musical America* (January): MA 14 ff.

Hill, Edward Burlingame. 1924. *Modern French Music.* Boston: Houghton Mifflin. Rpt. Westport, Conn.: Greenwood Press, 1970.

Hindemith, Paul. 1952. *A Composer's World.* Cambridge, Mass.: Harvard University Press.

Hinton-Braaten, Kathleen. 1979. "The Grand Old Man of the Flute." *The New York Times,* 1 July, Sec. 2, p. 19.

Hopkinson, C. 1954. *A Dictionary of Parisian Music Publishers 1700–1950.* London.

Horowitz, Joseph. 1988. *Understanding Toscanini.* Minneapolis: University of Minnesota Press.

Howe, M. A. De Wolfe. 1914. *The Boston Symphony Orchestra: An Historical Sketch.* Boston and New York: Houghton Mifflin Co.

James, Henry. 1990. *A Little Tour in France.* Rev. ed. New York: Houghton, Mifflin & Co.

Kaufmann, Richard. 1891. *Paris of Today.* Trans. Olga Flinch. Chicago: Thompson & Thomas.

Keefe, Linda. 1989. "The Magic of Moyse." *Flute Talk* (May/June): 21.

Kirk, H. L. 1974. *Pablo Casals.* New York: Holt, Rinehart & Winston.

Koechlin, Charles. 1945. *Gabriel Fauré.* London: Dennis Dobson Ltd. Rpt. New York: AMS Press, 1976.

Kozinn, Allan. 1981. "The Miracle of Marlboro: Rudolf Serkin's Musical Mecca." *Ovation* (June): 10 ff.

Kupferberg, Herbert. 1969. *Those Fabulous Philadelphians: The Life and Times of a Great Orchestra.* New York: Charles Scribner's Sons.

Laloy, Louis. 1906. "Les Concours du Conservatoire." *Le Mercure Musical* (August 15): 154–157.

Lavignac, Albert. 1895. *Music and Musicians*. Trans. William Marchant, ed. H. E. Krehbiel. New York: G. P. Putnam's Sons.

Lavignac, A., and L. de La Laurencie, eds. 1921–31. *Encyclopédie de la musique et dictionnaire du Conservatoire*. Paris: C. Delagrave.

Lawrence, Eleanor. 1979. "Interview with Marcel Moyse." *National Flute Association Newsletter* (February): 3, 5, 8–10.

Lesure, François, and Roger Nichols, eds. 1987. *Debussy Letters*. Trans. Roger Nichols. London: Faber and Faber.

Liebling, A. J. 1944. *The Road Back to Paris*. New York: Doubleday, Doran and Co. Rpt. New York: Paragon House, 1988.

———. 1964. *Mollie and Other War Pieces*. New York: Ballantine Books. Rpt. New York: Schocken Books, 1989.

Lippa, Si. 1979. "Notes from the Magic Flutist." *Women's Wear Daily*, 17–24 August.

Locke, Arthur Ware. 1920. *Music and the Romantic Movement in France*. London: K. Paul, Trench, Trubner & Co.

"Lost Moyse Manuscript: Publisher's Alert." 1985. *The Flutist Quarterly* (Summer): 27.

Lynch, Hannah. 1906. *French Rural and Provincial Life*. London: G. Putnam's & Sons.

Maitland, J. A. Fuller, ed. 1922. *Grove's Dictionary of Music and Musicians*. London: MacMillan Co.

"Marcel Moyse, Flutist, a Founder of Marlboro." 1984. *The New York Times*, 2 November, Sec. D, p. 18.

"Marcel Moyse: Publications and Records." 1979. *National Flute Association Newsletter* (February): 10 ff.

Marlboro Music School and Festival. 1992. *Marlboro Music: 1951–1991*. Marlboro, Vt.: Marlboro Music School and Festival.

Martinů, Charlotte. 1978. *My Life with Bohuslav Martinů*. Trans. Diderik C. D. DeJong. Prague: Orbis Press Agency.

Massenet, Jules. 1919. *My Recollections*. Trans. H. Villiers Barnett. Boston. First published in 1912 as *Mes souvenirs, 1848–1912*. Paris. New edition annotated by Gérard Condé. Paris, 1992.

McCutchan, Ann. 1989a. "Marcel Moyse: A Biographical Sketch." *Flute Talk* (May/June): 14–16.

———. 1989b. "Voice of the Flute: Remembering Marcel Moyse." *Chamber Music* (Summer): 18–19, 33; (Fall): 21–23, 37, 56.

Medicus, Emil, ed. 1920–28. *The Flutist*. January 1920–May 1928. Asheville, N.C.: Emil Medicus.

Melba, Nellie. 1926. *Melodies and Memories*. Rpt. New York: AMS Press, 1971.

Meylan, Raymond. 1974. *La Flûte*. Lausanne: Éditions Payot. Trans. Alfred Clayton as *The Flute*. Portland, Ore.: Amadeus Press, 1988.

———. 1985. "Mein Studienplan bei Marcel Moyse." *Tibia* 10 (1): 265–267.

Monteux, Doris. 1965. *It's All in the Music*. New York: Farrar, Straus & Giroux.

Montgomery, William. 1985. "Bernard Goldberg—Carrying On the Tradition." *Flute Talk* (January): 2–7.

Moran, William. 1985. *Nellie Melba: A Contemporary Review.* Westport, Conn.: Greenwood Press.

Moyse, Blanche. 1975. Interview with Marcel Moyse. Unedited audio footage for "Marcel Moyse Flute Seminars 1975" videotapes. Trans. Michel Moyse. Marcel Moyse Archives.

Moyse, Claude and Michel. 1980. Trans. Philip Gottling. Unedited interviews with Marcel Moyse for the film "Marcel Moyse, Grand Old Man of the Flute." Recorded May-August. Marcel Moyse Archives.

———. 1984. "Marcel Moyse, Grand Old Man of the Flute." Videotape. Brattleboro: Moyse Enterprises.

———. 1989. "Marcel Moyse Flute Seminars 1975." Set of eight videotapes. Brattleboro: Moyse Enterprises.

Moyse, Louis. 1977. "Homage to Marcel Moyse." Speech given at National Flute Association conference, Atlanta, Georgia, 21 August 1976. *National Flute Association Newsletter* (March): 7.

———. 1985. "My Father, Marcel Moyse: The Man, the Artist." *The Flutist Quarterly* (Summer): 35–38.

Moyse, Marcel. 1935. "M. Moyse nous parle de son enseignement de flûte." Ed. Jean Vuillermoz. *Musique et Concours* (October). Trans. Edward Blakeman, *Pan* (December),1985.

———. 1949. "Marcel Moyse on Flute Playing." Trans. Maud La Charme. *Symphony* (June/July): 5.

———. 1950. "The Unsolvable Problem: Considerations on Flute Vibrato." *Woodwind Magazine* (March): 14.

———. 1973. *The Flute and Its Problems: Tone Development Through Interpretation.* Tokyo: Muramatsu.

Nevill, Ralph. 1927. *Days and Nights in Montmartre and the Latin Quarter.* New York: Geoge H. Doran Co.

Older, Julia. 1979. "Marcel Moyse: The Magic Flutist." *Woodwind World Brass & Percussion* 18(4): 8–10.

Orenstein, Arbie, comp. and ed. 1990. *A Ravel Reader.* New York: Columbia University Press.

Otis, Philo Adams. 1924. *The Chicago Symphony Orchestra. Its Organization, Growth and Development, 1891–1924.* Chicago: Clayton F. Summy Co.

Perrin, Olivier, ed. 1960. *Prestigieux théâtres de France.* Paris.

Pinchemel, Philippe. 1969. *France: A Geographical Survey.* Trans. Christine Trollope and Arthur J. Hunt. New York: Frederic A. Praeger.

Pincherle, Marc. 1961. *Le Monde des Virtuoses.* Paris: Flammarion. Trans. Lucile H. Brockway as *The World of the Virtuoso.* New York: W. W. Norton, 1963.

Pitou, Spire. 1990. *The Paris Opéra: An Encyclopedia of Operas, Ballets, Composers and Performers.* Westport, Conn.: Greenwood Press.

"Remembrances of Marcel Moyse." 1984. *The Flutist Quarterly* (Winter): 12–17.

Rich, Alan. 1962. "Marlboro Octet Excels in Concert." *The New York Times,* 6 August.

Robison, Paula. 1992. "À Propos de Moyse." *Greater Boston Flute Association Newsletter* (May): 3–4.
Rosenstiel, Leonie. 1982. *Nadia Boulanger: A Life in Music.* New York: W. W. Norton.
Rubinstein, Artur. 1973. *My Young Years.* New York: Knopf.
Sadie, Stanley, ed. 1980. *The New Grove Dictionary of Music and Musicians.* London: MacMillan Publishers Ltd.
Saint-Saëns, Camille. 1919. *Musical Memories.* Trans. Edwin Gile Rich. Boston: Small, Maynard & Co.
_____. 1922. *Outspoken Essays on Music.* Trans. Fred Rothwell. London. Rpt. 1969.
Scobie, James R. 1971. *Argentina: A City and a Nation.* 2d ed. New York: Oxford University Press.
Serkin, Irene Busch, comp. 1991. *Adolf Busch: Letters–Pictures–Memories,* Vols. 1 and 2. Trans. Russell Stockman. Walpole, N.II.: Arts & Letters Press.
Shattuck, Roger. 1958. *The Banquet Years: The Origins of the Avant-Garde in France, 1885 to World War I.* Rev. ed. New York: Vintage Books, 1968.
Sonneck, O. G. 1949. *Early Concert Life in America, 1731–1800.* New York: Musurgia Publishers.
Steinheil, Marguerite. 1912. *My Memoirs.* New York: Sturgis & Walton Co.
Suckling, Norman. 1951. *Fauré.* London: Dent. Rpt. Westport, Conn.: Greenwood Press, 1979.
Swilley, Wanda Sue. 1978. *A Comprehensive Performance Project in Flute Literature with an Essay on Flute Embouchure Pedagogy in the United States from ca. 1925–1977 as Described in Selected Writings.* D.M.A. Dissertation, University of Iowa.
Thompson, Oscar. 1937. *Debussy: Man and Artist.* Rpt. New York: Dover Publications, 1965.
Toff, Nancy. 1985. *The Flute Book.* New York: Charles Scribner's Sons.
"A Tribute to Marcel Moyse." 1984. *The Flutist Quarterly* (Winter): 9 ff.
Vuillermoz, Émile. 1969. *Gabriel Fauré.* Trans. Kenneth Schapin. Philadelphia: Chilton Book Co.
Vuillermoz, Jean. 1935. "Marcel Moyse on His Method of Learning the Flute." *Musique et Concours* (October). Rpt. *The Flutist Quarterly* 1986 (Spring): 59–62. Trans. and intro. Edward Blakeman.
Weber, Eugen. 1986. *France, Fin de Siècle.* Cambridge, Mass.: Belknap Press.
Weinstock, Herbert. 1968. *Rossini: A Biography.* New York: Knopf.
Wood, Charles W. 1900. *In the Valley of the Rhone.* London: MacMillan & Co. Ltd.
Wye, Trevor. 1985a. "Marcel Moyse: An Appreciation." *Pan* (March): 33–38.
_____. 1985b. "Marcel Moyse 1889–1984." *Pan* (June): 57–58.
Zeldin, Theodore. 1973–77. *France, 1848–1945,* 2 vols. Oxford: Oxford University Press.

Publications of
Marcel Moyse

Leduc	Contract Date; Copyright Date
Études et exercices techniques	June 1921; 1921
Exercices journaliers	October 1922; 1923
25 études de virtuosité Czerny	September 1927; 1929
Mécanisme—chromatisme	July 1927; 1928
École de l'articulation	July 1927; 1928
25 études mélodiques avec variations	May 1928; 1932
Chopin: 12 études de grande virtuosité	June 1928; 1929
20 études d'après Kreutzer	June 1928; 1929
100 études faciles et progressives d'après Cramer (in two volumes)	September 1928; 1933
24 petites études mélodiques	September 1928; 1932
De la sonorité: art et technique	August 1932; 1934
Histoires, *Jacques Ibert* (transcription)	August 1932; 1933
48 études de virtuosité (in two volumes)	October 1932; 1933
Gammes et arpèges	October 1932; 1933
Le débutant flûtiste	August 1933; 1935
10 études d'après Kessler	August 1933; 1935
10 études d'après Wieniawski	August 1933; 1935
50 études mélodiques Demersseman (in two volumes)	August 1933; 1937
20 exercices ou études sur les grandes liaisons	August 1933; 1935
Bouquet de tons	May 1938; 1952
24 études Caprice	May 1938; 1948
24 études journalières d'après Soussman	May 1938; 1949
18 exercices Berbiguier	May 1938; 1949
Grandes études Berbiguier	May 1938; 1949

12 études Boehm	May 1938; 1949
26 exercices Fürstenau (in two volumes)	December 1939; 1949
Exercices Fürstenau	April 1940; 1949
6 grandes études Fürstenau	April 1940; 1949

McGinnis and Marx Music Publishers	**Copyright Date**
Tone Development Through Interpretation for the Flute and Other Wind Instruments: the study of expression, vibrato, color, suppleness, and their application to different styles	1962; corrected ed., 1978
50 Variations on the Allemande of Bach from the Sonata for Flute Alone for the study of articulation, embellishment, trills, groppetti, and grace notes	1964

Muramatsu	n.d.
The Flute and Its Problems: Tone Development Through Interpretation for the Flute	

Zen-On Music, Tokyo	
The Golden Age of the Flutists	1979

Self-Published

Comment j'ai pu maintenir ma forme (with English translation of text: *How I Stayed in Shape,* by Paul Douglas), West Brattleboro, Vermont	1974

Discography

by Susan Nelson and William Shaman

Table of Contents

INTRODUCTION

Marcel Moyse, already renowned as a soloist when the electrical recording process emerged in 1925, quite naturally became the first flutist of the prewar era to record extensively. He was not an especially prolific recording artist, however, when compared to the pianists and violinists of the same era who enjoyed a similar international reputation, but he did succeed in recording a representative cross-section of the flute's serious repertory over a period of more than two decades. In many cases, Moyse's remained the only interpretations available on disc for years. (As George Sutherland lamented in the February 1937 issue of *The Gramophone,* "Our wind instruments talent was never richer than it is to-day, but the meager output does it scant justice" [p. 376].) Yet Moyse was by no means a pioneer: flutists had been recording regularly since the 1890s. Many anonymous artists and members of famous military and concert bands had produced thousands of renditions of popular songs, marches, waltzes, and polkas. As early as 1910, the flute was well known to patrons of the gramophone, although not as a very serious or versatile instrument. Small ensembles of flute, violin, and harp poured out a seemingly endless stream of salon music on early records, while virtuoso piccolists performed amazing variations and musically portrayed every known species of bird.

Woodwind performers of serious reputation were not entirely neglected, but they were seldom courted by the recording industry prior to the advent of electrical recording. Many prominent flutists did record before Moyse, most notably some of his French predecessors. Philippe Gaubert and Adolphe Hennebains, both professors at the Paris Conservatory and acclaimed virtuosos, made acoustical recordings. Georges Barrère began recording in 1903 and continued at irregular intervals until 1941. René Le Roy, Moyse's most esteemed contemporary, was more active still, recording from the 1920s until after the war, while other prominent French flutists of the period—George Laurent, Gaston Blanquart, and Gaston Crunelle among them—recorded only sporadically. Among English flutists, Albert Fransella was an early and very active recording artist, his first discs having been made in the 1890s. Eli Hudson, more renowned perhaps as a piccolist, made many recordings during the acoustical period, while Robert Murchie; John Lemmone, an Australian; and John Amadio of New

Zealand made relatively few, but were among the most important early interpreters of more sophisticated repertory on records. Emil Prill, first flutist of the Berlin Staatsoper Orchestra, was recording more esoteric eighteenth-century works in Germany by the early 1920s, as was Georg Müller. In America, band musicians such as Frank V. Badollet, Darius Lyons, and Marshall Lufsky, as well as such orchestral and studio players as Clement Barone, Sr., dominated the catalogs, with little competition from any native concert virtuosos (many of America's leading flutists had by then been imported from Europe). John Wummer and William Kincaid, long-time first flutist of the Philadelphia Orchestra, were probably the first prominent American flute virtuosos to record consistently important repertory.

With the coming of electrical recording and the proliferation of serious instrumental music on record, including large-scale works, the woodwind repertory came gradually to assert itself as commercially viable. In this setting, Moyse began recording, both as a soloist and as a principal member of the numerous ensembles with which he was associated beginning in the 1910s: the Paris Opéra-Comique, Pasdeloup, Paris Conservatory, and Straram orchestras. His recording career was centered in the Paris studios of the Gramophone Company and Columbia Graphophone, but he also recorded in London for the English branches of both companies. His other records, which appeared on a variety of labels, all seem to have been made in Paris, with the possible exception of what may have been a Swiss session for Decca (items nos. 50–53) and an obscure group of French recordings for Nippon Columbia (items nos. 165–168). His only American recordings were privately made and issued first in the 1950s on his own "Marcel Moyse" label. Moyse's first known commercial solo recordings were made in 1927, his last in 1948, with private pedagogical recordings occupying him thereafter. There are no documented acoustical recordings, but it is entirely possible, considering the fact that he was active as a soloist prior to the First World War, that there were earlier recorded performances. Chamber music, played in ensemble, tended to dominate his commercial output both as a flutist and, near the end of his life, as a conductor, but there is ample evidence of his versatility in the many orchestral recordings made in the 1920s and 1930s in which he can be heard distinctly. Several European broadcasts have survived from the years 1934–50, as well as a remarkable film of the Paris Conservatory Orchestra, Philippe Gaubert conducting, made in the mid or late 1930s. This may be only one of several short films made by the orchestra (another, conducted by Robert Heger but not featuring Moyse, has also come to light recently).

The discography lists all the documented Moyse solo and ensemble recordings, published and unpublished, as well as his few recordings as a conductor, much of this information having been taken directly from the ledgers of EMI, the company responsible for the majority of his commercial releases. All known broadcast transcriptions and films have been listed, the latter including Moyse's appearances as an orchestral player, conductor, and teacher—in the apparent absence of any motion pictures of him on the concert platform. It seems very likely that more motion picture footage will eventually be discovered. Excluded from the discography are the many uncredited orchestral recordings in which he probably took part for a variety of labels including the Gramophone Company, Columbia, Pathé, and possibly others. Parts III and IV of the discography list those orchestral recordings on which Moyse is actually *identified* as a soloist and, in a few cases, recordings in which his participation has long been suspected.

ACKNOWLEDGEMENTS

Grateful acknowledgement is made to the following individuals for their generous assistance in compiling this discography: Sarah Hobbs and the staff of the EMI Music Archives, Hayes, Middlesex; Alan Kelly, Sheffield; William R. Moran, La Cañada, California; and Michel Moyse, Brattleboro, Vermont.

We are also grateful for the assistance of Marguerite Andreasson, Vermont; Kathy Andrew, Brattleboro; Nancy Andrew, Baltimore; Dr. Frederick Crane, Iowa City; Fredi Dünnenberger, Baar, Switzerland; Frank Erzinger, Wädenswil, Switzerland; Herbert Glass, Champaign, Illinois; Carol Hoeschen, St. Scholastica College, Duluth, Minnesota; Eleanor Lawrence, New York City; Betty Bang and Roger Mather, Iowa City; Marc Monneraye, Saint-Maur-des-Fossés, France; Claude Moyse, Vermont; Louis Moyse, Vermont; Alex Ogle, Brattleboro; the Sony-CBS Archives, New York City; Christopher Steward, Birmingham,

England; and John Strukel, St. John's University, Collegeville, Minnesota. Our thanks as well to author Ann McCutchan, Austin.

Special thanks is tendered to Peter Adamson, St. Andrews, Fife, for his expert sleuthing on obscure matters of repertory and European labels and to Blanche Moyse, Brattleboro, who graciously consented to be interviewed on the subject of her recordings with the Trio Moyse.

General Abbreviations

*	An asterisk placed before a discography number designates an endnote.
?	Unknown or uncertain
arr.	Arranged by
pf/	Piano accompaniment/pianist as named
pf/?	Piano accompaniment/pianist unknown
orch/	Orchestral accompaniment/conductor as named
orch/?	Orchestral accompaniment/conductor unknown
[]	Gramophone Company single-sided "face numbers," which were assigned to all pre-1934 double-sided issues, are given in brackets after the double-sided catalog numbers.

Discography Numbers

Individual discography numbers are assigned to each individual matrix or master recording. In the case of original microgroove recordings (items nos. 199–225), discography numbers are assigned to the individual selections on each side.

Performers

Performers' names are given first for each item in the discography, with soloists' names followed by those of accompanists and accompanying ensembles/conductors in parentheses.

Titles

Listed immediately after performers' names, titles of vocal works and excerpts are generally in the language used on the original record labels, followed by titles in the original language in brackets. Translations of titles and "nicknames" are also given after the title, in brackets and quotation marks.

All vocal recordings in which Moyse participated are in French.

Matrix Numbers

At the left of the discographical information, matrix numbers have a letter prefix and take-number suffix. All Moyse recordings included in this discography are electrical recordings.

His Master's Voice (HMV) matrix-number prefixes vary according to date and place of recording. Among the early variable HMV matrix prefixes, "OPG" and "2G" are ten- and twelve-inch Paris masters, respectively. Beginning with Moyse's 1935 HMV recordings, the "2LA" matrix prefix designates a twelve-inch master recorded in Paris and "OLA" a ten-inch Paris master; "2EA" designates a twelve-inch London master ("OEA" was the ten-inch London designation).

In the case of Moyse's many Columbia recordings, the "W" designates the early Western Electric cutter head, while "C" designates the later Columbia (Blumlein) head. "L" designates a Paris recording, "A" a London recording. "X" designates a twelve-inch master (ten-inch masters are designated by the absence of this third letter).

The other companies for which Moyse recorded did not use coded matrix-number prefixes, the size of masters being indicated instead by the catalog-number prefix assigned.

Take Numbers

These are the numerical suffixes to the matrix numbers. Unknown take numbers are indicated by a question mark following the matrix number: in such instances, it is not known which takes were made or issued. In cases where more than one take of a matrix was recorded during the same session, the issued take is underlined.

Gramophone Company take numbers ending "T1" were transfers, made most often to compensate for some inadequacy in the original master.

Recording Dates

The day, month, or year of the session(s) is listed immediately after the matrix numbers. When the exact date(s) of a recording are not known, a span of dates may be cited, based upon the available information: thus, "late 1928–early 1929" designates a recording made *between* rather than *through* those dates.

Catalog Numbers

To the right of the recording dates, catalog numbers from the *original* country of issue are given first for all recordings, followed by those of other countries in alphabetical order by catalog-number prefix. Subsequent issues have been stacked beneath the original catalog numbers.

Generally, European catalog numbers bear letter prefixes, while most American catalog numbers do not. Catalog numbers for most of the companies for which Moyse recorded (Odéon, Decca, Pathé, *L'Anthologie Sonore,* etc.) are explained in the headers for each section of the discography. For Columbia, the Gramophone Company, and Victor the following table is provided:

Columbia Graphophone Co., Ltd.
Columbia Phonograph Company, New York

26000	Argentina (12-inch)	DF	France (10-inch)
[5000]	U.K. (10-inch)	DFX	France (12-inch)
		DO	Australia (10-inch)
D 11000	France (12-inch)	DOX	Australia (12-inch)
D 13000	France (10-inch)	DX	U.K. (12-inch)
D 19000	France (10-inch)	GQX	Italy (12-inch)
D-suffix	U.S. *Masterworks*:	J	Czechoslavakia (10-inch)
	17000 (10-inch)	LF	France (10-inch)
	68000 (12-inch)	LFX	France (12-inch)
	69000 (12-inch)	LX	U.K. (12-inch)
	70000 (12-inch)	LWX	Germany (12-inch)
DB	U.K. (10-inch)		
		M-*suffix*	U.S. Masterworks: 4000 (10-inch)
		S	Japanese Nippono-phone/Nippon Columbia Co. Ltd.

The British 5000 catalog numbers continued a block which began at 1000.

The Gramophone Company, Ltd.,
Hayes, Middlesex ("His Master's Voice")
Compagnie Française du Gramophone,
Paris ("La Voix de Son Maître")

AW	Italy black label (12-inch)
C	U.K. plum label (12-inch)
DA	International "Celebrity" red label (10-inch)
DB	International "Celebrity" red label (12-inch)
ED	Australia black label (12-inch)
FKX	Switzerland plum label (12-inch)
K	France green label (10-inch)
L	France green label (12-inch)
P	France black label (10-inch)
SK	France blue label (10-inch)
SL	France blue label (12-inch)
W	France black label (12-inch)
G&T	Gramophone & Typewriter Ltd. (X: Long-Playing Reissues only)

Victor [RCA Manufacturing Company, Inc.]

4500-	10-inch Red Seal
11000-	12-inch Red Seal

I THE SOLO RECORDINGS

Compagnie Française du Gramophone
Paris

Recorded Paris, 1927

* 1. MARCEL MOYSE; flute (pf/R. Delor?): *ORFEO ED EURIDICE,*
     ACT II: "Dance of the Blessed Spirits" (Gluck)
     BFR 438-1   21–26 Mar 1927   K5266 [239158]

* 2. MARCEL MOYSE, flute (pf/R. Delor?): *L'ARLÉSIENNE* SUITE
     NO. 2: Minuet (Bizet–arr. Guiraud)
     BFR 439-1   21–26 Mar 1927   K5165 [239156]

* 3. MARCEL MOYSE, flute (pf/R. Delor?): SONATA IN G MAJOR,
     Op. 1, No. 5 (Handel)
     a) [Fifth movement]: Menuetto   b) [Second movement]: Allegro
     BFR 440-1, 2   21–26 Mar 1927   K5266 [239157]

* 4. MARCEL MOYSE, flute (pf/R. Delor?): "Carnaval de Venise,"
     Op. 14 (Paul Genin)
     BFR 441-1, 2   21–26 Mar 1927   K5165 [239155]

Columbia Graphophone Company, Ltd.
Paris

Recorded Paris, 1927?

MARCEL MOYSE, flute (pf/Georges Truc): "Fantaisie" (Georges Hüe)

* 5. Part 1:
     WLX 133-?   1927?   D11006

* 6. Part 2:
     WLX 163-1?   1927?   D11006

* 7. MARCEL MOYSE, flute (pf/Georges Truc): "Carnaval de Venise,"
     Op. 14 (Paul Genin)
     WLX 164-1   1927?   D11062

Odéon
Paris

Issued as green French Odéon (165.000 catalog numbers), brown
German Odéon (O-prefix catalog numbers), and maroon American
Decca imports ("Odéon-Parlophone Recording" series, 20000 catalog
numbers, sometimes prefixed "G-").

Recorded Paris, late 1927–early 1928

MARCEL MOYSE, flute; EUGÈNE GINOT, viola; LILY LASKINE, harp:
SONATA FOR FLUTE, VIOLA, AND HARP (Debussy)

* 8. Pastorale (first part)
      Ki 1527-1, 2   1927–28   165.243   O-26100   [G-]20085

* 9. Pastorale (conclusion)
      Ki 1528-1, 2   1927–28   165.243   O-26100   [G-]20085

*10. Interlude (first part)
      Ki 1529-1, 2   1927–28   165.244   O-26101   [G-]20086

*11. Interlude (conclusion)
      Ki 1530-1, 2   1927–28   165.244   O-26101   [G-]20086

*12. Final (first part)
      Ki 1531-1, 2   1927–28   165.245   O-26102   [G-]20087

*13. Final (conclusion)
      Ki 1532-1, 2   1927–28   165.245   O-26102   [G-]20087

Columbia Graphophone Company, Ltd.
Paris

Recorded Paris, 1928

*14. MARCEL MOYSE, flute (unaccompanied): "Syrinx" (Debussy)
      WL 853-1   16–18 Jan 1928   D19056

*15. MARCEL MOYSE, flute (pf/Georges Truc): "Andante pastorale"
      (Taffanel)
      WL 854-1   16–18 Jan 1928   D19056

*16. MARCEL MOYSE, flute (pf/Georges Truc): "Scherzettino"
      (Taffanel)
      WL 855-1, 2   16–18 Jan 1928   D19088

      MATRICES 856–857: NO INFORMATION/NOT USED

 17. MARCEL MOYSE, flute (pf/Georges Truc): SUITE NO. 2 IN B
      MINOR, BWV 1067 (J. S. Bach)
      a) Polonaise b) Badinerie
      WL 858-1   16–18 Jan 1928   D19088

MARCEL MOYSE, flute; GABRIEL PIERNÉ, piano; — LOPÈS, cello:
SONATA DA CAMERA, Op. 48 (Pierné)

*18. Prélude (first part)
      WL 1160-1   1928   D13063   5275

*19. Prélude (conclusion)
      WL 1161-1   1928   D13063   5275

*20. Sarabande sur le nom de Louis Fleury (first part)
      WL 1162-1   1928   D13064   5276

*21. Sarabande sur le nom de Louis Fleury (conclusion)
WL 1163-1   1928   D13064   5276

*22. Finale (first part)
WL 1164-1, 2   1928   D13065   5277

*23. Finale (conclusion)
WL 1165-1, 2   1928   D13065   5277

Compagnie Française du Gramophone
Paris
Recorded Paris, 1928

*24. YVONNE BROTHIER, soprano; MARCEL MOYSE, flute (orch/G. Diot): *LE PARDON DE PLOËRMEL [DINORAH]*, ACT II: "Ombre Légère" (Meyerbeer)
BT 4028-1, 2   7 Jun 1928   P831 [50-659]

YVONNE BROTHIER, soprano; MARCEL MOYSE, flute (orch/G. Diot): *LUCIA DI LAMMERMOOR*, ACT III: Mad Scene (Donizetti)

*25. "L'autel rayonne" ["Splendor le sacre facì intorno!"]
CT 4029-1, 2   7 Jun 1928   W966 [033290]

*26. "Je vais loin de la terre" ["Spargi d'amaro pianto il mio terrestre velo"]
CT 4030-1, 2   7 Jun 1928   W966 [033291]

Columbia Graphophone Company, Ltd.
Paris
Recorded Paris, 1929

MARCEL MOYSE, flute; MME. Y. BLEUZET, piano; LOUIS BLEUZET, oboe; LOUIS COSTES, clarinet; FERNAND OUBRADOUS, bassoon: *QUINTETTE* (G. Rumeau)

*27. a) Theme b) Variation 1 c) Variation 2 d) Variation 3
WLX 974-?   Mar–Apr 1929   D11060

*28. Variation 4
WLX 975-?   Mar–Apr 1929   D11060

*29. Variation 5
WLX 976-?   Mar–Apr 1929   D11061

*30. a) Variation 6 b) Variation 7 c) Variation 8 (first part)
WLX 977-?   Mar–Apr 1929   D11061

*31. a) Variation 8 (conclusion) b) Finale
WLX 978-?   Mar–Apr 1929   D11062

Odéon
Paris

Issued as green French Odéon (165.000 catalog numbers) and maroon American Decca imports ("Odéon-Parlophone Recording" series, 20000 catalog numbers, sometimes prefixed "G-"). There were no German issues.

Recorded Paris, 1929

*32. MARCEL MOYSE, flute (pf/?): "Fantaisie avec variations sur un air napolitain," Op. 8 (Paul Genin)
    Ki 2796-1, 2   Dec 1929 165.853   —   —

*33. MARCEL MOYSE, flute (pf/?): *SUITE,* Op. 116: Idylle (Godard)
    Ki 2797-1, 2   Dec 1929 165.853   —   —

*34. MARCEL MOYSE, flute (pf/?): "Variations sur un air tyrolienne," Op. 20 (Theobald Böhm)
    Ki 2798-1, 2   Dec 1929 165.854   —   —

*35. MARCEL MOYSE, flute (pf/?): "Carmen fantaisie brillante" (François Borne)
    Ki 2799-1, 2   Dec 1929 165.855   —   [G-]20535

*36. MARCEL MOYSE, flute (pf/?): *FANTAISIE PASTORALE HONGROISE,* Op. 26: Molto andante (Franz Doppler)
    Ki 2811-1, 2   Dec 1929 165.854   —   —

*37. MARCEL MOYSE, flute (pf/?): "Madrigal" (Gaubert)
    Ki 2812-1, 2   Dec 1929 165.855   —   [G-]20535

*38. MARCEL MOYSE, flute (pf/?): *LE CARNAVAL DES ANIMAUX:* "Le Cygne" (Saint-Saëns)
    Ki 2813-1, 2   Dec 1929 165.856   —   —

*39. MARCEL MOYSE, flute (pf/?): "Mélodie" (E. Noblot)
    Ki 2814-1, 2   Dec 1929 165.856   —   —

Compagnie Française du Gramophone
Paris

Recorded Paris, 1930

MARCEL MOYSE, flute (orch/Piero Coppola): CONCERTO NO. 2 IN D MAJOR, K. 314 (Mozart)

*40. Allegro aperto (first part)
    CF 3111-1   30–31 Mar 1930 L835 [52-748]   12477
                              C2258 [52-748]
                              FKX41 [52-748]
         -2   Mar–Apr? 1930 unpublished

*41. Allegro aperto (conclusion) [Cadenza by Donjon]
          CF 3112-1   30–31 Mar 1930 unpublished
                      -2   Mar–Apr? 1930 L835 [52-749]   12477
                                          C2258 [52-749]
                                          FKX41 [52-749]

*42. Andante ma non troppo
          CF 3113-1   30–31 Mar 1930 unpublished
                      -2   Mar–Apr? 1930 L836? [52-750]   12478?
                                          C2259 [52-750]
                                          FKX42? [52-750]

                      -2T1 1930?   L836 [52-750]   12478
                                          C2259 [52-750]
                                          FKX42 [52-750]

*43. Allegro [Cadenza by Donjon]
          CF 3114-1   30–31 Mar 1930 L836 [52-751]   12478
                                          C2259 [52-751]
                                          FKX42 [52-751]
                      -2   Mar–Apr? 1930 unpublished

Columbia Graphophone Company, Ltd.
Paris
Recorded Paris, 1930

MARCEL MOYSE, flute; MANUEL DE FALLA, harpsichord; GEORGE
BONNEAU, oboe; ÉMILE GODEAU, clarinet; MARCEL DARRIEUX,
violin; AUGUSTE CRUQUE, cello: CONCERTO FOR HARPSI-
CHORD, FLUTE, OBOE, CLARINET, VIOLIN, AND CELLO (De Falla)

*44. Allegro
          WLX 1366-1, [2, 3] 2 Jun 1930? unpublished
                      -4   7 Jun 1930? LFX 92 67922-D 266017
                                                      70408-D

*45. Lento (giubiloso ed energico) (first part)
          WLX 1367-1, [2, 3] 2 Jun 1930? unpublished
                      -4   7 Jun 1930? LFX 92 67922-D 266017
                                                      70409-D

*46. Lento (giubiloso ed energico) (conclusion)
          WLX 1417-1   2 Jun 1930? unpublished
                      -2, [3, 4] 7 Jun 1930? LFX 93 67923-D 266018
                                                      70409-D

*47. Finale: vivace (flessibile scherzando)
          WLX 1418-1   2 Jun 1930? unpublished
                      -2, [3, 4] 7 Jun 1930? LFX 93 67923-D 266018
                                                      70408-D

JOSEPH ROGATCHEWSKY, tenor; MARCEL MOYSE, flute (orch/Elie Cohen): *ARMIDE,* ACT II: "Plus j'observe ces lieux" ["Air de Renaud"] (Gluck)

*48. First part:
     WL 2832-1   Dec 1930   LF76   4127-M

*49. Second part:
     WL 2833-1   Dec 1930   LF76   4127-M

Decca Record Company Ltd.
Paris and/or Switzerland?

The original French and English pressings bear early purple labels with the Beethoven motif. The "T" and "TF" catalog prefixes are French; the "K" prefixes are British. Maroon American Decca imports (25000 catalog numbers) were issued in the "Odéon-Parlophone Recording" series.

Both the Beethoven Serenade and the Berlioz Trio appeared in the eleventh French Decca Supplement (1931), but only the Beethoven is listed in an English Supplement dated June 1931. There was apparently no British issue of TF.139.

It has not been possible to determine with certainty the national origin of the "SA" matrix prefix, but there is persuasive evidence that these records were Swiss, recorded in the studios of either Radio Suisse, Zurich; Radio Beromünster, Bern; or Victoria Hall, Geneva. French Polydor has been suggested as a possible source, the recordings having been made either in Le Bal Bullier, an old Parisian dance hall, or in their studio located near Pathé-Marconi on Rue Albert. It has also been claimed that the SA/SB block (twelve- and ten-inch, respectively) was recorded by Decca at the Salle Gaveau, Paris. The "FA" prefixes of the Berlioz were definitely Parisian. The chronology of the two Moyse Decca sessions is also uncertain, but late 1930–early 1931 for both seems likely.

Recorded Paris or Switzerland?, 1930–31

MARCEL MOYSE, flute; MARCEL DARRIEUX, violin; PIERRE PASQUIER, viola: SERENADE, Op. 25 (Beethoven)

*50. [First movement]: Entrata–Allegro
     SA 50-1, 2   1930–31   T.10002   K.582   G-25592

*51. [Second movement]: Tempo ordinario d'un Menuetto
     SA 51-1, 2   1930–31   T.10002   K.582   G-25592

*52. [Fourth movement]: Andante con Variazioni
     SA 52-1, 2   1930–31   T.10003   K.583   G-25593

*53. [Sixth movement]: Adagio–Allegro vivace e disinvolto
     SA 53-1, 2   1930–31   T.10003   K.583   G-25593

Recorded Paris, 1930–31

MARCEL MOYSE, flute; ALBERT MANOUVRIER, flute; LILY LASKINE, harp: *L'ENFANCE DU CHRIST,* Op. 25: Part III ["L'Arrivée à Saïs"], No. 3: "Trio of the Young Ishmaelites" ["Sérénade"] (Berlioz)

*54. Part 1
       FA 162-1, 2   1930–31   TF.139   —   G-25750
*55. Part 2
       FA 163-1, 2   1930–31   TF.139   —   G-25750

Compagnie Française du Gramophone
Paris
Recorded Paris, 1931

MARCEL MOYSE, flute; LILY LASKINE, harp (orch/Piero Coppola): CONCERTO IN C MAJOR FOR FLUTE AND HARP, K. 299 (Mozart)

*56. [Second movement]: Andantino (first part)
        2G 120-1, 2   26 Jan 1931 L877 [52-858]   11325
                                      C2388 [52-858]   11329
                                      FKX44 [52-858]   13223
                                      C7221 [52-858]

*57. [Second movement]: Andantino (conclusion) [Cadenza by Graener]
        2G 121-1,   26 Jan 1931 L877 [52-859]   11325
        1A, 2   C2388 [52-859]   11327
                                      FKX44 [52-859]   13223
                                      C7221 [52-859]

*58. [Third movement]: Rondo (first part)
        2G 122-1, 2   26 Jan 1931 L878 [52-860]   11326
                                      C2389 [52-860]   11328
                                      FKX45 [52-860]   13222
                                      C7220 [52-860]

*59. [Third movement]: Rondo (conclusion) [Cadenza by Graener]
        2G 123-1, 2   26 Jan 1931 L878 [52-861]   11326
                                      C2389 [52-861]   11329
                                      FKX45 [52-861]   13221
                                      C7219 [52-861]

*60. [First movement]: Allegro (first part)
        2G 347-1, 2   26 Feb 1931 L876 [52-856]   11324
                                      C2387 [52-856]   11327
                                      FKX43 [52-856]   13221
                                      C7219 [52-856]

*61. [First movement]: Allegro (conclusion) [Cadenza by Graener]
      2G 348-1, 2   26 Feb 1931 L876 [52-857]   11324
                                    C2387 [52-857]   11328
                                    FKX43 [52-857]   13222
                                    C7220 [52-857]

RÉGINE DE LORMOY, mezzo-soprano; MARCEL MOYSE, flute; —
PIERRE-MARIE, piano; LUCIEN SCHWARTZ? and — GALLAND,
violin; LUCIEN QUATTROCHI, viola; VICTOR PASCAL, cello:
SEPTUOR POUR VOIX DE MEZZO, Op. 3 (Paul Fort–Arthur Hoérée)

*62. a) Danse b) Chanson—"Le Bonheur"
      2G 403-1, 2   5 Mar 1931 L898 [52-918]

*63. Chante du Patrie (sic)
      2G 404-1, 2   5 Mar 1931 L898 [52-919]

Columbia Graphophone Company, Ltd.
Paris

Recorded Transoceanic Trading Company Studio, 61 Rue Albert, Paris, 1932

MARCEL MOYSE, flute; ÉMILE GODEAU, clarinet; GUSTAVE
DHÉRIN, MARIUS PIARD, bassoon; EUGÈNE FOVEAU, — VIGNAL,
trumpet; ANDRÉ LAFOSSE, RAPHAEL DELBOS, trombone; IGOR
STRAVINSKY, conductor: OCTET FOR WIND INSTRUMENTS
(Stravinsky)

*64. [Second movement]: Thème et variations (first part)
      WLX 1603-1 6 May 1932 LFX 287 GQX 11086 68203-D
                              LWX 222 LX 308   70431-D

*65. [First movement]: Sinfonia
      WLX 1604-1 6 May 1932 LFX 287 GQX 11086 68203-D
                              LWX 222 LX 308   70430-D
      MATRICES 1605–1606: see *PULCINELLA* SUITE (nos. 184 and
      185)
      MATRICES 1607–1608: NOT BY MOYSE

*66. [Second movement]: Thème et variations (conclusion)
      WLX 1609-1 9 May 1932 LFX 288 GQX 11087 68204-D
                              LWX 223 LX 309   70431-D

*67. [Third movement]: Finale
      WLX 1610-1 9 May 1932 LFX 288 GQX 11087 68204-D
                              LWX 223 LX 309   70430-D

Recorded Paris, 1933

*68. MARCEL MOYSE, flute (pf/?): "Fantaisie" (Reichert)
      CL 4440-?   Jun–Jul 1933   DF1312

*69.   MARCEL MOYSE, flute (pf/?): "Souvenir de Gand" (François
       Seghers)
          CL 4441-?   Jun–Jul 1933   DF1312

Recorded Paris, 1933

MARCEL MOYSE, flute (unaccompanied): *TROIS PIÈCES POUR FLÛTE
SEULE* (Pierre Ferroud)

*70.   a) Bergère captive   b) Jade
          CLX 1773-1   1933   DFX194   68433D

*71.   Toan-Yan (La fête du double cinq)
          CLX 1774-1   1933   DFX194   68433D

L'Anthologie Sonore
Paris

   The monumental *L'Anthologie Sonore,* subtitled "A Synthesis of the
Musical Arts/14th to 18th Centuries," was initiated in 1933 under the
artistic and musicological direction of Dr. Curt Sachs (1881–1959), former
professor of musicology at Berlin University who left Germany in 1933 for
political reasons. The project strove to present early music and chamber
music in a way that conformed to the most exacting standards of what we
now call "performance practice." The original notes to Volume III insist
that the recordings assured the

> strict authenticity of texts and strict adherence to the original instru-
> mentation insofar as accurate indications of the original scoring are
> available. *No liberties or arrangements of any sort have been tolerated and the
> collection absolutely guarantees accuracy of and fidelity to the original music.*

   Two volumes, each consisting of ten twelve-inch, double-sided discs
were issued annually by subscription (discs were not sold individually).
Volumes I and II (AS 1–10 and AS 11–20) appeared in 1933–34, while
Volumes III and IV (AS 21–20 and AS 31–40) were issued in late 1936 or
early 1937 (the notes for those volumes were copyrighted in 1936).
According to *The Gramophone Shop Encyclopedia of Recorded Music,* R. D.
Darrell, compiler (New York City: The Gramophone Shop, Inc., 1936), p.
552, this second set of issues was still "in preparation," and would
"probably be available in the summer or fall of 1936." Marcel Moyse
appeared on only two discs, AS 9 from the first volume and AS 26 from the
third (items nos. 120 and 121). His son, Louis, performed in a Bach cantata on AS 23. On both the elder Moyse's labels, Curt Sachs is credited as
the "Musicological Director"; in the original notes that accompanied the
second issue, it is further mentioned that the recordings were "carried out
entirely under the personal direction of Professor Sachs."
   Original French pressings bore either white and purple or black and
gold labels with a "L'Anthologie Sonore" motif, while American

pressings, issued exclusively by the Gramophone Shop, Inc., 18 East Forty-eighth Street, New York City, bore the Gramophone Shop banner motif above the spindle hole. The first American pressings had large, bright, gold and black labels. Subsequent American pressings bore large, yellow and black labels similar in all other respects to the first design. The last American 78 issues of the series had smaller labels with a dull, gold and black design. The earliest pressings were heavy laminates, while the late black and gold–label issues were not. The final 78 pressings— manufactured before the first *L'Anthologie Sonore* LPs were issued by the Haydn Society, Inc., of Boston—were vinylite discs with fine, smooth surfaces.

Recorded Paris, 1933–34

MARCEL MOYSE, flute; PAULINE AUBERT, harpsichord: SONATA IN D MINOR, Op. 2, No. 2 ["La Vibray"] (Blavet)

*72. a) Andante b) Allemande c) Les Caquets Gavotta
      AS 23   1933–34   *L'Anthologie Sonore* 9

*73. a) Sarabande b) Allegro
      AS 24   1933–34   *L'Anthologie Sonore* 9

Columbia Graphophone Company, Ltd.
Paris

Recorded Paris, 1935

MARCEL MOYSE, flute (pf/Joseph Benvenuti): *JOUEURS DE FLÛTE,* Op. 27 (Roussel)

*74. a) Pan b) Tityre
      CL 5244-1   Feb–Mar 1935   DF1800   17090-D

*75. M. de la Péjaudie
      CL 5245-1   Feb–Mar 1935   DF1800   17090-D

*76. MARCEL MOYSE, flute (unaccompanied): "Pièce pour flûte seule" (Ibert)
      CL 5246-1   Feb–Mar 1935   DF1801   17066-D

 77. MARCEL MOYSE, flute (unaccompanied): PARTITA IN A MINOR, BWV 1013: Sarabande (J. S. Bach)
      CL 5247-1   Feb–Mar 1935   DF1801   17066-D

Columbia Graphophone Company, Ltd.
London

Recorded London, 1935

 78. MARCEL MOYSE, flute (pf/Louis Moyse): STRING QUARTET NO. 1, Op. 11: Andante cantabile (Tchaikowsky)

CAX 7546-1   18–19 May 1935   DX721   DOX539 —
MATRICES 7547–7548: NOT BY MOYSE

*79.   MARCEL MOYSE, flute (pf/Louis Moyse): "Am Waldesbach" ["By the Brook"], Op. 33 (Paul Wetzger)
       CAX 7549-1, 2 18–19 May 1935   DX721   DOX539? —

*80.   MARCEL MOYSE, flute (pf/Louis Moyse): *LES MILLIONS D'ARLEQUIN*: "Serenade" (Riccardo Drigo)
       CA 15072-1   28–30 May 1935   DB1617   DO 1692

MARCEL MOYSE, flute (pf/Louis Moyse): *FANTAISIE PASTORALE HONGROISE,* Op. 26 (Franz Doppler)

*81.   Part 1
       CA 15073-1 28–30 May 1935 DB1630 DO1568 J2575 S30058

*82.   Part 2
       CA 15074-1 28–30 May 1935 DB1630 DO1568 J2575 S30058

*83.   Part 3
       CA 15075-1 28–30 May 1935 DB1631 DO1569 J2576 S30059

*84.   Part 4
       CA 15076-1 28–30 May 1935 DB1631 DO1569 J2576 S30059
       MATRICES 15077–15080: NO INFORMATION/NOT USED

85.   MARCEL MOYSE, flute (pf/Louis Moyse): "Serenade" (Woodall)
       CA 15081-1 28–30 May 1935 DB1645 DO1607   —

86.   MARCEL MOYSE, flute (pf/Louis Moyse): *PIÈCES DE CLAVECIN,* 3ᵉ Livre, 14ᵉ Ordre: "Le rossignol en amour" (François Couperin–arr. Fleury)
       CA 15082-1 28–30 May 1935 DB1645 DO1607   —

87.   MARCEL MOYSE, flute (pf/Louis Moyse): "Humoresque," Op. 101, No. 7 (Dvořák)
       CA 15083-1 28–30 May 1935 DB1617 DO1692   —

MARCEL MOYSE, flute; RUDOLF SERKIN, piano; ADOLF BUSCH, violin and conductor; BUSCH CHAMBER PLAYERS: BRANDENBURG CONCERTO NO. 5, BWV 1050 (J. S. Bach)

*88.   [First movement] Allegro (first part)
       CAX 7616-1 10 Oct 1935 LX444 GQX10798 LFX483 68442-D
                                                      69910-D

*89.   [First movement] Allegro (second part)
       CAX 7617-1 10 Oct 1935 LX444 GQX10798 LFX483 68442-D
                                                      69911-D

*90.   [First movement] Allegro (conclusion)
       CAX 7618-1 10 Oct 1935 LX445 GQX10799 LFX484 68443-D
                                                      69912-D

MATRIX 7619: NO INFORMATION/NOT USED
MATRICES 7120–7121: NOT BY MOYSE

*91. [Third movement]: Allegro (conclusion)
     CAX 7622-1 10 Oct 1935 LX446 GQX10800 LFX485 68444-D
                                                   69915-D

*92. [Second movement]: Affetuoso (conclusion) and [Third movement]: Allegro (first part)
     CAX 7623-1 10 Oct 1935 LX446 GQX10800 LFX485 68444-D
                                                   69914-D

*93. [Second movement]: Affetuoso (first part)
     CAX 7624-1 10 Oct 1935 LX445 GQX10799 LFX484 68443-D
                                                   69913-D

MATRICES 7625–7635: NOT BY MOYSE

MARCEL MOYSE, flute; LOUIS MOYSE, flute; ADOLF BUSCH, violin and conductor; BUSCH CHAMBER PLAYERS: BRANDENBURG CONCERTO NO. 4, BWV 1049 (J. S. Bach)

*94. [Second movement]: Andante
     CAX 7636-1 Oct 1935 LX442 GQX10797 LFX482 68441-D
                                                   69906-D

*95. [First movement]: Allegro (first part)
     CAX 7637-1 Oct 1935 LX441 GQX10796 LFX481 68440-D
                                                   69905-D

*96. [First movement]: Allegro (conclusion)
     CAX 7638-1 Oct 1935 LX441 GQX10796 LFX481 68440-D
                                                   69904-D

*97. [Third movement]: Presto
     CAX 7639-1 Oct 1935 LX442 GQX10797 LFX482 68441-D
                                                   69903-D

MARCEL MOYSE, flute; GEORGE ESKDALE, trumpet; EVELYN ROTHWELL, oboe; ADOLF BUSCH, violin and conductor; BUSCH CHAMBER PLAYERS: BRANDENBURG CONCERTO NO. 2, BWV 1047 (J. S. Bach)

*98. Allegro (first part)
     CAX 7640-1 Oct 1935 LX439 GQX10793 LFX439 68437-D
                                                   69907-D

*99. Allegro (conclusion)
     CAX 7641-1 Oct 1935 LX439 GQX10793 LFX439 68437-D
                                                   69908-D

*100. Andante
     CAX 7642-1 Oct 1935 LX440 GQX10794 LFX440 68438-D
                                                   69909-D

*101.   Allegro assai
        CAX 7643-1 Oct 1935 LX440 GQX10794 LFX440 68438-D
                                                                    69909-D

Compagnie Française du Gramophone
Paris

Recorded Paris, 1935–36

MARCEL MOYSE, flute (orch/Eugène Bigot): CONCERTO FOR FLUTE
AND ORCHESTRA (Ibert)

*102.   Allegro
        2LA 738-1   late November 1935   L1013

*103.   Andante (first part)
        2LA 739-1   late November 1935   L1013

*104.   a) Andante (conclusion) b) Allegro scherzando (first part)
        2LA 740-1   late November 1935   L1014

*105.   Allegro scherzando (conclusion)
        2LA 741-1   late November 1935   unpublished
              -2, 3   late November 1935?   L1014

MARCEL MOYSE, flute (orch/Eugène Bigot): CONCERTO NO. 1 IN G
MAJOR, K. 313 (Mozart)

*106.   Allegro maestoso (first part)
        2LA 903-1   February 1936   L1021   12123
                                                         12126
                                                         12853

*107.   Allegro maestoso (conclusion) [Cadenza by Taffanel]
        2LA 904-1   February 1936   L1021   12123
                                                         12127
                                                         12854

*108.   Adagio ma non troppo (first part)
        2LA 905-1   February 1936   L1022   12124
                                                         12128
                                                         12855

*109.   Adagio ma non troppo (conclusion) [Cadenza by Taffanel]
        2LA 906-1   February 1936   L1022   12124
                                                         12126
                                                         12855

*110.   Rondo–Tempo di menuetto (first part)
        2LA 907-1   February 1936   L1023   12125
                                                         12127
                                                         12854

*111.   Rondo–Tempo di menuetto (conclusion) [Cadenza by Taffanel]
        2LA 908-1   February 1936   L1023   12125
                                                              12128
                                                              12853

        MATRICES 909–910: NO INFORMATION/NOT USED
        MATRIX 911: NOT BY MOYSE

VINA BOVY, soprano; MARCEL MOYSE, flute (orch/Henri Busser):
LUCIA DI LAMMERMOOR, ACT III: Mad Scene (Donizetti)

*112.   "Splendez le sacre fani" ["Splendor le sacre facì intorno!"]
        2LA 912-1   February 1936   DB4998

*113.   "Je vais loin de la terre" ["Spargi d'amaro pianto il mio terrestre
        velo"]
        2LA 954-1   1936   DB4998

                    The Gramophone Company, Ltd.
                              London
Recorded Studio 2, Abbey Road, London, 28 October 1936

MARCEL MOYSE, flute (Busch Chamber Players/Adolf Busch): SUITE
NO. 2 IN B MINOR, BWV 1067 (J. S. Bach)

*114.   Overture (first part)
        2EA 3906-1   28 Oct 1936   DB3015   11996
                                              DB8195   11999
                                              ED1017   12993

*115.   Overture (conclusion)
        2EA 3907-1   28 Oct 1936   DB3015   11996
                                              DB8196   12000
                                              ED1017   12992

*116.   Rondeau
        2EA 3908-1   28 Oct 1936   DB3016   11997
                                              DB8197   12001
                                              ED1018   12991

*117.   Sarabande
        2EA 3909-1   28 Oct 1936   DB3016   11997
                                              DB8197   12002
                                              ED1018   12990

*118.   a) Bourrée No. 1 b) Bourrée No. 2 c) Polonaise
        2EA 3910-1   28 Oct 1936   DB3017   11998
                                              DB8196   12003
                                              ED1019   12989

*119.   a) Menuet b) Badinerie
          2EA 3911-1   28 Oct 1936   DB3017   11998
                                             DB8195   12004
                                             ED1019   12988

L'Anthologie Sonore
Paris
See note preceding items nos. 72 and 73 above.

Recorded Paris, 1936

MARCEL MOYSE, flute; JEAN PASQUIER, violin; ÉTIENNE PASQUIER, cello; RUGGIERO GERLIN, harpsichord: *TAFELMUSIK, III, No. 2:* Quartet in E minor (Telemann)

*120.   a) Adagio b) Allegro
          AS 60   1936   *L'Anthologie Sonore* 26

*121.   a) Allegro b) Dolce
          AS 61   1936   *L'Anthologie Sonore* 26

Pathé
Paris
Recorded Paris?, circa 1937–38

MARCEL MOYSE, flute; LOUIS BLEUZET, oboe; MARGUERITE ROESGEN-CHAMPION, piano (Évrard Female Orchestra/Jane Évrard): *SUITE JEUNES FILLES* (Marguerite Roesgen-Champion)

*122.   a) Bavardes b) À la danse
          matrix unknown   1937–38   Pathé PAT 141

*123.   MARCEL   MOYSE,   flute;   LOUIS   BLEUZET,   oboe; MARGUERITE ROESGEN-CHAMPION, piano (Évrard Female Orchestra/Jane Évrard): "Étoiles filantes" (Marguerite Roesgen-Champion)
          matrix unknown   1937–38   Pathé PAT 141

Compagnie Française du Gramophone
Paris
Recorded Paris, 1938

MARCEL MOYSE, flute; BLANCHE HONEGGER, violin; LOUIS MOYSE, piano: SONATA FOR FLUTE, VIOLIN, AND PIANO (Martinů)

*124.   Part 1
          2LA 2253-1   Jan 1938   L1047   12493

*125. Part 2
        2LA 2254-1   Jan 1938   L1047   12493

*126. Part 3
        2LA 2255-1   Jan 1938   L1048   12494

*127. Part 4
        2LA 2256-1   Jan 1938   L1048   12494

MARCEL MOYSE, flute; LILY LASKINE, harp; ULYSSE DELECLUSE, clarinet; CALVET QUARTET: INTRODUCTION AND ALLEGRO IN G-FLAT MAJOR (Ravel)

*128. Part 1
        OLA 2397-1   Jan–Feb 1938   K8168   4509

*129. Part 2
        OLA 2398-1   Jan–Feb 1938   K8168   4509

*130. Part 3
        OLA 2399-1   Jan–Feb 1938   K8169   4510

*131. Part 4
        OLA 2400-1   Jan–Feb 1938   K8169   4510
        MATRICES 2401–2413: NOT BY MOYSE

MARCEL MOYSE, flute; BLANCHE HONEGGER, violin; LOUIS MOYSE, piano: TRIO SONATA IN G, BWV 1038 (J. S. Bach)

*132. Largo
        2LA 2414-1   7? Feb 1938   unpublished
              -2, 3   25? Apr 1938   DB5076   13591
                                                ED431?

*133. a) Vivace b) Adagio c) Presto
        2LA 2415-1   7? Feb 1938   DB5076   13591
                                                ED431?
              [-2, 3]   25? Apr 1938   unpublished

*134. MARCEL MOYSE, flute; BLANCHE HONEGGER, viola: DUET
        IN B-FLAT MAJOR, Op. 10, No. 3: [Second movement] Adagio
        (Neubauer)
        2LA 2416-1   7? Feb 1938   unpublished
              -2, 3   25? Apr 1938   DB5080   12492

*135. MARCEL MOYSE, flute; LOUIS MOYSE, flute: SONATA NO. 1
        IN E MINOR FOR TWO FLUTES (J. C. Schultze–attributed to
        Handel)
        a) [Third movement] Lento b) [Fourth movement] Allegretto
        2LA 2417-1   7? Feb 1938   DB5080   12492
              [-2, 3]   25? Apr 1938   unpublished

French Polydor
Paris
[Deutsche Grammophon-Gesellschaft G.m.b.H.]

Recorded Paris, 1938

*136.   MARCEL MOYSE, flute; LOUIS MOYSE, flute: *PETITE SUITE EN TROIS PARTIES:* Second Movement (Honegger)

11004 HPP	1938	unpublished
11004½ HPP	1938	Chant du Monde 519
		Chant du Monde 530

*137.   MARCEL MOYSE, flute; JEAN LAFON, guitar: "Entr'acte" (Ibert)

11005 HPP	1938	unpublished
11005½ HPP	1938	Chant du Monde 518
		Chant du Monde 530

Compagnie Française du Gramophone
Paris

Recorded Paris, 1938

MARCEL MOYSE, flute; ALICE MERCKEL, viola; LILY LASKINE, harp: SONATA FOR FLUTE, VIOLA, AND HARP (Debussy)

*138.   a) Pastorale (conclusion)   b) Interlude (first part)

2LA 2857-1	7 Nov 1938	L1066	13810
			13813

*139.   Pastorale (first part)

2LA 2858-1	7 Nov 1938	L1066	13810
			13812

*140.   Interlude (conclusion)

2LA 2859-1	7 Nov 1938	L1067	13811
			13813

*141.   Finale

2LA 2860-1	7 Nov 1938	L1067	13811
			13812

Éditions de l'Oiseau-Lyre
Louise B. M. Dyer
122, Rue de Grenelle, Paris VIIᵉ

Similar in intent to *L'Anthologie Sonore,* the *Éditions de l'Oiseau-Lyre* were issued by subscription and intended to meet the needs of the most discriminating enthusiasts of early, contemporary, and chamber music.

Unlike that of *L'Anthologie Sonore,* however, *L'Oiseau-Lyre*'s series was a domestic French product pressed by Pathé-Marconi and was available elsewhere only as an import. All prewar 78-rpm issues bore purple labels with gold print and the familiar lyrebird motif. In most, if not all cases, the recordings were intended to accompany *L'Oiseau-Lyre*'s printed editions of the works performed.

OL 81–82 are twelve-inch; OL 20, 25, and 26 are ten-inch.

Recorded Paris, circa 1938

MARCEL MOYSE, flute (pf/Louis Moyse): SONATA, Op. 11 (Stanley Bate)

*142. Allegro
PART 1155   circa late 1938   *L'Oiseau-Lyre* OL25

*143. Andante
PART 1156   circa late 1938   *L'Oiseau-Lyre* OL25

*144. Presto
PART 1157   circa late 1938   *L'Oiseau-Lyre* OL26

MARCEL MOYSE, flute; BLANCHE HONEGGER, violin; LOUIS MOYSE, piano: *ESSERCIZII MUSICII*: No. 9, Trio Sonata in E major (Telemann)

*145. a) Soave b) Presto
PART 1171   circa late 1938   *L'Oiseau-Lyre* OL20

*146. a) Andante b) Scherzando
PART 1172   circa late 1938   *L'Oiseau-Lyre* OL20

*147. MARCEL MOYSE, flute; LOUIS MOYSE, flute: SONATA IN B MINOR FOR TWO FLUTES, Op. 6, No. 1 (Jacques-Christophe Naudot)
a) Largo b) Allegro
PART 1173   circa late 1938   *L'Oiseau-Lyre* OL26

MARCEL MOYSE, flute; FERNAND OUBRADOUS, bassoon; NOËL GALLON, piano: TRIO IN G, Wo.O 37 (Beethoven)

*148. Allegro (first part)
PART 1354-1   circa late 1938   *L'Oiseau-Lyre* OL81

*149. Allegro (conclusion)
PART 1355-1   circa late 1938   *L'Oiseau-Lyre* OL81

*150. Adagio
PART 1356-1   circa late 1938   *L'Oiseau-Lyre* OL82

*151. Theme and Variations
PART 1357-1   circa late 1938   *L'Oiseau-Lyre* OL82

The Gramophone Company, Ltd.
London

Recorded Studio 3, Abbey Road, London, 21 July 1947

MARCEL MOYSE, flute; BLANCHE HONEGGER MOYSE, violin; LOUIS MOYSE, piano: TRIO SONATA IN G, BWV 1038 (J. S. Bach)

*152. Largo
           2EA 12202-1, 2   21 Jul 1947   C3671
                                                  ED431?

*153. a) Vivace   b) Adagio   c) Presto
           2EA 12203-1, 2   21 Jul 1947   C3671
                                                  ED431?

*154. MARCEL MOYSE, flute (unaccompanied): "Syrinx" (Debussy)
           OEA 12204-1, 2   21 Jul 1947   unpublished

*155. MARCEL MOYSE, flute (pf/Louis Moyse): CAPRICE NO. 2: Scherzo for Flute and Piano (Louis Moyse)
           OEA 12205-1, 2   21 Jul 1947   unpublished

*156. MARCEL MOYSE, flute; LOUIS MOYSE, flute (unaccompanied): SONATA FOR TWO FLUTES: a) [Third movement]: Lento   b) [Fourth movement]: Allegretto (J. C. Schultze–attributed to Handel)
           2EA 12206-1, 2   21 Jul 1947   unpublished

*157. MARCEL MOYSE, flute (unaccompanied): PARTITA IN A MINOR, BWV 1013: Sarabande (J. S. Bach)
           2EA 12207-1, 2   21 Jul 1947   unpublished

Compagnie Française du Gramophone
Paris
Recorded Paris, 1948

*158. MARCEL MOYSE, flute; LOUIS MOYSE, flute; BLANCHE HONEGGER MOYSE, violin: "Aubade printanière" (Marcel Gennaro)
           OLA 5476-?   1948   SK106

*159. MARCEL MOYSE, flute; LOUIS MOYSE, flute; BLANCHE HONEGGER MOYSE, viola: SUITE IN C FOR TWO FLUTES AND VIOLA: Serenade (Louis Moyse)
           OLA 5477-?   1948   SK106
       MATRICES 5478–5481: NO INFORMATION/NOT USED

MARCEL MOYSE, flute; LOUIS MOYSE, flute (L'Orchestre de l'Association des Concerts Lamoureux/Eugène Bigot): CONCERTO FOR TWO FLUTES AND ORCHESTRA (Domenico Cimarosa)

*160. Allegro vivo (first part)
       2LA 5482-1   1948   SL131

*161. Allegro vivo (conclusion)
       2LA 5483-1   1948   SL131

*162. Largo
       2LA 5484-1   1948   SL132

*163. Rondo [Cadenza by Louis Moyse]
       2LA 5485-1   1948   SL132

II   UNDATED SOLO RECORDINGS

Étoile
Paris?

Recorded Paris?, date unknown

*164. ALICE LUMBROSO (vocalist); MARCEL MOYSE, flute; LILY
       LASKINE, harp (orch/Georges Dervaux): "Le Sablier" [Mélodie]
       (La Comtesse Tolstoi–Fernande Decruck)
       AB11233   Étoile 11233

Nipponophone/Nippon Columbia Company Ltd.
(Japanese Columbia)

Recorded Paris, 1935–37 (see "Pre-Press Note," p. 310)

MARCEL MOYSE, flute (pf/?)

*165. "Kojo no tsuki" ["Moon at a Desolate Castle"] (Rentaro Taki)
       matrix unknown   Japanese   S-30103   OZ-7554-N
                         Columbia

*166. "Yoi michagusa" ("Yoimachi-Gusa") ["The Evening Primrose"]
       (Tadasuke Ohno)
       matrix unknown   Japanese   JX 1176
                         Columbia   S-30103   OZ-7554-N

*167. "Karatachi no hana" ["Trifoliate Orange Blossom"] (Kosaku
       Yamada)
       matrix unknown   Japanese   ?   OZ-7554-N
                         Columbia

*168. a) "Comin' thro' the rye" (Traditional Scottish) b) "Hanayome
       ningyo" ["The Doll Bride"] (Haseo Sugiyama)
       matrix unknown   Japanese   ?   OZ-7554-N
                         Columbia

III ORCHESTRAL SOLOS: PARTICIPATION ESTABLISHED

The following orchestral solos are credited to Moyse on the original disc labels.

Columbia Graphophone Company, Ltd.
Paris

Recorded Paris, 1927

MARCEL MOYSE, flute (L'Orchestre Symphonique de Paris/Georges Truc): *LE CARNAVAL DES ANIMAUX* (Saint-Saëns)

*169. "Aquarium"

WLX78-?	1927	9520	12505? 12506?	67381-D

*170. "Volière"

WLX79-?	1927	9520	12505? 12507?	67381-D

Recorded Paris, 1929

MARCEL MOYSE, flute (L'Orchestre Symphonique de Paris/Elie Cohen): *ORFEO ED EURIDICE,* ACT II: "Dance of the Blessed Spirits" (Gluck)

*171. Part 1
        WLX 992-1, 2   Mar–Apr 1929   DX60

        MATRIX 993: NO INFORMATION/NOT USED

*172. Part 2
        WLX 994-1, 2   Mar–Apr 1929   DX60

Compagnie Française du Gramophone
Paris

Recorded Paris, 1931

*173. MARCEL MOYSE, flute (L'Orchestre de la Société des Concerts du Conservatoire de Paris/Piero Coppola): *NAMOUNA,* Suite No. 1, No. 4a: "Parade de foire" (Lalo)
        2G 244-1, 2   11 Feb 1931   W1173 [52-828]

Pathé
Paris

Recorded Paris, 1935

This abridged performance, issued on sixteen 12-inch sides, was released on French Pathé PDT 20–27, British Columbia Masterworks Album 43 (manual sequence, LX 425–432; automatic sequence, 8186–8193), American Columbia Set OP/MOP-15 (manual sequence, 11000/11007-D; automatic sequence, 11008/11015-D and 11497/11504-D), Spanish Odéon 121166–121173, Argentinian Odéon 125054–125061, and as a re-recording on American Vox LP PTL 6780 (1950) and OPX 200 (1962). American Columbia 69250-D was a single-disc issue coupled with the Act I "Dance of the Furies."

Moyse is the featured soloist on the well-known "Dance of the Blessed Spirits" (his name appears on the various labels in small type) and no doubt played on the rest of the recording.

MARCEL MOYSE, flute (L'Orchestre Symphonique de Paris/Henri Tomasi): *ORFEO ED EURIDICE,* ACT II: "Dance of the Blessed Spirits" (Gluck)

*174.   Part 1

CPTX 56-1, 2	1935	PDT 24	LX429	69250-D	121169
			LX 8192	11003-D	125057
				11014-D	
				11503-D	

Compagnie Française du Gramophone
Paris

Recorded Paris, 1932

MARCEL MOYSE, flute (L'Orchestre de la Société des Concerts du Conservatoire de Paris/Piero Coppola): *GUILLAUME TELL*: Overture (Rossini)

175.   Part 1

OPG 213-1, 2	Oct–Nov 1932	DA4833

176.   Part 2

OPG 214-1, 2	Oct–Nov 1932	DA4833

177.   Part 3

OPG 215-1, 2	Oct–Nov 1932	DA4834

178.   Part 4

OPG 216-1, 2	Oct–Nov 1932	DA4834

IV   ORCHESTRAL SOLOS: PARTICIPATION UNCERTAIN

These are orchestral performances with flute solos for which Moyse is not credited on the original disc labels, but for which his participation has long been suspected. It seems likely that the vast majority of Columbia recordings by the Straram Orchestra, under various conductors, and by L'Orchestre de la Société des Concerts du Conservatoire, under the direction of Philippe Gaubert, included Moyse, but only a few of the more prominent solos are given here.

Columbia Graphophone Company, Ltd.
Paris

Recorded Paris, 1927–28

179.   MARCEL MOYSE, flute (L'Orchestre Symphonique de Paris/Elie Cohen): *CARMEN,* ACT III: Entr'acte (Bizet)
WLX 229-1, 2, <u>3</u>   1927–28   D14230   9535

Recorded Paris, 1930

MARCEL MOYSE, flute (Walther Straram Orchestra/Walther Straram): *PRÉLUDE À "L'APRÈS-MIDI D'UN FAUNE"* (Debussy)

*180.   Part 1
WLX 1289-1   1930 LFX30 DX279 GQX10638 68010-D

*181.   Part 2
WLX 1290-1, <u>2</u> 1930 LFX30 DX279 GQX10638 68010-D

Compagnie Française du Gramophone
Paris

Recorded Paris, 1930

MARCEL MOYSE, flute (Gramophone Symphony Orchestra/Piero Coppola): *PRÉLUDE À "L'APRÈS-MIDI D'UN FAUNE"* (Debussy)

*182.   Part 1
CF 2795-1, 2   1930   unpub?
      -2T1   1930   W1150   AW281

*183.   Part 2
CF 2796-1   1930   W1150   AW281

Columbia Graphophone Company, Ltd.
Paris
Recorded Transoceanic Trading Company Studio, 61 Rue Albert, Paris, 1932

MARCEL MOYSE, flute (Instrumental Ensemble/Igor Stravinsky): *PULCINELLA* SUITE (excerpts)

*184.   Fifth movement: Toccata
        WLX 1605-1   6 May 1932   LFX 289   68187-D
                                                68573-D (X-36)
                                                70448-D (MX-36)

*185.   Sixth movement: Gavotta con due Variazioni
        WLX 1606-1   6 May 1932   LFX 289   68187-D
                                                68573-D (X-36)
                                                70449-D (MX-36)

V   BROADCAST TRANSCRIPTIONS

DANMARKS RADIO (DANISH RADIO), Copenhagen?, 1934

*186.   MARCEL MOYSE, flute (Danish Radio Symphony Orchestra/Paul Paray): *NOCTURNE ET ALLEGRO SCHERZANDO* (Gaubert)
        Broadcast, DANMARKS RADIO, Copenhagen?, 4 Jan 1934
        LP: Danacord DACO 135

OFFICE DE RADIODIFFUSION–TÉLÉVISION FRANÇAISE (ORTF), Paris, 1947–48

Musique de Chambre

*187.   MARCEL MOYSE, flute; LOUIS MOYSE?, piano: "Conte d'avril" (Widor)

*188.   MARCEL MOYSE, flute; BLANCHE HONEGGER MOYSE, violin; LOUIS MOYSE, piano: TRIO FOR FLUTE, VIOLIN, AND PIANO (Rabaud)

*[189]. MARCEL MOYSE?, flute; LOUIS MOYSE?, flute; BLANCHE HONEGGER MOYSE?, piano: "Divertissement grec pour deux flûtes et piano" (Gaubert)
        Broadcast, ORTF, Paris, date unknown
        Disc master, recorded 31 January 1947
        53 minutes

Musique de Chambre de Orban, Hahn, et Marras

*190.   MARCEL MOYSE, flute; LOUIS MOYSE, flute: "Sonatine for two flutes" (Orban)

*191.   MARCEL MOYSE, flute; LOUIS MOYSE?, piano: "Variations on a theme by Mozart, for flute and piano" (Reynaldo Hahn)
         Broadcast, ORTF, Paris, date unknown
         Disc master, recorded 8 January 1948
         49 minutes

OFFICE DE RADIODIFFUSION–TÉLÉVISION FRANÇAISE (ORTF), Paris, 1950

Les Instruments à Vent dans la Musique Contemporaine

*192.   FERNAND OUBRADOUS, bassoon; MARC EDMOND, ?; MICHEL GÉRARD, ?; DEVENY, ?; and MARCEL MOYSE?, flute: Work(s) not identified
         Broadcast, ORTF, Paris, 11 March 1950 (*sic*)
         Disc master, recorded 10 March 1950 (*sic*)
         56 minutes

OFFICE DE RADIODIFFUSION–TÉLÉVISION FRANÇAISE? (ORTF), Paris, date unknown

*193.   MARCEL MOYSE, flute; LOUIS MOYSE, flute (orch/?): CONCERTO IN G MAJOR FOR TWO FLUTES AND ORCHESTRA (Cimarosa)
         Broadcast, ORTF?, Paris, date unknown
         Disc or tape master, date unknown
         LP: Marcel Moyse LP T4RM 1161

SOCIÉTÉ NATIONALE DE RADIODIFFUSION (RADIO FRANCE), Paris, 1977

Cours d'Interprétation 1

*194.   MARCEL MOYSE, flute; DENISE MEGEVAND, ?: "Solo No. 13" (Dulon)
         Broadcast, RADIO FRANCE, Paris, 4 April 1977
         Tape master, recorded 17 January 1977
         25 minutes

Cours d'Interprétation 2

*195.   MARCEL MOYSE, flute; DENISE MEGEVAND, ?: SONATA NO. 5 IN E MINOR, BWV 1034 (J. S. Bach)
         Broadcast, RADIO FRANCE, Paris, 5 April 1977
         Tape master, recorded 18 January 1977
         25 minutes

Cours d'Interprétation 3

*196. MARCEL MOYSE, flute; DENISE MEGEVAND, ?: "Étude No.
3" (Andersen)
Broadcast, RADIO FRANCE, Paris, 6 April 1977
Tape master, recorded 19 January 1977
25 minutes

Cours d'Interprétation 4

*197. MARCEL MOYSE, flute; DENISE MEGEVAND, ?: "Carnaval de
Venise," Op. 14 (Genin)
Broadcast, RADIO FRANCE, Paris, 7 April 1977
Tape master, recorded 20 January 1977
25 minutes

Cours d'Interprétation 5

*198. MARCEL MOYSE, flute; DENISE MEGEVAND, ?: "Menuet[?]"
(Mozart)
Broadcast, RADIO FRANCE, Paris, 8 April 1977
Tape master, recorded 21 January 1977
25 minutes

VI   ORIGINAL MICROGROOVE RECORDINGS

Marcel Moyse Records
Only two of the six Marcel Moyse–label LPs contained *original* recordings by Moyse not previously issued in some other form. The entire set of
Marcel Moyse LPs (and the Muramatsu reissues of M-99 and M-101) is
documented in Part X of the discography, Long-Playing Reissues (nos.
23.1–24.6) The alternate titles on nos. M-99 and M-101 are found on the
backs of the jackets.

The French School at Home—How to Practice
Marcel Moyse Records M-99 (issued circa 1954)
Muramatsu MGF 1001 (reissue)

SIDE 1: matrix G8-OP-8995

MARCEL MOYSE, flute (unaccompanied):
*199. *24 SMALL MELODIC STUDIES*: Nos. 1, 2, 3, 4, 8, 10, 7 (Marcel
Moyse)
*200. *25 MELODIC STUDIES*: No. 10 (Marcel Moyse)
*201. *24 SMALL MELODIC STUDIES*: No. 9 (Marcel Moyse)
*202. *25 MELODIC STUDIES*: Nos. 25, 3 (Marcel Moyse)
*203. *24 SMALL MELODIC STUDIES*: Nos. 15, 22 (Marcel Moyse)

*204. *24 DAILY STUDIES*: No. 15 (Heinrich Soussman)
*205. *BOUQUET DES TONS,* Op. 125: No. 9 (Anton Fürstenau)

SIDE 2: matrix G8-OP-8996

MARCEL MOYSE, flute (unaccompanied):
*206. *24 STUDIES,* Op. 15: Nos. 8, 16, 18, 15, 4a, 3 (Joachim Andersen)
*207. *24 DAILY STUDIES*: No. 22 (Heinrich Soussman)

Marcel Moyse, Flutist [Tone Development Through Interpretation/Sixteen (sic)
Classical Selections for Flute]
Marcel Moyse Records M-101 (issued circa 1954)
Muramatsu MGF 1002 (reissue)

SIDE 1: matrix KP 3601-E1

MARCEL MOYSE, flute (pf/Louis Moyse):
*208. *FORTUNIO,* ACT II: "J'aimais la vicille maison grise" ["La maison grise"] (Messager)
*209. *SAPHO,* ACT I: "Qu'il est loin, mon pays!" (Massenet)
*210. *L'ATTAQUE DE MOULIN,* ACT ?: "Adieu, forêt profonde" (Bruneau)
*211. *OBERON,* ACT II, Finale: "O wie wogt es sich schön" (Weber–arr. Demersseman)
*212. *WERTHER,* ACT IV, Entr'acte: "Il notte de natale" (Massenet)
*213. (unaccompanied): "O Magali" [Provençal song]
*214. *IL TROVATORE,* ACT IV: "Mira, di acerbe lagrime" (Verdi–arr. Moyse)

SIDE 2: matrix KP 3602-E2

MARCEL MOYSE, flute (pf/Louis Moyse):
*215. "Fantaisie mélancolique," Op. 1: Introduction and Theme (Reichert)
*216. *OBERON,* ACT III: "Arabien, mein Heimatland" (Weber–arr. Dermersseman)
*217. "Air Écossais" ["Fantaisie"]: Andante (Jean-Louis Tulou)
*218. *L'ARLÉSIENNE* SUITE NO. 1: Adagietto (Bizet)
*219. SONATA IN B-FLAT FOR FLUTE AND PIANO, K Anh.4: Largo (Beethoven)
*220. MARCEL MOYSE, flute; LOUIS MOYSE, flute; BLANCHE HONEGGER MOYSE, piano: TRIO SONATA IN G MINOR, BWV 1039: Adagio (J. S. Bach)
*221. MARCEL MOYSE, flute; BLANCHE HONEGGER MOYSE, violin; LOUIS MOYSE, piano: TRIO SONATA IN C MINOR, Op. 2, No. 1: Adagio (Handel)

VII MOYSE AS CONDUCTOR

Recorded New York?, 30 Oct 1957

Issued as *Chamber Music from Marlboro* (ML 5426 and MS 6116)
  Music from Marlboro (M 33527)

*222. MARLBORO FESTIVAL OCTET/Marcel Moyse: OCTET FOR
  WINDS IN E-FLAT MAJOR, Op. 103 (Beethoven)
  xxLP-48286-1   Columbia ML 5426 (Mono)
  xxSM-48679-1   Columbia MS 6116 (Stereo)
  xxSM-48679-2   Columbia M 33527 (Stereo)

[OCTET: oboe/Alfred Genovese, Earl Schuster; clarinet/ Richard
Lesser, Harold Wright; horn/Myron Bloom, Richard Mackey;
bassoon/Anthony Checchia, Roland Small]

Recorded at the Marlboro Festival, Marlboro, Vermont, 26 July? 1975

Issued as SERENADE IN B-FLAT MAJOR, K. 361 (MRS 11 and MRSC 11)

[MARLBORO ENSEMBLE]/Marcel Moyse: SERENADE NO. 10 IN B-
FLAT MAJOR ["Gran partita"] K. 361 (Mozart)

*223. No. 1. Largo
  No. 2. Menuetto
  No. 3. Adagio
    MRS-11A [29176]   Marlboro Recording Society MRS 11
        (Stereo LP)
      Marlboro Recording Society MRSC 11
        (Stereo cassette)
      Sony SMK-46248 (Stereo CD: ADD)
      Sony SMT-46248 (Stereo cassette)

*224. No. 4. Menuetto
  No. 5. Romanza
  No. 6. Thema mit Variazione
  No. 7. Rondo
    MRS-11B [29176]   Marlboro Recording Society MRS 11
        (Stereo LP)
      Marlboro Recording Society MRSC 11
        (Stereo cassette)
      Sony SMK-46248 (Stereo CD: ADD)
      Sony SMT-46248 (Stereo cassette)

[MARLBORO ENSEMBLE: oboe/Rudolph Vrbsky, Randall
Wolfgang; clarinet/Richard Stoltzman, David Singer; bassett
horn/Frank Cohen, Eli Eban; bassoon/Alexander Heller,
Christopher Millard; horn/Robert Routch, Meir Rimon, E. Scott
Brubaker, John Serkin; double bass/Jack Kulowitch]

Recorded at the Boston Symphony Hall, 25–26 February 1980

Issued as *Marcel Moyse Conducting the Marlboro Alumni* (NR 56)

*225.   [MARLBORO ALUMNI]/Marcel Moyse: SERENADE NO. 10 IN
        B-FLAT MAJOR ["Gran partita"] K. 361 (Mozart)
            [DIDZ 10012]   Nautilus Recordings NR56 (CD: ADD)

VIII   FILMOGRAPHY

226. SYMPHONY ORCHESTRA OF PARIS *(sic)*/Philippe Gaubert:
      "Roman Carnival Overture" (Berlioz)
      1 reel (8:45 minutes); B&W; n.d. (circa mid to late 1930s)

A one-reel short subject, re-packaged in the U.S. in the late 1940s
or early 1950s under the series title "Musical Masterpieces" (a *DER
FLIEGENDE HOLLÄNDER* Overture from the same series,
conducted by Robert Heger, played by an ensemble appearing
under the same name, has also been seen, but the orchestral personnel is markedly different and there is no sign of Moyse among
the flutes). No further information about the Berlioz film could be
found, including U.S. copyright information, under the title of the
film or the series. Gaubert died on 8 July 1941, so the film can at
least be provisionally dated as above. The title card gives the
orchestra as "The Symphony Orchestra of Paris," and while this
may be "L'Orchestre Symphonique de Paris," as credited on
French Columbia records, it has been identified by Louis Moyse
as "L'Orchestre de la Société des Concerts du Conservatoire de
Paris," which Gaubert conducted from 1919 to 1938, and with
which he made a great many recordings for French Columbia (see
note for section IV). Indeed, Louis Moyse was able to identify the
hall as the Old Conservatory at 2 bis Rue du Conservatoire, Paris,
and several of the musicians. Along with Moyse, who is visible
throughout the film as first-chair flutist, Albert Manouvrier is the
second flute and piccolo; Gobert, English horn; probably Bleuzet,
oboe; Costes and Guyot, clarinets; Fernand Oubradous, bassoon;
Vuillermoz, French horn; Vignal and Meriguet, trumpets;
Couillaud, Raphael Delbos, and Tudesq, trombones; Perret, tim-
pani; Auguste Cruque, cello; Drouet, viola; Just, bass; and
Merckel, Seigneur, and Dumont, violins.
      Many of these players were not listed among the 1930
orchestra personnel, lending some credibility, given certain
physical aspects of the film itself, to the likelihood that it was produced no earlier than about 1935.

227. *Marcel Moyse et Son Pays*

> Documentary, circa 1969–70
> Director: François Gir
> Assistant Director: Pierre Cavassilas
> Script: Catherine Moinot
> Editors: Claude Dufour and Mindla Coronel
> Director of Photography: Henri Martin
> Cameraman: Jean-Claude Thuillier
> Sound Engineer: Bernard Bleicher
> Copyright and release date unknown
> Running time unknown

> This documentary, provisionally dated above by those who have seen it, may have been a French Television production.

228. *Marcel Moyse, Grand Old Man of the Flute*

> Producers: Claude and Michel Moyse
> Director: Michel Moyse
> Assistants: Christopher Andreasson, Cathy Meinzer, Luke Meinzer, Joshua Moyse, and Monique Moyse
> Editor: Michel Moyse
> Assistant Editor: Toby Bernstein
> Cinematographer: Claude Moyse
> Sound Recordists: Cyril K. Helle and Judith Sherman
> Narrators: Neal Welner and James Galway
> Marcel Moyse Voice-over (Narration): Thomas Panzera
> Copyright Claude and Michel Moyse 1984; 1985
> 58 minutes; color
> 16mm film, ¼-inch open reel sound

> Filmed in May 1979 (Moyse teaching flute and woodwind seminars in Michel Moyse's studio in Brattleboro, Vermont); summer 1979 and 1980 (Moyse teaching and conducting at the Marlboro Music Festival); and summer 1980 (Moyse at St. Amour in Jura, France). Footage of Moyse teaching students at his home in West Brattleboro was shot mainly in 1979–80, although director Michel Moyse has reported that the total footage was collected in 1979–82.

> Special thanks is tendered in the closing credits to Anthony Checchia, Walter DeHoog, Jacqueline Hofto, Pierre Honegger, Stuart Lieberman, Dominique Steinberg, Linda Moyse, Alex Ogle, Dorothy Olson, Debra O'Neil, Peter Quackenbush, Susan Rotholz, Frank Solomon, Carol Wincenc, Harold Wright, Ruth Wright, Marlboro College, Marlboro Music Festival, and the Vermont Council on the Arts.

Marcel Moyse Flute Seminars 1975

> Filming: Claude Moyse
> Editors: Claude and Michel Moyse
> Copyright Moyse Enterprises 1989
> Set of eight videotapes (nos. 229–236)

229. Videotape #1: "Conversation with Blanche Moyse"
Color, 55 minutes

230. Videotape #2: Flutist: Carol Wincenc (Lesson #1)
Color, 55 minutes
Music: CONCERTO NO. 1 IN G MAJOR (Mozart)

231. Videotape #3: Flutist: Carol Wincenc (Lesson #2)
Color, 48 minutes
Music: CONCERTO NO. 1 IN G MAJOR (Mozart)

232. Videotape #4: Flutist: Julia Bogorad (Lesson #1)
Color, 52 minutes
Music: "Fantaisie mélancolique," Op. 1 (Matheus André Reichert)

233. Videotape #5: Flutist: Julia Bogorad (Lesson #2)
Color, 43 minutes
Music: "Fantaisie mélancolique," Op. 1 (Matheus André Reichert)

*234. Videotape #6: Flutist: Chris Potter
Color, 49 minutes
Music: 24 SMALL MELODIC STUDIES: Nos. 1–5 (Marcel Moyse)

235. Videotape #7: Flutists: Sara Tutland and Marie Herseth
Color, 43 minutes
Music: Sarah Tutland: 24 SMALL MELODIC STUDIES: No. 9
(Marcel Moyse)
Marie Herseth: "Syrinx" (Debussy)

*236. Videotape #8: Flutists: Julia Bogorad, Alex Ogle, Max Schoen-
feld, and Susan Hyman
Color, 45 minutes
Music: Julia Bogorad, Alex Ogle, and Max Schoenfeld: TRIO,
Op. 65 ["Les trois amis"]: [First movement]: Allegro
(Tulou)
Susan Hyman: "Air varié de la molinara," Op. 4 (Böhm)

IX NOTES TO THE DISCOGRAPHY

Frequent references are made in the notes to four major contemporary discographical works:

The Gramophone Shop Encyclopedia of the World's Best Recorded Music (1930 and 1931 editions), various compilers (New York: The Gramophone Shop, Inc., 1930 and 1931).

The Gramophone Shop Encyclopedia of Recorded Music (1936, 1942, and 1948 editions), various compilers and editors (New York: The Gramophone Shop, 1936; New York: Simon and Schuster, 1942; New York: Crown, 1948).

[*WERM*] Clough, Francis F., and G. J. Cuming. *The World's Encyclopaedia of Recorded Music* (London: London Gramophone Corporation and Sidgwick and Jackson Ltd., 1952); *First Supplement* (1952); *Second Supplement* (London: London Records Inc. and Sidgwick and Jackson Ltd., 1953); *Third Supplement* (London: Sidgwick and Jackson Ltd. and Decca Record Company Ltd., 1957)

[*Rigler-Deutsch*] *The Rigler-Deutsch Index,* 977 microfilm reels. Washington D.C: The Association for Recorded Sound Collections/Dist.: NY: Mi-Kal County-Matic, Inc., 1981–83.

Items nos. 1–4: The Paris recording sheets say only "week ending 26 March" (1927). Tentative identification of the pianist for these items is based on information taken from Moyse's own reissue of the "Carnaval de Venise" (item no. 4) on Marcel Moyse Records M-102 (LP no. 23.3), where the pianist for this selection is given as "R. Delor." If this attribution is correct, Delor would in all likelihood have been the accompanist for the entire session. Company ledgers apparently contain no information on the pianist.

Item no. 2: While often attributed to Bizet, the second suite based on his incidental music for *L'ARLÉSIENNE* was arranged by the French composer Ernest Guiraud (1837–1892). The minuet was appropriated by Guiraud from the third act of Bizet's 1866 opera *LA JOLIE FILLE DE PERTH*.

Item no. 3: The Handel is identified, ostensibly, as "Sonate no. 3, Menuet et Allegro" on the original HMV label, but it is in fact the fifth of the fifteen Opus 1 sonatas. The Muramatsu LP (no. 24.4) identifies it as "Sonata in G, Op. 1, No. 5." Moyse did not record the remaining three movements of the sonata.

Item no. 4: Paul Agricole Genin (1832–1903) wrote this set of variations on the popular theme in 1857. Moskovitz's list of Moyse recordings in *Woodwind Magazine,* No. 2 (January 1950), p. 10, gives this as Victor 4-81313, but no such number could be documented. There simply was no American Victor issue of the recording nor any Victor number of this type from any country. Nor is this a misrepresentation of the HMV "face" or single-sided number, which was 239155.

Items nos. 5–6. Georges Hüe (1858–1948) composed the "Fantaisie" in 1913 for flute and orchestra. These matrices could not be dated exactly. They are among the first electrical recordings of this twelve-inch French Columbia LX series ("W" designating the Western Electric recording system, "L" a French master, and "X" the size). The matrix gaps between part 1 (WLX 133) and part 2 (WLX 163) cannot be explained, but considering the spread, they were probably recorded at different sessions.

The take numbers are not known, as copies of the original discs could not be examined.

Items nos. 5–7: Georges Truc, a music director in Columbia's French branch during the 1920s and 1930s, was, as a conductor, a prolific recorder, presiding over many of the sets issued during the early electrical period. Nothing else about him, including his dates, has been documented.

Item no. 7: This "Carnaval de Venise" was used to fill the final side of the Rameau *QUINTETTE* (nos. 27–31), issued in the U.S. on Columbia D11061–D11062 as Gramophone Shop Album Set 25.

Items nos. 8–13: Moyse's surname is spelled "Moise" on the original French Odéon labels. The Debussy was issued as Gramophone Shop Album Set 20. The Pearl LP (no. 12) gives the recording date as 1927, but Paris Odéon matrices Ki 1671–1678 (Mistinguett), all second takes, have been reliably dated 3 May 1928, making late 1927 or early 1928 equally likely dates of the Moyse matrices, Ki 1527–1532.

The late American Decca pressings were often (but not always) prefixed "G-," but copies of the Moyse issues were not examined to verify this. There is some indication that the Debussy SONATA, if not the other Moyse Odéons (see items nos. 32–39), may have been issued in a short-lived series of American Columbia Odéon issues in 1932–35 (on "Royal Blue" shellac), but this cannot be verified. It is very likely, however, since many of the German and French Odéons issued later by Decca first appeared in this country on Columbia.

Item no. 14: "Syrinx," composed in 1913, was dedicated to the eminent French flutist Louis Fleury (1878–1926).

Items nos. 15–16: Paul Taffanel (1844–1908) composed the "Andante pastorale et scherzettino" to serve as a "Morceau de concours" for the Paris Conservatory's annual examination in 1907.

Matrices 856–857 are unaccounted for.

Items nos. 18–23: Gabriel Pierné (1863–1937) composed this trio in 1927. The SONATA DA CAMERA was dedicated to the memory of flutist Louis Fleury, with "Fleury" serving as a thematic anagram for the second movement. The forename of the cellist cannot be found. He is given as "Lopez" on British Columbia labels and in the 1931 *Gramophone Shop Encyclopedia of the World's Best Recorded Music,* but as "Lopès" in other sources and non-British labels.

The British issue, Columbia 5275–5277, was released in April 1929. British pressings were issued in the U.S. as Gramophone Shop Album Set 108.

Items nos. 24–26: Sung in French. The *DINORAH* aria is coupled with Brothier's "Adieu tout ce que j'aime" ["Addio del passato"] from *LA TRAVIATA* on HMV P831. Though recorded in 1928, the recording was first announced in the French HMV supplement of March 1930, hence the late face-number.

Items nos. 27–31: See note for item no. 7. The composer of the *QUINTETTE* may be Gaston Rumeau, dates unknown; the British Columbia Records Supplement 41 (1 May 1930) lists the composer of the quintet as "G. Rumeau," while the 1931 *Gramophone Shop Encyclopedia of the World's Best Recorded Music* carries the following note: "As we go to press no information seems available, in America, regarding this composer. The music is undoubtedly late XIX Century. Certainly, not 'Rameau.'" Ironically, "Rameau" is then incorrectly given under Moyse's name in the Artist Index to this edition!

The take numbers have not been found.

Items nos. 32–39: The first four matrices of this group of Moyse Odéons were probably recorded no later than the third week of December 1929, the third take of Paris matrix Ki 2783 (Mistinguett) having been reliably dated 4 December. Items nos. 36–39 were likely to have been recorded a few days later. See also the note for items 8–13 regarding American Decca pressings and possible American Columbia pressings.

Item no. 34: Labeled "Air suisse." These "Variations sur un air tyrolienne," Op. 20, of Theobald Böhm (1794–1881) are also known under the alternate title "Variations brilliantes sur un air suisse."

Item no. 35: François Borne was a professor at the Toulouse Conservatory who also experimented with flute design. His dates were not found.

Item no. 36: Moyse plays only the first 48 measures ("Molto andante") of the *FANTAISIE PASTORALE HONGROISE.*

Item no. 37: Gaubert composed this solo in 1908. Moyse's performance was coupled on American Decca with the Borne "Carmen fantaisie."

Item no. 39: No composer with the surname "Noblot" could be documented. An Odéon leaflet dated October 1930 reports the composer as E. Noblot. It seems unlikely that the "Mélodie" is the work of French organist and harpsichordist *Charles* Noblet (1715–1769).

Items nos. 40–43: The Mozart D Major Concerto was issued in the U.S. as Victor Set M-589. The Victor books show that take 2 of the "Andante ma non troppo" (CF 3113) was issued on Victor 12478, but take 2T1, a dubbing, has been documented on prewar copies, hence the question marks following the Victor as well as the French and Swiss issues of this side for take 2.

Numerous sources (including the unsigned article on Moyse in the fifth edition of *Grove's Dictionary of Music and Musicians,* Vol. 12, p. 661) have claimed that this recording received a 1928 *Grand Prix du Disque*—two years before the recording was made. It was actually among the prize recipients of 1932. An announcement for the first *Grand Prix du Disque* awards, by Louis Quiévereux, appeared in the July 1931 issue of *The Gramophone,* p. 63: "The French literary weekly *Candide,* edited in Paris," it begins, "has vigorously stood up in the defence of what the men-in-the-street would call 'highbrow' music by instituting the annual 'Grand Prix du Disque.' " The panel of judges for both the 1931 and 1932 awards included composers Gustave Charpentier and Maurice Ravel, singers Lucienne Bréval and Jean Périer, and writer Colette. The first recipient of the orchestral award (1931) was the Straram recording of Debussy's *PRÉLUDE À "L'APRÈS-MIDI D'UN FAUNE"* (items nos. 180 and 181), which almost certainly featured Moyse. The Mozart D Major Concerto was listed among the second year's "Instruments" winners, announced by Quiévreux in the June 1932 issue of *The Gramophone,* p. 38. The prize was 6000 francs.

The French HMV catalog of 1935, p. 348, notes that the recording received the "1er Prix d'Instruments, Fondation Candide 1932," while the 1936 catalog, p. 227, says simply "Prix 'Candide' 1932." Both catalogs describe Moyse as "Professeur au Conservatoire de Paris" and "Soliste de la Société des Concerts du Conservatoire."

Accounts of which movements feature cadenzas vary from one source to another (*WERM,* company catalogs, etc.). The listing in the discography reflects what is actually heard in the recording.

Items nos. 44–47: Christopher Steward's Moyse listing in Claude Dorgeuille's *The French Flute School 1860–1950,* English edition (London: Tony Bingham, 1986), p. 124, gives the recording dates of the De Falla Concerto as 2 and 7 June 1930, but this has not been confirmed.

De Falla wrote this concerto between 1923 and 1926. The performance was originally issued in the U.S. as Columbia set X-9.

Items nos. 48–49: Moyse is heard in both parts of this Rogatchewsky recording and to great advantage in the lengthy solo introduction to the first part.

Items nos. 50–53: *WERM,* p. 51, notes "movements 3 and 6 omitted," which, barring any ambiguity of the movement numbers, would imply that movements 1, 2, 4, and 5 were recorded, which is not correct. The 1936 *Gramophone Shop Encyclopedia* lists both the French and British issues (no movements given), while the 1942 edition of the same work notes in error, "movements 1 and 2 only."

The French issue, purple-label Decca T.10002/3, appears in the French Decca Supplement 11 dated 1931. British Decca K.582 and K.583, originally issued as purple label, then blue label, were issued in Britain in early June 1931, and appeared in the mid-June 1931 supplement. *The Gramophone* (July 1931), p. 49, describes them as "two jolly records" and notes that the third movement (marked only "Allegro molto" in the score) is omitted. The fifth movement of the trio, "Allegro scherzando e vivace," is also omitted.

Items nos. 54–55: Steward's Moyse listing (op. cit.), p. 122, includes an *additional* performance of this work with Moyse, Laskine, and Louis Moyse rather than Albert Manouvrier. He assigns French Columbia D25750 as the catalog number, with no matrix number given. This citation may have been taken from the 1942 *Gramophone Shop Encyclopedia of Recorded Music,* where the "D" suffix is in fact meant to designate American Decca, not the French Columbia catalog-number prefix, "D."

Items nos. 56–61: Issued in the U.S. as Victor Set M-141 (manual), AM-141 (automatic), and DM-141 (drop sequence). C7219–C7221 were the automatic HMV couplings.

Victor assigned their own domestic matrix numbers to this set, CVS 72469–CVS 72474 for nos. 56–61, respectively, with the appropriate take suffixes.

Note that the movements were recorded out of sequence. Although the HMV ledgers indicate that take -1A was the one released on HMV LX877, Victor pressings bearing take -1 have been documented (these are the same performance in any event, simply recorded on different lathes). The takes used on the various other HMV issues have not all been confirmed.

Steward's listing (op. cit.), p. 127, notes that nos. 56 and 57, the "Andantino," bear the *additional* matrix numbers 2G 13^I and 2G 14^I, respectively; *Rigler-Deutsch,* p. 52680, claims that the *first* part of the "Andantino" (no. 56) bears matrix 2G 14, with no take number given. In fact, matrices OG 13 and OG 14 (the ten-inch recordings that actually consumed these serial numbers) were recorded in Casablanca! What these "extra" matrix numbers designate has not been determined. The HMV ledgers give the matrix numbers in the sequence cited in the discography.

Items nos. 62–63: Arthur Hoérée (1897–1986) was a Belgian composer and music critic. The *SEPTUOR* was composed in 1923 and (first?) performed at the Zurich Festival of the International Society for

Contemporary Music, 23 June 1926. The text of the second movement, "Le Bonheur," is by French poet Paul Fort (1872–1960).

Items nos. 64–67: The OCTET, composed 1922–23, was recorded during a three-day session at the studios of the Transoceanic Trading Company, Paris, on 6, 7, and 9 May 1932, the composer conducting. On Friday, 6 May, the first four parts of *L'HISTOIRE DU SOLDAT* were recorded (matrices WLX 1599-1/1600-1/1601-1/1602-2), along with the first and second parts of the OCTET (in reverse order) and the "Toccata" and "Gavotte" of the *PULCINELLA* SUITE (WLX 1605-1/1606-1). The last two sides of *L'HISTOIRE DU SOLDAT* (WLX 1607-1/1608-2) were recorded on Saturday, 7 May, and the third and fourth sides of the OCTET on Monday, 9 May. *L'HISTOIRE DU SOLDAT* is scored for clarinet, bassoon, trumpet, trombone, violin, double-bass, and percussion, and so could not have involved Moyse.

WERM identifies the performing ensemble as the "Paris Wind Octet," but this name does not appear on either pre- or postwar French or American labels, which, instead, give the names of the musicians.

The OCTET was originally issued in the U.S. as Columbia set X-25 (68203-D/68204-D) and reissued as Masterworks set MX-25 (70430-D/70431-D).

Stravinsky appears to have conducted an earlier recording of the OCTET for the Bernard Roux Studio, Maison Pleyel, Rue Rochechouart, Paris, around November 1923, personnel unknown (the work had made its debut in a Paris Koussevitzky concert on 18 October of that year). Only the first and second movements were recorded complete (the Finale was truncated through a technical mishap). The recording was probably never published or was privately circulated on a very limited basis; in any event, it has not survived. It has not been documented that Moyse participated in either the premiere of the work or in this early recording session, but the possibility is not entirely remote. See Philip Stuart's *Igor Stravinsky—The Composer in the Recording Studio* (Westport, Conn.: Greenwood Press, 1991 [*Discographies,* No. 45]), pp. 4–5 and 26, for a detailed account of the recordings.

See also notes for items nos. 184–185.

Item no. 68: Matheus André Reichert (1830–1880), also identified as Mathieu André Reichert, was a Dutch flutist and composer who lived in Brazil from 1859 until his death. This recording is probably Reichert's "Fantaisie mélancolique," Op. 1, which Moyse subsequently recorded on Marcel Moyse LP M-101 (item no. 215). The takes are unknown. An excerpt from the piece was included in Moyse's *Tone Development Through Interpretation* (New York: McGinnis and Marx, 1962).

Item no. 69: François Seghers (1801–1881) was a Belgian violinist and composer. His forename has also been found as Frédéric. Alphonse

Leduc, Paris, published an edition of the "Souvenir de Gand" as revised by Moyse in 1936.

Items nos. 70–71: Pierre Ferroud (1900–1936) wrote these three unaccompanied works on "Chinese" themes in 1921–22.

Items nos. 72–73: Blavet (1700–1768) was a French flutist and composer of ballets, operas, and a great many works for the flute. The Opus 2 sonatas were published in 1732. The realization of the figured bass for this Moyse performance is credited to Pauline Aubert in the original notes to the first volume of *L'Anthologie Sonore,* in which this sonata appeared.

Items nos. 74–75: The *JOUEURS DE FLÛTE* (1924) consists of four works, each depicting a different flutist in legend or fiction. Moyse did not record the third piece, "Krishna."

Item no. 76: Ibert's "Pièce pour flûte seule" was published in Paris by A. Leduc in 1936.

Item no. 79: This well-traveled piece by Paul Wetzger (1870–?) is known variously under its German title, "Am Waldesbach"; its literal translations, "By the Brook" and "Brook in the Wood"; and as "Idylle," possibly a subtitle.

The coupling of Australian Columbia DOX539 could not be confirmed, but it seems likely considering the British coupling, DX721.

Item no. 80: The ballet *LES MILLIONS D'ARLEQUIN* was composed in 1900 and first performed in St. Petersburg under its Russian title, "Arlekinada."

Items nos. 81–84: The two Japanese (78-rpm) catalog numbers were listed in a 1956 Nippon Columbia Co. Ltd. catalog, having remained in print in that form for over twenty years.

The Czech J-prefix catalog numbers are cited in *Rigler-Deutsch,* but have not been verified elsewhere: "J" suffixes usually designated 12-inch recordings.

Items nos. 88–93: In the U.S., the BRANDENBURG CONCERTOS Nos. 5 and 6 were coupled in Columbia Set M/MM-250 under the title "Brandenburg Concertos, Vol. 2." The intervening matrix CA[X] 7619 is untraced; matrices CAX 7620 and CAX 7621 are part of the third concerto, recorded on 10 October 1935. Matrices CAX 7625–7635 are part of the first and sixth concertos.

Items nos. 88–101: International catalog numbers for the entire set of the six BRANDENBURG CONCERTOS, originally issued in January 1936,

were as follows (Moyse performed only in Nos. 2, 4, and 5):
    U.S.: 68434-D–68447-D (sets M-/MM-249 and M-/MM-250)
    Italy: GQX 10790–10803
    U.K.: LX 436–449
    France: LFX 434–436; 439–440; 480–488

Items nos. 94–101: In the U.S., Columbia released the first four
BRANDENBURG CONCERTOS (BWV 1046–1049) as Set M-249 (MM-
249) under the title "Brandenburg Concertos, Vol. 1." Note that the movements of the fourth concerto were recorded out of sequence.

Items nos. 102–105: The Ibert concerto was written for Moyse, and he
premiered the work in Paris on 25 February 1934. Unpublished second
and third takes for the first three sides (matrices 2LA 738–2LA 740) are
likely but were not documented from recording sheets.

Items nos. 106–111: Released in the U.S. as Victor Set M-396 (manual) and
AM-396 (automatic). Victor seems not to have assigned domestic matrix
numbers on these four sides.

Items nos. 106–113: No recording sheets were found in the EMI company ledgers for matrices OLA/2LA 903–912 and 2LA 954, so that the
matrices between items nos. 106–111 and 112–113 (909–910) could not be
traced. Paris matrix 852 was recorded on 31 January 1936; matrix 1018
was recorded on 4 April 1936, hence the provisional date for the Mozart
CONCERTO NO. 1 and Bovy's *LUCIA* aria.

Items nos. 112–113: Sung in French. Based on a transcription of the
record label, *Rigler-Deutsch,* p. 52683, claims that the first part of the aria
begins at "Splendor le sacre faci," to quote the original Italian text; John R.
Bennett and Eric Hughes's *Voices of the Past,* Vol. 4 [*International Red Catalog,
Book I-'DB'*] (Lingfield, Surrey: Oakwood Press, 1967?), p. 180, gives the
starting place of the first side as two measures before, at "Ardon
gl'incensi."
    Soprano Vina Bovy was born in Ghent (1900–1983). After numerous
successful operatic seasons in Europe and South America, she was
engaged by the Metropolitan Opera for the 1936–39 seasons. Her interpretation of the French and Italian coloratura repertory was especially
notable. Bovy matrix 2LA 911-1, the *TRAVIATA* "Ah! fors è lui," is coupled
with 2LA 823-1, the "Sempre libera," on DB 5004; neither features Moyse.
There are no cards at EMI documenting matrixes 909 and 910.

Items nos. 114–119: The SUITE NO. 2 IN B MINOR, coupled with the
SUITE NO. 1 IN C MAJOR, was issued in the U.S. as Victor Set
M/AM/DM-332 in December of 1936. Victor assigned and machined in
the wax of the records the domestic matrix numbers CVS-06000/CVS-

06005 (all designated as first takes), corresponding to the original HMV matrices 2EA 3906–3911, respectively.

The complete suites, performed by the Busch Chamber Players, were released by Victor in two sets: M/AM/DM-332 (Suites 1 and 2) and M/AM/DM-339 (Suites 3 and 4). DB3015–DB3017 were issued in HMV Set 268A (with SUITE NO. 1). The U.K. issues of all four suites were DB3012–DB3022 (manual) and DB8195–DB8205 (automatic); the Australian HMV issue was ED1014–ED1024.

Items nos. 120–121: A Gaveau harpsichord is credited for this performance in the original notes to the third volume of *L'Anthologie Sonore,* in which AS 26 appeared.

Items nos. 122–123: Marguerite Roesgen-Champion (1894–1976) was a composer, pianist, and harpsichordist and recorded extensively on both instruments. As a composer she sometimes used the pseudonym Jean Delysse.

The attributions of the flute-playing on these recordings have proven inconsistent: Steward (op. cit.) and the 1948 *Gramophone Shop Encyclopedia of Recorded Music* cite Marcel Moyse, while *WERM* gives Louis Moyse. In a 23 October 1984 reply to Steward's inquiry, Louis Moyse mentioned, "I don't remember at all playing on a record for Mrs. M. Roesgen-Champion. . . . I think that the recording you are talking about should be attributed to my father."

No notice of issue for the recordings could be found: no mention or advertisement for them appeared in *The Gramophone* between 1937 and 1940, but the catalog numbers seem to indicate a 1937–38 issue. With pianist J. Doyen, Roesgen-Champion recorded three of her own waltzes, "Valse romantique," "Valse, 1930," and "Valse triste," probably at the same sessions, as issued on Pathé PAT 140.

Items nos. 124–127: This Martinů SONATA was composed in 1936. The Victor files note that catalog numbers 12493 and 12494 were "not used" and, elsewhere, that the set was "withdrawn from 1939 [Victor] connoisseur's catalog." However, the 1939–40 Victor general catalog, p. R76, lists the discs as Album M-597 under the "Moyse Trio" in the Red Seal section, with the composer given in error as "Martini." It was probably not available in the U.S. for more than a year, as it was not listed in either the 1938 or 1940 Victor catalogs.

Blanche Honegger (not a daughter of Arthur, as was sometimes erroneously assumed, but a distant relative) married Louis Moyse on 7 November 1939. She is identified as "Blanche Honegger" on these and other pre-1939 record labels. On most later recordings she is identified as Blanche Honegger Moyse or simply as Blanche Moyse.

Items nos. 128–131: The Ravel INTRODUCTION AND ALLEGRO was composed in 1905. At the time of its founding, the Calvet Quartet consisted of Joseph Calvet and Daniel Guilevitch, violins; Leon Pascal, viola; and Paul Mas, violoncello. This performance was not released as a set by Victor. There are no recording sheets for Paris matrices OLA 2397–OLA 2400, but matrix 2506 was made on 4 May 1938.

Items nos. 132–133: *WERM* gives DB5076 as the catalog number of the "old version" (meaning this 1938 performance rather than the 1947 performance, items nos. 152–153). HMV C3671 was the British catalog number used for the 1947 version; it is not clear whether Australian ED431 corresponds to the early version only, as it may have been used at one time or another for *both* performances. It can only be assumed, not documented, that second and third takes were also made of matrix 2LA 2415.

The Victor issue, 13591, was announced in the October/December 1940–April 1941 "Recently Released Victor Records" supplement to the 1940 general catalog. In error, the 1942 *Gramophone Shop Encyclopedia* assigned this number to the same work as performed by the Danish Quartet (Blanquart, flutist), issued by HMV as DB 5221, but not by Victor. *WERM* gives the Victor number incorrectly as *15391*, an earlier catalog number from a different Red Seal series issued in 1939. David Hall's *The Record Book Supplement* (New York: Smith & Durrell, 1941) and *The Record Book International Edition* (New York: Oliver Durrell, 1948) cite 13591.

BWV 1038 is among Bach's "doubtful and spurious" works and may have been written by one of the composer's sons or students. It employs the thorough-bass of BWV 1021, the SONATA IN G FOR VIOLIN AND CONTINUO composed at Cöthen prior to 1720.

The recording was awarded the *Grand Prix du Disque* on 5 December 1938, and was so advertised in the January 1939 La Voix de Son Maître supplement.

Items nos. 132–135: The recording dates assigned to the Bach (circa 7 February 1938 for the first takes, circa 25 April 1938 for the third takes) are based on documentation of the *Chatou Galvanoplasty* "workshop" numbers, which appeared embossed on all French pressings manufactured by Pathé-Marconi from the early 1930s on. These can certainly be extended, considering their proximity of matrix numbers, to the Neubauer and Schultze. Apparently these "M6"-prefixed numbers functioned as "in house" recording numbers, unrelated to the actual company (HMV) matrix numbers. For the Bach, matrix 2LA 2414-3 is M6-93524 and matrix 2LA 2415-1 is M6-92522; for the Neubauer, matrix 2LA 2416-3 is M6-93525; and for the Schultze, matrix 2LA 2417-1 is M6-92524. The first takes from February were obviously allotted sequential *Chatou Galvanoplasty* numbers, as were the published third takes from the following April.

Items nos. 134–135: The Victor books give 2LA 2416 and 2LA 2417 as the respective matrix numbers, but do not list takes, so it is not known if alternate takes were issued in the U.S. It seems likely that second and third takes were also made of matrix 2LA 2417.

The composer of the "Adagio" is Franz Christoph Neubauer (c. 1760–1795), a Bohemian violinist and composer. The three Opus 10 duets were originally scored for violin and viola.

Item no. 135: *WERM*, p. 263, notes: "Sonata, 2 Flutes, E minor, ascribed to Handel on G.DB5080; Vic 12492, is really by J. C. Schultze (being 3rd and 4th movements of his Sonata no. 1, E minor)." The original French HMV label reads simply: "Sonata pour deux flûtes/Haendel." The composer could not be identified in reliable current sources. The title "Six sonates à deux flûtes traversière" by Johann Christoph Schultze (c. 1733–1813) is listed in *The National Union Catalog Pre–1956 Imprints* (London: Mansell, 1977), Vol. 531, p. 499, with reference made to Handel as the "supposed composer." Based upon entries found in the *British Museum Catalogue of Printed Music*, *NUC*'s Handel entry (Vol. 225, p. 423) lists J. C. Schultze as the "attributed composer." The 1948 *Gramophone Shop Encyclopedia*, p. 253, says only that the authenticity of the sonata is "doubtful."

Items nos. 136–137: The *PETITE SUITE*, composed in 1934, consists of three movements, the second of which is scored for two unaccompanied flutes. The first movement is scored for saxophone and piano, the third for violin, clarinet, and piano. The performers for the other movements, also on Chant du Monde 519 and 530, are G. Hamelin, clarinet; F. L'Homme, saxophone; A. Locatelli, violin; and J. Manuel, piano.

The *SUITE* was originally coupled on Chant du Monde 519 with Auric's "Impromptus" in E major and G major, performed by pianist Jacques Février. The Honegger and the Ibert (item no. 137) were later coupled as Chant du Monde 530.

The Ibert "Entr'acte" was composed in 1935. *WERM* lists the original catalog number as 518, coupled with Henri Sauveplane's *HABANERA*, performed by violinist R. Charmy and pianist J. Manuel.

"Chant du Monde" was a French Polydor (Deutsche Grammophon) label intended for the issue of esoteric repertory.

Items nos. 138–141: The SONATA was released in America as Victor Set M/DM-873. Victor assigned domestic matrix numbers CVS 069059–CVS 069062 to the original French matrix numbers 2LA 2857–2LA 2860, respectively. Note that the first and second parts were recorded out of sequence.

Items nos. 142–144: Stanley Bate (1911–1959) was a prolific English composer and pianist, a pupil of Vaughan Williams, Boulanger, and Arthur Benjamin (piano).

Items nos. 142–151: The recording dates for the *Éditions de l'Oiseau-Lyre* performances could not be determined, but it is known that the Telemann and Beethoven Trios (items nos. 145–146 and 148–151) were issued in January 1939, so late 1938 seems the likeliest recording date for the entire set.

Items nos. 145–146: Blanche Moyse recalled in a 1993 interview that Curt Sachs served as a musicological/artistic supervisor for *L'Oiseau-Lyre,* and that he proposed a recording of Bach's *EIN MUSIKALISCHES OPFER* with the Trio Moyse, but the project was not realized. Sachs did serve in this capacity for *L'Anthologie Sonore*, but there is no indication that he was ever involved with *L'Oiseau-Lyre*. However, *EIN MUSIKALISCHES OPFER* was eventually recorded for the label, as arranged and conducted by Fernand Oubradous and played by "L'Oiseau-Lyre Orchestral Ensemble," as issued on OL 130–135.

Item no. 147: Jacques-Christophe Naudot (c. 1690–1762) was a French composer, flutist, and teacher, also identified as "Jean-Jacques Naudot." His Opus 6 duets were published by 1731.

Items nos. 152–153: See note for items nos. 132–133 regarding the Australian issue, ED431, and the TRIO SONATA itself.

Items nos. 152–157: This session, recorded in Studio 3, Abbey Road, London, was originally scheduled for Saturday, 19 July, and Sunday, 20 July (10:00 A.M. to 1:00 P.M.), but was rescheduled for Monday, 21 July 1947. The company "Instructions for Recording" were originally prepared on 18 July and were received at Hayes on 22 July.
    Two takes each were made of the six masters cut (12202–12207). Both takes of the four unpublished titles are marked "res," designating "reserve," as are the unpublished second takes of the Bach TRIO SONATA, items nos. 152–153.

Item no. 156: See note for item no. 135. It is assumed that this is the Schultze sonata. The recording sheet says only "LENTO AND ALLEGRETTO FROM SONATA FOR 2 FLUTES/Handel."

Items nos. 158–159: Cobbett's *Cyclopedic Survey of Chamber Music*, 2nd ed., 3 vols. (London: Oxford University Press, 1963), Vol. 1, p. 444, lists a woodwind trio by composer "Marcel Gennaro," but no information about the "Aubade printanière" has been found.
    The take numbers of matrices OLA 5476 and 5477 are unknown.

Items nos. 158–163: These late recordings appeared first in an HMV "Continental Issues" supplement dated March 1950. They were recorded in 1948 (Paris matrix numbers 5375 and 5663 were recorded 24 November 1947 and 15 December 1949 respectively) but were not issued until late 1949 or early 1950.

Items nos. 160–163: The labels for HMV SL 131 apparently cite "Révision de Louis Moyse," while the label for the third movement adds "Révision et Cadence de Louis Moyse."

Item no. 164: The label of this rare issue credits the music to "F. Decruck," meaning Fernande Breilh Decruck (1896–?), wife and frequent collaborator of Maurice Decruck (1896–1954), a French saxophonist, who was at one time a soloist with the New York Philharmonic. The text, by the Countess Tolstoy (most likely Sofyia Andreevna Tolstaia-Esenina, 1844–1919), could not be documented. Nor was anything about vocalist Lumbroso or conductor Georges Dervaux found. Conductor *Pierre* Dervaux (1917–), son of a trombone player in the Colonne Orchestra, made his debut on the podium in 1945, conducting the Pasdeloup Orchestra: but the recording is obviously prewar, an early electric. The credited symphony orchestra consists only of strings, and appears to be a quartet.

The gold-on-black label reads "LE SABLIER Mélodie/Chantée par Alice LUMBROSO/Par de La Comtesse TOLSTOI—Mus. de F. DECRUCK/Orch. Symphonique sous la dir. de Georges Dervaux/avec Lily Laskine, harpiste et Marcel Moyse, flûtiste/LES ÉDITIONS DE PARIS." The label name, "Étoile," surmounts a complex logo that, in addition to a star, includes what appear to be both the Arc de Triomphe and the Eiffel Tower, the latter with small rays emanating from its top, a motif suggestive of broadcasting. The legend "Chaque exécution à la Radio ou au Pick-Up doit être mentionnée sur les programmes de la S.A.C.E.M." (Société des Auteurs, Compositeurs et Éditeurs de Musique) appears on either side of the spindle hole. "Pick-Up" here may mean either a microphone or a record player, the definitions assigned in the *Grand Larousse de la Langue Française* (1976) as corresponding to 1932 and 1935, respectively. It is much more likely, however, that the latter is the intended meaning of the inscription. This establishes that the recording is electrical, of course, and that it dates from 1932 to about 1935. Indeed, of the Decruck Les Éditions de Paris scores traced, all were published between 1932 and 1934. Virtually nothing else is known of the "Étoile" label except that some issues were distributed for cinema (interval) use, and that dance music also appeared on the label. Bearing this imprimatur, the performance may be a private studio recording, or derive from a live performance (acetate) transcription or even a broadcast. It may have been pressed in limited quantities and sold privately or by subscription. The number appears as "11233" on the label, probably a catalog number, and as "AB 11233" in the wax, undoubtedly the matrix number. "Le Sablier" is coupled with Lumbroso's performance of Decruck's "Le Rigaudon" (11234).

The only other *known* label bearing this name is of a much earlier vintage: the star-shaped design for a French "Étoile" label manufactured by Pantophone was deposited for registration on 15 February 1905 (no. 88582) by Lazar Morhange. Only baritone Jean Lassalle's recording of

Pierné's "Le sait-tu [sic] bien" (matrix 1913) has been traced to this label. Possibly the two labels are related, though it seems unlikely that this Pantophone make survived past the mid-1920s or, indeed, past the acoustical era.

Items nos. 165–168: Christopher Steward (op. cit.) lists these recordings as "Japanese Columbia (LP) OZ-7554-N./[c. 1938]." He gives no matrix numbers. OZ-7554-N was in fact a conventional monaural LP *reissue* of the original Moyse 78s and carries more than one "SP" (phonogram) date: 1930, 1937, 1939, and 1940, corresponding undoubtedly to the recordings by other artists included on the same record: cellists Emanuel Feuermann and Maurice Maréchal, pianist Leonid Kreutzer, and violinist Efrem Zimbalist.

The Japanese Columbia 78-rpm issue (S-30103) was still available in the 1956 catalog of the Nippon Columbia Co. Ltd., Kawasaki, Japan. JX 1176 is reported to have been a mixed coupling with Feuermann, whose Japanese recordings may date from as early as 1934. It remains to be seen if the Moyse recordings were made as early as 1938 or perhaps even earlier, or whether they could have been recorded in Japan. They are extremely good recordings, however, and sound as if they were recorded considerably later. See "Pre-Press Note" (p. 310).

Item no. 165: Rentaro Taki (1879–1903) composed "Kojo no tsuki" in 1901.

Item no. 167: Kosaku Yamada (1886–1965) composed "Karatachi no hana" in 1923.

Items nos. 169–170: The complete *CARNAVAL DES ANIMAUX* was issued as British Columbia 9519–9522 (later 12504–12507) and American Columbia Set M-81 (67380-D/67383-D). It has not been determined if the British 12000 numbers were manual or automatic couplings, hence the question marks following the two possible catalog numbers assigned to these sides. Pianists Maurice Fauré and Becher (?); cellist Joseph Fauré; and Delmas Boussagol, contrabass, were the featured soloists along with Moyse.

Items nos. 171–172: *WERM* identifies the orchestra as the "Paris Philharmonic."

Item no. 173: Lalo's ballet *NAMOUNA* was composed in 1881–82. This selection is one of four sides constituting the SUITE NO. 1 of music excerpted from the ballet. The first movement, "Prélude," is omitted. The rest of the suite is as follows:
>   SOCIÉTÉ DES CONCERTS DU CONSERVATOIRE/Piero
>   Coppola: *NAMOUNA* (Lalo)
>   No. 4b. Fête Foraine

2G 245-1, 2	11 Feb 31	W1173	[52-829]
No. 2. Sérénade			
2G 246-1, 2	11 Feb 31	W1172	[52-827]
No. 3. Thème varié			
2G 247-1, 2	11 Feb 31	W1172	[52-826]

Item no. 174. This abridged performance, sung in French and released in 1936, included only numbers 1–2, 7–8, 13, 15, 19–20, 22, 30, 32–33, 41, 43, and 45 of the original score, as well as an interpolation of "Le Dieu de Paphos" from the composer's last opera, *ÉCHO ET NARCISSE* (1779). The cast included Alice Raveau (Orphée), Germaine Féraldy (Eurydice), Jany Delille (L'Amour), and the D'Alexis Vlassov Russian Choir. Raveau's Act III "J'ai perdu mon Eurydice" was issued separately as Pathé PDT 38.

Items nos. 180–181: This recording was the first orchestral performance to win the *Grand Prix du Disque*, awarded in 1931 by the Parisian literary weekly *Candide*. See the extensive note on the prize for items nos. 40–43.

Items nos. 182–183: Listed in *WERM* as issued on W1150 and confirmed in the EMI ledgers. Christopher Steward's Moyse listing (op. cit.) gives the catalog number W937 in error.

HMV W937 is in fact a performance of Stan Golestan's *RAPSODIE ROUMAINE* by the Orchestre Symphonique du Gramophone, conducted by Coppola (matrices CT 4061-1/CT 4062-1), recorded in Paris, 12 June 1928.

Take 2T1 of the first part of the Debussy, a dubbing, is the only take marked in the EMI ledgers as having been issued.

Items nos. 184–185: See also notes for items nos. 64–67. The *PULCINELLA* SUITE excerpts, recorded at the 6 May 1932 session immediately after the first two sides of the OCTET, are credited on labels simply to "Instrumental Ensemble." Considering their instrumentation (the "Toccata" is scored for flute and piccolo and the "Gavotte con due Variazioni" for two flutes) and the fact that they were recorded at the same session that produced the OCTET, there is good reason to assume that Moyse played in these items, hence their inclusion in the listing.

In the U.S., the "Toccata" and "Gavotte" were reissued in 1934 as part of a *PULCINELLA* SUITE set, X-36, coupled with the "Duettino," "Minuetto," and "Finale" recorded in the Théâtre des Champs-Élysees, Paris, on 12 November 1928 by the Walther Straram Concerts Orchestra, Stravinsky conducting. Set X-36 consisted of catalogue numbers 68573-D and 68574-D, manually coupled. These, in turn, were reissued in 1937 as Set MX-36, bearing the automatic coupling, 70448-D and 70449-D. Both these American sets were titled "Pulcinella: Suite for Small Orchestra," with the ensemble credited only as "Symphony Orchestra."

In France, these *PULCINELLA* SUITE excerpts were not combined, but issued separately as D15126 (1928) and LFX289 (1932). The 1928 Straram excerpts were not issued in any form in England or elsewhere in Europe.

Details of the 1928 Straram Orchestra *PULCINELLA* SUITE are as follows:

a) Movement VII: Duetto, and Movement VIIa: Minuetto

WLX 626-1	12 Nov? 1928	unpublished		
-2	12 Nov 1928	D15126	67694-D	
			68574-D	(X-36)
			70449-D	(MX-36)

b) Movement VIIIb: Finale

WLX 627-1	12 Nov 1928	D15126	67694-D	
			68574-D	(X-36)
			70448-D	(MX-36)

The "Duetto," "Minuetto," and "Finale" are all scored for two flutes. Because Moyse is known to have been active in the Straram Orchestra between 1922 and 1933, it is very likely that he participated in this 12 November 1928 Paris recording session as well as in the other Paris Stravinsky sessions with the orchestra that preceded and followed: November 1928 (the *FIREBIRD* SUITE), May 1929 (*THE RITE OF SPRING*), May 1930 (*CAPRICCIO*), and February 1931 (*SYMPHONY OF PSALMS*).

In addition to added metronome markings, the "Duetto" was retitled "Vivo" in the revised 1949 edition of the score, originally published in 1924.

Item no. 186: Gaubert's *NOCTURNE ET ALLEGRO SCHERZANDO* was written in 1906 as an examination piece for the Paris Conservatory. Danacord LP DACO 135 is the only known issue of this early broadcast performance, the circumstances of which are unknown. The LP is a compilation of various artists in selections secretly recorded, it is said, by an attending engineer.

Items nos. 187–198: With the exception of item no. 193, nos. 187–198 are from the collection of the "Phonothèque de Radio Française." Because they were not available to us, it is uncertain in a few cases which musicians play on each selection. In other instances, the 11 March 1950 broadcast for example (item no. 192), there is the possibility that much of the content is non-musical, and may in fact consist of interviews, discussions, or lectures.

Item no. 187: Widor's "Conte d'avril", Op. 64, was written as incidental music to a four-act comedy of that title by Auguste Dorchain (1857–1930). The play, based on Shakespeare's *TWELFTH NIGHT*, premiered at the Paris Odéon on 22 September 1885.

For this broadcast, an arrangement or medley based on the original orchestral score was probably used.

Item no. 188: Because Henri Rabaud (1873–1949) composed numerous chamber works of a similar nature, definite identification of the piece performed here by the Trio Moyse is not possible, but it may be the "Andante et Scherzetto," Op. 8, for flute, violin, and piano, copyright 1926.

Item no. 189: The "Divertissement grec" was composed in 1909.

Item no. 190: It is likely that the composer of this work is Marcel Orban (1884–1958). However, another French composer of the same name was born in 1918. As no additional information was given in the Phonothèque's listing of the broadcasts, further identification is not possible.

Item no. 192: Moyse came to reside in Vermont in 1949 (having left South America in September of that year), so the listing of "Moyse" in this prerecorded broadcast, dated "10 March 1950" in the catalog of the Phonothèque de Radio Française, must be in error. Indeed, the Moyse Trio gave a concert at the Library of Congress on 10 March 1950, obviously precluding even the possibility of his participation. Louis Moyse was adamant that his father did not return to Paris until 1977. Mention of this broadcast in the discography has been retained in deference to the fact that no other information has become available.

Item no. 193: Marcel Moyse LP T4RM 1161 lists this as a Paris broadcast, date unknown. Marcel and Louis Moyse did make a commercial recording of this Cimarosa concerto (items nos. 160–163), but it was not available for comparison.

Items nos. 194–198: It is not known whether Moyse actually plays on these five broadcasts from 1977. Each is subtitled "Marcel Moyse, flûtiste: analyse et commentaires sur l'interprétation." It has been reported that these were the result of a series of master classes given by Moyse in Paris and broadcast a few months later. Considering the format of the videotaped Moyse master classes (items nos. 229–236), it is likely that students play on the recordings as Moyse lectures and demonstrates. Denise Megevand, a harpist, may be the interviewer and announcer.

Item no. 194: Friedrich Ludwig Dulon (1769–1826) was a German flutist and composer.

Item no. 196: The Danish flutist Karl Joachim Andersen (1847–1909) produced a vast repertory of flute solos and etudes.

Items nos. 199–221: According to a 1993 interview with Blanche Honegger Moyse, Marcel Moyse LPs M-99 and M-101 were recorded at Moyse's home in Brattleboro, Vermont, with his son, Louis, serving as recording engineer when not playing himself.

Items nos. 199–207: The composers of the etudes were all noted flutists: Andersen, Anton Fürstenau·(1792–1852), and Heinrich Soussman (1796–1848).

Items nos. 208–221: Side 1 and the first four selections of side 2 were published in Moyse's collection of operatic, orchestral, and instrumental themes, *Tone Development Through Interpretation* (op. cit.). This recording was probably intended to enhance that collection. Indeed, the back jacket of the album bears the subtitle "Marcel Moyse Teaching Record."
      Although the album cover carries the description "Sixteen classical selections for flute," there are only fourteen excerpts in all. In the album's list of contents for the first side, "O Magali" and the *WERTHER* Entr'acte are reversed.
      Among the less well-known French composers represented in the collection are flutist Jules Dermersseman (1833–1866) and Jean-Louis Tulou (1786–1865), also a famous flutist and professor of flute at the Paris Conservatory.
      The Beethoven SONATA IN B-FLAT is a work of doubtful authenticity.

Item no. 213: Marcel Moyse LP M-101 lists this item only as a "popular song" under the title "O Magali," while Moyse's *Tone Development Through Interpretation* (op. cit.) lists it as an excerpt from *SAPHO*. This is in fact the same "Chanson provençale" interpolated into Massenet's 1897 opera *SAPHO* by the creator of the title role, soprano Emma Calvé (1858–1942). Calvé recorded the song in London in 1902 on G&T 3282 (matrix 2059F).

Item no. 222: This LP was titled "Chamber Music from Marlboro" in its original monaural and stereo issue (ML 5426/MS 6116) and "Music from Marlboro" when it was reissued (using the same matrix numbers) as M 33527 in June 1975. ML 5426 and MS 6116 were released on 7 March 1960.
      ML 5426 and MS 6116 were coupled with Dvořák's SERENADE FOR WINDS AND STRINGS IN D MINOR, Op. 44, played by the Marlboro Wind Ensemble, Louis Moyse conducting (matrices xxLP 48287-1 and xxSM 48680-1, respectively, recorded 29 August 1957).
      M 33527 was recoupled with Rudolf Serkin, piano; Rudolf Vrbsky, oboe; Richard Stoltzman, clarinet; Alexander Heller, bassoon; and Robert Routch, horn, playing the Beethoven QUINTET IN E-FLAT MAJOR, Op. 16 (matrix MAL 33527-1, recorded 14 and 18 August 1974). This 1975 reissue was produced by Mischa Schneider, with liner notes by Jean K. Wolf.

Items nos. 223–224: The Marlboro Recording Society began issuing Marlboro performances early in 1970. Eighteen issues on the MRS label have appeared to date. Funding for the Marlboro Recording Society—an agency of the Marlboro Festival, Marlboro, Vermont, and the Marlboro School of Music, Inc.—is credited on the jacket of MRS 11 to Dr. and Mrs. André Aisenstadt. The original recording was produced by Mischa Schneider and engineered by Mark Seiden and Andrew Kazdin, with liner notes by Frederick Dorian.

MRS[C] 11 was reissued on a Sony compact disc (SMK-46248) and stereo cassette (SMT-46248) in August 1990 as part of a Marlboro Festival "40th Anniversary Series."

The performers featured in this recording match those listed in *Marlboro Music 1951–1991* (Marlboro, Vt.: Marlboro Music School and Festival, n.d.), p. 471, for a performance (at Marlboro) of the same work on 26 July 1975.

Item no. 225: The performers on this Nautilus compact disc are listed only as the "Marlboro Alumni." Some of the original participants in this performance were said to be dissatisfied with the results, but the tapes were eventually sold to the now-defunct Nautilus label, which issued the compact disc in 1983. The circumstances of the recording (live or studio) are not known.

Item no. 234: Although the title gives the musical contents as *STUDIES 1–5*, the student flutist is heard playing only nos. 1–4 from Moyse's *24 SMALL MELODIC STUDIES* (1932).

Item no. 236: Moyse speaks throughout most of this session—the three flutists play through only the first movement of the Tulou TRIO at the end of the film.

X LONG-PLAYING REISSUES

The long-playing reissues (vinyl LPs and compact discs) are listed alphabetically by label and further ordered by catalog-number prefix and catalog numbers.

The Marcel Moyse Records and Muramatsu LPs are given last as *sets* with modified, single item numbers.

The contents of the LPs are listed by Discography Number.

Note that many of the Angel [EMI] LPs from various countries are simply domestic variations.

1. *Brandenburg Concertos*
    Angel [EMI] COLC 13/14 [2 LPs: Mono]

French issue [*Gravures illustrés* series]: 1957
U.K. issue: 1957
U.S. issue: 1958
Contents: 88–101

2. *Great Recordings of the Century*
    Angel [EMI] GR 2226 [1 LP: Mono]
    Japanese issue: 197?
    Contents: 128–131

3. *Suites (Complete), Vol. 1*
    Angel [EMI] GR 2248 [1 LP: Mono]
    Japanese issue: 1973
    Contents: 114–119

4. *Great Recordings of the Century*
    Angel [EMI] GR 2250 [1 LP: Mono]
    Japanese issue: 197?
    Contents: 98–101

5. *Great Recordings of the Century*
    Angel [EMI] GR 2251 [1 LP: Mono]
    Japanese issue: 197?
    Contents: 88–97

6. *Great Recordings of the Century*
    Angel [EMI] GR 2321 [1 LP: Mono]
    Japanese issue: 197?
    Contents: 114–119

7. *Great Recordings of the Century*
    Angel [EMI] GR 70047 [1 LP: Mono]
    Japanese issue: 1983?
    Contents: 40–43 and 106–111

8. *Joseph Rogatchewsky*
    Club 99 CL 99-44 [1 LP: Mono]
    U.S. issue: date unknown
    Contents: 48, 49

9. [TITLE?]
    Japanese Columbia OZ-7554-N [1 LP: Mono]
    Japanese issue: date unknown
    Contents: 165–168

10. *[Bach: Orchestral Suites and Brandenburg Concertos]*
    EMI Classics CHS 7 64047 2 [3 CDs: AAD]
    U.K. issue: 1991
    EMI Classics CDHC 64047 [3 CDs: AAD]
    U.S. issue: 1991?
    Contents: 88–101 and 114–119

11. *Gluck Opera Recital*
    Eterna 495/757 [1 LP: Mono]
    U.S. issue: circa 1955/reissued circa 1963
    Contents: 48–49

12. *The Great Flautists,* [Vol. 1]
    Pearl GEMM 284 [1 LP: Mono]
    GEMM CD 9284 [1 CD: Mono-AAD]
    U.K. issue: 1985
    Contents: 8–13, 80, and 87

13. *The Great Flautists, Vol. 2*
    Pearl GEMM 302 [1 LP: Mono]
    GEMM CD 9302 [1 CD: Mono-AAD]
    U.K. issue: 1986
    Contents: 4, 33, 50–53, and 171–172
    [NOTE: Charles Haynes's notes for the first volume of *The Great Flautists* contain a curious error which may have come from Terry Fadden's liner notes for Seraphim LP 60357 (no. 15), which claim that Moyse played the premiere of Debussy's *PRÉLUDE À "L'APRÈS-MIDI D'UN FAUNE"* in 1913, Igor Stravinsky conducting (the piece actually premiered in 1894 and was conducted by Gustave Doret). This probably confused the Debussy with Stravinsky's *LE SACRE DU PRINTEMPS,* which did make its debut under the composer's baton in Paris on 29 May 1913, and in which it seems almost certain that Moyse played. It has also been suggested that Moyse might have played the premiere of Nijinsky's ballet to *PRÉLUDE À "L'APRÈS-MIDI D'UN FAUNE"* (1912), which may have been responsible for this persistent attribution.]

14. *Debussy Sonatas*
    Pearl GEMM CD 9348 [1 CD: Mono-AAD]
    U.K. issue: 1989
    Contents: 8–13

15. *Marcel Moyse*
    Seraphim [EMI] 60357 [1 LP: Mono]
    U.S. issue: 1980
    Contents: 88–93 and 114–119

16. *Age of the Great Instrumentalists,* [Vol. 1]
    Seraphim [EMI] 6043 [3 LPs: Mono]
    U.S. issue: circa August 1969
    Contents: 88–93

17. *Concertos pour flûte*
    La Voix de Son Maître [EMI] 2C 051-73056M [1 LP: Mono]
    French issue: 1983?
    Contents: 40–43 and 106–111

18. *Le Quatour Calvet*
     La Voix de Son Maître [Pathé-Marconi] 2C 061-11.305 M [1 LP: Mono]
     Les Gravures illustrés (series)
     French issue: 196?
     Contents: 128–131

19. *Concertos brandenbourgeois*
     La Voix de son Maître [EMI] 2C 151-43.067/068 [2 LPs: Mono]
     French issue: 198?
     Contents: 88–101

20. *Orphée et Eurydice*
     Vox PTL 6780 [1 LP: Mono]
     U.S. issue: 1950
     Contents: 174

21. *Orphée et Eurydice*
     Vox OPX 200 [1 LP: Mono]
     U.S. issue: 1962
     Contents: 174

22. [Title unknown]
     World Records SHB-68 [2 LPs: Mono]
     U.K. issue: before 1982
     Contents: 114–119 (with other suites as performed by Busch et al.)
     [NOTE: An article on Moyse in David Hamilton's *The Listener's Guide
        to the Great Instrumentalists* (New York: Quarto Marketing/
        Facts on File, 1982, p. 73) mentions that a complete release
        of the Busch Brandenburg Concertos was also planned at
        that time by World Records.]

Marcel Moyse Records, U.S.A. (LP only)

Given below is the complete Marcel Moyse Records series of LPs produced by Moyse beginning in about 1954 and extending at least into the late 1960s. The first two entries, M-99 and M-101, contain *original* recordings, not simply transfers of Moyse's commercial 78s, and so are also listed among the original microgroove recordings (Part VI) as Discography items 199–207 and 208–221, respectively.

Moyse's efforts to acquire the rights to reissue his own HMV and Columbia 78s on the Marcel Moyse label have been documented from a 1967 letter reporting the results of various legal inquiries on his behalf. Moyse wanted to use one of his recordings of the "Dance of the Blessed Spirits" from *ORFEO ED EURIDICE* (items nos. 1, 171–172, and 174), the 1936 Mozart G Major Concerto (items nos. 106–111), the Hüe "Fantaisie" (items nos. 5–6), the 1930 Mozart D Major Concerto (items nos. 40–43), and the Debussy SONATA FOR FLUTE, VIOLA, AND HARP (items nos. 138–141). Columbia disclaimed ownership of the Hüe, but in fact it was their record (issued as Columbia D11006); RCA Victor, which released both the Mozart D Major Concerto and the Debussy SONATA FOR FLUTE, VIOLA, AND HARP, was consulted about these recordings, but deferred all inquiries to the rightful owner, EMI, with whom they had severed relations some ten years earlier. As of 19 April 1967, no reply had been received from Pathé-Marconi regarding the materials they controlled.

The manager of EMI's copyright office at Hayes responded on 3 May 1967 to a 27 April 1967 inquiry, saying that though

> we are normally unwilling to permit the re-recording of our commercial records, . . . in the present instance . . . we are very pleased to be of assistance to Marcel Moyse and are therefore willing to permit the transfer of the 78 r.p.m. records . . . provided this is solely for the personal use of Marcel Moyse including such musical instruction as he may be giving at the Marlboro School of Music in Vermont.

The letter was offered as "sufficient authorisation" for the use of the recordings.

This explains why Moyse was allowed legal access to so many of his commercial HMV recordings and why the LPs were probably not circulated on a regular commercial basis.

Transfers from Moyse's commercial 78s are given with the respective Discography numbers of the original recordings. In a few instances, where more than one version of a selection was recorded, the identity of individual excerpts has not been determined conclusively.

Except for the first two LPs, which are known to have appeared in about 1954, the Marcel Moyse LPs have not been precisely dated.

23.1. *The French School at Home—How to Practice*
       Marcel Moyse Records M-99
       Issued circa 1954

SIDE 1: matrix G8-OP-8995 [Discography items nos. 199–205]
MARCEL MOYSE, flute (unaccompanied):
1. *24 SMALL MELODIC STUDIES:* Nos. 1, 2, 3, 4, 8, 10, 7 (Marcel Moyse)
2. *25 MELODIC STUDIES:* No. 10 (Marcel Moyse)
3. *24 SMALL MELODIC STUDIES:* No. 9 (Marcel Moyse)
4. *25 MELODIC STUDIES:* Nos. 25, 3 (Marcel Moyse)
5. *24 SMALL MELODIC STUDIES:* Nos. 15, 22 (Marcel Moyse)
6. *24 DAILY STUDIES:* No. 15 (Heinrich Soussman)
7. *BOUQUET DES TONS,* Op. 125: No. 9 (Anton Fürstenau)

SIDE 2: matrix G8-OP-8996 [Discography items nos. 206–207]
MARCEL MOYSE, flute (unaccompanied):
1. *24 STUDIES,* Op. 15: Nos. 8, 16, 18, 15, 4a, 3 (Joachim Andersen)
2. *24 DAILY STUDIES:* No. 22 (Heinrich Soussman)

23.2. *Marcel Moyse, Flutist [Tone Development Through Interpretation/Sixteen* (sic) *Classical Selections for Flute]*
Marcel Moyse Records M-101
Issued circa 1954

SIDE 1: matrix KP 3601-E1 [Discography items nos. 208–214]
MARCEL MOYSE, flute (pf/Louis Moyse):
1. *FORTUNIO,* ACT II: "J'aimais la vieille maison grise" ["La maison grise"] (Messager)
2. *SAPHO,* ACT I: "Qu'il est loin, mon pays!" (Massenet)
3. *L'ATTAQUE DE MOULIN,* ACT ?: "Adieu, forêt profonde" (Bruneau)
4. *OBERON,* ACT II, Finale: "O wie wogt es sich schön" (Weber–arr. Demersseman)
5. *WERTHER,* ACT IV, Entr'acte: "Il notte de natale" (Massenet)
6. (unaccompanied): "O Magali" [Provençal song]
7. *IL TROVATORE,* ACT IV: "Mira, di acerbe lagrime" (Verdi–arr. Moyse)

SIDE 2: matrix KP 3602-E2 [Discography items nos. 215–221]
MARCEL MOYSE, flute (pf/Louis Moyse):
1. "Fantaisie mélancolique," Op. 1: Introduction and Theme (Reichert)
2. *OBERON,* ACT III: "Arabien, mein Heimatland" (Weber–arr. Dermersseman)
3. "Air Écossais" ["Fantaisie"]: Andante (Jean-Louis Tulou)
4. *L'ARLÉSIENNE* SUITE NO. 1: Adagietto (Bizet)
5. SONATA IN B-FLAT FOR FLUTE AND PIANO, K Anh.4: Largo (Beethoven)
6. MARCEL MOYSE, flute; LOUIS MOYSE, flute; BLANCHE HONEGGER MOYSE, piano: TRIO SONATA IN G MINOR, BWV 1039: Adagio (J. S. Bach)
7. MARCEL MOYSE, flute; BLANCHE HONEGGER MOYSE, violin; LOUIS MOYSE, piano: TRIO SONATA IN C MINOR, Op. 2, No. 1: Adagio (Handel)

23.3. *Marcel Moyse, Flutist [A Marcel Moyse Flute Recital]*
Marcel Moyse Records M-102
Issue date unknown

SIDE 1: matrix J80P-4281 1-A1
MARCEL MOYSE, flute (pf/Louis Moyse):
1. (unaccompanied): "Syrinx" (Debussy): Discography no. 14
2. "Kojo no tsuki" (R. Taki–arr. Louis Moyse): Discography no. 165?
3. "Andante pastorale" (Taffanel): Discography no. 15
4. "Am Waldesbach" ["By the Brook"], Op. 33 (Paul Wetzger): Discography no. 79
5. STRING QUARTET NO. 1, Op. 11: Andante cantabile (Tchaikowsky): Discography no. 78

6. (pf/R. Delor?): "Carnaval de Venise," Op. 14 (Paul Genin): Discography no. 4

SIDE 2: matrix J8-P-4282 1-A1
MARCEL MOYSE, flute (pf/Louis Moyse):
1. *PIÈCES DE CLAVECIN,* 3ᵉ Livre, 14ᵉ Ordre: "Le rossignol en amour" (Couperin): Discography no. 86
2. *FANTAISIE PASTORALE HONGROISE,* Op. 26 (Doppler): Discography nos. 81–84
3. (unaccompanied): *TROIS PIÈCES POUR FLÛTE SEULE:* Toan-Yan (Ferroud): Discography no. 71
4. "Humoresque," Op. 101, No. 7 (Dvořák): Discography no. 87
5. *JOUEURS DE FLÛTE,* Op. 27: M. de la Péjaudie (Roussel): Discography no. 75
6. *JOUEURS DE FLÛTE,* Op. 27: Tityre (Roussel): Discography no. 74(b)

23.4. *Marcel Moyse, Flutist*
Marcel Moyse Records M-103
Issue date unknown

SIDE 1: matrix X4RM-0828-1
1. MARCEL MOYSE, flute (L'Orchestre Symphonique de Paris/Coppola): CONCERTO NO. 2 IN D MAJOR, K. 314 (Mozart): Discography nos. 40–43
2. MARCEL MOYSE, flute; BLANCHE HONEGGER MOYSE, violin; LOUIS MOYSE, piano: TRIO SONATA IN G MAJOR, BWV 1038 (J. S. Bach): Discography nos. 132–133 or 152–153

SIDE 2: matrix X4RM-0829-1
1. MARCEL MOYSE, flute (orch/Bigot): CONCERTO NO. 1 IN G MAJOR, K. 313: Rondo (Mozart): Discography nos. 110–111
2. MARCEL MOYSE, flute (pf or orch): *ORFEO ED EURIDICE,* ACT II: "Dance of the Blessed Spirits" (Gluck): Discography no. 1 (pf) or 171–172 or 174 (orch)
3. MARCEL MOYSE, flute; BLANCHE HONEGGER, violin; LOUIS MOYSE, piano: SONATA FOR FLUTE, VIOLIN, AND PIANO (Martinů): Discography nos. 124–127

23.5. *The French School of Flute Playing*
Marcel Moyse Records M-110
Issue date unknown

SIDE 1: no matrix number
1. MARCEL MOYSE, flute: (unaccompanied): "O Magali" [Provençal song]: Discography no. 213
2. MARCEL MOYSE, flute (pf/Louis Moyse): *OBERON,* ACT II, Finale: "O wie wogt es sich schön" (Weber–arr. Demersseman): Discography no. 211, or *OBERON,* ACT III: "Arabien, mein

Heimatland" (Weber–arr. Dermersseman): Discography no.
216
3. ADOLPHE HENNEBAINS (pf/?): "German air and variations"
(Böhm)
5641h   G&T 39184 and G&T 39198   Paris, 1908
4. ADOLPHE HENNEBAINS (pf/?): *ARMIDE,* ACT IV: "Sicilienne"
(Gluck)
5565h   G&T 39189 and G&T 39197   Paris, 1908
5. ADOLPHE HENNEBAINS (pf/?): *SUITE,* Op. 116: Allegretto
(Godard)
5564h   G&T 39188 and G&T 39196   Paris, 1908
6. ADOLPHE HENNEBAINS (pf/?): *FANTAISIE PASTORALE
HONGROISE* (Doppler)
5560h   G&T 39184 and G&T 39198   Paris, 1908
7. ADOLPHE HENNEBAINS (pf/?): "Nocturne," Op. 15, No. 2
(Chopin–arr. Taffanel)
5562h   G&T 39186 and G&T 39200   Paris, 1908
8. ADOLPHE HENNEBAINS (pf/?) "Waltz in D-flat," Op. 64, No. 1
["Minute Waltz"] (Chopin–arr. Taffanel)
5563h   G&T 39187 and G&T 39201   Paris, 1908
9. ADOLPHE HENNEBAINS (pf/?): *LE TREMOLO:* a) Introduction
et Thème b) Variations (Demersseman)
5638h   G&T 39190 and G&T 39206   Paris, 1908
5639h   G&T 39191 and G&T 39207   Paris, 1908

SIDE 2: no matrix number
1. MARCEL MOYSE, flute; LOUIS MOYSE, flute; BLANCHE
HONEGGER MOYSE, violin: "Aubade printanière" (Marcel
Gennaro): Discography no. 158
2. MARCEL MOYSE, flute (pf/Louis Moyse): *L'ARLÉSIENNE* SUITE
NO. 1: Adagietto (Bizet): Discography no. 218
3. ADOLPHE HENNEBAINS (pf/?): *ORFEO ED EURIDICE,* ACT II:
"Dance of the Blessed Spirits" (Gluck)
5640h   G&T 39194 and G&T 39204   Paris, 1908
4. ADOLPHE HENNEBAINS (orch/?): "Romance," E-flat major
(Pessard)
5637h   G&T 39193 and G&T 39203   Paris, 1908
5. PHILIPPE GAUBERT, flute (pf/?): "Madrigal" (Gaubert)
769aj   HMV W 303   Paris, 1919
6. PHILIPPE GAUBERT, flute (pf/?): "Nocturne," Op. 15, No. 2
(Chopin–arr. Taffanel)
770aj   HMV W 303   Paris, 1919
7. PHILIPPE GAUBERT, flute (pf/): *CHILDREN'S CORNER SUITE:*
The Little Shepherd (Debussy–arr. Hennebains)
03328v   HMV W 380   Paris, 3 March 1920
8. PHILIPPE GAUBERT, flute (pf/?): *ASCANIO:* Air de Ballet (Saint-
Saëns)
03330v   HMV W 380   Paris, 3 March 1920

[NOTE: The excerpt from *OBERON* on side 1 of M-110 is identified only as "Mélodie," and it is assumed that this is one of the same *OBERON* excerpts found on M-101. Louis Moyse is given as the pianist. The 1908 Hennebains recordings were renumbered twice on Gramophone and Typewriter, and were subsequently reissued on green French Disque Zon-o-phone.]

23.6.   Untitled
        Marcel Moyse Records T4RM 1161-2 (matrices only)
        Issue date unknown

SIDE 1: matrix T4RM 1161
    1. MARCEL MOYSE, flute, and LOUIS MOYSE, flute (orch/Bigot or ?): CONCERTO IN G MAJOR FOR TWO FLUTES AND ORCHESTRA (Cimarosa): Discography nos. 160–163? or broadcast, source and date unknown (no. 193)

SIDE 2: matrix T4RM 1162
    1. LOUIS MOYSE, flute; BLANCHE HONEGGER MOYSE, violin: FOUR DANCES FOR FLUTE AND VIOLIN (Louis Moyse): Broadcast?, source and date unknown
    2. LOUIS MOYSE, flute; ORNULF GULBRANSEN, flute; BLANCHE HONEGGER MOYSE, viola: SUITE IN C FOR TWO FLUTES AND VIOLA (Louis Moyse): Broadcast?, source and date unknown
        [NOTE: Ornulf Gulbransen, a flutist from Oslo and a close friend of Louis Moyse for many years, was also Marcel Moyse's pupil. He performed at Marlboro and later went on to teach in Canada and Norway. The label of T4RM 1161-2 claims that the performance of Louis Moyse's SUITE IN C FOR TWO FLUTES AND VIOLA was taken from an Oslo broadcast. In fact, Gulbransen invited Louis and Blanche Moyse to perform in Oslo; Mme. Moyse remembers a performance of the SUITE IN C as having been *recorded* there during their visit, but it is not certain that the performance on this LP is necessarily the same Oslo recording she mentioned, though it is likely. As Gulbransen's first season at Marlboro was in the summer of 1959, this performance could have taken place any time between that year and 1971. The information on the label, as well as Dale Higbee's review of this LP in *American Recorder,* 12/3 (November 1971), pp. 136–139, identifies each of the selections as broadcast performances, although this has not been confirmed. The Cimarosa was supposedly "recorded in Paris, France, during a broadcast." Similar notes place the FOUR DANCES in Geneva and the SUITE IN C in Oslo.]

Muramatsu, Japan (LPs and Compact Discs)

In 1970, Moyse sold several tapes, presumably those used for the Marcel Moyse label LPs, and the rights to manufacture pressings from them to the Muramatsu Music Instruments Manufacturing Co., Ltd., of Japan. Muramatsu then began issuing the LPs gradually, using the material provided. The first three Muramatsu releases (MGF 1001, 1002, 1003) were, item for item, reissues of the first three Marcel Moyse LPs (Marcel Moyse M-99, M-101, and M-102, respectively). According to copies of Moyse's 1970 contracts with Muramatsu, the master tapes for M-99 and M-101 were purchased in February 1970 and those for M-102 in April of that year. A contract from September 1970 outlines the sale of two more tapes, identified as "Flute Recital No. 2" and "Moyse in chamber music"; it is likely that the latter provided the contents of MGF 1004. All the contracts were signed by Osamu Muramatsu, Toshio Takahashi, and Marcel Moyse and have been preserved. In view of the quantity of Moyse material eventually released by Muramatsu on LP (reissued recently on CD), other tapes were obviously sold to the company at some point.

It has been reported that Moyse, at least initially, intended to reissue more of his performances on the "Marcel Moyse" label in America and that he stipulated that Muramatsu not make their releases available in the United States, ostensibly to eliminate competition. As a result, none of the Muramatsu LPs or CDs are commercially available in the U.S.

Precise issue dates for the individual Muramatsu LPs and dates for their transfer to compact disc are not known.

24.1.   *The French Flute School at Home*
        [Reissue of Marcel Moyse Records LP M-99]
        MURAMATSU MGF 1001 (LP)

SIDE 1 [Discography items nos. 199–205]
MARCEL MOYSE, flute (unaccompanied):
  1. *24 SMALL MELODIC STUDIES:* Nos. 1, 2, 3, 4, 8, 10, 7 (Marcel Moyse)
  2. *25 MELODIC STUDIES:* No. 10 (Marcel Moyse)
  3. *24 SMALL MELODIC STUDIES:* No. 9 (Marcel Moyse)
  4. *25 MELODIC STUDIES:* Nos. 25, 3 (Marcel Moyse)
  5. *24 SMALL MELODIC STUDIES:* Nos. 15, 22 (Marcel Moyse)
  6. *24 DAILY STUDIES:* No. 15 (Heinrich Soussman)
  7. *BOUQUET DES TONS,* Op. 125: No. 9 (Anton Fürstenau)

SIDE 2 [Discography items nos. 206–207]
MARCEL MOYSE, flute (unaccompanied):
  1. *24 STUDIES,* Op. 15: Nos. 8, 16, 18, 15, 4a, 3 (Joachim Andersen)
  2. *24 DAILY STUDIES:* No. 22 (Heinrich Soussman)

24.2. *Tone Development Through Interpretation*
[Reissue of Marcel Moyse Records LP M-101]
MURAMATSU MGF 1002 (LP)

SIDE 1 [Discography items nos. 208–214]
MARCEL MOYSE, flute (pf/Louis Moyse):
1. *FORTUNIO,* ACT II: "J'aimais la vieille maison grise" ["La maison grise"] (Messager)
2. *SAPHO,* ACT I: "Qu'il est loin, mon pays!" (Massenet)
3. *L'ATTAQUE DE MOULIN,* ACT ?: "Adieu, forêt profonde" (Bruneau)
4. *OBERON,* ACT II, Finale: "O wie wogt es sich schön" (Weber–arr. Demersseman)
5. *WERTHER,* ACT IV, Entr'acte: "Il notte de natale" (Massenet)
6. (unaccompanied): "O Magali" [Provençal song]
7. *IL TROVATORE,* ACT IV: "Mira, di acerbe lagrime" (Verdi–arr. Moyse)

SIDE 2 [Discography items nos. 215–221]
MARCEL MOYSE, flute (pf/Louis Moyse):
1. "Fantaisie mélancolique," Op. 1: Introduction and Theme (Reichert)
2. *OBERON,* ACT III: "Arabien, mein Heimatland" (Weber–arr. Dermersseman)
3. "Air Écossais," ["Fantaisie"]: Andante (Jean-Louis Tulou)
4. *L'ARLÉSIENNE* SUITE NO. 1: Adagietto (Bizet)
5. SONATA IN B-FLAT FOR FLUTE AND PIANO, K Anh.4: Largo (Beethoven)
6. MARCEL MOYSE, flute; and LOUIS MOYSE, flute; BLANCHE HONEGGER MOYSE, piano: TRIO SONATA IN G MINOR, BWV 1039: Adagio (J. S. Bach)
7. MARCEL MOYSE, flute; BLANCHE HONEGGER MOYSE, violin; LOUIS MOYSE, piano: TRIO SONATA IN C MINOR, Op. 2, No. 1: Adagio (Handel)

24.3 *Marcel Moyse Flute Recital*
[Reissue of Marcel Moyse Records LP M-102]
MURAMATSU MGF-1003 (LP)

SIDE 1:
MARCEL MOYSE, flute (pf/Louis Moyse):
1. (unaccompanied): "Syrinx" (Debussy): Discography no. 14
2. "Kojo no tsuki" (R. Taki–arr. Louis Moyse): Discography no. 165?
3. "Andante pastorale" (Taffanel): Discography no. 15
4. "Am Waldesbach" ["By the Brook"], Op. 33 (Paul Wetzger): Discography no. 79

5. STRING QUARTET NO. 1, Op. 11, "Andante cantabile" (Tchaikowsky): Discography no. 78
6. (pf/R. Delor?): "Carnaval de Venise," Op. 14 (Paul Genin): Discography no. 4

SIDE 2:
MARCEL MOYSE, flute (pf/Louis Moyse):
1. *PIÈCES DE CLAVECIN,* 3ᵉ Livre, 14ᵉ Ordre: "Le rossignol en amour" (Couperin): Discography no. 86
2. *FANTAISIE PASTORALE HONGROISE,* Op. 26 (Doppler): Discography nos. 81–84
3. *TROIS PIÈCES POUR FLÛTE SEULE:* Toan-Yan (Ferroud) (unaccompanied): Discography no. 71
4. "Humoresque," Op. 101, No. 7 (Dvořák): Discography no. 87
5. *JOUEURS DE FLÛTE,* Op. 27: M. de la Péjaudie (Roussel): Discography no. 75
6. *JOUEURS DE FLÛTE,* Op. 27: Tityre (Roussel): Discography no. 74(b)

24.4. *Marcel Moyse's Flute Classics*
MURAMATSU MGF-1004 (LP)

SIDE 1:
1. MARCEL MOYSE, flute; MARCEL DARRIEUX, violin; PIERRE PASQUIER, viola: SERENADE, Op. 25: a) Entrata-Allegro b) Tempo ordinario d'un Menuetto c) Andante con Variazioni d) Adagio–Allegro vivace e disinvolto (Beethoven): Discography nos. 50–53
2. MARCEL MOYSE, flute; BLANCHE HONEGGER, viola: DUET IN B-FLAT MAJOR, Op. 10, No. 3: [Second movement] Adagio (Neubauer): Discography no. 134

SIDE 2:
1. MARCEL MOYSE, flute; FERNAND OUBRADOUS, bassoon; NOËL GALLON, piano: TRIO IN G, Wo.O 37 (Beethoven): Discography nos. 148–151
2. MARCEL MOYSE, flute, and LOUIS MOYSE, flute: SONATA NO. 1 IN E MINOR FOR TWO FLUTES, a) Lento b) Allegretto (J. C. Schultze–attributed to Handel): Discography no. 135
3. MARCEL MOYSE, flute (pf/?): SONATA IN G MAJOR, Op. 1, No. 5: a) [Fifth movement]: Menuetto b) [Second movement]: Allegro (Handel): Discography no. 3

24.5. *Immortal Flutist Marcel Moyse*
MURAMATSU MGF-1005 (LP)

SIDE 1:
1. MARCEL MOYSE, flute; PAULINE AUBERT, harpsichord: SONATA IN D MINOR, Op. 2, No. 2 ["La Vibray"] (Blavet):

Discography nos. 72–73

2. MARCEL MOYSE, flute; BLANCHE HONEGGER, violin; LOUIS MOYSE, piano: *ESSERCIZII MUSICII:* No. 9, Trio Sonata in E major (Telemann): Discography nos. 145–146

3. MARCEL MOYSE, flute, and LOUIS MOYSE, flute: SONATA IN B MINOR, Op. 6, No. 1: a) Largo b) Allegro (Naudot): Discography no. 147

4. MARCEL MOYSE, flute (pf/Louis Moyse): "Serenade" (Woodall): Discography no. 85

SIDE 2:

1. MARCEL MOYSE, flute (unaccompanied): *TROIS PIÈCES POUR FLÛTE SEULE* (Ferroud): Discography nos. 70–71

2. MARCEL MOYSE, flute (pf/Louis Moyse): *JOUEURS DE FLÛTE,* Op. 27: a) Pan b) M. de la Péjaudie c) Tityre (Roussel): Discography nos. 74–75

3. MARCEL MOYSE, flute; LOUIS MOYSE, flute; BLANCHE HONEGGER MOYSE, violin: "Aubade printanière" (Gennaro): Discography no. 158

4. MARCEL MOYSE, flute; LOUIS MOYSE, flute; BLANCHE HONEGGER MOYSE, viola: SUITE IN C FOR TWO FLUTES AND VIOLA: Serenade (Louis Moyse): Discography no. 159

24.6. *Marcel Moyse's French Favorites*
MURAMATSU MGF-1006 (LP)

SIDE 1:

1. MARCEL MOYSE, flute (orch/Bigot): CONCERTO FOR FLUTE AND ORCHESTRA: Allegro (Ibert): Discography no. 102

2. MARCEL MOYSE, flute (unaccompanied): "Pièce pour flûte seule" (Ibert): Discography no. 76

3. MARCEL MOYSE, flute; JEAN LAFON, guitar: "Entr'acte" (Ibert): Discography no. 137

4. MARCEL MOYSE, flute (pf/Louis Moyse): SONATA, Op. 11 (Stanley Bate): Discography nos. 142–144

SIDE 2:

1. MARCEL MOYSE, flute; (pf/?): "Fantaisie avec variations sur un air napolitain," Op. 8 (Genin): Discography no. 32

2. MARCEL MOYSE, flute; (pf/?): *L'ARLÉSIENNE* SUITE NO. 2: Minuet (Bizet–arr. Guiraud): Discography no. 2

3. MARCEL MOYSE, flute; (pf/?): "Carmen fantaisie brillante" (Borne): Discography no. 35

4. MARCEL MOYSE, flute (pf/Georges Truc): "Fantaisie" (Hüe): Discography nos. 5–6

ADDENDUM

The "Kojo no tsuki" included on Marcel Moyse LP M-102 ("Marcel Moyse, Flutist") and the subsequent Muramatsu LP and CD reissues is *not* Discography item no. 165. It is in fact a later recording of the piece, probably made in Brattleboro, Vermont, during the same sessions that produced the other original microgroove recordings (items 199–221) featured on Marcel Moyse LPs M-99 and M-101. The piano accompaniments of the two versions vary significantly, as do Moyse's phrasing and overall interpretation. This single item from LP M-102 should be listed in the Discography proper as an *original* recording, inserted as item 221a.

The Muramatsu LPs (MGF-1001 through MGF-1006) were later issued on five compact discs, MGCD 1001–1005. The CDs are identical in content to the LPs; only the order has been slightly altered. MGCD-1003 (the compact disc version of MGF-1003) contains all *three* of the selections from Roussel's *JOUEURS DE FLÛTE* recorded by Moyse; Ferroud's *TROIS PIÈCES POUR FLÛTE SEULE* is found complete on MGCD-1005, rather than scattered over two LPs; and the contents of LPs MGF-1004 through MGF-1006 are contained on only two compact discs (MGCD-1004 and MGCD-1005). All the compact discs bear the deceptive title *Marcel Moyse/The Complete Works of the Great Flautist,* although this is certainly not the case any more than it was on the original Muramatsu LPs.

The Art of Marcel Moyse, a set of four compact discs produced by Japanese EMI, circa 1991, was issued as set TOCE 7491-94 (2DJ-4106 through 2DJ-4109). Contents, indicated by Discography numbers, are:
Disc 1: 114–119, 94–97, 88–93
Disc 2: 106–111, 40–43
Disc 3: 56–61, 171, 87, 2, 81–84, 32, 4
Disc 4: 8–13, 18–23, 128–131, 102, 15, 14
Our thanks to Mark Dannenbring, Taichung, Taiwan, for these details.

PRE-PRESS NOTE: Thanks to Mr. Irving Levin of Rego Park, New York, for details of three test pressings that shed light on the piano-accompanied "Japanese" Nipponophone recordings in Section II (items nos. 165–168). These were recorded by French Columbia in Paris between December 1935 and January 1937. The labels read "P.F./R.C. Seine 74.361/Échantillon/INVENDABLE/MADE IN FRANCE" and bear the following information:

1. [Unidentified (Japanese?) theme with variations]: "do la la la mi re do/CL 5546ᴵᴵ/B.B./???/Japonais/Un petit claqu[emen]t au milieu, légers gratt[ement]s au s[illon] final"
2. ["Kojo no tsuki"]: "la re mi fa la fa si la/CL 5547ᴵᴵ/Japonais/B.B./Bruits étranges, légers gratt[ement]s par places et au s[illon] final" (This is *not* the take issued on either S-30103 or OZ-7554-N.)
3. ["Comin' thro' the rye/Hanayome ningyo"]: "CL 6040⎯/Moyse/1° Comin' thro' the rye/2° Hanayome ningyo/22/1/37"

XI   LONG-PLAYING CONCORDANCE
TO THE DISCOGRAPHY

In order that LP and compact disc transfers of the original Moyse recordings may be traced from the originals to the reissues, the following concordance is given. The discography numbers of the original recordings are shown at the left, with the corresponding LP or compact disc number(s) at the right:

DISCOGRAPHY NUMBER	LONG-PLAYING REISSUE	DISCOGRAPHY NUMBER	LONG-PLAYING REISSUE
1	23.4?	106–109	7, 17
2	24.6	110–111	7, 17, 23.4
3	24.4	114–119	3, 6, 10, 15, 22
4	13, 23.3, 24.3	124–127	23.4
5–6	24.6	128–131	2, 18
8–13	12, 14	132–133	23.4?
14	23.3, 24.3	134	24.4
15	23.3, 24.3	135	24.4
32	24.6	137	24.6
33	13	142–144	24.6
35	24.6	145–146	24.5
40–43	7, 17, 23.4	147	24.5
48–49	8, 11	148–151	24.4
50–53	13, 24.4	152–153	23.4?
70	24.5	158	23.5, 24.5
71	23.3, 24.3, 24.5	159	24.5
72–73	24.5	160–163	23.6?
74	24.5	165–168	9
74(b)	23.3, 24.3	165	23.3?, 24.3?
75	23.3, 24.3, 24.5	171–172	13, 23.4?
76	24.6	174	20, 21, 23.4?
78	23.3, 24.3	193	23.6?
79	23.3, 24.3	199–207	23.1, 24.1
80	12	208–210	23.2, 24.2
81–84	23.3, 24.3	211	23.2, 23.5?, 24.2
85	24.5	212	23.2, 24.2
86	23.3, 24.3	213	23.2, 23.5, 24.2
87	12, 23.3, 24.3	214–215	23.2, 24.2
88–93	1, 5, 10, 15, 16, 19	216	23.2, 23.5?, 24.2
94–97	1, 5, 10, 19	217	23.2, 24.2
98–101	1, 4, 10, 19	218	23.2, 23.5, 24.2
102	24.6	219–221	23.2, 24.2

XII   ARTIST INDEX
(with corresponding Discography numbers)

PIERNÉ, GABRIEL, piano (1863–1937): 18–23
PIERRE-MARIE, —, piano: 62–63
POTTER, CHRIS, flute: 234

QUATTROCHI, LUCIEN, viola: 62–63

RIMON, MEIR, horn: 223–224
ROESGEN-CHAMPION, MARGUERITE, piano (1894–1976): 122–123
ROGATCHEWSKY, JOSEPH, tenor (1891–): 48–49
ROTHWELL, EVELYN, oboe (b. 1911): 98–101
ROUTCH, ROBERT, horn: 223–224

SCHOENFELD, MAX, flute: 236
SCHUSTER, EARL, oboe: 222
SCHWARTZ, LUCIEN?, violin: 62–63
SERKIN, JOHN, horn: 223–224
SERKIN, RUDOLF, piano (1903–1991): 88–93
SINGER, DAVID, clarinet: 223–224
SMALL, ROLAND, bassoon: 222
STOLTZMAN, RICHARD, clarinet: 223–224
STRARAM, WALTHER, conductor (1876–1933): 180–181
STRAVINSKY, IGOR, conductor (1882–1971): 64–67, 184–185

TOMASI, HENRI, conductor (1901–1971): 174
TRUC, GEORGES, conductor: 169–170
TRUC, GEORGES, piano: 5–7, 15–17
TUTLAND, SARA, flute: 235

VIGNAL, —, trumpet: 64–67
VRBSKY, RUDOLPH, oboe: 223–224

WALTHER STRARAM ORCHESTRA: 180–181
WINCENC, CAROL, flute: 230–231
WOLFGANG, RANDALL, oboe: 223–224
WRIGHT, HAROLD, clarinet: 222

XIII   INDEX OF WORKS PERFORMED
(with corresponding Discography numbers)

24 DAILY STUDIES: No. 15 (Soussman): 204
24 DAILY STUDIES: No. 22 (Soussman): 207
24 SMALL MELODIC STUDIES: Nos. 1, 2, 3, 4, 7, 8, 10 (Marcel Moyse): 199
24 SMALL MELODIC STUDIES: No. 9 (Marcel Moyse): 201
24 SMALL MELODIC STUDIES: Nos. 15, 22 (Marcel Moyse): 203
25 MELODIC STUDIES: No. 10 (Marcel Moyse): 200
25 MELODIC STUDIES: Nos. 25, 3 (Marcel Moyse): 202
24 STUDIES, Op. 15: Nos. 3, 4a, 8, 15, 16, 18 (Andersen): 206

"Variations on a theme by Mozart" (Hahn): 191
"Variations sur un air tyrolienne," Op. 20 (Böhm): 34
"La Vibray" (see SONATA IN D MINOR, Op. 2, No. 2) (Blavet)

WERTHER, ACT IV, Entr'acte: "Il notte di natale" (Massenet): 212

"Yoi michagusa" ["Yoimachi-Gusa"] ["The Evening Primrose"] (Ohno):
    166

Index